POLITICS
& POETIC VALUE

POLITICS
& POETIC VALUE

Edited by Robert von Hallberg

The University of Chicago Press
Chicago and London

Most of the essays in this volume originally appeared in CRITICAL INQUIRY: Spring 1987 (vol. 13, no. 3).

The University of Chicago Press, Chicago 60637
The University of Chicago Press, Ltd., London

Printed in the United States of America
94 93 92 91 90 89 88 87 5 4 3 2 1

Library of Congress Cataloging-in-Publication Data

Politics & poetic value.

Includes bibliographical references.
1. Poetry—History and criticism. 2. Politics in literature. 3. Politics and literature. 4. Poets—Political and social views. I. Von Hallberg, Robert, 1946– . II. Title: Politics and poetic value.
PN1081.P65 1987 809.1'9358 87-16231
ISBN 0-226-86495-2
ISBN 0-226-86496-0 (pbk.)

The paper used in this publication meets the minimum requirements of American National Standard for Information Sciences—Permanence of Paper for Printed Library Material, ANSI Z39.48-1984.∞

Cover design by Richard Sessions.

Contents

Introduction

In recent literary interpretation there is renewed interest in the political meaning, explicit or implicit, intentional or inadvertent, of all sorts of texts. One often now reads that some novel, play, poem, or essay is only apparently unrelated to political issues contemporary with either the text's production or our current reading of it. This sort of interpretation, which is fast becoming conventional, sometimes slides too easily, I think, toward evaluation: on one hand, insofar as a text is shown to veil its author's self-interest (often understood as the interest of a class or gender) with claims to larger concerns, the critic nudges this title a little out of the canon of currently engaging texts; on the other, a text expressive of a progressive political position is retrieved from the neglect it suffered from critics who veiled their self-interest (that is, the interest of their class or gender) with misleading talk of aesthetic standards. Either way, self-interest is now thought of as the most authentic motive an interpreter can divulge in a text. This kind of political interpretation can be defended as a healthy reaction to what is remembered as a time, now more than twenty years gone, when extrinsic criteria were disavowed and literature was said to be valuable primarily *as literature*. But how far has this reaction gone beyond formalism on one hand and ideological conformity on the other toward fresh, rich terms for evaluative criticism? Not far, I think. Without strong evaluative criticism it seems unlikely, as E. D. Hirsch has argued, that academic literary criticism can intervene in the institutions of literary instruction, or indeed in the production and reception of the poetry of our contemporaries, which is my own large interest (insofar as I have any).

It should be said too that the current trend toward political interpretation owes a good deal to our own narrow professional self-interest: as fewer institutional and economic resources have been directed toward the study of literature in the 1970s and 1980s, we can all remember fondly the importance that ideas, especially political ideas, seemed to hold in the 1960s. Some recent political interpretation seems to be motivated not just by a desire to maintain faith with the concerns of the 1960s, but as well by a need of scholars of humanities to generate terms that render the study of literature—or culture generally—obviously important. The political shifts of the late 1960s and early 1970s took money, jobs, and even a sense of consequence away from humanities departments. The recent move is to restore at least a sense of consequence to literary criticism. However worthy that objective, there is no reason to think that self-legitimation will lead to the development of evaluative standards appropriate to the study and enjoyment of poetry in America in 1987.

The essays collected here bear almost exclusively on obviously political poetry. All of the critics were invited to look more critically than is now customary at the difficulties of evaluating political poetry. My intention in framing the issue this way was not to suggest that poetry is most meaningful politically when it is explicitly so, but rather to ensure that the disclosure of a political meaning in some poem or other would not be the end of an argument. These essays are intended to move beyond interpretation. The poets discussed are not regarded as symptomatic of one or another political phenomenon; instead, Pindar, Horace, Milton, Clare, Cardenal, and others are taken as writers whose direct and deliberate engagement with the relations between poetry and politics are instructive to American literary intellectuals now.

The Arnoldian notion that criticism, or even poetry, is ever disinterested is now fully discredited in American academic circles. The essays gathered here start from this consensus, but they go well beyond it in measuring just where and how far the political intentions of poets are actually compatible with criteria of excellence in poetry that were employed back in those old days when literature was said to be valuable on aesthetic or formalist grounds. Alicia Ostriker states plainly that what she looks for in poetry generally—wit, grace, passion, eloquence, playfulness, compression, vitality, and freshness—is just what she finds in the political poems she most admires. Her implication is that certain literary qualities are valuable in all sorts of poetry, that political poems do not require evaluative criteria specific to that genre. There is much agreement in this collection that political poetry does not require that critics invent some new set of standards, but that it does require that certain qualities of poetry, which I will enumerate here, be regarded as problematic.

The first of these is surely the impulse of some poets to write poems expressing a desire to transcend the limits of time and space. Most of the critics here hold to the notion that the ability of poems to transcend their moments of origin has been wrongly stressed. There are of course many cases of poems coming to have meaning that their authors could not possibly have foreseen. Rob Nixon writes about how *The Tempest* took on highly pointed meaning for African and Caribbean writers of the 1950s–1970s. In one sense the play is indeed universal, but its interpretation by postcolonial authors derives less from qualities inherent to the play than from the political and cultural needs of communities of our own century. There is no reason to dissociate the capacity of great literature to develop new meaning (its universality) from the political concerns of writers and readers. Michael André Bernstein shows that Horace knew well that the demands of a particular political situation will in the end make themselves felt, even when cultural conventions, such as measuring syllables, or declaring a holiday, seem to insulate us from ordinary responsibilities. There are ultimately no holidays from the political significance of our statements, as Horace's slave is reminded at the end of the seventh satire.

In place of aspirations to universality, political poets often aim at forceful particularity; but no single precept, like Pound's "Go in fear of abstraction," will do to help critics and political poets set a proper relationship between particularity and generality. Reginald Gibbons invokes the satiric tradition of naming names, cursing villains, in his analysis of Ernesto Cardenal's poem on Somoza; according to this view, political poetry is most responsible when it remains insistently particular. Anne Burnett shows how Pindar's art successfully brings particular political figures, not only named but present when the poems were first performed, into meaningful relation with abstract qualities, such as Good Order, Justice, Tranquility, Truth, and Maturity. Elizabeth Helsinger's essay on John Clare, though, cautions that the resort to general terms can lead a poet to a too comfortable relationship with his or her audience. Only when he writes of a particular landscape familiar to him does Clare, in "Summer Images," get away from the generalized passages he composed "for sale to a middle-class audience." His insistence on particularity in his poems, Helsinger argues, is intended to establish a rapport with his readers like that of an actual meeting of two people who hope not to be confined to behavior typical of their social classes. Gibbons points out that the English critical tradition esteems "acute discriminations and vividness of detail" in poetry generally. It was just this that led Auden to claim that poets are "singularly ill-equipped to understand politics or economics."[1] And Susan Schweik claims that this criterion of particularity in war poetry reinforces the prerogatives of a male literary tradition. It was against the idea of the soldier poet, who could speak authoritatively from his own experience, that Marianne Moore wrote "In Distrust of Merits."

With what authority, then, can a poet speak politically? Yeats' admission that "in truth / We have no gift to set a statesman right" seems, after Pound, Eliot, and Yeats himself, sadly true of modern Anglo-American poets, though this is not a new problem. Socially, Clare was an outsider to his own readers, and his poetry faltered at those moments, as in "The Mores," when he was uncertain of the authority with which he might speak. There is a sense in which poets are now expected to be social

1. *Poetry and Politics,* ed. Richard Jones (New York, 1985), p. 47; all further references to this work will be included in the text.

outsiders, regardless of their social class. And outsiders, though they enjoy certain privileges, are just the same limited in political discourse by their status. Burnett says that Pindar, who was no outsider, in praising certain athletes necessarily praised and supported the aristocratic social structure that enabled the games. He sang as one wholly and willingly complicitous with the society he addressed. Bernstein shows that Horace was fully aware of his own involvement in the hierarchy and power of Augustan Rome. Janel Mueller argues that Milton's strongest political poem is "On the new forcers of Conscience," exactly because his balancing of contingent detail and philosophical universals allowed him to write as a citizen in advocacy of a practical political position in 1647–48. But few poets now—Cardenal is of the few—are complicitous in this way. More commonly poets speak of their political involvement subjectively. Robert Bly, for instance, says that "a true political poem is a quarrel with ourselves, and the rhetoric is as harmful in that sort of poem as in the personal poem" (pp. 133–34). There is clearly a rhetorical danger that a poet may pretend to authority and settle for grandiosity. More important, though, poets who express their own participation in the acts and choices of those they criticize or praise show at least some awareness of the political danger of any citizen disclaiming responsibility for the state's activities. More narrowly, in terms of the literary culture, they refuse the professional-outsider status given them by their audience's conception of the poetic. Which is to say that a case can be made for poets in democratic societies invoking only the authority of citizens participating in the social and cultural institutions we speak of as the state. However much seriousness literary tradition provides to poets, they are only figuratively visionaries speaking to prisoners; literally, they are citizens speaking to other citizens.

All of the essays here refer to the ways in which aesthetic value is determined collaboratively by readers and authors in particular historical contexts. Robert Pinsky describes how a society's idea of the poetic is transformed or rebutted by individual poets. The difference between transformation and rebuttal is plainly great. Even once it seems settled that poetic value is not transcendent or transhistorical, but instead established by a community, the exact relationship of the poet to that established value can be viewed differently. Anne McClintock tells the story of how editors and writers in South Africa quite deliberately set out to exploit a politically useful sense of poetic value in the 1970s. Jerome McGann, on the other hand, speaks of the need for poets to contest and disrupt ideas of the poetic, because such preconceptions uphold not only aesthetic but social and linguistic orders as well. The disagreement between these two critics is not attributable, I think, to ideology but rather to their different views of the function of poetry. An ambitious poet, according to McGann, undermines imperialism by invoking conventions counter to narrative, chronology, and causation generally. The black South African poets, and Cardenal too, who put their art at the disposal of a political movement, were not answering to the highest call of their art.

However, McClintock and Gibbons might claim that McGann mistakenly has too much confidence in the political significance of particular literary forms. Pound, after all, was Cardenal's formal model. Part of the issue here is the extent to which poetic form itself is properly understood to address political values. The straightforward notion that a poem's form ought to imitate its subject has long been regarded as fallacious by critics, though it has remained attractive to poets. McGann's claim is rather that the form of a poem properly criticizes the political orders that rest upon linguistic structures. Auden believed something like this too.

> A society which was really like a good poem, embodying the aesthetic virtues of beauty, order, economy and subordination of detail to the whole, would be a nightmare of horror for, given the historical reality of actual men, such a society could only come into being through selective breeding, extermination of the physically and mentally unfit, absolute obedience to its Director, and a large slave class kept out of sight in cellars. [P. 48]

This is why he concluded that a poet could not be a responsible critic of liberal democratic society. Because poets are lovers of order, George Steiner has recently argued, theirs is an inherently reactionary art.[2] McGann, like Ostriker, prefers rebellious (anarchistic?) poets. And the rebellion for him begins with poetic form. In an imperial state, he would have poets constantly refuse to collaborate with their readers in the establishment of values.

These essays are not intended to put forward any one approach to the evaluation of political poetry; I have deliberately assembled a collection of practical essays without any purely theoretical pieces. It does not seem to me, nor to the other contributors, that political poetry demands peculiar evaluative standards, though the case of political poetry does make especially clear how much is entailed by an esteem for universality or an expectation of particularity in poetry, in a poet's effort to speak authoritatively or complicitously, and in the commonly held notion that a poet's formal choices reflect ideological priorities. These essays do not speak with one voice to any of these topics, but they show where some of the difficulties arise when poetry and politics are brought together directly. Although the evaluative criteria proposed in these essays are not defended with systematic logical argument, they can indeed be tested: the poetry quoted constitutes a large part of their claim to validity. And beyond validity of this traditional sort there is hope: these essays state what some critics want poetry to be in our political lives.

2. George Steiner, "Criticisms of Life, Voices of Protest," review of *The Faber Book of Political Verse,* ed. Tom Paulin, *TLS* (23 May 1986), p. 547.

For this reprinting of the special issue of *Critical Inquiry* on politics and poetic value, I have added two new essays, two short responses by Charles Altieri and Jed Rasula to particular pieces already printed, McGann's response to Altieri, and a general response by David Bromwich to all of the essays printed here now. Donald Davie's essay on Goldsmith comes directly at the problematic relation of particularity to generality in political poetry: he urges us to consider whether in this kind of writing the value of particularity may not in fact (contra Gibbons) be inadequately accounted for by our customary critical principles, and whether too our usual assessments of political poetry do not give short shrift to the sort of poem that names its concerns directly and in detail. Turner Cassity's essay on Kipling addresses some of the issues I have already discussed (in particular, the relation of detail to type and the value of a poet's actual political experience), but he raises a more general point too: whether poetry about other people, especially narrative poetry, is not an especially valuable sort of writing in political terms; his claim is that the history of English poetry does not make it easy for poets now to write well about other people. These new essays, as well as many of those published before, focus on the points of strain that emerge not only when poets choose to engage political subjects directly, but also when critics and scholars attempt to fit the language of criticism to poetry and politics.

Robert von Hallberg

Responsibilities of the Poet

Robert Pinsky

Certain general ideas come up repeatedly, in various guises, when contemporary poetry is discussed. One of these might be described as the question of what, if anything, is our social responsibility as poets.

That is, there are things a poet may owe the art of poetry—work, perhaps. And in a sense there are things writers owe themselves—emotional truthfulness, attention toward one's own feelings. But what, if anything, can a poet be said to owe other people in general, considered as a community? For what is the poet answerable? This is a more immediate—though more limited—way of putting the question than such familiar terms as "political poetry."

Another recurring topic is what might be called Poetry Gloom. I mean the sourness and kvetching that sometimes come into our feelings about our art: the mysterious disaffections, the querulous doubts, the dispirited mood in which we ask ourselves, has contemporary poetry gone downhill, does anyone at all read it, has poetry become a mere hobby, do only one's friends do it well, and so forth. This matter often comes up in the form of questions about the "popularity" or "audience" of poetry.

Possibly the appetite for poetry really was greater in the good old days, in other societies. After the total disaster at Syracuse, when the Athenians, their great imperialist adventure failed, were being massacred, or branded as slaves with the image of a horse burned into the forehead,

This essay was first delivered as a "craft lecture" at the Napa Poetry Conference in August 1984.

a few were saved for the sake of Euripides, whose work, it seems, was well thought of by the Syracusans. "Many of the captives who got safe back to Athens," writes Plutarch,

> are said, after they reached home, to have gone and made their acknowledgments to Euripides, relating how some of them had been released from their slavery by teaching what they could remember of his poems and others, when straggling after the fight, had been relieved with meat and drink for repeating some of his lyrics.

This is enviable; but I think that at some vital level our answer must be, *so what?* Jarrell wrote about those people who say they "just can't read modern poetry" in a tone that implies their happiest hours are spent in front of the fireplace with a volume of Blake or Racine. To court such readers, or to envy Euripides, would be understandable, but futile, impulses.

And I think they are even frivolous impulses, beside the point. Of course every artist is in competition with the movies, in the sense that art tries to be as interesting as it can. But tailoring one's work to an audience any less hungry for one's art than oneself probably makes for bad movies and bad poems. And whether that is true or not, most poets would be bad at such tailoring anyway. Daydreams aside, more urgent questions are: what is our job? And: what are the roots of good and bad morale about it?

The second question is strange, if I am right in supposing that poetry is the very art of being interesting. The two most interesting things in the world, for our species, are ideas and the individual human body, two elements that poetry uniquely joins together. It is the nature of poetry to emphasize constantly that the physical sounds of words come from a particular body, one at a time, in a certain order. By memorizing lines of Euripides, the Athenian soldiers had incorporated certain precise shades of conception. This dual concern, bodily and conceptual, is what Pound means by saying that poetry is a centaur: prose hits the target with its arrow; poetry does the same from horseback. If you are too stupid, or too cerebral, you may miss half of it.

Here I arrive at the relation between the two questions, morale and responsibility. In the root sense of the glamourless word "responsibility,"

Robert Pinsky teaches at the University of California, Berkeley. His most recent book of poems, *History of My Heart,* was awarded the William Carlos Williams Prize. His other books include *Sadness and Happiness, An Explanation of America,* and a volume of criticism, *The Situation of Poetry. Mindwheel,* his narrative entertainment for computer, has been issued by Brøderbund Software.

people crave not only answers but also answerability. Involving a promise or engagement, the word is related to "sponsor" and "spouse." We want our answers to be craved as in the testing and reassuring of any animal parent and child, or the mutual nudge and call of two liturgical voices. The corporeal, memorizable quality of verse carries with it a sense of social exchange. The image of the horse burned into the living human body says one thing; the memorized cadence of words, without exactly contradicting that statement, answers it with another.

An artist needs, not so much an audience, as to feel a need to answer, a promise to respond. The response may be a contradiction, it may be unwanted, it may go unheeded, it may be embraced but twisted (William Blake the most quoted author in the modern House of Commons!)—but it is owed, and the sense that it is owed is a basic requirement for the poet's good feeling about the art. This need to answer, as firm as a borrowed object or a cash debt, is the ground where the centaur walks.

A critic, a passionate writer on poetry, culture and politics, once said to me, "When I ask American poets if they are concerned about United States foreign policy in Latin America, they all say yes, they are. But practically none of them write about it: why not?"

My response to this question was not dazzling. "I don't know," I said. And then, thinking about it for another moment: "It certainly isn't that they don't want to." The desire to make a good work, or the desire to deal with a given subject—in theory, the desire to deal with every subject—isn't automatically fulfilled.

The desire to see, and the desire to feel obliged to answer, are valuable, perhaps indispensable parts of the poet's feelings about the art. But in themselves they are not enough. In some way, before an artist can see a subject—foreign policy, or any other subject—the artist must transform it: answer the received cultural imagination of the subject with something utterly different. This need to answer by transforming is primary; it comes before everything else.

Something of the kind may explain the interesting phenomenon of bad work by good artists. Even a gifted, hard-working writer with a large and appreciative audience may write badly, I think, if this sense of an obligation to answer—a promised pushing-back or re-sponding—is lacking. Irresponsibility subtly deadens the work. Conversely, a dutiful editorializing work, devoid of the kind of transformation I mean, may also be dead.

To put it differently, the idea of social responsibility seems to raise a powerful contradiction, in the light of another intuited principle, freedom. The poet needs to feel utterly free, yet answerable. This paradox underlies and confounds much discussion of our art; poetry is so bodily and yet so explicit, so capable of subjects and yet so subtly transforming of them, that it seems recurrently to be quite like the rest of life, and yet different.

One anecdotal example: I have a friend who drives a car impatiently, sometimes with a vivid running commentary on other drivers. One day while I sat next to him the car in front of us behaved in a notably indecisive, unpredictable, petulant, dog-in-the-manger manner. But my friend was calm, he did not gesture and he certainly did not honk. I asked him why, and his explanation was, "I never hassle anybody who is taking care of small children."

This self-conscious respect for child care seems to me more than simply sweet. It exemplifies a basic form of social responsibility, an element of communal life more basic even than the boss-and-henchmen *comitatus* celebrated in *Beowulf.* People in a bus or restaurant where there is a small child like to think, I believe, that in an emergency they would protect the child, despite gulfs of social class or race or mere difference that might intervene.

The feeling is not goodness, exactly, but rather the desire to think well of ourselves—the first civic virtue, the fission of subject and object emitting the bubble reputation. That desire is part of our nature as social animals whose hairless, pudgy offspring pass through a long period of learning and vulnerability. We live together, rather than separately like Cyclopes, or otherwise perish in a generation. We living in our majority need to mediate between the dead, who took care of us, and not only the young, but the unborn.

And as poets, too, one of our responsibilities is to mediate between the dead and the unborn: we must feel ready to answer, as if asked by the dead if we have handed on what they gave us, or asked by the unborn what we have for them. This is one answer, the great conservative answer, to the question of what responsibility the poet bears to society. By practicing an art learned partly from the dead, one keeps it alive for the unborn.

Arts do, after all, die. In a way it is their survival that is surprising. When I was in primary school, they showed us films provided by the paper industry or the glass industry showing, with diagrams and footage of incredibly elaborate machines, the steps in making the innumerable kinds of paper, or glass jars and lenses and fiberglass curtains and fusilages. I remember thinking with some panic that it would soon all decay and fall apart: that the kids I knew in my own generation would be unable to learn those complex processes in time. When the adults died, we would botch the machines; I knew this with certainty, because I knew my peers and myself.

This fear still makes sense to me, and yet some of us went on not only to master those arcane processes and elaborate machines, but to improve them. Some people who were grubby, bored ten-year-olds in 1950 are now experts in fiber-optic controls in the manufacturing of semi-vitreous components, or in the editing of Provençal manuscripts.

So one great task we have to answer for is the keeping of an art that we did not invent, but were given, so that others who come after us can have it if they want it, as free to choose it and change it as we have been. A second task has been defined by Carolyn Forché, in a remarkable essay, as "a poetry of witness": we must use the art to behold the actual evidence before us. We must answer for what we see.

Witness may or may not involve advocacy, and the line between the two is rarely sharp; but the strange truth about witness is that though it may include both advocacy and judgment, it includes more than them, as well. If political or moral advocacy were all we had to answer for, that would be almost easy. Witness goes further, I think, because it involves the challenge of not flinching from the evidence. It proceeds from judgment to testimony.

In the most uncompromising sense, this means that whatever important experience seems least poetic to me is likely to be my job. Forché, for example, writes:

> In those days I kept my work as a poet and journalist separate, of two distinct *mentalités,* but I could not keep El Salvador from my poems because it had become so much a part of my life. I was cautioned to avoid mixing art and politics, that one damages the other, and it was some time before I realized that "political poetry" often means the poetry of protest, accused of polemical didacticism, and not the poetry which implicitly celebrates politically acceptable values.[1]

That is, the poet realized that what had seemed "unpoetic" or fit only for journalism, because it was supposedly contaminated with particular political implications, was her task. The "contamination" of "politics" was her responsibility, what she had to answer for as if she had promised something about it when she undertook the art of poetry. A corollary realization is that "all poetry is political": what is politically acceptable to some particular observer may seem "unpolitical" to that observer.

Where does the debilitating falseness come from, that tempts us to look away from evidence, or fit it into some allegedly "poetic" pattern, with the inevitable result of Poetry Gloom? Forché continues, a few sentences later:

> From our tradition we inherit a poetic, a sense of appropriate subjects, styles, forms and levels of diction; that poetic might insist that we be attuned to the individual in isolation, to particular sensitivity in the face of "nature," to special ingenuity in inventing metaphor.[2]

1. Carolyn Forché, "El Salvador: An Aide Memoire," *American Poetry Review* 10 (July/Aug. 1981): 6.
2. Ibid.

The need to notice, to include the evidence as a true and reliable witness, can be confused and dulled by the other, conserving responsibility of mediation between the dead and the unborn. And just as society can vaguely, quietly diffuse an invisible, apparently "apolitical" political ideology, culture can efficiently assimilate and enforce an invisible idea of what is poetic. In a dim view of the dialectic, it seems that society's tribute to poetry is to incorporate each new, at first resisted sense of the poetic, and so to spread it—and blunt it—for each new generation. Even while seeming not to taste each new poetic, the world swallows it.

Two nearly paradoxical formulations emerge from this process. First, only the challenge of what may seem unpoetic, that which has not already been made poetic by the tradition, can keep the art truly pure and alive. Put to no new use, the art rots. Second, the habits and visions of the art itself, which we are responsible for keeping alive, can seem to conspire against that act of use or witness. The material or rhetoric that seems already, on the face of it, proper to poetry may have been made poetic already by Baudelaire, or Wordsworth, or Rilke, or Neruda.

To put it simply, and only a little fancifully, we have in our care and for our use and pleasure a valuable gift, and we must answer both for preserving it, and for changing it. And the second we fail to make good answer on either score, the gift stops giving pleasure, and makes us feel bad, instead.

Since there is no way to say what evidence will seem pressing but difficult to a given artist—Central America, the human body, taking care of one's paraplegic sister, theology, farming, American electoral politics, the art of domestic design—no subject ever is forbidden. Society depends on the poet to witness something, and yet the poet can discover that thing only by looking away from what society has learned to see poetically.

Thus, there is a dialectic between the poet and his culture: the culture presents us with poetry, and with implicit definitions of what materials and means are poetic. The answer we must promise to give is "no." Real works revise the received idea of what poetry is; by mysterious cultural means the revisions are assimilated and then presented as the next definition to be resisted, violated and renewed. What poets must answer for is the unpoetic. And before we can identify it, or witness it, an act of judgment is necessary. This act of judgment can only be exemplified.

Here is one of the most valued poems in our language. In quoting the poem, I particularly want to point out the insistently repeated absolutes, especially the words "*every*" and "*most*":

London

I wander thro' each charter'd street,
Near where the charter'd Thames does flow,
And mark in every face I meet
Marks of weakness, marks of woe.

In every cry of every Man,
In every Infant's cry of fear,
In every voice, in every ban,
The mind-forg'd manacles I hear:

How the Chimney-sweeper's cry
Every blackning Church appalls,
And the hapless Soldier's sigh
Runs in blood down Palace walls.

But most thro' midnight streets I hear
How the youthful Harlot's curse
Blasts the new-born Infant's tear
And blights with plagues the Marriage hearse.

The word "every" throbs through all of the stanzas except the final one, repeated five times in the drumlike second stanza. This insistent chain of "every's" leads to the capping, climactic movement of the conclusion, with its contrary, superlative "But *most*": the immense force of the ending comes partly from the way "But most" piles its weight onto the already doubled and redoubled momentum of "every" and "every" and "every."

One thing that "every" and "every" brings into the poem is the sense of a social whole: it is all of us, we are part of it, no utter exception is possible, it is like a family, and a family that bears a "mark." And though my brother and not I may have poured your blood or blighted your tear, it would be stupid of me to think that your response to me—or mine to you—could go uncolored by what you know of my family. The poem witnesses the legal entity of a city in a way that transforms it into this social whole.

Blake's "most" is reserved for the blighting of future generations—the extension of social corruption forward, into the future, through the infection of those still *in utero.* This continuation forward in time of the omnipresent blight and pain, under the climactic "but most," suggests both of the broad kinds of answerability: it is literally conservative, and it reminds us that we are witnesses for the future. Those who want to know about London in Blake's time read this poem. They may read the contemporary journalism, as well, but for an inward understanding of such evidence, they will again read Blake. If someone in the future wants to understand *Newsweek* and *Time,* or the *CBS Evening News,* our poems must answer to the purpose. We are supposed to mark the evidence, as well as continue the art.

In "London," all this is accomplished by the violently wholesale quality of what is "marked" in both senses, witnessed and scarred. The "unpoetic" part of the poem is the rhetoric that invents or enacts the vision of society as a kind of nightmarish, total family rather than an orderly contractual, chartered arrangement. Formally, the poem is a transformed hymn, the cadences of communal binding turned against the institutions of the visible community. And in a sense, Blake had to transform the city imaginatively, put the mark of his judgment upon it, before he could see it.

If all poems were like "London," the question might seem relatively simple. But not all poems invite a social understanding of themselves nearly as strongly as this. And few of us were attracted to poetry to start with by the idea of being a good witness, still less the idea of mediating between the dead and the unborn. Most of us were attracted to poetry because of language that gave us enormous, unmistakable pleasure: not only the physical pleasure of beaded bubbles winking at the brim, but also the intellectual pleasure of thinking of the thin men of Haddam who rode over Connecticut in a glass coach, how they are both creatures of fantasy and suburban commuters on the train.

Such transformation seems to precede witness, in the working of poetry and in the history of our need for poetry. Its relation to witness is like that suggested by a passage in Ben Jonson's great poem "To Heaven":

> As thou art all, so be thou all to me,
> First, midst, and last, converted one, and three;
> My faith, my hope, my love: and in this state
> My judge, my witness, and my advocate.

Faith in the absolute fairness of a judge like the Father is parallel to hope regarding a witness (the Holy Ghost) and love for an advocate, whose Christian mercy extends beyond justice. In keeping with the biblical and religious models, the transforming certainty of judgment precedes the processes of witness and advocacy. Jonson's intellectually elegant inversion of the courtroom sequence (evidence, argument, judgment) reflects the way that poetry seems to depend upon a prior and tremendously confident process of transformation.

Transformation, too, is a social role of poetry: its oldest, clearest form must be epideictic, the praising of heroes, celebrating one whose physical or moral gifts have brought gain or glory to the tribe: the woman in Edwin Arlington Robinson's "Eros Turannos," whose catastrophic love affair makes "all the town and harbor side / Vibrate with her seclusion" is a peculiar, American provincial version of such a figure. She makes the town more heroic, and the gossiping townfolk make her story more heroic:

> She fears him, and will always ask
>   What fated her to choose him;
> She meets in his engaging mask
>   All reasons to refuse him;

But what she meets and what she fears
Are less than are the downward years,
Drawn slowly to the foamless weirs
　Of age, were she to lose him.

Between a blurred sagacity
　That once had power to sound him,
And Love, that will not let him be
　The Judas that she found him,
Her pride assuages her almost,
As if it were alone the cost.
He sees that he will not be lost,
　And waits and looks around him.

A sense of ocean and old trees
　Envelops and allures him;
Tradition, touching all he sees,
　Beguiles and reassures him;
And all her doubts of what he says
Are dimmed with what she knows of days—
Till even prejudice delays
　And fades, and she secures him.

The falling leaf inaugurates
　The reign of her confusion;
The pounding wave reverberates
　The dirge of her illusion;
And home, where passion lived and died,
Becomes a place where she can hide,
While all the town and harbor side
　Vibrate with her seclusion.

We tell you, tapping on our brows,
　The story as it should be,
As if the story of a house
　Were told, or ever could be;
We'll have no kindly veil between
Her visions and those we have seen,
As if we guessed what hers have been,
　Or what they are or would be.

Meanwhile we do no harm; for they
　That with a god have striven,
Not hearing much of what we say,
　Take what the god has given;
Though like waves breaking it may be,
Or like a changed familiar tree,
Or like a stairway to the sea
　Where down the blind are driven.

The mean-minded little town, the superior, desperate woman, the vulgar man, even perhaps the complacent, spavined literary culture whose editors had no use for Robinson's work, all are resisted and transformed by a rhetoric that includes the coming together of the poem's peculiar form, its powerful narrative, and the heroic symbol of the ocean.

Formally, the resistant or "unpoetic" element in "Eros Turannos" is a kind of hypertrophy. As if in response to an insufficiently communal or folkloric relation between artist and audience, or heroine and community—even between the seemingly omniscient narrator of the beginning and the "we" speaking the ending—the poem exaggerates the formal, communal elements of the poem. With its feminine rhymes and triple rhymes and extension of ballad structure the poem is almost a parody ballad. The hypertrophy of traditional folk or ritualistic formal means resists an idea of poetic language, and of poetry in relation to social reality, by exaggeration. In its own terms this virtuoso exaggeration is as violent as the sweeping terms of Blake's "London."

Based on a mighty, prior act of transforming judgment, "London" takes the rhetorical mode of witnessing ("I mark"); what is on trial is a transformed London, and the poet's eye roams through it like the Holy Ghost, seeing more than any literal social reality could make possible. His repeated "every" is in part a mark of ubiquity. Robinson's poem of tragic celebration, full of mercy and advocacy in relation to its heroine, evokes images and rhetoric of judgment; and judgment is formally emphasized almost to the point of parody by the quality of incantation. Yet the perspective in "Eros Turannos," too, is preternatural. Certainly, the viewpoint is more than socially located. It is the multiple perspective of the ubiquitous witness:

> Meanwhile we do no harm; for they
>   That with a god have striven,
> Not hearing much of what we say,
>   Take what the god has given;
> Though like waves breaking it may be
> Or like a changed familiar tree,
> Or like a stairway to the sea
>   Where down the blind are driven.

What "we" see or say; what is known of "her" fears and questions; what "they" hear or take; what the god gives; what "it" may be like—all of these narrated materials gain their authority from the underlying, invisible certainty that he has seen anew. That certainty appears in the "changed familiar tree," and its invisible, generative power leads to the stairway "Where down the blind are driven." The poet's own voice changes from impersonal omniscience at the outset to a communal first person plural by the close.

These examples suggest to me that society forms an idea of the poetic, an idea which has implications about social reality, and that the poet needs to respond by answering with a rebuttal or transformation of terms. But what about a poem that is deliberately irresponsible, that is anarchic or unacceptable in its social attitude? What, for example, about Frank O'Hara's poem "Ave Maria"?

Mothers of America
let your kids go to the movies!
get them out of the house so they won't know what you're up to
it's true that fresh air is good for the body
but what about the soul
that grows in darkness, embossed by silvery images
and when you grow old as grow old you must
they won't hate you
they won't criticize you they won't know
they'll be in some glamorous country
they first saw on a Saturday afternoon or playing hookey
they may even be grateful to you
for their first sexual experience
which only cost you a quarter
and didn't upset the peaceful home
they will know where candy bars come from
and gratuitous bags of popcorn
as gratuitous as leaving the movie before it's over
with a pleasant stranger whose apartment is in the Heaven on Earth Bldg
near the Williamsburg Bridge
oh mothers you will have made the little tykes
so happy because if nobody does pick them up in the movies
they won't know the difference
and if somebody does it'll be sheer gravy
and they'll have been truly entertained either way
instead of hanging around the yard
or up in their room hating you
prematurely since you won't have done anything horribly mean yet
except keeping them from life's darker joys
it's unforgivable the latter
so don't blame me if you won't take this advice
and the family breaks up
and your children grow old and blind in front of a TV set
seeing
movies you wouldn't let them see when they were young

The language of this poem dodges and charges so brilliantly on its way, with energy that is so happily demotic, that a reader is likely to want to keep up, to want to show that one can keep up. Among other things, the poem expresses love for the flawed, for imperfection—especially American imperfection—and the dark. O'Hara sprints happily through this terrain, leaping between such oppositions as "silvery images" versus "the peaceful home," to find the genuinely friendly, intimate and democratic note of "sheer gravy" and "so don't blame me if you won't take this advice." It is a contest between glamour and decency, apparently settled by an appeal to American idiom. His understanding of such speech, and by implication of the movies, is so clear and vivid that we want to share it, to assure ourselves that we, too, understand the dark, stained charm of Heaven on Earth as it appears in an actual New York. The language streaks forward impatiently and we want to go along.

One thing we are invited to go along with is the idea that children young enough to need permission to go to the movies may benefit from sexual use by adult strangers; that they may be grateful for it. Considered as advocacy, this is distinctly not nice. It is as if O'Hara chose the most repulsive proposition he could think of, to embed in the middle of his poem.

Various matters of rhetoric may soften or deflect the issue of unacceptability: since the group "Mothers of America" will for the most part not hear, and surely not heed, this oration, it can be looked on as not literal advocacy but mock-advocacy. And more legalistically, the seduction is conjectural: they "*may*" even be grateful. So the advocacy is hemmed by irony and disclaimer, with the outrageous jokes of "only cost you a quarter" and "sheer gravy" signaling how very much in the realm of rhetoric we are—an exuberant homosexual *schpritzing*.

But just the same, there is an element of the unacceptable in the poem, a violation of social boundaries. And far from seeming a regrettable, separable blemish, this repugnant element seems essential. It is what makes us believe the "darker joys," asking in effect if pleasure in the poem has a component of inexpensive, vicarious sexual naughtiness. Ultimately, I think it asks us to entertain the possibility of some one unusual eleven-year-old (should we imagine the lines as actual or fantasized autobiography?) who might conceivably feel grateful to his mother for the opportunity described.

In other words, the poem breaks or bends ideas about poetic method and content. And this resistant act seems prior to the poem, part of a preceding judgment that underlies what is seen and argued. Perhaps one thing I like so much in the poem is the daring and clarity with which it plays—and so clearly plays—at the definitive terms of judgment:

> . . . keeping them from life's darker joys
> it's unforgivable the latter

or the ratiocinative terms of advocacy:

. . . because if nobody does pick them up in the movies
they won't know the difference
and if somebody does it'll be sheer gravy

The democratic, almost conspirational note of "sheer gravy," and "horribly mean," deftly contrasted with language like "prematurely" and "the latter," invites an alliance in imperfection. The poem happily witnesses a great communal imperfection ("what you're up to," "horribly mean") and excitement in American life, all the grotesque, glorious fantasy life associated with the movies. The bite of the poem comes from its comic perspectives: the imagination of a scene where the poet addresses the Mothers, the imagination of the future at the end of the poem, the imagination of idyllic sexual initiation for "tykes."

He is willing to share his sense of the movies, and of our culture, with us, and his willingness is rooted in his will to transform our idea of what is acceptable, in poetry or in the imagined oration itself. Other works of those late Eisenhower years get higher marks in the category "does not advocate awful crimes," but we do not read them with the pleasure and recognition this one gives, with its stern standard of being "truly entertained." In one way, the poem is a daring, ebullient prank; in another, it embodies the process whereby the vision and rhetoric of a poem spring from a prior resistance to what the culture has given.

"All poetry is political." The act of judgment prior to the vision of any poem is a social judgment. It always embodies, I believe, a resistance or transformation of communal values: Blake's indictment of totally visible, monolithic London; Robinson's dry rage that an aristocracy of grace and moral insight has no worldly force; O'Hara's celebration of what is cheerfully lawless in American life. Even when Emily Dickinson defines the ultimate privacy of the soul, she does it in terms that originate in social judgment:

The soul selects her own Society—
Then—shuts the Door.

As one of the best-known lines in contemporary poetry indicates, the unpredictable effect upon a community of what one writes may be less to the point than discharging the responsibility:

America I'm putting my queer shoulder to the wheel.

The poet's first social responsibility, to continue the art, can be filled only through the second, opposed responsibility to change the terms of the art as given—and it is given socially, which is to say politically. What that will mean in the next poem anyone writes is by definition unknowable, with all the possibility of art.

The Scrutiny of Song: Pindar, Politics, and Poetry

Anne Burnett

Pindar's songs were composed for men at play, but his poetry was political in its impulse and in its function. The men in question were rich and powerful, and their games were a display of exclusive class attributes, vicariously shared by lesser mortals who responded with gratitude and loyalty (for example, *Pythia* 5.43–44). Victories were counted as princely benefactions (compare *Olympia* 5.3 and 15, 7.94, 8.87, *Isthmia* 6.69) and laid up as city treasure like the wealth deposited in the treasuries at Delphi (*Pythia* 6.5). Athletic victory was thus both a manifestation and an enhancement of aristocratic domination, which meant that the poet who praised those who boxed and raced in pan-Hellenic games necessarily praised the social structure that depended on them.

Pindar understood his political function and was proud of it—"I would consort with victors" (*Olympia* 1.115b).[1] He believed in athletic contest as a model for all human life. He believed in the aristocratic system: "Inherited governance of cities lies properly with the nobility" (*Pythia* 10.71–72). He believed also that praise poetry could regulate as well as laud that system, and he believed finally that such poetry was itself incorruptible. Games, song, and princely rulers were all parts of a single brilliant order, and this truth had a linguistic reflection, for the bit that tames a horse, the meter of a poetic line, and the moderation of a ruler were all called by the same name—*metron*. "Measure (*metron*) inheres in everything" (*Olympia* 13.47 and throughout).

1. All translations are my own.

As Pindar saw it, there was only one pursuit open to a man, whether he was a prince or a poet or an ordinary citizen, and that was to search out the superlative and try to embody it in his own sort of action. And the search was not difficult because in the world as in song the best—the topmost element in any hierarchy—was plainly marked by its beauty. One could not fail to recognize it because all creation fell into natural categories in which one item had its evident and lovely dominance: water among the elements, gold among the metals, sun among the planets, Olympia among the games, and among men the princely victor (*Olympia* 1.1–7; compare *Olympia* 3.42–45). "Magnificence takes manifold forms but its extremest peak is reached in princes. Look no higher," he says in praise of a victorious tyrant (*Olympia* 1.113–15). The wealthy aristocrat, winning and spending with splendor, was the "bastion" of his city and also its "eye"—its most beautiful part—because the world was so organized that pragmatic and aesthetic values were in agreement (*Pythia* 5.55–57; compare *Olympia* 14.1–7, where the Charites are involved alike in wisdom, physical beauty, and social preeminence). Beauty was, in fact, a kind of moral imperative: "If a man be fair himself, and if he act in harmony with his appearance, he mounts to the topmost height of manhood" (*Nemea* 3.19). And for a demonstration of the coincidence of beauty with excellence one had only to look at the games where the aristocracy, through disciplined exertions toward supremacy, discovered to the world its own superlative qualities: the victor was "fair himself, his exploits like his looks" (*Nemea* 3.19). Wealth was a prerequisite, just as strength was (*Pythia* 3.110), but the particular virtue that was put on display was a combination of courage, judgment, desire to please ancestors and gods, and a will to distinguish oneself (*Isthmia* 6–10). This was the best that lay in human nature, and it took a form that was outwardly beautiful, making its appearance in the flesh of blooded horses and the bodies of young victors as lovely as Ganymede (*Olympia* 10.103–5).

At the games aristocrats, the most beautiful of men, vied among themselves in the most beautiful of pastimes to discover the most beautiful embodiments of their own best qualities (compare, for example, *Olympia* 9.94–100). And since success derived finally from god, the victor's triumph had no danger in it. "All the machinery of mortal excellence comes from god" (*Pythia* 1.41; compare, for example, *Nemea* 9.45). The victor, his competitors, the spectators, and the world at large were all reminded, precisely through the wreath that was put around his head, "won not

---

Anne Burnett is professor of classical languages and literature at the University of Chicago. Her most recent publications are *Three Archaic Poets: Archilochus, Alcaeus, Sappho* (1983) and *The Art of Bacchylides* (1985). A monograph on choral poetry, with focus on the Sicilian poet Stesichorus, is forthcoming.

without the aid of god" (*Pythia* 2.6–7; compare *Olympia* 6.79, 8.18, *Pythia* 8.61–69), of the nonhuman power that defined and reduced even the achievements of victors and kings. This meant that the victory poet did not praise a particular man in his strength; rather, he praised the success (*kudos,* as at *Olympia* 3.39, 5.7, *Pythia* 4.66) that was a divine gift bestowed upon one representative of a class of men. Ultimately, he praised god: "I come as a suppliant, O Zeus . . . sighing through Lydian flutes, begging you to deck this city out with deeds of manly virtue" (*Olympia* 5.19, 21–22). Furthermore, his own poetic success, exactly like that of the athlete, was in the same divine hands (*Olympia* 9.27–29, 11.10, *Pythia* 8.76, *Nemea* 4.41–43). Only with god's help would he be able to give the beauty of the moment of victory a musical reduplication and, by translating it to the realm of what is remembered, rescue it from the dissolution that necessarily marks all human action.

Athletic contest was thus a metaphor for the test of action which must be accepted by anyone who would give his innate quality its finest outward expression. "Only in trial is the fulness of a man's excellence made plain" (*Nemea* 3.70; compare *Olympia* 4.22, *Isthmia* 4.33). The games also represented the natural visibility of excellence: there could be no lying about prizes present or past, for the herald had cried out the names, and so Olympia was "Mistress of Truth" (*Olympia* 8.2; compare phrases in which the games are said to "know" a man, as at *Olympia* 7.83). And finally the athletic contest figured, in its spectators, the passive recognition and approbation which must be accorded to all the superlatives that cap the world's various priamels. "There is a rule among men that a splendid accomplishment must not fall and be covered in silence" (*Nemea* 9.6). The contest's double demand of action and acclamation defined man's life at its best, whatever his class or profession, and the poet was in the peculiar position of answering both imperatives at once. The act of composing a song was congruent with the act of competing in the games, as the poet made trial of his own powers and put the manifestation of his best in competition with the songs of others. At the same time, his praise of the victor was congruent with the applause of the spectators, though it was a more artful show of admiration. Epinician poetry thus differed from other pursuits, whether athletic, political, or technical, only by being doubly functional and doubly beautiful.

Such was Pindar's largest view of the interaction of politics, contest, and the poetry of praise. About the excellence of the aristocracy he was confident. It was his belief that men were not born equal (*Nemea* 7.5 and 54), that the qualities of temper and strength (*Nemea* 1.57; compare *Nemea* 2.14–15) lived in the seed of certain families (*Pythia* 8.44; compare *Olympia* 7.92–93, 9.100, *Pythia* 10.11–12) where they were present even in infants and children (*Nemea* 1.57, 3.44). This was a universal law—

"It is by nature that a noble temper predominates, passing from father to child" (*Pythia* 8.44)—and the only exception Pindar would allow was the possibility that such blood-virtue might lie dormant in a generation of less assertive men (*Nemea* 6.8b–11, 11.37–43). Since a man was a single whole ("like the speed of feet, so the strength of arm and the greatness of heart," *Olympia* 4.28–29; compare *Olympia* 8.19), one with the native qualities of nobility would use them to fight forward along "direct paths" of open and splendid deeds (*Nemea* 1.25; compare *Isthmia* 5.22, where the road of action is "pure"), because there was a familial fame (*Nemea* 3.40) and a familial destiny (a *daimon genethlios, Olympia* 13.105; compare *Isthmia* 1.39, *Nemea* 5.40) shaping his life. Nevertheless, each noble individual had to "track down" his own inborn virtue (*Nemea* 6.14), and having apprehended it, he had to exert himself because only action had significance, and action was always risky and difficult: "Toil and expenditure ever struggle for excellence in the deed that is wrapped in danger" (*Olympia* 5.16–17; compare *Olympia* 6.9–10). Whatever the danger, however, it had to be faced because inactivity was like sitting at home by one's mother while others went out to find a cure for death in courageous deeds (*Pythia* 4.185–87; compare *Olympia* 1.81–84).

Superb powers came from a superb inheritance and that inheritance was an obligation: one could not spot the fair fame of one's family (see especially *Pythia* 6). The opportunity to exercise such powers, however, came not from one's blood but from god. The grand risk (*Olympia* 1.81, usually called *kairos*), once recognized, had to be taken with a kind of modesty—one was its companion but not its master (*Pythia* 4.287)—and the success that was gained in the end was no more man's creation than the original chance had been, for the beginning and the end of every action was with god. The wealth that naturally belonged to an aristocrat (*Pythia* 10.17) played its part, of course, allowing him to pursue the "wilder ambitions" (*Olympia* 2.54) of contest and war. "If god give soft wealth to me, I can hope to find the height of fame in future time" (*Pythia* 3.110; compare *Pythia* 8.92). Nevertheless, it was only with divine help that a man might, "with luck from the gods and not betraying his own courage" (*Olympia* 8.67), mix his wealth with inherited virtue and use it in individual risk so that his familial fame should be renewed and revived. "Let him spend in joy, / let him put divinely given qualities to work, then / god will make fair reputation grow for him and he, / with heaven's honors plain, will cast his anchor on / the furthest shores of blessedness" (*Isthmia* 6.10; compare the opening of *Pythia* 5).

In theory, then, all was well as splendid men, licensed by splendid gods, performed splendid deeds which were given splendid praise by poets who added permanence to this redundancy of perfections. Nevertheless, neither Pindar nor his clients nor his audiences were simpletons, and all knew that imperfections, not to say corruptions, existed in the world. Most particularly did they all know, as Greeks, that one could lie—and lie beautifully if one were a poet (*Olympia* 1.29)—even about beauty. A man could cheat, using power that was either political or poetical, so as to impose a lesser substitute for a natural superlative; he could cover over what was really finest and exhibit something second-rate. This danger existed even inside the sanctified spaces of the great games, and outside in the secular world it was everywhere, menacing statesmen and singers as well as ordinary men. It could touch even the true aristocrat, for all his innate virtue, because especially in a moment of success a man might run mad and, with something other than his ordinary character ("with maddened heart," *Pythia* 2.26), commit an outrage. He might be in the midst of a fair action and yet, by means of false oaths, flattery, or calumny, he might create something ugly: a city in which the best men did not predominate, a praise poem that aroused only vulgar envy or, if he were a mythic hero, a monster that was neither god nor man nor beast.

Pindar saw these dangers but he also knew, or thought he knew, of elements within the aristocratic culture that would check them. In the first place, nobles moved by a desire for deathless renown (and such a desire was presumably a generic trait with them) could not expect to cheat Time, the eventual judge of all actions (*Olympia* 10.53–55). "The manner of one's life is told forth in the words or songs of after-coming men" (*Pythia* 1.92–94). And in the second place, even if this ideal failed to inhibit them, the actual would, for these men lived in the extreme openness of small and talkative communities. As leaders they were necessarily conspicuous and consequently the true quality of each of their moves, whether clean or sordid, was observable by all. They "walked the road where all could see," with every possession bearing witness to its source (*Olympia* 6.72). Furthermore, their wealth and success made them subject to a prying, envious blame that grudged proper acclamation but made out every misdeed (*phthonos, Pythia* 11.29; *momos, Olympia* 6.74). Neighbors were quick to spread evil tales (*Olympia* 1.47; compare *Olympia* 2.95), and consequently wealth and success were enjoyable only when a man behaved so as to be well thought of among his fellow citizens (*Pythia* 11.45; compare *Pythia* 11.28, *Nemea* 8.38).

Though it had no constituted power the public was thus a kind of check upon the aristocracy, while song itself provided a more far-reaching instrument of scrutiny. In order to be sure of an undying glory, the victor had to entrust his reputation to an epinician poet, for "Though he has wrought fair deeds, if a man go to Hades without song, his panting labor is hollow and his joy brief" (*Olympia* 10.91–93; compare *Pythia* 3.114, *Nemea* 7.12). Since the song he (or his family) commissioned would be performed by a multiplicity of a singers before a greater number of guests, this was tantamount to his presentation of his good fame to his fellow citizens for their examination. True, only a small number of fellow aristocrats would be present at the poem's single performance, but the young chorus members would certainly repeat its lines throughout the town, so that the song would become a public statement. With it the victor said in effect: "What I have done (which is the same thing as what I am) is here presented to you in the full glare of poetry: I am no Clytemnestra with something to hide, but a man who has gained the force of wealth without violence, one who now uses it in tranquility" (compare *Pythia* 11, and especially 54–56). The song's production was thus the victor's pledge to his community, his assertion that he did indeed care primarily for its opinion and was in consequence kept from any wrongdoing by the many eyes that were upon him. Before such a number of witnesses the statesman or prince could not afford to give off false sparks, but had to sharpen his tongue on the anvil of truth (*Pythia* 1.87–88). And by extension, though he paid a poet to celebrate his victory, that poet could only commemorate a glory that already existed, one created by impeccable actions of courage and manliness.

This, indeed, is only the narrowest description of song's power of review, because the victory ode offered its client's deeds not just to a local public but to the entire Hellenic community. "I am no statue-maker whose image stands fixed on its base; I go out from Aegina in every ship, a sweet song-cargo" (*Nemea* 5.1–3). The ode, moreover, reached even beyond a man's contemporaries, for it found an audience among the dead: "They listen with underground minds, when great deeds are sprinkled with the soft dewdrops of song" (*Pythia* 5.96–103; compare *Olympia* 8.77–80). And finally, an epinician was heard in heaven by the gods it so frequently addressed, and this was no conceit but an actuality, for its performance mode was borrowed from the danced songs of magic and worship, its gestures and melodies close to those of cult. Praise poetry was thus the medium through which a great man's actions were, by his own command, tested against the norms of a collective Hellenic morality. The epinician was a "faithful seal" (*Olympia* 11.6) affixed to a life that dared affront an audience of ghosts and daimones as well as the mortal envy of peers and inferiors. Furthermore, because virtue came to fulfillment only "slowly, by way of splendid songs" (*Pythia* 3.114), the ode had an influence that was not merely retrospective. In all the preliminary choices and exercises meant to lead to a desired success, a man had to keep this melodious investigation in mind. His every move had to be of the sort that would lend itself to future celebration by flutes and lyres, and consequently Pindar could say that the "grace" of music acted as an "overseer" in the lives of successful men (*Charis . . . epopteuei, Olympia* 7.11).

Success was forever splendid only when it had been sung, and this truth had a negative corollary that gave to music in addition an almost punitive power (symbolically stated in the unfriendly effects of the lyre at *Pythia* 1.13–14 and of Hesychia at *Pythia* 8.8–12). Actions that failed or were flawed were deprived of music, for they demanded its opposite, the shadow of silence and forgetfulness (*Nemea* 5.18). Indeed, this condemnation reached even to simple inaction, for Pindar speaks of "the unrecognized silences of things left untried" (*Isthmia* 4.32). Poetry could punish simply by refusing to come into being, thus creating the silence that would suffocate a man's fame. In actuality there was a particular kind of poetry that went further, defying the law by which the unsightly should be suppressed to sing out a verbalized blame, "fattening itself on heavy words of hatred" (*Pythia* 2.55–56). The praise poet was of course debarred by definition from any such practice, but Pindar nevertheless liked to remind his clients, on occasion, that there are times when open blame would be appropriate. He points ostentatiously to the silence to which he has sentenced certain unworthy actions (*Olympia* 13.91, *Nemea* 5.14b, and so on), thus suggesting that they might have been denounced, and in the case of the tyrant Phalaris he actually finds a way of voicing silence by making his chorus sing, "An evil reputation holds him captive, nor do lyres join the murmuring of young voices to make sweet sound for him" (*Pythia* 1.96). Again and again, with one of his favorite conceits, he describes his own acts of celebration as a form of "attack." He "does battle with" his client's many victories (*Olympia* 13.44); the victor cannot "escape" his song (*Olympia* 6.6), for his words are "arrows" shot at courage (*Olympia* 1.112), and the Muse has put many into his quiver (*Olympia* 6.6, 9.8). All this is arch and playful, but Pindar once shifts his metaphor to become a poet-wolf who might leap from hiding upon his enemy (*Pythia* 2.84–85). Even a praise poet, he warns, could learn to sing another sort of song if goaded by flagrant iniquity.

Since evil or base actions demanded silence, the praise poet in principle would refuse to sing any victory that was tainted or any victor who was beneath the standard of aristocratic virtue. Theoretically he accepted a commission only when he recognized an occasion as one in which the Muse, Memory, Festivity, and Tranquility the daughter of Justice might be willing to join. Epinician poetry thus acted as a censor, ever dividing what was worthy of blame from what was worthy of praise, and Pindar, at any rate, thought it right to continue in this work of discrimination even as he composed his laudatory odes. What he praised, after all, was splendid action crowned by success; it was victory, not the victorious man, that was to be rescued from forgetfulness and fixed in men's memory. The wreath alone was perfect and immortal, whereas the man who wore it was necessarily imperfect and mortal. Other deeds of his might fall far short of the superlative, or he might go madly on into violence and excess, and Pindar did not tire of mentioning these possibilities. His commission might come from a haughty northern nobleman or even from a tyrant with a reputation for cruelty; still, he would presume to offer counsels of moderation, even admonitions aimed at faults, if they seemed appropriate.

Such presumption from a powerless hireling was at the very least rash, but Pindar was encouraged in it by traditions that had long identified poets with prophets, and he also found his own ways of dressing out his negative warnings. In the guise of sympathy, he dared to sing about the physical ailments of Hieron of Syracuse, insisting that he, the harshest tyrant of his time, would have to die exactly as all the rest of mankind dies (*Pythia* 3). The poet would like to bring him the starlight of rescue from death (ll. 72–76), but of course he cannot since even Asclepius was not allowed to reverse the process of dying. Only insofar as Hieron has been a true ruler, gentle to his people, fair to his nobility, and open to strangers (ll. 70–71, this to the man credited with having invented the secret police!) can he hope. And his hope will be no more than what is common to all men: that immortality will come when virtue at last finds its completion in continuing songs (l. 114). Similarly, in the guise of piety, Pindar presumed to insist upon this same tyrant's dependence upon god's aid for his success, and then to suggest that such aid might not be always forthcoming. "It is god who governs your ambitions and has the care of your power and fame, Hieron. As long as he does not abandon you, you may hope for more victories" (*Olympia* 1.106–11). The overt statement is a happy one, but it rests on the ominous assumption that the divine prop might yet be withdrawn. The same suggestion is made to a noble family of Aegina who is reminded with a prayer ("May Time not tire in its support!") that the strength of their island, resting as it does with god, could still crumble and fall like a column (*Olympia* 8.25–30; compare *Olympia* 4.16, 13.25–26 and 105, *Pythia* 5.117–21).

Those, however, were mere insinuations. For real admonition Pindar borrowed a sophisticated tool from earlier poets: the indirect but inarguable demonstration grounded in myth. Mythic scenes were, after all, generic to choral poetry, and Pindar was liberal with freestanding instantaneous glimpses of familiar figures from the gigantic drama that was always being played just outside of time. Danced by the chorus, such tableaux traditionally served to attach present ephemeral festivities to the world of permanence. They were employed as well by the epinician poets as reinforcement to the thought pattern of an ode, for they could give the super-actuality of fiction to general notions such as the presence of god in the world's order or the inefficacy even of error in the face of fate. To these two uses of myth Pindar added a third. Exploiting the multitude of meanings that each myth contained, he would sometimes bring a story forward in ostensible support of his general praise but load it with an opposite, ominous message as well. In this way he could maintain the suave and laudatory surface of his hymn, and yet produce solemn warnings that seemed to rise directly from the most ancient Hellenic conclusions about the shape of human existence.

The best-known example of the monitory myth occurs in the First Olympian Ode, where shifting instants from the story of Pelops are being activated. The song is for Hieron, and the mythic demonstration is apparently suited to the tyrant's praised success, since it too culminates in a chariot victory. Nevertheless there is a second strand to the story, one that ends with the eternal punishments of another hero who did not know how to use success. Tantalus, forever tortured by unappeased appetites, was a model for anyone who—like Hieron—had known prosperity far beyond that of others (*Olympia* 1.54–55; 103–5) but could not "digest" his advantages. Forgetting that he was a receiver and not a giver of divine favor, he tried to usurp powers that were not his, and his consequent fall was immediate and cruel. Put this way, the application to Hieron's almost superhuman arrogance is blatant, but Pindar has provided every possible distraction: the hint (via repudiation) of divine cannibalism, the self-conscious proclamation of originality, the glancing erotic reference to Ganymede, and above all a poetic language which, as he reminds us, could charm belief into the unbelievable (l. 31). Here it works to add enchantment to the unpalatable, but nevertheless it is finally the myth itself that lets the poet do his work. Pindar is able to tell the tyrant that tyrannical behavior is dangerous only because myth allows him to do so in signs instead of in words.

The same effect of mythic admonition is achieved in the Second Pythian Ode, also made for Hieron. Again Pindar chooses the tale of one who stood at the peak of divine favor but forgot that there was an absolute difference between man and god. Ixion, like Tantalus, tried to take prerogatives (sexual, this time, instead of dietary) that were denied him by the constitution of the universe, and he too was given an endless punishment. His adventure signifies the danger and ugliness of ingratitude, and in the ostensible movement of the ode it provides a grotesque foil for the grateful response which the present music offers to the benefactions of Hieron. Ixion's ingratitude created a monster, whereas the thankfulness of Syracuse creates the ode now being sung. As the poem proceeds, however, the parallel between the enormous bliss of Ixion before his misstep and the enormous bliss of Hieron at the present moment induces a sense of discomfort (ll. 58–61). And the result is that when the end of the ode is invaded by beasts representing the various distortions of a healthy public, there is an unspoken indication that Hieron, too, may be about to engender monsters by going beyond the bounds of permitted political aspirations. If he does, he will be almost as conspicuous in his fall as Ixion on his wheel. The passage in which the poet suggests that tyranny and mob rule are a pair of extremes between which lies the admirable mean—rule by the wise (l. 88)—is purposely obscure, but in the final lines the victor is plainly included in a leveling exhortation. The great ruler of Syracuse, the shockingly rich horse-trainer tyrant, must bear the yoke of divine superiority along with the rest of mankind and, like a beast, answer to god's goad (ll. 93–96).

Myth allowed Pindar to object to the misuse of power, but his more characteristic political pressures were positive. In every ode he urged victors and the class that produced them to be in fact the best—to be a literal aristocracy. And in doing so he went beyond exhortation and took up a mode of magical duress, the precedent for which he found in earlier religious poetry. In prayers and hymns petitioners had tried, like sorcerers, to trap a divinity into showing a favorable aspect, using a time-honored method. First they described the god to himself as having the desired quality, using traditional epithets that he could not deny, and then they told him of past actions which he must, in consistency with himself, repeat once more. In this way the god was caught in the inescapable obligations of his own nature, and when the process was carried out simultaneously by a number of worshippers he was bound to respond. (This same idea of prayer as a binding spell is expressed, incidentally, in Donne's Sermon on Psalm 90:14, and Anglicans still, when asking for mercy, say "For thou art the same Lord, whose property is always to have mercy. . . . ")

It was this almost universal technique of prayer that Pindar borrowed, realizing that the victory ode, a secular hymn danced by a number of performers, could exert a like coercion upon its client. Once the magical words of a group of dancers had formally described a man (or a family or a class or a city) as having a certain quality, that subject would be bound in faith to itself to continue in a display of the same. Pindar expressed the purely practical side of this notion when he said that good fame "masters" or "takes control of" a man (*Olympia* 6.10), but he understood as well the more occult force of his chorus. When once he had ritually reminded Hieron of his ideal aspect as a ruler (a lordly first among peers, one who used his wealth in freedom of spirit, bold in youth and wise in maturity), he spoke like the magician who knows that his spell has been properly performed. To the summoned spirit of Hieron's favorable aspect he gave this simple command: "Now BE what you have learned yourself to be!" (*Pythia* 2.72).

Hieron was not the only one thus bound by Pindar's hymns. Victors, and with them their friends and families, were reminded again and again of their innate excellence, of the virtues that grew like plants within their natures (for example, *Olympia* 9.16), and also of their proper association with such nonviolent world-forces as Good Order, Justice, Tranquility, Truth, and Maturity (for example, *Olympia* 9.15–16). These repeated descriptions are parallel to the invocation of a true prayer, where the god's particular powers are revived and contained even as he is called ("O thou whose strength it is to . . . "). And having thus invoked his aristocrats, what Pindar urged upon them was the defense of the present order, properly understood. Eunomia, that balanced and peaceful political mode in which the nobles rejoiced, was not their own construction to do with as they pleased. It was instead the gift of the same god who had established music, prophecy, and healing medicines (*Pythia* 5.63–69), and the principles of all four had to be kept congruent. One word, *nomos,* could be used both for a melodic line (*Nemea* 5.25) and for traditional law (*Pythia* 1.62). Another word, *tethmos,* served for the rules that established song (*Olympia* 7.88, 13.29, *Isthmia* 6.20, *Nemea* 4.33) and for those that established contest (*Olympia* 6.69, 13.40), as well as for the ancient Doric constitution (*Pythia* 1.64; compare *Paean* 4.43, where reference is to the Kean customs) and also for the divine favor granted to a city (*Olympia* 8.25). These were not philological accidents but linguistic evidences of the single divine harmony—authoritative and inalterable—that rulers were meant to protect.

Pindar thus urged an active conservatism upon his noble victors, invoking them as powerful but reminding them that they moved within a fixed and transcendent scheme. Certainly they flew as eagles, while lesser men cowered below (*Nemea* 3.81–82), but they occupied a hierarchical position that was superb only when viewed from the ground. Within the cosmos they were at best only imitators of the mighty ones above: a tyrant might drive away enemies and create a new city, but those exploits shrank beside their cosmic doublet wherein Zeus crushed a gigantic chaos monster under a volcano and created the concept of order (*Pythia* 1). Every act of strength and governance was enhanced but also minimized by a like absolute model, a truth most plainly stated in the Eighth Isthmian, where the present athletic victory, the repulse of the Persians, and even the legendary taking of Troy are all magnified but diminished as well by the example of Zeus in victory over a potential rival. The ascendancy of the nobles was only a lesser projection of the royal and statesmanlike rule of Zeus. It had its limitations, and these Pindar attempted to bind upon it, even as he invoked the nobility at the height of its powers.

The victor class was described to itself as turning its back on unjust violence (*Olympia* 7.92, *Pythia* 11.55b; compare *Pythia* 8.12, where Hesychia thrusts hybris into the bilge). It was reminded that it used wealth only when that wealth came in justice, willingly (*Pythia* 5.4, 14, *Pythia* 3.105) and as a healthy thing (*Olympia* 5.25), for noble souls were superior to riches (*Nemea* 9.32). An aristocrat scorned oath breaking, flattery, and calumny. Even more important, he was above envy, which meant that he could recognize and acclaim true superiority. He was not quarrelsome and ready to fight for evil ends, nor was he bent simply on winning—neither *dyseris* nor *philonikos* (from Adrastus' praise of his former enemy at *Olympia* 6.19). Consequently he would not disrupt the polity by sordid struggles for dominance. Furthermore, he could not be swayed by bribery or bad counsel but would "orphan the evil tongue of its bright sound, and know / how to hate all acts of selfish violence" (from the description of Damophilus as the ideal citizen at *Pythia* 4.283). Trained by the games, he would acclaim the opinion that proved to be best in today's political contest, knowing that all played by the same rules, "upholding and resisting policies with moderation, / their tongues in line with their hearts" (of the Aeginetan Phylacids at *Isthmia* 6.71–72).

An ideal such as this was naturally anti-autocratic and Pindar, when he could, used his chorus to involve the noble community in a public and solemn abjuration of tyranny. Thus at Aegina he caused the citizen singers to renounce with their general voice the kind of conspiracy that could bring undeserved dominance to a cunning man, while they swore to subject one another to a constant, friendly review:

> Falsehood does violence to what is bright
> and offers rotten fame to the obscure.
> Let this never be my way, O father Zeus!
> Let me take the simple paths
> not those of duplicity,
> that when I die I may not leave my sons
> ill-fame. Some pray for gold,
> some for boundless lands,
> but I would wish to please my fellow townsmen,
> then hide my limbs beneath the ground
> as one who praised the man deserving praise
> and sprinkled blame upon iniquity.
>
> [*Nemea* 8.34–45]

At home in Thebes Pindar bound the citizens even more explicitly in an aristocratic creed hostile to tyranny, giving his chorus these words to sing:

> In city matters I find out the middle way
> that longer flowers with prosperity, for I reject
> the tyrant's lot.
> I reach instead towards virtues common to all noble men;
> thus the envious are held at bay.
> The man who takes the bloom of noble deeds,
> steers his life in quietude
> and turns his back on dire violence
> will have a finer passing into black death
> for offering his sweet continuing race
> this best prize as its inheritance—
> the grace of good repute.
>
> [*Pythia* 11.52–60]

Statements such as these, solemnly proclaimed in a multiple first-person voice and magically reinforced by choral gesture, were not unlike the oaths sworn in certain ancient sodalities. With them Pindar meant to fix the nobles for whom his odes were made in a common allegiance to traditional aristocratic forms.

Music was necessary to the aristocracy because it was the source of immortalizing glory. This meant that the poet had an enormous influence since, in theory at least, the reserved powers of review, admonition, and exhortation lodged in the epinician ode could not be suppressed. But what kept the poet from simply selling this influence or using his control over princely fame in an unscrupulous fashion? This question clearly troubled Pindar, for his odes are filled not only with pointed self-vindication but also with general meditations on the honesty of song. He knows that even those who have the highest endowments may be open to bribery—Asclepius himself sold his powers unlawfully (*Pythia* 3.54). He blames other men for useless chatter (*Olympia* 2.87), dangerous slander (*Pythia* 2.54–56), or vain croaking boasts (*Olympia* 9.38–39), and he admits that lies may be decked out with elaborate beguilements so as to impose themselves as truth (*Olympia* 1.28b–29). Worse yet, one may commit an act of killing injustice by refusing praise to the deserving and giving it to a lesser man; this, he says, is what the Achaeans (and Homer) did in the case of Ajax and Odysseus (*Nemea* 7.20; compare *Nemea* 8.23). Such are the possible perversions of praise, but he, Pindar, feels secure in his profession because true poets, like true aristocrats, are part of the appointed order of things. They too are invested by nature with their special virtue (*Olympia* 2.86), given their opportunities by god-made splendors, and granted success only by the Muses. The man who sings with such a vocation imitates eternal songs that have been shaped in heaven (*Nemea* 5.22–25, *Isthmia* 8.63–66), and this means that, though his work may be imperfect, it cannot be false. Furthermore, the poet, again like the aristocrat, is driven by his own need for good fame, and he too is scrutinized in the envious openness of small communities. "To make a new song and give it over to trial on the touchstone—that is danger in full!" (*Nemea* 8.20–21; compare *Pythia* 1.84). When he takes a commission he is thus like a charioteer entering a race (*Olympia* 9.81–82) or an athlete descending into the playing space (*Olympia* 8.54, *Olympia* 13.93, *Pythia* 2.44). He needs all his daring (*Olympia* 13.11), for he is engaging his particular excellence in that risky public toil which is man's only means of escaping the non-life of obscure inaction. In such an endeavor anyone would be a fool to be other than true.

Convinced of such sublimities Pindar could approach even the question of his own pay. True, his compositions were bought, but all work had its natural wage. Shepherds, birdcatchers, and fishermen worked to keep themselves from hunger; poets worked for pay, and the class whose work was contest and war earned its own proper wage, paid in the words that the poets produced (*Isthmia* 1.47; compare *Nemea* 7.63, *Olympia* 7.16). Pindar's clients did not purchase his praise; rather, their actions—when they were inwrought with virtue—demanded it. Thus in fact he was paying them, not the other way around. The fee covered the rehearsing and costuming of a chorus, presumably leaving something over for the poet to take home, but the duty of acclamation had been imposed directly by the victory. "Crowns laid upon curling heads force this god-made duty upon me . . . and Pisa too bids me to speak" (*Olympia* 3.6–9; compare *Pythia* 7.10–13).

The fundamental notion was one of just recompense, often seen as answering light with light. "Wherever god-given brightness comes, a brilliant light lies upon men and a sweet spate of days" (*Pythia* 8.96–97). Every superlative achievement was luminous, as were also youth, wealth, fame, and salvation (*Nemea* 8.34; compare *Nemea* 3.64, 3.84, 4.13; youth, *Nemea* 7.3; wealth, *Olympia* 2.55–56; fame, *Olympia* 1.23; salvation, *Pythia* 3.75). Especially at the games did innate excellence shine out in each contest (*Isthmia* 1.22; compare *Nemea* 3.84, 9.42, and *Isthmia* 2.17, where the victor brings light to his city), and such light could be prolonged indefinitely by the light of superlative poetry (the chorus equals light at *Olympia* 4.12; compare *Olympia* 9.22). A victor could lead a portion of song up into the light, reviving the actions of his forefathers (*Isthmia* 6.62; compare *Olympia* 5.15 where the victor leads his city into light), and he himself could burn bright with the Muses (*Isthmia* 7.23) because poetry was like a torch (*Isthmia* 4.47) that shone back inextinguishable upon the beam of a fine accomplishment. And light, like air and water, was incorruptible.

As Pindar saw it, the power of poets was checked exactly as the power of princes was: by the divine order that dealt out natural endowments, by the need for good fame and the appetite for glory, by the ready criticism of peers, and by the unseen audience of Time and the Olympians. Poetry, moreover, (at any rate his own) was asked to undergo a further regulation, for Pindar invited the public to scrutinize not just his finished work but also his creative processes. A Pindaric ode presents itself not as a final and impervious object, but rather as a performance under construction. There is a constant wavering between inception and finality, intention and effect. There is a dizzying shift of temporal occasion, which at one point may seem to be the winning of the victory, at another the commissioning of the ode or the instruction of the chorus; sometimes the public performance describes itself, but again the poetic moment may seem to be one of private communion between poet and Muse. And all this is reflected in a hybrid persona, for the frequent "I" of the odes may refer to an "I, poet" (for example, *Olympia* 6.84, *Isthmia* 1.1), an "I, poem" (*Nemea* 5.3), an "I, chorus" (*Olympia* 14.18), or a combination of the three (*Olympia* 9.20). And what this mixed "voice of the ode" repeatedly asks is that an audience assumed to be close at hand observe each gesture and test each ingredient in the semimagical praise process.

The ruling fiction is that the song is dynamic; it is taking form before the eyes and ears of the spectators. Furthermore, it is fallible and in need of encouragement and confirmation. "Have I made an idle boast?" (*Pythia* 10.4). "Would anyone call this the work of a Boeotian pig?" (*Olympia* 6.89–90). The negations provoked by questions such as these involve the audience in a kind of complicity in the act of praise. When difficult choices are to be made, listeners may be asked to participate. "Which of your glories, Thebes, would you hear sung?" is the explicit demand at the opening of *Isthmia* 7, and the same kind of appeal may be made implicitly, as when the chorus confesses that the praise of a tyrant is more difficult than that of a king (*Pythia* 2.13–18), with the unspoken appeal: How then shall we proceed? Sometimes a song will expose a stress point in its structure, so that the audience will seem to supervise the search for a solution (for example, *Olympia* 13.40–46b, *Nemea* 7.53). Again, an ode may explain that just here a long list of victories might be offered but will not appear because "deep in their hidden hearts men resent the praise of others' virtues" (*Pythia* 1.84; compare, for example, *Pythia* 8.31–32). An alternate motif will be proposed and the listener who has been treated with such comradely courtesy is bound to approve; indeed, the poem's next phase will seem to have originated with him.

These are of course tricks of style, useful for emphasis and also for a kind of irony, a classic technique for involving an audience. Thus, having chosen to evoke the figure of Clytemnestra (as a negative foil to a conspicuous but guiltless victor), the chorus of *Pythia* 11 pretends to be at a loss. Whirling in its dance it sings, "Friends, I am whirled at a crossroads, though I was going on so well—surely some wind has blown me off course!" (ll. 38–40), which, "translated," means, "Admire the apt unconventionality of our myth and ponder its meaning!" The notion that the audience might catch the dancers in some sort of *faux pas* is a favorite conceit (*Olympia* 9.35–36, *Pythia* 10.51, *Nemea* 3.26–27), but it is also an invitation to collaboration, as is the Pindaric habit of making the song describe itself. Having struck up in a mode called the Castorian, a chorus will chant: "I would yoke my victor to a Castorian hymn" (*Isthmia* 1.16). Or alternatively, in the Dorian: "Muse, stand by me as I devise a bright new way to yoke the Dorian mode to the voice of the komos-singer" (*Olympia* 3.4–5). Placing an initial image, the singers say, "I shall place golden columns at this broad porch . . . " (*Olympia* 6.1–3); breaking off a narrative (and perhaps coming to a choreographed halt) the dancers sing: "I come to a stop" (*Nemea* 5.16). Song is action; action is decision, danger, and the grasping of opportunities, and the audience is forced to share the risk with techniques such as these.

Some of these practices are generic, deriving from the self-description of magical operations; a certain number of them are to be found as well in the epinicians of Bacchylides. Nevertheless there is a pervasive assumption of close assistance from an audience that sets Pindar's metapoetical passages apart from others. He insists upon discussing the performance with those who watch it, breaking through its facade so that the inner contrivances are visible. This is of course only one more contrivance, but it expresses Pindar's sense of his political function. He does praise those in power; he must, for that is his profession. Nevertheless he announces with these programmatic appeals that his praise is (or should be) a fully popular affair. His chorus stands as one, but it represents the commonality (it is *idios en koinōi, Olympia* 13.49).

It would be foolish to try to assess the immediate influence of Pindar's political thought. There is no way to know if Thebans and Aeginetans did actually behave according to the civic creeds repeated for them by Pindaric choruses. Nor can anyone say whether Hieron in any way moderated his arrogance after watching the Tantalus example danced out in his halls. Did Arcesilaus, king of Cyrene, in fact try to mix pure virtue with his wealth because his singers had told him he did? The question is ephemeral as well as unanswerable, for he was soon overthrown. Indeed, the continuing events of the fifth century seem to accuse Pindar of bad political prophecy, as city after city saw aristocratic governments (reflections of the eternal harmonies of Apollo's lyre) edged out by what Pindar called the "loud-mouthed mob" (*Pythia* 2.87). Time in its longer reaches, however, makes another sort of judgment. In every generation since his own, certain men have been moved afresh by Pindar's vision of government by men who were both strong and fine. The notion of poetic scrutiny is gone but some still dream—according to the two great Pindaric metaphors—of political rivalry as an open and glorious contest, and of political entities as festive places where Quietude suppresses violence and rejoices in all the forms of graciousness (*Pythia* 8.1–5).

"O Totiens Servus": Saturnalia and Servitude in Augustan Rome

Michael André Bernstein

> Who can speak broader than he that has no house to put his head in? Such may rail against great buildings.
>
> —SHAKESPEARE, *Timon of Athens*

To pose the question of evaluating political poetry is, of course, itself already a polemical move, since it insists on distinctions that command neither general critical consent nor methodological specificity. Repudiating the pertinence of such concerns to poetry has been, after all, the principal thrust of some of the most influential texts in modern literary theory. Indeed, considered historically, the struggle to separate aesthetic from both moral and political considerations can be seen as constituting the inaugural, grounding act of poetics as a distinct discipline. In such a view, the words of a poem, by their very nature, are radically divorced from their usage in the quotidian world of shared human activities, so that although a text may contain political themes among its *materia poetica,* insofar as it succeeds as a work of art these must function purely as internal and autonomous elements in the structure of the piece, not as arguments seeking to participate in a wider discourse. Because the language of poetry is unique and self-sufficient, thematic considerations are strictly irrelevant, and the issue of evaluation is identical regardless of the ostensible subject matter of the poem. Political poetry, in other words, is a meaningless term: a work is either a poem or it is not, and any attempt to include

In its full context, the present essay will constitute part of a larger exploration of the Saturnalian dialogue entitled *When the Carnival Turns Bitter: A Study of the Abject Hero.*

political concerns in its creation or evaluation is simply to abandon the domain of art for what Mallarmé dismissed as the debased idiom of "les journaux."[1]

Yet the very need to keep insisting on so categorical a distinction reveals that contamination is always possible, that the chasm may prove only a threshold habitually traversed by the words of any poem. And in fact, for every instance of a Mallarméan insistence upon the autonomy of the poem, there exists a counterpolemic stressing the link between word and world and, more pertinently still, between the language of verse and a search for values applicable to the communal experiences of both author and readers.[2] But as I remarked earlier, the very heterogeneity of these arguments tends to deprive them of any methodological specificity, and all too often discussions of political poetry have done little more than catalog judgments about the ideological stance of a given work according to a critic's fixed conception of which attitudes merit approval and which deserve censure. There is a crucial distinction between reading political poetry and reading poetry politically. In the latter case, the concern is less with the characteristics, let alone the evaluation, of political poetry per se than with judging how effectively the poem either champions or contests positions whose independent authority is always already guaranteed and which, in principle, are only to be illustrated, not questioned or modified, by literary texts.

Clearly both perspectives—the Mallarméan and what, for want of a better term, I can only call the poem-as-polemical-illustration—are unable to engage the tensions and ambiguities that political verse, as much as any other kind, often reveals. I am not convinced, however, that another general, theoretical analysis of the topic will do much to

1. Mallarmé's formulation here is both categorical and powerful: "cette donnée exacte, qu'il faut, si l'on fait de la littérature, parler autrement que les journaux" (Stéphane Mallarmé, *Correspondance*, ed. Henri Mondor and Lloyd James Austin, 11 vols. [Paris, 1959–85], 3:67).

2. I discuss the terms of the quarrel between what the French called *la poésie pure* and poetry specifically committed to political and social effectiveness in *The Tale of the Tribe: Ezra Pound and the Modern Verse Epic* (Princeton, N.J., 1980).

Michael André Bernstein, associate professor of English and comparative literature at the University of California, Berkeley, is the author of *The Tale of the Tribe: Ezra Pound and the Modern Verse Epic* (1980) and *Prima della Rivoluzione* (1984), a volume of verse. He is currently completing a book on the Abject Hero and a study, *Talent and the Individual Tradition in Modern Poetry.*

further our understanding. Because *all* of the terms of the question are themselves historical in nature, functioning quite differently in the context and rhetoric of different eras, a series of individual studies is likely to prove far more profitable than any global claims. Accordingly, my own concern here will be with a poem whose setting—the Roman Saturnalia—has been regarded as virtually the archetypal embodiment of human desire for freedom from cast and cant, a glimpse of a utopian moment in which our longing for a prelapsarian world of unfettered communication and social equality finds its decisive literary expression. Saturnalian poetry is political in the deepest sense, precisely because it owes allegiance to no particular party or temporary interests. Its themes, although expressed through carnival laughter and festive license, are always directly about power and servitude, and its entire *raison d'être* is to challenge the claims of a dominant hierarchy by giving voice to everyone whom that hierarchy has silenced in the maintenance of its rule. Because the carnivalization of all normally inflexible distinctions governs both the argument and idiom of a Saturnalian poem, its political thrust is registered as much formally as thematically, and because its articulation is not linked to the championing of any one ideology, the Saturnalian text has been celebrated by critics like Mikhail Bakhtin as the paradigmatic instance of literature's capacity to speak for a less repressive human dispensation.[3]

But as soon as one begins to question the nature of the topos without yielding to the seductively optimistic descriptions of writers like Bakhtin, the Saturnalia acquires a darker and more complex character. What is needed here, I believe, is first to understand better the curious function of the Saturnalian carnival *as a modern critical fiction.* From the perspective opened by this questioning, we can then see how a poet like Horace employed the conventions of the Saturnalian dialogue to fashion a self-examination that is more painful and more politically unsettling than habitual readings have been prepared to recognize.

> We stand in the tumult of a festival.
> What festival? This loud, disordered mooch?
> —Wallace Stevens, "The Auroras of Autumn"

3. The powerful appeal of the Saturnalia to Bakhtin's imagination is evident throughout his writings. See, particularly, Mikhail Bakhtin, *Rabelais and His World,* trans. Helene Iswolsky (Cambridge, Mass., 1968); *The Dialogic Imagination: Four Essays,* ed. Michael Holquist, trans. Caryl Emerson and Holquist (Austin, Tex., 1981); *Problems of Dostoevsky's Poetics,* ed. and trans. Emerson (Minneapolis, 1984); and *Speech Genres and Other Late Essays,* ed. Holquist and Emerson, Slavic Series no. 8 (Austin, Tex., 1987). This aspect of Bakhtin, and its connection to his other concerns, is discussed in *Bakhtin: Essays and Dialogues on His Work,* ed. Gary Saul Morson (Chicago, 1986). Tzvetan Todorov's *Mikhail Bakhtin: The Dialogical Principle,* trans. Wlad Godzich (Minneapolis, 1984), provides a valuable reading of Bakhtin's major works. The most lucid brief account of Bakhtin that I have read in English remains Morson's essay, "The Heresiarch of *Meta,*" *Poetics and Theory of Literature* 3 (Oct. 1978): 407–27.

Like so much else in contemporary theory, our newfound faith in the liberating power of carnival laughter returns for much of its rhetoric to the cardinal example of Friedrich Nietzsche. In *Jenseits von Gut und Böse,* for example, Nietzsche claims for his own age a unique preparedness

> for a carnival in the grand style, for the laughter and high spirits of the most spiritual revelry, for the transcendental heights of the highest nonsense and Aristophanean derision of the world. Perhaps this is where we shall discover the realm of our *invention,* that realm in which we, too, can still be original, say, as parodists of world history and God's buffoons—perhaps, even if nothing else today has any future, our *laughter* may yet have a future.[4]

Yet even this affirmation, regularly quoted as a kind of crystallization in advance of the whole modern longing for the cathartic energy of the Saturnalia, is more equivocal than is commonly recognized.[5] A phrase like "that realm in which we, too, can still be original" betrays a profound anxiety about the possibility of finding any sphere in which to invent the new, and Nietzsche's solution is itself so dependent on that which it would replace—a parodist, no matter how brilliant, is always in a derivative relationship to the object of his parody—that it hardly seems to satisfy the demand for an "original" future. But if my reading of this passage as more like an Aristophanean derision of the hope for a transcendental carnival than any straightforward announcement of a program seems overly pessimistic, consider how much darker it becomes when placed beside another typical Nietzschean formulation:

> How can man have pleasure in nonsense? . . . The overthrowing of experience into its opposite, of purposefulness into purposelessness, of necessity into what is wished for, but in such a way that this process causes [us] no harm, but is simply imagined once out of wanton exuberance, delights [mankind] because it liberates us *momentarily* from the compulsion of necessity, of what is appropriate to [quotidian human] purpose and experience in which we ordinarily see our inexorable masters. We play and laugh when the expected (which usually makes us afraid and tense) reveals

4. Friedrich Nietzsche, *Jenseits von Gut und Böse,* in *Werke in sechs Bände,* ed. K. Schlechta (Munich, 1980), 4:686 (sec. 223). The translation is from Nietzsche, *Beyond Good and Evil: Prelude to a Philosophy of the Future,* trans. Walter Kaufman (New York, 1966), p. 150.

5. As an example of such an affirmative reading of Nietzsche, consider Michel Foucault's celebrated essay, "Nietzsche, Genealogy, History," in *Language, Counter-Memory, Practice,* ed. D. F. Bouchard (Ithaca, N.Y., 1977), pp. 139–64. I realize, of course, that Foucault is scarcely ever regarded as an affirmative writer, but his attitude toward the liberating power of carnival laughter in this essay seems to me much more celebratory than Nietzsche's own. On p. 161, for example, Foucault quotes the same passage from *Jenseits von Gut und Böse* as I have done, but he seems to miss the grim humor in Nietzsche's description and reads it as a straightforward homage to the "parodists of world history and God's buffoons."

itself without causing harm. It is the slave's pleasure at the Saturnalia.[6]

Throughout his writings, the word "slave" served Nietzsche as a synecdoche for a whole range of contemptible moral and intellectual qualities, and in this passage from *Human, All Too Human* his scorn for the slave's joy at the temporary license of the carnival is unmistakable.

One reason for such scorn is the very fact of the Saturnalia's brevity ("it liberates us *momentarily* from the compulsion of necessity"). For someone who believes as deeply as Nietzsche that "alle Lust will Ewigkeit-, / -will tiefe, tiefe Ewigkeit! (all desire longs for eternity-, / -wants deep, deep eternity),"[7] a joy that is confined, as the very condition of its existence, to a preordained time table must seem trivial, and an officially sanctioned reversal of conventional hierarchies must appear more like a parody than a genuine instance of liberation.

The strict temporal limits of the Saturnalia and its character as an official state holiday do not seem to trouble Bakhtin, and he describes the "essence of carnival" as "most clearly expressed and experienced in the Roman Saturnalias."[8] Bakhtin goes on to recognize that "the tradition of the Saturnalias remained unbroken and alive in the medieval carnival, which expressed this universal renewal and was vividly felt as an escape from the usual official way of life,"[9] and sees its final triumphant expression in Rabelais' tales.

But while the continuity between the Roman Saturnalia and the festivals of medieval and Renaissance Europe has been recognized for a long time, there is certainly no agreement about which fictional works best embody "the quintessence of the Saturnalia."[10] Instead, what unites the diverse characterizations of the Saturnalia is the nostalgic appeal with which such rituals are invested by theoreticians as part of an argument about a more desirable society. In his study of "la fête," Roger Chartier challenges such readings by showing how the contemporary carnival is always seen as a degradation of an earlier, more vital one, and how different theories about the meaning of festivals all tend to merge into

6. Nietzsche, *Menschliches, Allzumenschliches*, in *Werke in sechs Bände*, 2:572 (sec. 213); my translation.

7. Nietzsche, *Also Sprach Zarathustra*, in *Werke in sechs Bände*, 3:558 (pt. 4, sec. 12); my translation.

8. Bakhtin, *Rabelais and His World*, p. 7.

9. Ibid., p. 8.

10. Enid Welsford, for example, devotes very little space to Rabelais, but finds that in *Twelfth Night* "Shakespeare transmutes into poetry the quintessence of the Saturnalia" (Welsford, *The Fool: His Social and Literary History* [Garden City, N.Y., 1961], p. 253).

the projection of an imaginary and idealized collective past.[11] Chartier further warns that the whole relationship between the narration or representation of a carnival, whether in literature, folk art, or paintings, and the festival as a collectively lived social experience is far more problematic than writers like Bakhtin acknowledge. But in spite of any specific divergences, when one examines the use of historical, ethnographic, and literary data in the descriptions of Saturnalian carnivals proposed by contemporary theoreticians, three general principles emerge with remarkable consistency.

The first is the prevalence across numerous cultures, whether literate or not, of some ritual occasion during which, as with the Ashanti of central Ghana, "our forebears . . . ordained a time, once every year, when every man and woman, free man and slave, should have freedom to speak out just what was in their head, to tell their neighbors just what they thought of them . . . [and] also [of] the king or chief."[12] The second is that the carnivalesque ceremony can be interpreted as a specific kind of language through which the tensions present in a society can be articulated and made visible.[13] The third principle is the most crucial for our purposes, since it addresses the polemical function of carnival rites when they are invoked as models for a less restrictively hierarchic, more tolerant and spontaneous social organization. It is largely because of such longings that literary scholars find accounts of ceremonies like the Ashanti's *Apo* festival or the medieval Feast of Fools so attractive a guide for their interpretations of Western Saturnalian texts. Often in these interpretations ethnographic data is introduced in a more or less random manner, and insufficient attention is given to the distinction Chartier stresses "between the textual usages of the festival and the [real] festival rituals."[14] With this caution in mind, my concern here will be limited to the use of the Saturnalia as represented in a fictional narrative or theoretical speculation, and the actual history of such festivals will only figure in the discussion when it can directly illuminate the image of the carnival as a specifically literary topos.

In its classical incarnation in Roman culture, the Saturnalia designated a distinct religious festival held in honor of the mythical Golden Age of Saturn. During the time of the Saturnalia (17–19 December) a special license to speak their minds freely was accorded to everyone, irrespective of rank. It is usually only this one aspect of the festival that poets used

11. Roger Chartier, "La fête en question: retour sur un colloque" and "Des fêtes de l'Ancien Régime à la fête révolutionnaire: problèmes de lecture," in *La Fête en question*, ed. Karin R. Gürttler and Monique Sarfati-Arnaud (Montreal, 1979), pp. 1–4 and 35–56.

12. Robert C. Elliott, *The Power of Satire: Magic, Ritual, Art* (Princeton, N.J., 1966), p. 80.

13. See Chartier's comment, "la fête est aussi un langage où peuvent se dire et se donner à voir les tensions qui traversent une société," in *La fête en question*, p. 2.

14. Ibid., p. 3 ("entre les pratiques textuelles de la fête et ses pratiques rituelles").

in their descriptions: other, equally crucial, features of the actual Saturnalian rites, such as the agrarian celebrations linked to the sowing of crops, the ritual exchange of presents, and so forth, are often not treated at all in Saturnalian texts like the two satires Horace set during the festival period. From the beginning, that is, writers did not seek to represent Saturnalia as such but to exploit the inherent literary potential of certain specific features. Foremost among these was, of course, the right of slaves to criticize their masters. As a literary setting, the Saturnalia lends itself particularly well to satiric attacks both on specific individuals and on the larger customs of the age because criticism can be introduced into the work with a minimum of prefatory explanation to justify their audacity. Moreover, by placing these attacks in the mouth of someone without any social standing, the satirist can permit himself a degree of acerbity in his observations that might be unseemly, or even dangerous, if uttered in his own voice. This literary use of a slave as ironist only follows Aristotle's advice in his *Rhetoric:* "There are some things which . . . you cannot say about your opponent without seeming abusive or ill-bred. Put such remarks, therefore, into the mouth of some third person."[15] The Saturnalian freedom of everyone to speak his mind also affords the artist considerable technical as well as thematic opportunities; it allows him, that is, to experiment with mixed tones, expressions, and idioms that would violate the decorum appropriate to most other narrative situations.[16]

The questioning and rebellious stance permissible in a Saturnalian context also proved particularly fruitful for utopian speculations, with the description of a better society either explicitly narrated or at least unmistakably implied as the direct opposite of an unsatisfactory present. Thus, as Robert C. Elliott rightly argues, satire, Saturnalia, and utopia are linked in a clear continuum, but this continuum is determined as much by the formal possibilities inherent in the convention as by the universal longing that Elliott posits for a carnivalesque suspension of daily norms.[17] Such a distinction is worth emphasizing because literary

15. Aristotle *Rhetoric* 3.17.1418. I have used *The Rhetoric of Aristotle,* ed. John E. Sandys, trans. Sir Richard Claverhouse Jebb (Cambridge, 1909), p. 194, but have somewhat modified Jebb's translation in the version quoted here.

16. It is precisely this kind of liberty to which Martial appealed in defending his verses from the charge of obscenity:

> versus hos tamen esse tu memento
> Saturnalicios, Apollinaris:
> mores non habet hic meos libellus.

> But remember, Apollinaris, these poems are meant to be read in the spirit of the Saturnalia: this little book doesn't voice my personal morals.

(Martial *Epigrams* 11.15.11–13. The translation appears in the edition of Walter C. A. Ker, [London, 1930], 2:248–249. I have modified Ker's translation somewhat).

17. See Elliott, *The Shape of Utopia: Studies in a Literary Genre* (Chicago, 1970), pp. 18–25.

historians have been tempted to apply such powerful accounts of the festival's capacity to abolish time and history to the fictional presentations of a carnival as well.[18] In works like *Le Mythe de l'Eternel Retour,* for instance, Eliade describes the participants in a ritual as experiencing an unmediated contemporaneity with the timeless world of myth. This abolition of their daily consciousness is, however, precisely what characters like Davus, the slave in Horace's Saturnalian poem, cannot feel, since the threat of the coming day's punishment intrudes even into their hours of festive liberty. Nor can a satirist like Horace pretend that his poem returns us to the timeless and undifferentiated equivalence of the Golden Age, since the act of writing itself already draws attention to the separation between mythic experience and literary artifice. It is worth reminding ourselves that in a Saturnalian dialogue like Horace's 2.7 we do not overhear the complaint of a slave suddenly able to give voice to his grievances. Rather, we read the poet exercising his consummate metrical skill in the creation of Davus' speech, and it is the craftsman's cunning in satisfying the expectations of the satiric form and in expanding the genre's thematic range that gives his text its authority.

But even as a literary topos, the Saturnalia is considerably more ambiguous than descriptions like Bakhtin's or Elliott's suggest. If Saturn (Saturnus, "the sower," later identified with the Greek Cronus) introduced agriculture to Rome and founded the citadel on the Capitol, he also, as Erwin Panofsky and Elliott both point out, castrated his father and ate his children.[19] Saturn was thus linked both with a time of earthly paradise and with a threatening malignancy, a sense that still carried meaning in the Renaissance notion of a "saturnine" temperament, one embittered or melancholy as a result of Saturn's influence. Even in Latin poetry, moreover, the Age of Saturn was not necessarily associated with an epoch of human freedom from labor and class divisions. In the *Aeneid,* for example, Virgil describes the Golden Age of Saturn as an era marked not by anarchic license but by the people's natural orderliness and just behavior, maintained through their own free choice rather than under the compulsion of the law:

> . . . neue ignorate Latinos
> Saturni gentem haud uinclo nec legibus aequam,
> sponte sua ueterisque dei se more tenetem.[20]

18. See especially Mircea Eliade, *Le Mythe de l'eternel retour: Archetypes et repetition* (Paris, 1969), and *Le Sacré et le profane* (Paris, 1965) for two influential expressions of this tendency.

19. See Elliott, *The Shape of Utopia,* pp. 18–19. See also Erwin Panofsky, *Studies in Iconology: Humanistic Themes in the Art of the Renaissance* (New York, 1939) and Raymond Klibansky, Panofsky, and Fritz Saxl, *Saturn and Melancholy: Studies in the History of Natural Philosophy, Religion, and Art* (London, 1964).

20. Vergil *Opera* (Oxford, 1969, ed. R. A. B. Mynors), 7:202–4. The translation below is from *The Aeneid,* trans. Robert Fitzgerald (New York, 1983), p. 202.

Know that our Latins
Come of Saturn's race, that we are just—
Not by constraint or laws, but by our choice.

No matter how the mythical Age of Saturn was conceived, however, there is no doubt that for poets of Horace's generation (65 B.C.–8 B.C.), the idea of a carnivalesque suspension of social norms had very little appeal since much of their lives had been spent witnessing or, as in Horace's case, briefly participating in the chaos and brutal internecine warfare that marked the end of the Roman Republic. Horace, as W. R. Johnson reminds us, was sixteen when Caesar and Pompey fought for supremacy in the Latin world, twenty-one when Caesar was murdered, and twenty-three when, as a student in Athens, he joined Brutus' army as a military tribune, only to flee "sensi relicta non bene parmula (leaving my shield ingloriously behind)" in the rout at Philippi in November 42 B.C.[21] One historian estimates that "in the twenty years after Caesar crossed the Rubicon, some 200,000 Italians were often under arms."[22] Throughout this period, moreover, Rome itself suffered through a series of bloody proscriptions, during one of which "Appian puts the number of those murdered as high as two thousand knights and three hundred senators."[23] Even after Horace's safe return to Rome, pardoned but bankrupt, he still had to experience the protracted struggle among Caesar's successors, and not until Augustus' victory at Actium in 31 B.C. did a measure of enduring peace return to the Empire. As Niall Rudd observes, "when, after Actium, Octavian finally turned to the task of rebuilding the Roman state, the wonder is that there was anything left to rebuild."[24]

I cite these facts in order to emphasize that Horace's famous advocacy of moderation and balance was formulated in the aftermath of wholesale and almost continuous violence during which much of the social order in which he believed perished, and that the tone of reasoned civility which has provided generations of schoolmasters with elegant tags apparently justifying a life of leisured inoffensiveness was purchased with far more strain and under far greater pressures than traditional readings recognize. Horace is both a darker and a more disturbing writer than

21. For this account of Horace's career, see W. R. Johnson's foreword in Burton Raffel, trans., *The Essential Horace: Odes, Epodes, Satires, and Epistles* (San Francisco, 1983), pp. vii–xiii. Horace's description of his inglorious flight at Philippi is from *Odes* 2.7.10; the translation appears in *Odes and Epodes,* ed. and trans. C. E. Bennett (Cambridge, Mass., 1927), p. 122. However, for a skeptical discussion of the historical accuracy of Horace's description of his battle experiences and an analysis of the famous phrase *relicta non bene parmula,* see Eduard Fraenkel, *Horace* (Oxford, 1957), p. 11.

22. P. A. Brunt, "The Army and the Land in the Roman Revolution," *Journal of Roman Studies* 52 (1962): 75.

23. Niall Rudd, *The Satires of Horace: A Study* (London, 1966), pp. 36–37.

24. Ibid., p. 37.

his conventional image suggests, and Johnson's account of the poet's situation provides a valuable corrective to that image:

> Horace was not a man between two worlds. He was a poet at the edge of a chasm beyond which he could not see. What he saw was a ruin of the world he loved and the death of freedom. His vision was the more bitter because, for a while, he had almost learned to hope against hope, that his culture would not collapse and his freedom would not die. But when that hope had vanished, though he could not hope again, he would not give up. The desolation of outward freedom ultimately forced him to search out the inner freedom of the heart that each man has if he wills to find it. Political crisis and cultural crisis had provoked from Horace an astonishing number of complex successful songs in which hope warred against despair and celebration of the human spirit warred against dark intuitions of abiding failure and futility.[25]

But even so acute a reader as Johnson is misleading, I believe, when he speaks of "the inner freedom of the heart that each man has if he wills to find it," since it is precisely such liberty which Horace is also compelled to cast into doubt or, perhaps more accurately, on whose possession Horace keeps overinsisting as a kind of barrier against the suspicion that in Augustan Rome private freedom, too, has become only a particularly alluring form of self-deception. François Furet describes a postrevolution situation as replacing "the conflict of interest for power with a competition of discourses for the appropriation of legitimacy," and it is clear that Augustus saw the work of his favorite poets as a powerful weapon in the legitimization of his own regime.[26] Although

25. Johnson, foreword to *The Essential Horace,* p. x.

26. In context, Furet is speaking of the French Revolution. I do not mean to suggest that the situation in Augustus' Rome was similar to that in Republican Paris, but rather that his account seems to me accurate as a description of how every new government that is established through the violent overthrow of its predecessor strives to confirm its right to continue holding power. Furet's lines are quoted in Alan Forrest, "Life-cycle of a Circle," *Times Literary Supplement,* 1 November 1985, p. 1226. Richard Jenkyns' description of Augustus' use of the arts as political instruments seems to me quite helpful in relating the success of imperial policy to similar attempts in later cultures: "It was by political propaganda expressed through poetry that both Augustus and Elizabeth [Elizabeth I of England] imposed upon posterity the idea of themselves as presiding geniuses of a culminating age" (Jenkyns, *Three Classical Poets: Sappho, Catullus, and Juvenal* [London, 1982], p. 182 n. 21). The centrality of political undercurrents in the verse of the major Augustan poets, even when they were writing on seemingly quite different themes, is powerfully demonstrated in the collection of essays assembled by Tony Woodman and David West, *Poetry and Politics in the Age of Augustus* (Cambridge, 1984). Woodman's own contribution to the volume ("Horace's First Roman Ode," pp. 83–94), for example, offers a persuasive reading of Horace's *Odes* 3.1 ("Odi profanum vulgus et arceo") as a subtly modulated argument for the emperor's program of social reform. In *Propertius: "Love" and "War," Individual and*

history has confirmed the brilliance of the emperor's and Maecenas' choices for imperial approval and patronage, the responsibility of the poets so honored to the Augustan party line was, if delicately imposed, nonetheless quite unmistakable.[27]

And so, if Horace learned the narrow limits of political integrity and justice from the public events of his era, his own spectacularly successful career showed just how uncertain a thing "inner liberty" was, and how vulnerable all his claims to independence might prove when challenged. That Horace had to endure such challenges on numerous occasions is clear from the repeated insistence in the satires, odes, and epistles on his enemies' *invidia* (envy) to account for the hostility he seems to have encountered throughout his career.[28] But his self-defense, although presented with disarming straightforwardness, itself only helps to keep the issue alive, and a tone of aggrieved uneasiness resonates very close to the surface of such seemingly untroubled narratives as the famous account of Horace's own childhood and early career in book 1, satire 6.[29] When

---

State under Augustus (Berkeley and Los Angeles, 1985), Hans-Peter Stahl describes the tensions between literature and politics in the Augustan elegy, and traces the struggle of poets like Propertius to express a "personal voice in a publicly uniform and therefore homogenizing environment" (p. 3).

27. The counterexample of Ovid, whom Augustus personally banished for life to Tomis, a wretched village on the coast of the Black Sea, indicates how poetic genius alone could not save a writer of the "wrong" sort. Indeed, the very severity of Ovid's punishment suggests that his poems, with their steady undercurrent of irony at the whole Augustan ethos, were in good measure responsible for the emperor's harshness. In "History: Ovid and the Augustan Myth," for example, Rudd argues that Ovid's erotic poems, by their very themes and tone, enacted a semideliberate mockery not only of Augustan values but of the imperial family itself and thus helped to ensure the poet's miserable fate. See Rudd, *Lines of Enquiry: Studies in Latin Poetry* (Cambridge, 1976), pp. 1–31.

28. I have not done a systematic count of all the uses of *invidia* as an explanation for his opponents' motives in Horace's work, but the following examples, although far from exhaustive, will help give some sense of how important a force Horace felt envy was in explaining human behavior: *Satires* 1.3.61; 2.1.77; 2.6.48; *Odes* 2.20.4; 4.3.16; or *Epistles* 1.14.37–38, where the word itself does not occur, but the idea is strikingly presented: "non istic obliquo oculo mea commoda quisquam / limat, non odio obscuro morsuque venenat (Where you live, no one with eye askance detracts from my comforts, or poisons them with the bite of secret hate)" (Horace *Epistles* 1.14.37–38; this translation and those from the *Satires* which appear throughout the text—modified where necessary—appear in H. Rushton Fairclough, ed., *Satires, Epistles, and Ars Poetica* [New York, 1929]). Indeed, when Horace envisages his own future immortality, he cites a final victory over the *invidia* of his enemies as one of its principal benefits: "Non usitata nec tenui ferar / pinna biformis per liquidum aethera / vates, neque in terris morabor / longius *invidiaque* maior / urbes relinquam (On no common or feeble pinion shall I soar in double form through the liquid air, a poet still, nor linger more on earth, but victorious over envy I shall quit the towns of men)" (*Odes* 2.20.1–5; my emphasis; translation appears in C. E. Bennett, ed., *Odes and Epodes,* p. 165).

29. In an important essay, "The Roman Socrates: Horace and His Satires," William S. Anderson argues that the "Horace" of the *Sermones* must be understood as a persona created by the satires, and that this figure cannot be interpreted coherently by an appeal

his antagonist is one of the Roman patricians, shocked by the intimacy this freedman's son and ex-rebel enjoys with Augustus and Maecenas, Horace always deflects the implicit charge of toadying to the great by pointing out his indifference to politics and his entire disinterestedness in the struggle for influence or position. One of the poet's favorite strategies is to reverse roles and, as in book 1, satire 9, to show his loathing for those courting favors from the great, thus implicitly demonstrating how aloof he himself remains from such ignoble desires.[30]

In a sense, the higher the rank and presumption of his challenger the easier it is for Horace to marshal his most effective *apologia* and counteraccusations. But the situation is entirely different when the accuser's voice is that of a household slave, speaking not with the arrogance of an aristocrat's *invidia,* but with the license of a single day to vent a whole year's accumulated irritation. The speaker, of course, is merely a Davus—almost the generic name for impertinent slaves in Roman comedy—but the questions are those of Horace himself, distanced, no doubt, but nonetheless edged with genuine force.[31] In *Satires* 2.7, as in its most notable descendant, *Le Neveu de Rameau,* the satire's leveling is directed not only against society's stale conventions but against the carefully built up self-image of the author whose life and consciousness constitute the real "tumult" of the festival's "loud disordered mooch."

---

to the poet's own biography: "The main point is that Horace produced a Socratic satirist probably quite unrepresentative of himself; and this satirist, the speaker in his *Sermones,* is one of the greatest achievements of Horatian poetry" (Anderson, *Essays on Roman Satire* [Princeton, N.J., 1982], p. 29). But for all its persuasiveness, Anderson's point must be considered a necessary corrective to the facile assimilation of the author to the speaker of the verses rather than a barrier against exploring tensions created within and by the poems themselves. Indeed, part of Horace's mastery consists precisely in the ways in which his persona succeeds in alternately evading or triumphing over the pressures of the poet's actual circumstances. If the poems strive to create a certain voice and viewpoint, they do not do so with uniform success. Both the fissures in the representation and the moments of curious overemphasis on seemingly trivial points require their own kinds of explanation. My own reading of *Satires* 2.7, for example, does not so much contest Anderson's claim as seek to uncover some of the cost—technical as well as emotional—of Horace's effort to maintain the persona of a "Socratic satirist" with any consistency. It is when the characterization begins to waver, when the poem's tone and structure become momentarily uncertain, that the strain of Horace's effort raises questions a strictly New Critical reading cannot fully register or account for.

30. For an enlightening discussion of this point, see D. R. Shackleton Bailey, *Profile of Horace* (Cambridge, Mass., 1982), pp. 20–22.

31. In *Satires* 1.10.40–43, for example, Horace mentions "Davus" as the typical slave-trickster of the comic stage, who helps to fool the old father for the sake of the play's lovers. Again, in *Satires* 2.5.91–92, Horace has Tiresias advise Ulysses: "Davus sis comicus atque / stes capite obstipo, multum similis metuenti (Act like the Davus of the comedy, and stand with head bowed, much like one [pretending to be] overawed)." Later satirists continued Horace's own borrowings from Roman comedy by calling the slave in their poems Davus as well (e.g., Persius' fifth satire, ll. 161–81).

Dulcis inexpertis cultura potentis amici:
expertus metuit.

—HORACE, *Epistles* 1.18

Those who have never tried think it pleasant to court a friend in power; experience teaches one to fear it.

Like most of the satires in book 2, "Iamdudum ausculto" is cast as a dialogue in which Horace is not an instructor but rather the more or less captive audience to someone else's unsolicited urge to give advice. Yet Horace is careful to frame the poem with a clear indication of the limits within which the conversation takes place. Davus is eager to talk to Horace, but he knows his position well enough to resist doing so until given permission by the poet. Note that although the Saturnalia has already begun, it requires his master's formal acknowledgment of Davus' rights before the slave dares to use the traditional freedom of the holiday period:

Iamdudum ausculto et cupiens tibi dicere servus
pauca, reformido. . . .
. . . age, libertate Decembri,
quando ita maiores voluerunt, utere; narra.

[2.7.1–2, 4–5]

I've been listening for some time, and wishing to speak to you, but as a slave I dare not. . . . Come, use the license December allows, since our fathers willed it so. Have your say.

Similarly, at the satire's conclusion, Horace reasserts his authority by threatening his slave, first playfully with stones and arrows (2.7.116) and then, more plausibly, with transforming Davus from a household servant to a farm laborer:

. . . Ocius hinc te
ni rapis, accedes opera agro nona Sabino.

[2.7.117–18]

If you don't take yourself off in a jiffy, you'll make the ninth laborer on my Sabine farm.

The central part of the poem is thus framed by the guarantee of a "normal" world order in which the relationship of master and slave will continue untroubled by its brief suspension. But the confidence that such a frame inspires and the petty status of his interlocutor, both intellectually and personally, permit Horace to introduce questions whose resonance he might have been less willing to confront in a different context. In essence, the entire satire turns on the question of who is a slave, and the centrality of this theme is clearly signaled by the way the poem's opening hexameter ends on the word *servus*. There are, of course, two ways to define a slave, one legal and the other moral-philosophical, and Davus is careful to point out that in the latter sense his master is conspicuously lacking in true freedom. The bill of charges moves through several distinct stages with increasing specificity as Davus gains in both vehemence and audacity. At first (2.7.6–20), Davus limits himself to safe generalizations on the order of "man is a slave because of his inconsistency, unable to stay firmly committed to any course of action whether noble or vicious" (*vixit inaequalis*, 2.7.10). Here Davus, as though not yet daring to implicate his master directly, draws his examples from behavior of others like Priscus, the senator, whose life had no unity of purpose or character, as opposed to the obsessive gambler, Volanerius, who at least maintained a certain constancy, if only in his mania. Rudd points out that "the problem of consistency, which in morals involves the integration of the personality and in art the achievement of unity amid variety, held a special interest for Horace."[32] Such an interest, it may be worth adding, must surely have been augmented, or at least nourished, by the example of Caesar Augustus, a man whose single-mindedness and ambition resulted in such spectacular accomplishments. But in spite of his admiration for men whose lives testified to the intensity of a single aim, Horace appeals to us precisely because of his own mercurial temperament and because of his skill in exploiting that fickleness as an essential characteristic of his literary persona.[33]

After a brief transition (2.7.21–22), in which Horace virtually compels Davus to explain the point of all these examples, the slave begins to take direct aim at the poet himself (*ad te, inquam*, 2.7.22). In rapid succession, Horace stands accused of wavering in his proclaimed values, of being divided in his desires, of a readiness to change his mind under circumstances that suggest rank opportunism, of hypocrisy in his self-description, and, finally, of being even a greater fool (*stultior*) than is Davus himself (2.7.23–45). The most interesting aspect of Davus' catalog is introduced with seeming casualness amidst the deluge of other charges: Horace is not only a weak man but a parasite, as subject to Maecenas' whims as the poet's own *scurrae* or hangers-on are subject to his:

> . . . si nusquam es forte vocatus
> ad cenam, laudas securum holus ac, velut usquam
> vinctus eas, ita te felicem dicis amasque,

32. Rudd, *The Satires of Horace*, p. 138.

33. Rudd's description here seems to me entirely accurate, both of Horace and later of Diderot as well: "Horace had a genuine respect for men of homogeneous character. He recognized their potential heroism, and could formulate the ideal in memorable terms. . . . But he evinces no affection for such men, and it is clear that he himself was made of quite different stuff" (Rudd, *The Satires of Horace*, p. 199).

> quod nusquam tibi sit potandum. iusserit ad se
> Maecenas serum sub lumina prima venire
> convivam: 'nemon oleum feret ocius? ecquis
> audit?' cum magno blateras clamore fugisque.
> [2.7.29–35]

> If it happens that you aren't asked out to supper, you praise your quiet dish of herbs and, as though you were in chains when you do go anywhere, you call yourself lucky, and hug yourself, because you don't have to go out for some carousal. Let but Maecenas bid you at a late hour come to him as a guest, just at lamp-lighting time: "Won't somebody bring me oil this instant? Does nobody hear me?" So you scream and bawl, then tear off.

Although couched in the conventional satiric topos of the dinner party and deliberately denied any prominence by being merely one of a torrent of insults, Davus' observation is of particular significance in light of Horace's customary insistence on his liberty. In *Satires* 1.6 and 1.9, for example, Horace emphasizes that his relationship to the second most powerful man in the empire was one of friend to friend, and that neither Maecenas' wealth and position nor the poet's poverty determined the nature of their interaction. Yet here we see Maecenas inviting Horace as a kind of afterthought, apparently needing him to fill an empty couch at his banquet, and Horace is only too eager to oblige. Beneath the ostensible charge of fickleness and gluttony, the far more serious one of servility is unmistakable, and Horace's own anxiety about his ascendancy into the inner circle of Rome's rulers is at least partially acknowledged. If the "Epistle to Lollius," from which my epigraph about learning fear in the company of the powerful is drawn, shows one side of Horace's experience, he was also not above an occasional tone of boasting about his success. In *Satires* 2.1, for example, he declares:

> . . . tamen me
> cum magnis vixisse invita fatebitur usque
> invidia . . .
> [2.1.75–77]

> yet Envy, in spite of herself, will ever admit that I have lived with the great

Much of Horace's ambivalence about his position is crystallized in the juxtaposition of the lines from epistle 1:18 and *Satires* 2.1, but in neither poem is the issue pressed as far or with as much polemical energy as in Davus' image of the poet as Maecenas' all too eager dinner guest. As though to deflect attention from so painful a picture, the poem immediately continues with a further inventory of distinctly minor instances of Horace's weaknesses, most extendedly of his supposed sexual misadventures

(2.7.46–67). Although the Stoic philosophers (whose precepts Davus mangles, having acquired their teachings not from Crispinus but from his janitor) condemn sexual servitude as another instance of man's enslavement to his baser instincts, Davus' moralizing is curiously beside the point. In *Satires* 1.2, Horace had already shown a remarkably practical view of sexual matters, arguing for the advantages, in terms of personal safety, reputation, and cost, of liaisons with a *meretrix* or common prostitute rather than with a well-born Roman matron (2.1.57–59), and now the poet merely answers Davus with the simple declaration, "I am no adulterer" (2.7.72).

Readers have often been puzzled why the satire should devote so much space to a theme that touches its target only tangentially, and Davus' own explanation within the poem, that it is only cowardice which prevents Horace's fall into this particular vice, is notably feeble. A typical defense for this sequence is offered by Rudd who recognizes how clumsily the argument proceeds but adds that "this point takes the argument to another, more purely Stoic, level. For while the Cynics and Epicureans condemned adultery because of its risks, the Stoics concentrated on the unhealthy state of the offender's soul. Even if there were no risks, they said, the virtuous man would abstain because of his inner discipline. This helps to prepare us for the noble description of the truly free man."[34] Thematically as well as poetically, however, so extended a digression is hardly a very satisfying preparation "for the noble description of the truly free man," and it seems that a better strategy might be to ask why Horace was eager to introduce the digression in the first place; what function, in other words, is served by a lengthy accusation which the poet could refute in a single phrase?

I think the operative principle here is a particularly cunning form of "innocence by association." The earlier attack that Horace was only Maecenas' *scurra* had raised too much anxiety either to be openly acknowledged or laughingly brushed aside, and the digression on adultery enables Horace to deflect some of the threat of the previous image. Since Davus is manifestly wrong about Horace's sexual conduct, his earlier accusations are now likewise less convincing, especially since the proportion between them (roughly two to one) makes it clear that, for Davus, the sexual is by far the more serious of the two issues. When Davus charges his master with sexual misconduct, he is not only inaccurate: he effectively returns the whole satire to the safe ground of traditional Roman comedy in which the slave is usually heavily involved in his owner's sexual intrigues. The image of Horace as typical *jeune premier* of classical stage comedies is obviously intended to be amusing in its implausibility, but both its very conventionality and its peculiar placement within the satire raises rather than disarms suspicion. There are times, in other words, when the reliance

34. Ibid., p. 192.

upon generic models seems as much a strategic search for refuge as a coherent poetic decision.[35]

Such a reading also helps explain the famous image which ends this section of the poem, since Davus now returns to the theme of Horace's own servitude under another master:

> tune mihi dominus, rerum imperiis hominumque
> tot tantisque minor, quem ter vindicta quaterque
> imposita haud umquam misera formidine privet?
> adde super dictis quod non levius valeat: nam
> sive vicarius est, qui servo paret, uti mos
> vester ait, seu conservus, tibi quid sum ego? nempe
> tu, mihi qui imperitas, alii servis miser atque
> duceris ut nervis alienis mobile lignum.
>
> [2.7.75–82]

> Are you my master, you, a slave to the dominion of so many men and things—you, whom the praetor's rod, though placed on your head three or four times over, never frees from base terror? And over and above what I have said, add something of no less weight: whether one who obeys a slave is an underslave, as the custom of your class names him, or a fellow-slave, what am I in respect to you? Why, you, who lord over me, are the wretched slave of another master, and you are moved like a wooden puppet by wires that others pull.

Writers like Diderot have found this peroration sufficiently powerful to appropriate for their own purposes, but in the immediate context of Davus' grievances the very vehemence of the image makes it appear curiously excessive.[36] As a summary of Horace's supposed cowardice and

35. See also Cicero *Paradoxa Stoicorum* (London, 1953, ed. A. G. Lee). The fifth of Cicero's six essays takes as its theme the proposition, "Omnes sapientes liberos esse et stultos omnes servos (All wise men are free and everyone without wisdom is a slave)," and rehearses many of the same motifs that Horace draws upon in his satire. For example, Edward P. Morris' edition of *Horace: Satires and Epistles* (Norman, Okla., 1974) notes that the satire "follows in part the same line of reasoning [as Cicero's *Parad.* 5], using in vss. 89 ff. the illustration of the lover enslaved by a woman and in vss. 95 ff. the illustration of the infatuated admirer of works of art, almost precisely as they are used by Cicero" (p. 234). Often in criticism, the discovery of a canonical source has been regarded as providing a sufficient answer to questions of interpretation. But no matter how complete such an inventory may be, and without denying the enormous value of such discoveries, the listing of echoes and borrowings cannot settle the issue of why an author chose that particular model at a specific moment in his own text. In this instance, for example, Horace's decision to make Davus' list of accusations recapitulate all of the typical comic vices in so seemingly arbitrary a sequence raises rather than resolves difficulties in the satire's structure and tone.

36. In *Le Neveu de Rameau,* Lui describes his own rebellion against the demands of the Bertin household by saying, "On useroit un pantin d'acier a tirer la ficelle du matin

sexual indiscretion, the lines seem both too charged and insufficiently focused. But as a return to the earlier description of Horace's excessive eagerness to please Maecenas, the image acquires an immediate and vicious sting. In a sense, the authority of the reproach extends beyond Horace to everyone in Augustus' Rome: senators, slaves, and poets alike all moved "like wooden puppets by wires that another pulls," and although Horace's intimacy with Rome's rulers might mitigate the rawness of their commands, it could scarcely conceal the strength with which the wires were secured. Thus, when Davus calls his master "O totiens servus" (2.7.70), a slave many times over, the grounds of the charge are only incidentally touched on in the description of the anxious adulterer. Instead, Horace is accused not only of being the court poet to an absolute master, one with the same power over the poet as Horace exercises over Davus, but of lying to himself about his real position, thereby only adding the inner chains of self-deception to his outward political subjection.

For the Stoics, a refusal to recognize one's situation clearly is both certain evidence of folly and a guarantee that one will remain forever a moral slave, and it is in contrast to this quite specific image of Horace's role that Davus embarks upon the portrait of the noble sage, free from outside control or untamed desires (2.7.83–88). The Stoic wise man lives self-containedly, *et in se ipso totus* (complete within himself, 2.7.86), in vivid opposition to men like Priscus who lead lives of random inconstancy. Horace, according to Davus, utterly fails to live up to this standard, and in the penultimate section of the poem he continues to berate his master for a host of greater and lesser vices, including, once again, sexual misconduct, gluttony, and the rather curious new charge of affectation in judging works of art.[37] However, Davus does make one final striking point. The real consequence of not being free is to be always in flight from oneself, and Horace tries in vain to "baffle Care" only to feel it pursuing him like a runaway fugitive:

---

au soir et du soir au matin (You'd wear out even a steel puppet if you kept pulling its string from morning to night every day)" (Denis Diderot, *Le Neveu de Rameau,* ed. Jean Fabre [Geneva, 1963], p. 65; my translation). Originally, in *Satires* 2.7, however, it was Davus who applied the puppet image to Horace, not to himself, and the transformation in the thrust of the simile is a perfect index of the ways in which an "abject hero" differs from a "licensed fool."

37. It is fascinating to note here that although Diderot obviously enjoyed the whole idea of a Saturnalian license, he was unwilling to grant Davus his liberties when the issue turned to art. In the *Salon de 1767,* Diderot again quotes from Horace's *Satires* 2.7, and cites both the original Latin and his own translation of lines 95–98. But this time, unlike in *Le Neveu de Rameau,* he does so to defend the idea of taste and refinement against the slave's mockery. Diderot the art lover calls Davus' accusation foolish and insists that taste in painting, as in literature, must be acquired by diligent study. See Diderot, *Salons,* ed. Jean Seznec and Jean Adhémar, 3 vols. (Oxford, 1963), 3:241.

. . . adde, quod idem
non horam tecum esse potes, non otia recte
ponere, teque ipsum vitas fugitivus et erro,
iam vino quaerens, iam somno fallere Curam;
frustra: nam comes atra premit sequiturque fugacem.
[2.7.111–14][38]

And again, you cannot yourself bear to be in your own company, you cannot employ your leisure aright, you shun yourself, a runaway and vagabond, seeking now with wine, and now with sleep, to baffle Care. In vain: that black consort dogs and follows your flight.

By now, however, Davus' complaints have begun to be both repetitious, and, in the main, ill-directed, and Horace interrupts the harangue with the threats that close the poem's Saturnalian frame and reestablish the postfestival power relationships in all their stark inequality. The license to speak freely has expired; neither master nor slave seems to have changed as a consequence of the right, and nothing suggests that next season's Saturnalia will differ in kind or effectiveness from this one. But the day has been rich in literary consequences: a pair of antagonists has been delineated, a dialogue set in motion, and a host of questions raised which will make us read the rest of Horace's satires, as well as the long list of their fictional descendants, both "more truly and more strange."

All important decisions are tested on nobodies.
—MAX APPLE, "Free Agents"

Thus far, I have emphasized those elements in Davus' criticisms which seem to cause Horace himself the greatest anxiety, or which strike most directly at the comfortable image that the poet has constructed with such care in his other satires. In 2.7 Horace stands accused of precisely the same faults for which he had mocked others in earlier poems, and the inversion of positions suits perfectly the spirit of the Saturnalia itself.

38. It is interesting to compare the vividness of Horace's image here with Lucretius' didactic manner of expressing a very similar idea:

hoc se quisque modo fugit, at quem scilicet, ut fit,
effugere haud potis est, ingratis haeret et odit
propterea, morbi quia causam non tenet aeger.

In this way each man struggles to escape himself: yet, despite his will he clings to the self, which, we may be sure, in fact he cannot shun, and hates himself, because in his sickness he knows not the cause of his malady.

(Lucretius *De Rerum Natura* 3.1068–70. The translation appears in the edition of Cyril Bailey [Oxford, 1947], pp. 141–42).

But the more pressing issue of who is a slave and who is free, with its stinging rebuke that Horace is deficient not only according to the strict tenets of the Stoic sage but also according to his own proudly announced principles of personal integrity and independence, is not untouched by Saturnalian irony either. Positions presented in such a satire, no matter how serious they might be in another context, cannot fail to be affected—and infected—by the comic extravagances of the depicted situation as a whole and by the formal expectations inherent in the genre itself. In this poem, for example, a slave like Davus, who himself confesses to gluttony, laziness, and excessive love of wine, is hardly offered as a reliable guide to the characteristics of a free man in either the legal or the moral/philosophical sense. Davus is, as the scholiast notes, a *sperhmológos* (a picker-up of learning's crumbs),[39] and his reliance on the philosophical authority of a Stoic teacher's doorkeeper is not designed to give us much faith in the slave's discernment. In fact, the poem, much like Erasmus' *Praise of Folly,* relies on the common paradox of a member of a discredited group describing someone else as having that group's characteristics—a version, that is, of the Cretan Epimenides' claim that all Cretans are liars. Since the manipulation of such logical conundrums was an essential part of Stoic training, its use in this satire helps to subject Stoicism itself to a kind of Saturnalian upheaval by pitting one doctrine ("only the wise man is free") against another ("a slave cannot adequately know or describe what it means to be free").[40] Many of Davus' accusations are also, as we have seen, unconvincing, and thus neither Horace nor his slave is left in a position of moral authority at the satire's end: the roles, in other words, are not so much reversed, as they are set awhirl until self-deception and servitude seem, again like Erasmian folly, the common property of everyone in the text.[41]

For all its complexity, however, Horace's satire is not ambiguous in the same way that some of its literary progeny are. Neither Horace nor Davus approaches the wisdom of the truly free man, but the pertinence

39. Fairclough, ed., *Satires, Epistles, and Ars Poetica,* p. 228 n. b.

40. For two valuable discussions of the place of dialectical argumentation in Stoicism and the relationship of this kind of mental training to ethical considerations, see A. A. Long, "Dialectic and the Stoic Sage," and G. B. Kerferd, "What Does the Wise Man Know?" in *The Stoics,* ed. John M. Rist (Berkeley and Los Angeles, 1978), pp. 101–24 and 125–36.

41. Kerferd points out that "early Stoic theory divided mankind sharply into two classes, the wise and the foolish, and there was no overlap between these two classes. No one who is foolish has knowledge; this is possessed only by the wise man, and it seems clear that the wise man is wise in virtue of the knowledge that he possesses" (Kerferd, "What Does the Wise Man Know?" in *The Stoics,* p. 125). Although he later became more sympathetic to Stoicism, it is clear that in the *Satires* Horace mocks the absoluteness of such distinctions. A Saturnalian subversion of all hierarchic divisions, including that separating wisdom from folly, is therefore a particularly appropriate strategy for challenging Stoic tenets.

of that ideal is itself never questioned seriously. Beyond its rehearsal of the Stoic apothegms about freedom and self-knowledge, however, the subtlety of the poem is due largely to two distinct features—first, its technical mastery, especially Horace's ease in framing so fluid and mercurial a dialogue within the hexameter's metrical exigencies and the vividness of the images with which Davus and the poet embellish their dispute; and second, the ways in which the text keeps touching on—only to withdraw again as though in contact with too nakedly exposed a nerve ending—the anxieties Horace felt about his role as Maecenas' dependent.[42] But neither the two characters nor the reader are ever troubled in their fundamental sense of which values are to be defended and which condemned. The Saturnalian transformation of all values applies, that is, to the worthiness of the men holding those beliefs rather than to the beliefs as such, and it is not difficult, when reading the poem, to determine the degree of justice with which each speaker frames his utterances and the extent to which he is deluded about himself. Horace and Davus know, as the opening lines make clear, that they are participating in a time-honored ritual ("since our fathers willed it so"), but this knowledge itself only enables a dialogue to take place; it does not directly penetrate the argument or stance of either interlocutor. The fact that this particular master and slave are only the latest in a long series of prior Saturnalian pairings is not regarded as itself possessing any thematic or psychological importance, and the very availability of the convention in so untroubled a manner ensures both the dialogue's internal coherence and the re-emergence of a normative social order at the poem's close.

42. In this regard, it is fascinating to see the change in Horace's relationship to his great patron during the poet's later years. In the first epistle, Horace refuses Maecenas' request that he continue writing lyric poetry, but he does so with great tact and with the powerful argument that it is time now to devote himself to philosophy. By the time of the seventh epistle, however, Horace insists on his right to remain in the country in spite of Maecenas' plea that he hurry back to Rome, and this time the poet asserts his personal independence with surprising aggressiveness, even going so far as to declare his readiness to return everything Maecenas had given him if that is the price of freedom. The offer has been seen as a "manly and dignified reply" (Fairclough, ed., *Satires, Epistles, and Ars Poetica,* p. 293), but to me it seems singularly crude since it is clear that Maecenas would never stoop to accept back any of his gifts, and at this stage in Horace's career he is sufficiently secure not to require any further patronage. D. R. Shackleton Bailey makes the interesting point that Maecenas himself "seems to have lost ground with the Emperor following the execution of his brother-in-law Varro Murena in 22. After the publication of the first Book of Epistles his name disappears from Horace's writings except for one affectionate reference in the fourth Book of Odes. Maecenas' message to Augustus in his will, 'Remember Horatius Flaccus as you remember me,' may not have been entirely innocent of *sous-entendu*" (Shackleton Bailey, *Profile of Horace,* p. 56 n. 25). I am not convinced by Shackleton Bailey's last supposition, but there is no doubt that once he was able to establish his full independence, Horace took a distinctly different tone to Maecenas than the one he had adopted earlier. The change is sufficiently striking, at any rate, to make Horace's initial claims that his regard for Maecenas was innocent of all calculation more than a little suspect.

Horace may be amused to hear the recital of some of his more venal failings. In a darker vein, he may be deeply troubled by the thought of his willing complicity in a network of political and social subjection, but his role as a master compelled by tradition to hear his slave's grievances does not cause him any anxiety. The Saturnalian convention, to put the matter as starkly as possible, is itself not subject to Saturnalian derision, and not until that final twist of the paradigm is incorporated into its possibilities in Diderot's *Le Neveu de Rameau* is the reader really discomforted. Davus, with some justice, calls his master "you slave many times over." But what if participating in such a form is itself already a guarantee of enslavement, of servitude not to any particular vices or inadequacies but to the increasingly uncomfortable demands of the Saturnalian dialogue itself? What if, in other words, the mere fact of finding oneself a participant in a Saturnalian dialogue were already sufficient proof that one deserved to be called *totiens servus,* and if all that one could do was reluctantly play one's accustomed part, waiting for the inevitable, and irrefutable, accusations?

> . . . satur est cum dicit Horatius "euhoe!"
>
> —JUVENAL, *Satires* 7

Horace's belly was well filled when he cried out, "Euhoe."

In this passage, as so often in his poems, Juvenal complains about the difficulties he endured attempting to write verse without the luxury of either personal wealth or influential patrons.[43] Juvenal admired Horace immensely as a satirist, but it is clear that he also felt his most famous predecessor in the genre had enjoyed an unfair advantage over any of his literary descendants. And as though to take up the terms of Juvenal's quarrel as its own, modern criticism too has found itself far more at ease applauding the social voice of poets either alienated from or in open defiance of the established rulers of their era. There are times, for example, when the tone of a poet like Horace, much of whose career was spent in intimate contact and even personal friendship with an imperial autocracy, begins to seem suspect, as though the rewards his verse earned him

43. Juvenal is specifically mocking the Horace of *Odes* 2.19. Jenkyns, a critic notably sympathetic to what he regards as Juvenal's difficult situation, describes this passage as "a brilliant display of Juvenal's sensitivity as a reader, for he has seized upon an example of Horace at his most tiresomely bogus: *Odes* 2.19, a work of laboured correctitude in which the poet claims to be carried away by bacchic frenzy" (Jenkyns, *Three Classical Poets,* p. 160). There is no need, however, to go quite so far in one's criticism of the *Odes'* occasionally forced tone of visionary inspiration (a tone, in any case, which has more to do with the particular genre and decorum of the poems than with Horace's supposed self-aggrandizement) to appreciate the malicious wit in Juvenal's citation.

somehow undermine its authenticity.[44] As I indicated in the opening pages of this essay, one of the chief problems regularly thwarting the evaluation of political poetry was the critic's tendency to read the work according to an already determined scale of values whose independent authority is never brought into question, and it is as well to recognize that this problem affects our evaluation of classical poets as much as it does of more recent ones.

Usually, however, in the case of the canonical Greco-Latin authors, the issue of evaluation as a political problem arises not so much in the discussion of an individual poet on his own terms as in the course of a comparison among writers of the same era. Thus, for example, Hans-Peter Stahl's recent study, *Propertius: "Love" and "War," Individual and State under Augustus,* regularly contrasts Propertius' subtle criticisms of the emperor's claims as bringer of peace and justice to the Roman world with the acceptance of those claims by Horace and Virgil. Stahl's central question, the one on which his thorough and cogent reading of Propertius depends, is formulated with exemplary clarity:

> Would the poet, in the difficult situation after Actium, dare to give his readers a glimpse of his true attitude if he does not agree with the new régime? Among scholars, this question is hotly contested, and thus cannot be answered categorically. Much depends on the interpreter's evaluation of the climate at Rome after the civil war has been decided: could a dissenter feel free to speak openly or not? . . . Historians tend to answer the question differently from literary critics; the latter often see Propertius in the light of Horace and Virgil, who found their way early to feeling reconciled to Octavian's cause.[45]

It is fascinating to observe, though, how the care Stahl brings to the reading of his chosen author is accompanied by a corresponding blindness toward the works of the other principal Augustan poets. Not only is Horace accused of what amounts to little better than sheer opportunism,

44. I am thinking here not only of the many passages in the *Odes* like 1.2, in which Horace sings the praise of Augustus as a semidivinity come to redeem Rome's iniquities and reign as the empire's beloved "pater atque princeps (father and prince)" (1.2.50), but, more subtly, of satires like 1.9 where the whole portrait of the ambitious bore implicitly flatters the taste and discernment of Maecenas. As Rudd comments,

> Maecenas and his friends knew very well that this was their poem. Not only were they the objects of the pest's endeavours, but without them the whole episode would have been inconceivable. As they listened to Horace's account of the fellow's efforts to ingratiate himself their amusement must have been spiced with a dash of self-congratulation. . . . No one is pained by flattery when it is offered with such tact, and it may be assumed that Horace's friends liked him all the more for inviting them to admire themselves. [Rudd, *The Satires of Horace,* pp. 82–83]

45. Stahl, *Propertius: "Love" and "War,"* p. 103.

but the *Aeneid* is criticized in turn for its celebration of "Octavian's rule as impartial, objective, and god-sent."[46] For Stahl, even so ambiguous a passage as Aeneas' spurning of Dido becomes merely another piece of evidence confirming Virgil's ready acceptance of Augustan *mores* as a whole and, more specifically, of the Julio-Claudian family's political ambitions.[47] My immediate concern, however, is less to challenge Stahl's account of either Horace or Virgil than to emphasize the dangers of positing a neat opposition between the political stance of the poet one wants to champion (almost invariably regarded as the sole voice of dissent) and those of his (supposedly accommodationist) contemporaries. To use a poet like Horace "as a foil which offers a sharper picture of Propertius' un-Augustan position"[48] is almost inevitably to invite a distorted judgment, if only because the temptation never to inquire closely into the true metal of one's foil is so strong.

It is only fair to emphasize that the view of Propertius which Stahl advocates is remarkably persuasive and that his capacity to recognize only one kind of political resistance does little to weaken the major claims of his study. But I have chosen to emphasize this kind of limitation precisely because there are few poets more suitable than Horace to make us confront the inadequacy of facile categories. Horace represents a kind of limit case because the central issues of his poems (constancy, candor, personal integrity, and evenhandedness) are raised in the context of a period when their very mention is fraught with political significance, but after the outcome of actual political struggles had been effectively settled. Rather than continue to resist that outcome, Horace was willing to accept its terms, in large measure, I think, because he had seen already the appalling nature of the other possible alternatives. But what poems like the Saturnalian dialogue (or, in a different genre, such "political" pieces as *Odes* 1.27, the "Cleopatra Ode") show us is the human cost of that acceptance. For all the benefits he personally enjoyed from the new regime, and for all his certainty that Rome too shared at least some of those benefits, Horace knew how dear a price had been paid for them. The self-accusation in a phrase like "o totiens servus" implicates author and audience alike in the most permanent of political questions: in the search for a livable space between the rival needs of a stable social order and the individual's longing to locate his identity and sense of worth in a domain that is not thoroughly saturated by the dictates of hierarchy and power. The fact that the results of the search are deeply discouraging

46. Ibid., p. 127.

47. See ibid., pp. 153–55. For a reading that emphasizes Virgil's questioning, not only of Rome's imperial "destiny" and Aeneas' heroism but of the whole ethics of heroism itself, see Johnson, *Darkness Visible: A Study of Vergil's Aeneid* (Berkeley and Los Angeles, 1976).

48. Stahl, *Propertius: "Love" and "War,"* p. 153.

in poems like *Satires* 2.7 only confirms (rather than vitiates, as in Stahl's view) the rigor with which Horace was able to probe the political possibilities of Augustan life in his art. To follow Horace's careful scrutiny of his situation is to develop a finer sense of how central a category "political poetry" can really be, and how much we will need to stretch our understanding of its scope before a meaningful evaluation is possible. And if we emerge from that evaluation with a chastened sense of our own authority to pass judgment on a poet "according to his agreement with or erring divergence from our own principles,"[49] then, I believe, the vision of a darker and less celebratory Saturnalia, first glimpsed in Horace and elaborated by his literary successors, will begin to trouble many of the easy affirmations cherished in our current critical pieties.[50]

49. I have adopted, for my own purposes here, a characteristic aphorism from Robert Musil's *Der Mann ohne Eigenschaften.* Musil describes one of his figures as "zeitlebens gehindert, in einem Buch etwas anderes zu erkennen als übereinstimmung oder irrende Abweichung von seinen eigenen Grundsätzen" (Musil, *Der Mann ohne Eigenschaften* [Hamburg, 1952], p. 89).

50. In a forthcoming book, *When the Carnival Turns Bitter: A Study of the Abject Hero,* I trace the theme of a grimly destructive and pessimistic Saturnalian dialogue from its origins in Horace's *Satires* to its modern consequences in authors like Diderot, Dostoyevski, and Céline.

The Mastery of Decorum: Politics as Poetry in Milton's Sonnets

Janel Mueller

Even friendly readers may condescend to political poetry for certain presumptive deficiencies. To those who associate poetry with private concerns as well as a personal voice, political poetry may seem unpoetic in its public concerns. Quite apart from such associations, the quotient of public concerns may prove troubling. Political poetry steeps itself in its own occasion. It can be counted on to take a position or declare for some view. When, as often, it also plunges a reader into a welter of specific references, topical weight compounds with a programmatic burden that seems to threaten accessibility and interest if not the status of this poetry as art. Can political poetry be justified as poetry? It looks at first as if it can, if we draw a few qualitative distinctions. Versified or not, propaganda remains propaganda, but this fact has no bearing on the poetic treatment of social values and social choices. Lines crammed with names and catchwords may reduce to journalism without entailing that circumstantiality and public events are unfit materials for poetry. A closer look, however, shows the inadequacy of trying to justify political poetry on the basis of qualitative distinctions alone. Political poetry poses a special dilemma for theorizing about the nature of poetry along lines that Aristotle's *Poetics* made definitive for much subsequent criticism and practice.

It is a pleasure to acknowledge incisive critiques of the first draft of this essay from my colleagues James Chandler, W. J. T. Mitchell, and Robert von Hallberg. Several other colleagues—they know who they are—offered useful comments on an intermediate draft read at a departmental colloquium. Joshua Scodel and Richard Strier gave me the added benefit of written comments on that draft. After all this help, only I can be held responsible for remaining faults.

If we supply a missing connection in the master text of English Renaissance poetic theory, we can bring the dilemma posed by political poetry into sharp relief. Sidney's *Defence of Poesie* seeks to confirm the supremacy of the poet's power over human minds by invoking the celebrated three-way distinction between poetry, philosophy, and history in the *Poetics.* According to Sidney, the proper question to ask of poetry is not "whether it were better to have a particular act truly or falsely set down" but "whether it be better to have it set down as it should be, . . . for your own use and learning." On this criterion, the philosopher shows himself too devoted to "knowledge" that "standeth upon the abstract and general," to the "precept," to "what should be." The historian attends too much to "the particular truth of things and not to the general reason of things," to the "example," to "what is." Only the poet "coupleth the general notion with the particular example" in "the speaking picture of poesy," thus synthesizing through his "imaginative and judging power" the best that the philosophical and historical domains can offer. "Aristotle himself," concludes Sidney, "plainly determineth this question, saying that poetry . . . is more philosophical and more studiously serious than history . . . because poesy dealeth with . . . the universal consideration, and the history with . . . the particular." Yet in mounting his *Defence of Poesie,* Sidney fails to give due force to a related and equally important distinction drawn in the *Poetics.* Aristotle ranks poetry below philosophy—and, by implication, history as well—at the crucial juncture where ontology and epistemology meet. He exclusively credits philosophical universals with rational "necessity." Poetic universals are recognized as having imaginative "likelihood," but no more than this.[1] Under this second three-way distinction, the domain proper to poetry turns out to be neither the realm of historical fact nor that of philosophical truth but some half-region of the truthlike, the verisimilar, disjoint from the plane of knowledge.

The dilemma of political poetry arises at the crossing of the two Aristotelian distinctions, bringing questions of its nature to the forefront.

1. The core distinctions are drawn by Aristotle in chap. 9, secs. 2–4, of the *Poetics;* also see chap. 1, sec. 1 of the *Topics* on the distinction between demonstration, based on reasoning from true knowledge, and dialectic, based on reasoning from what is generally accepted as probable. The quotations in this paragraph are from *Sidney: A Defence of Poetry,* ed. J. A. Van Dorsten (Oxford, 1966), pp. 35, 32, 33, 35.

Janel Mueller is professor of English and humanities at the University of Chicago. She has published mainly on poetry and prose of the earlier English Renaissance, culminating in her book *The Native Tongue and the Word: Developments in English Prose Style, 1380–1580.* An interest in Milton, however, has drawn her more recently to work in the later part of this period. She is writing a book on nature, culture, and gender in Milton's major poems.

If poetry is to claim a political dimension, on what basis and with what consequences does it do so? In engaging with social values and social choices, what can such poetry offer that political philosophy does not? How, moreover, can such poetry remain poetic while pursuing a primary commitment to political actuality? In taking subjects that are the materials of history, what will it make of these as poetry? Will it inevitably make too much, distorting or fabricating, or too little, dissolving universality in particulars?

Milton coped with the questions intrinsic to political poetry during the decade from 1642 to 1652 when he rose to prominence as a pamphleteer on public issues and concurrently pioneered the writing of political sonnets in English. This essay examines the responses he made, in part in his prose but mainly in the composition of seven sonnets. Political poems in a root sense, these sonnets concern themselves with human agency channeled into the functions of the state, with power manifested through governance. After exploratory and uneven beginnings, the group as a whole goes a fair way toward vindicating the enterprise of political poetry and offering one set of criteria for a good political poem.

While working within a fundamentally Aristotelian poetics, Milton in these sonnets nonetheless compels us to rethink the theoretical and hierarchical distinctions that Aristotle drew for the respective domains of philosophy, history, and poetry. One device in particular, we will find, proves indispensable to Milton's making of poetry from politics. He keys his use of the present tense within his text to a moment in present time outside the text, synchronizing the "now" of direct address with an occasion or event that is just "now" being experienced. In so doing, he seizes upon the immediacy of the political moment and makes poetry of its imperatives to action before these can either pass into the historical record or become objects of philosophical reflection. At the same time, private and public concerns require full integration in these sonnets. Without it, personal urgency and contemplative insight cannot attain the lyric equipoise Milton needs to mediate poetically between the historical and philosophical poles. Far from standing at odds with one another, poetic creation and political engagement turn out to be intimately connected. The artistry of the sonnets keeps pace with advances in Milton's specifically political understanding of events, parties, and leaders as well as his sense of their significance to himself and his nation as political entities.

When he broke into print as a prose writer with five tracts (May 1641–June 1642) advocating Presbyterian church government in England, Milton continued to regard and represent himself as a poet. The autobiographical excursus in *The Reason of Church Government* first opposes poetry and prose as kinds of composition. But it then finds a more fundamental consonance in their divine authorization and public function. Because poetic abilities, like the ministerial calling, "are the inspired guift of God," Milton claims for poetry a "power beside the office of a pulpit, to imbreed and cherish in a great people the seeds of vertu, and publick civility."[2] He goes on to credit the classical and biblical repertory of poetry—its major genres, its serious subjects and themes, its range of styles—as a source of its public power. But the heavier emphasis by far in Milton's characterization of himself as an author in the early tracts falls on a sanctified *furor poeticus* that is of a piece with his prophetic mandate for writing prose.[3] Whichever he writes, prose or poetry, he sees himself as giving inspired utterance to God's present will and purposes for the English nation. At this period Milton's attention was evidently caught by the sonnet form—which he called the "Petrarchian stanza"—when he decided to translate some lines from Petrarch's fiercely antipapal sonnet "Fontana di dolore, albergo d'ira." He used these in *Of Reformation*'s call for recognition that several great poets had been among the earliest attackers of ecclesiastical corruption.[4] The scattered leads in the prose of 1641–42 point to the likelihood that, if Milton were to turn the English sonnet to political ends, he would do so as a latter-day Petrarch, as a poet-prophet of divine vengeance.

But the very first of Milton's political sonnets strikes out in an altogether different direction. It anchors his inception of the mode in the secular context of human agency. The occasion, as inscribed in the manuscript titles which Milton gave all of these sonnets, was first noted thus, "On his dore when ye City expected an assault," and later revised to read more impersonally, "When the assault was intended to ye Citty." The "assault" in question was the impending invasion of London by royalist troops in November 1642 from the northeast, where Milton's house stood.[5] Milton broke into political verse under the threat posed to him

2. Milton, *The Reason of Church Government, Complete Prose Works of John Milton,* ed. Don M. Wolfe et al. (New Haven, Conn., 1953–82), 1:6–17. All further references to this edition, abbreviated *CPW* and with volume and page numbers, will be included in the text.

3. For early vignettes of the Miltonic persona uttering inspired strains that raise himself and uplift his people, see, respectively, *Reason of Church Government* (*CPW* 1:808) and *Of Reformation* (*CPW* 1:616). Compare the tribute Milton is glad to wrest—"the voice of three kingdomes," "a hymne in prose"—from an opponent's strictures on one of his "*astounding*" passages (*Apology for Smectymnuus, CPW* 1:930) and his parallel conception of the imperatives laid on the prophet Jeremiah and on himself "to take the trumpet and blow a dolorous or a jarring blast" for "the cause of God and his Church" (*CPW* 1:803, 805).

4. See *Of Reformation* (*CPW* 1:559) for the Petrarch translation in context; the allusion to an enclosed sonnet as "a Petrarchian stanza" occurs in his draft letter to an unidentified friend (ca. 1633) preserved in the Trinity College manuscript (*CPW* 1:320).

5. All Trinity College manuscript readings are cited from Harris Francis Fletcher's critical text edition of *John Milton's Complete Poetical Works Reproduced in Photographic Facsimile,* 4 vols. (Urbana, Ill., 1943); see 1:396 for these titles. All further references, abbreviated *F* and with volume and page numbers, will be included in the text. For an unconvincing proposal to predate the occasion of Milton's first political sonnet to the spring of 1641, see *Milton's Sonnets,* ed. E. A. J. Honigmann (London, 1966), pp. 101–3. All further references to this edition, abbreviated *S*(H), will be included in the text.

personally as a political being, that is, a property owner, by agents of arbitrary royal power.[6] What he had charged broadly in his prose tracts against the bishops—that they prompted the king to make illegal inroads on the possessions and liberties of Englishmen—now loomed at a mere sword's or musket's length from his own front door. He met the occasion with these lines:

> Captain or Colonel, or Knight in Arms,
> Whose chance on these defenceless dores may sease,
> If deed of honour did thee ever please,
> Guard them, and him within protect from harms,
> He can requite thee, for he knows the charms
> That call Fame on such gentle acts as these,
> And he can spred thy Name o're Lands and Seas,
> What ever clime the Suns bright circle warms.
> Lift not thy spear against the Muses Bowre,
> The great *Emathian* Conqueror bid spare
> The house of *Pindarus,* when Temple and Towre
> Went to the ground: And the repeated air
> Of sad *Electra*'s Poet had the power
> To save th'*Athenian* Walls from ruine bare.
>
> [*S*(H), no. 8]

Milton recognizes the moment, for all its extremity of personal emotion, as a political one, and he bids for recognition as a political participant through his poetry. Yet he also exhibits unsureness by casting his sonnet in the ancient poetic form of an inscription.[7] One of the commonest uses of the inscription poem promoted its funerary and memorial associations: the inscription-as-charm. Although the poetic inscription was a public form, its funerary and memorial associations tended to make it apolitical. The inscription-as-charm evolved in classical antiquity as a mode of utterance associated with a set locale: an edifice or monument bearing a versified appeal to the passing stranger to perform some act of respect or fellow-feeling. If such an inscription poem was to work its charm, it first had to rouse emotion at some fact of fatality and then direct that emotion into a humane gesture of compensation. The possibilities for strong affect, which tend toward universality and transcendence in the inscription-as-charm, clearly attracted Milton, and he sought to turn the

6. I develop this case in "On Genesis in Genre: Milton's Politicizing of the Sonnet in 'Captain or Colonel,'" in *Renaissance Genres,* ed. Barbara K. Lewalski, Harvard English Studies 14 (Cambridge, Mass., 1986), pp. 213–40.

7. On pertinent aspects of the history of this form, see Werner Peek's introduction to *Griechische Grabgedichte* (Berlin, 1960), pp. 1–42; Richmond Lattimore, *Themes in Greek and Latin Epitaphs* (Urbana, Ill., 1962), pp. 230–37; John N. Finley, "Milton and Horace: A Study of Milton's Sonnets," *Harvard Studies in Classical Philology* 48 (1937): 36–37; and Gordon Williams, *Tradition and Originality in Roman Poetry* (Oxford, 1968), pp. 172–94.

form toward political ends. The result is a magnificent rhetorical construct but an ultimately elusive handling of the challenge that prompts this sonnet: the issue of the present exercise of power.

Addressing the officer of the Crown whom he expects at any moment, Milton adapts to poetry the rhetorical justification that had standardly been given for history-writing since classical antiquity.[8] The fame that spurs public figures to perform great deeds lives on in works that continue to be read. In the long run, then, the officer's power is contingent on the poet's. In the immediate situation, the poet aims to cast a charm over the officer with his rhetoric, to work a verbal magic that will literally disarm his armed opposite. Lines 1–9 enact the transformative impact on power relations which is claimed for rhetoric throughout this sonnet. The grammatical mood that first lodges a plea ("Guard them, and him within protect from harms") converts in short order to a command ("Lift not thy spear against the Muses Bowre"). Meanwhile the poet steps up the force of his rhetorical claim. He "knows the charms" that not only work upon this officer but "call Fame on . . . gentle acts" in "What ever clime the Suns bright circle warms." Here, already in conjunction, are the elements from which Milton makes political poetry: a present moment, a figure of power directly addressed, an issue involving the exercise of power raised and pointed toward a resolution.

Yet the movement toward closure in "Captain or Colonel" dissolves the conjunction of elements that make for political engagement. The poet gestures beyond himself—to distant places and times, to immortal verse written and recognized as such—ostensibly to clinch his claim to superior power. In the analogies worked by allusion in the last five lines, flattery raises the rhetoric to one height of magnification—in the implied grouping of the royalist officer with Alexander the Great and the Spartan general Lysander—while poetic aspiration raises it to another—in the implied grouping of the poet-speaker with Pindar and Euripides. Sublime receding vistas and an aura of transcendence supplant all focus on the London emergency of 1642 that generated this Miltonic display of poetic power in the first place. Finally the sweep of rhetoric all but neutralizes the politics in the poetry—an effect tacitly registered in Milton's printing of "Captain or Colonel" among his *Poems* of 1645. This was the only political sonnet that he would release for publication before the *Poems*

8. The autobiographical excursus in *The Reason of Church Government* does bring this historiographical aim too—"to be an interpreter & relater of the best and sagest things among mine own Citizens throughout this Iland in the mother dialect"—within the vast scope of Milton's authorial aspirations for the future (*CPW* 1:811–12). Irene Samuel shows how rhetorical conceptions of history eventually decline in importance for Milton in "Milton and the Ancients on the Writing of History," *Milton Studies* 2 (1970): 131–48. In any event the prophetic mandate is much more emphasized in the early prose. William Kerrigan's *The Prophetic Milton* (Charlottesville, Va., 1974) traces this dimension through appropriate contexts for all of Milton's career.

of 1673, in the last year of his life. It is probably most accurate to term "Captain or Colonel" proto-political.

Two-and-a-half years would elapse before Milton wrote his next political sonnets, in a pair. The interim registered another outpouring of prose works from his pen. A first and then a much enlarged second edition of *The Doctrine and Discipline of Divorce* as well as *Of Education, The Judgement of Martin Bucer, Areopagitica, Tetrachordon,* and *Colasterion* all appeared between August 1643 and March 1645. This is the period covered by the decisive first civil war, which saw the royal power broken first by Parliament in conjunction with the pulpits and the press, then by military defeat. It seemed possible that England would be radically reconstituted. Milton exulted in the revolutionary ferment that graced itself with the soberer label of reformation, openly placing himself in the vanguard of free inquiry and expression and claiming leadership on such issues as the lifting of state censorship and the legitimating of divorce. In the matter of divorce he felt his preeminence especially as "the sole advocate of a discount'nanc't truth" (*CPW* 2:224). A political activist to the hilt at this period, Milton nevertheless made time and space for reflections on how to form sound citizens with independent, instructed capacities for thought and action. We find him in his brief but pithy *Of Education* (June 1644) rereading and rethinking an array of texts as he defines his objectives, explains his program of studies, and selects the items of his curriculum. As we watch him at work on a kind of system which for him always stood in close relation to a poetics, we can trace how Milton arrived at a connection between the formation of sound character and the formulation of sound policy as reciprocal functions of a unitary norm for choice. The tract prospectively illuminates the mind of the political poet, not only that of the educator.

The influence of Aristotle, as primary source and as interpreted by later writers, greatly predominates over Plato's in *Of Education.* It is not difficult to see why. Ethics, politics, and poetry are compatible for Aristotle as they never could be for Plato, whose severities in the *Republic* and the *Laws* Milton half-tries to palliate in *Areopagitica* (*CPW* 1:522–23, 526). The appeal of Aristotle's broadly integrative aims comes through clearly in the borrowed terminology of Milton's central definition. "I call," says Milton, "a compleate and generous Education that which fits a man to perform justly, skilfully and magnanimously all the offices both private and publike of peace and war" (*CPW* 2:377–79). In the *Politics* Aristotle, dividing "the life of citizenship" into "the employments of war and those of peace," proposes "the aims that ought to be kept in view in the education of the citizens." These he specifies as follows: "In regard to modes of life and choices of conduct, a man should be capable of engaging in . . . war, but still more capable of living in peace . . .; and he should do what is necessary and useful, but still more should he do what is noble." "What is noble" and "what is useful"—the Greek counterparts of Milton's "magnanimously" and "skilfully" here—hark back to an important earlier definition in the *Politics* which equates the two: "To goods of the soul not only the term 'noble' but also the term 'useful' can be properly applied. . . . To do well is impossible save for those who do good actions, and there is no good action either of a man or of a state without . . . courage, justice and wisdom." These virtues, adds Aristotle, have "the same meaning and form" when they belong to a state as when they bestow "the titles of just and wise and temperate on an individual human being."[9]

Originating in Aristotle's clarification of how the private and public aspects of wisdom and virtue interconnect, this equation of the noble and the useful became a key notion which Cicero would extend and elaborate for politics, and Tasso for poetics. All three sources contribute to the formulation of a norm for choice which is the aim of Milton's educational scheme. He hails this norm by name at the climax of his discussion of curriculum: it is "decorum," "the grand master peece to observe" (*CPW* 1:405). The immediate Miltonic context points to poetic connotations of "decorum," the Latin rendering of the Greek for "rightness" in the sense of fitting, suitable, appropriate (*to prepon*). Aristotle's *Poetics,* which Milton has just cited, refers this quality to the poet's creation of characters who reveal themselves through *proairesis,* the kinds of choice they make, and through their "ability to say what is possible and appropriate"—in other words, to articulate the thought that shaped their choice. Rightness in this sense—the articulation of possible and appropriate choices—is also, according to Aristotle, "the function of the statesman's or the rhetorician's art."[10] In the *Nicomachean Ethics* and the *Politics* he subjects *proairesis* to further analysis as a course of voluntary action based in reason, the kind of choice that defines moral virtue.[11] Milton registers his familiarity with these Aristotelian contexts earlier in *Of Education* when he declares students ready for advanced studies as soon as they are able to perform "that act of reason which in *Ethics* is call'd *Proairesis:* that they may with some judgement contemplat upon morall good and evil" (*CPW* 2:396).

9. Aristotle *Politics* (London, 1932; trans. H. Rackham), 1.2.14; 7.13.9; 7.1.5 (pp. 23, 607–9, 537–39). "Magnanimity" itself originates as a technical term in Aristotle (see *Nicomachean Ethics* 2.7.7–8; 4.3.1–34) although Milton reflects later trends in using it to cover virtue in its manifold realizations (see *CPW* 1:795), much as Spenser uses "magnificence" in his "Letter to Raleigh" on the philosophical underpinnings of the *Faerie Queene.*

10. Aristotle *Poetics* (London, 1927; trans. W. Hamilton Frye), pp. 27, 29. In point of fact, Aristotle does not use *to prepon* in this passage (chap. 6, secs. 22–24) but rather a synonym, *ton harmottonton,* which is also rendered "decorum" in Latin. For a highly relevant occurrence of *to prepon* in Aristotle, see the last sentence of the (unfinished) *Politics,* which sums up what he has been saying about the education of youth: "It is clear therefore that we should lay down these three canons to guide education: moderation, possibility, and suitability (*to prepon*)" (*Politics* 8.7.11; trans. Rackham, p. 675).

11. See Aristotle *Nicomachean Ethics* 2.6.15; 3.2.17; *Politics* 7.12.5.

It is Cicero, in *De Officiis,* who takes up Aristotle's equation of intellectual and moral choice and teases out its implications in an argument for decorum as the supreme virtue of human and, especially, of political life. Cicero is also aware of the link Aristotle drew between poetic and moral choice, but it scarcely figures with him. He invokes it merely to illustrate what he regards as a far more vital connection between rightness of mind and rightness of action. Decorum—or propriety, in the ensuing translation—is the element in choice that assures this connection. "Such is its essential nature," says Cicero of decorum, "that it is inseparable from moral goodness; for what is proper is morally right, and what is morally right is proper. . . . For whatever propriety may be, it is manifested only when there is pre-existing moral rectitude." While fully aware that decorum, insofar as it renders the Greek *to prepon,* must be correlated with the virtue of moderation or temperance, Cicero continues to insist on the validity of "a general sort of propriety, which is found in moral goodness as a whole." He emphasizes that this is a uniquely human attribute: "Propriety is that which harmonizes with man's superiority in those respects in which his nature differs from that of the rest of the animal creation."[12]

In its general as opposed to its specific sense, decorum thus encompasses and empowers the exercise of the other primary virtues: "that which is in its nature clear-sighted and penetrating (Wisdom), that which is adapted to promote and strengthen society (Justice), and that which is strong and courageous (Fortitude)." Cicero sums up on decorum in its general sense as the norm governing the sequence of right choices that constitute someone as a moral person: "If there is any such thing as propriety at all, it can be nothing more than uniform consistency in the course of our life as a whole and all its individual actions." He then turns to a revisionary treatment of the primary virtues in their political manifestations. Abruptly dethroning wisdom in its Aristotelian sense of speculative knowledge, Cicero argues that "the claims of human society and the bonds that unite men together take precedence over the pursuit of speculative knowledge."[13] These claims and bonds require us to recognize temperance or moderation—decorum in its general sense—as the supreme virtue. It is the principle governing the workings of the political order, as a system of right choices.

Although *De Officiis* is not cited in *Of Education,* it will become clear in due course how much the constructive aspects of Milton's political sonnets owe to Cicero's formulations in this work. Milton does, however, cite Tasso in close proximity to Aristotle in the passage that ends by hailing decorum as "the grand master peece to observe." Tasso's own influential discussion of decorum is found in book 3 of his *Discourses on the Heroic Poem.* Closely echoing salient phrases from *De Officiis,* this

12. Cicero *De Officiis* (London, 1913; trans. Walter Miller), 1:27.
13. Ibid., 1.31, 43–45.

discussion bends Cicero's authority to Tasso's own ends. He will develop the implications of the other Aristotelian equation, the comment in the *Poetics* that moral choice and poetic choice manifest a single decorum. "Decorum gets confused with virtue," says Tasso; "decorum cannot be separated from honour . . . : if there is any difference between them, it is more easily understood than explained. This decorum is of two sorts: one general, luminous in every honourable deed, the other dependent on the first, recognized in the components of honour. We know this is so when we consider the decorum observed by poets, who win more praise in proportion as they observe what is fitting." In Tasso's view, Virgil's character-drawing establishes him as the poet who best understood the "notion of general decorum: in Aeneas he gave shape to piety, religion, temperance, strength, magnanimity, justice, and every other . . . virtue."[14] Like Aristotle, Tasso considers that virtues take shape in a character through the choices he is shown to make. Later, in books 4 and 5 of the *Discourses,* Tasso also sustains Aristotle's emphasis on bringing thought to appropriate expression in the articulation of a given choice. He contends that lyric poets can join with epic poets as praisers and upholders of the complex of values signified by decorum if they select subjects to which they can apply the devices for "greatness and magnificence of speech" copiously illustrated from the sonnets of Petrarch, Tasso's father Bernardo, della Casa, and others.[15]

Milton deals with the norm of right choice in other writings of 1644, but it takes on a different aspect. Now it does not figure as the powerfully synthetic concept of decorum that Cicero and Tasso raised on Aristotelian foundations, but rather as a right so fundamental to Englishmen that nothing can be allowed to block its exercise. *Areopagitica* puts the case against censorship on behalf of a whole nation of virtuously intentioned choosers. The divorce tracts, too, argue that nature and Scripture both mandate a second chance for persons who innocently made a disastrous choice of a marriage partner the first time around. Milton expected his proposals for a free but accountable press and for divorce on grounds of incompatibility to be received as vital contributions toward the refounding of English society. However, by the fall and winter of 1644–45 three Presbyterian ministers had denounced the divorce tracts: Herbert Palmer, in a sermon to both houses of Parliament, and William Prynne and Daniel Featley in print. Palmer held that Milton had abused the liberty of the

14. Torquato Tasso, *Discourses on the Heroic Poem,* trans. Mariella Cavalchini and Irene Samuel (Oxford, 1973), pp. 92, 94.

15. Tasso, *Discourses,* pp. 114, 137, 137, 140, 166. For discussions of Milton's indebtedness to Tasso and della Casa for the features of the magnificent style that characterize his own sonnets, see John S. Smart, ed., *The Sonnets of Milton* (Glasgow, 1921), pp. 30–33, and F. T. Prince, *The Italian Element in Milton's Verse* (Oxford, 1954), pp. 14–33, 89–107. All further references to the Smart edition of the sonnets, abbreviated *S*(S), will be included in the text.

press by failing to secure a license to print a book "deserving to be burnt," and Milton was summoned for examination on his noncompliance with licensing regulations by two justices in December 1644. Featley decried not procedures but content: he charged Milton with overturning Jesus' teachings on divorce and with letting "the bonds of marriage . . . loose to inordinate lust and putting away wives for many . . . causes" (*S*[H], pp. 114–17). In *Colasterion* Milton countered wrathfully through the public medium of prose. In the notebook we know as the Trinity College manuscript, he entered two sonnets under the heading "On the detraction w[ch] follow'd upon my writing certain treatises." The first reads as follows:

> I did but prompt the age to quit their cloggs
> By the known rules of antient libertie,
> When strait a barbarous noise environs me
> Of Owles and Cuckoes, Asses, Apes and Doggs.
> As when those Hinds that were transform'd to Froggs
> Raild at *Latona's* twin-born progenie
> Which after held the Sun and Moon in fee.
> But this is got by casting Pearl to Hoggs;
> That bawle for freedom in their senceless mood,
> And still revolt when truth would set them free.
> Licence they mean when they cry libertie;
> For who loves that, must first be wise and good;
> But from that mark how far they roave we see
> For all this wast of wealth, and loss of blood.
>
> [*S*(H), no. 11]

The magnificent sound texture of this sonnet—the hissing of sibilants and the variations on tense and lax vocalic features of *o*'s and *a*'s—serves savage effects that finally evade the speaker's control. The lack of control emerges only by degrees; the savagery obtrudes virtually from the start. Laying aside the sketchy social context of the first two lines, Milton characterizes his opponents as producers of sheer animal sound. They are "Owles and Cuckoes, Asses, Apes and Doggs" who "rail," "bawle," and "cry." He appears to have labored over this imagery. The allusion to the myth from *Metamorphoses* 6.331–81 reads as if the rustics who threatened and cursed the goddess Latona when she requested a drink of water for herself and her infant twins, Apollo and Diana, did so in the guise of frogs ("those Hinds that were transform'd to Froggs / Raild"). But Milton's source, Ovid, states that they were transformed as a punishment for their treatment of divinity. Line 4 in manuscript read "buzzards" before it read "Cuckoes" (*F* 1:444). The revision highlights the feature of an inhuman cry and contributes to Milton's re-etymologizing of "barbarous noise." The ancient Greeks called all non-Greek speakers barbarians because their languages sounded like bar-bar-bar.

Milton's self-representation begins with somewhat oblique references to his humanity in terms of the prerogatives of a freeborn citizen ("I did but prompt the age . . . By the known rules of antient libertie"). But when he begins to represent his opponents as animals, he correspondingly upgrades his own associations from humanity to divinity. He has been dealt with "as" the goddess Latona was: a simile that commentators have drawn into a miniature allegory, identifying the divine twins with *Tetrachordon* and *Colasterion* (both published on 4 March 1645) and noting that Latona and Milton both suffered hostility in bringing their twins into the world (*S*[H], pp. 118–19). Well on this side of allegorizing, however, there are two unmistakable connections forged between the reception of the divorce tracts and the reception of the gospel: "But this is got by casting Pearl to Hoggs" echoes Jesus' warning regarding impious hearers, "Neither cast ye your pearls before swine" (Matthew 7:6), and "when truth would set them free" echoes Jesus' ringing characterization of his preaching, "Ye shall know the truth, and the truth shall set you free" (John 8:32).

When the sonnet closes without specifying further the "rules of antient libertie" that were declared "known" in line 1, we are tempted to take Jesus' reference to preaching the truth that sets men free and read this back as the sense of the phrase, "rules of antient libertie." But thus to resolve the unspecificity in the poetry is tantamount to accepting at face value and full strength Milton's argument in *The Doctrine and Discipline of Divorce* and *Tetrachordon.* It runs like this. Since it is impossible for Old Testament law to be freer—less stringent and more charitable—than the New Testament gospel, and since Moses is read as pronouncing more leniently than Jesus on the grounds for divorce, Jesus' words cannot mean what they seem to say. Milton considered that he had disencumbered Christ's true meaning and "set free the minds of ingenuous and apprehensive men from needless thraldome" to literalism and social conformity (*CPW* 2:239), but this, of course, was just what his opponents disputed with him. In cultivating these key allusive links between his divorce writings and Jesus' preaching, Milton imports into his poetry the sense of a prophetic mandate expressed in his earliest prose and gives it the loftiest possible construction. When he also ranges over against himself as a Christ-figure a whole (Presbyterian) menagerie, he gives all too evident imaginative rein to his personal rage at his contemporaries' rejection of the scholarship and leadership he had offered them.

The poetic tide swamps political possibility. A situation dichotomized between divinity and animality is one with no place for politics. Aristotle (*Politics* 1.1.12) and Cicero (*De Officiis* 1.11, 12) were standard sources for the observation that man is a political animal because he can differentiate right from wrong and communicate his perceptions in speech. Although men are endowed by nature with the potential and the desire for community, the leadership of outstandingly wise and good men has also proved necessary for organizing and sustaining the specifically political entity of the state. The state is a uniquely human product brought into being by conscious intent, something for which the instinctual lower animals have no capacity and the self-sufficient gods have no need. In "I did but prompt the age" Milton denies his community with beings who lack just these qualities of speech and moral judgment, and his consequent isolation is emphasized by the absence of direct address. Third-person references attest the distance between the observer and those he observes. The one "we" in line 13 must be the speaker's plural of majesty, for there is no sign of his having anyone to address but himself.

At the end of the octave, however, Milton falters and starts to undercut his own dichotomy. It is an interesting and precarious juncture. Recalling his authorial intentions ("But this is got by casting Pearl," "truth would set them free"), he proves unable to hold to the identity of a self-sufficient god, all the while that he wraps himself in connotations of divinity. Feeling his own political impulsions—that is to say, his humanity—too keenly, he moves abruptly to constitute a political realm in the sonnet's remaining lines. Beings he had represented solely as animals are now held accountable as humans for political failures that only humans can incur. Speech and moral judgment figure along with imputations of conscious intent. Their "mood," not their nature, is branded as "senceless." Before they will stop confusing "licence" and "libertie" they "must first be wise and good." We recognize the equation of wisdom and virtue as the Aristotelian basis on which Cicero rears his treatment of decorum. This recognition, in turn, furnishes a likely rationale for the late, high-handed switch in the terms of representation. When Milton at last acknowledges his opponents no longer as animals but as failed political animals, he can try to say where their choices went wrong and what responsibility they bear for them.

The charge that political degeneracy consists in mistaking *licentia* for *libertas* has been traced to its Roman republican sources in Cicero and Livy (*S*[S], pp. 68–69). "Licence" has been read alternatively as a pun on the licensing with which the Presbyterians aimed at control of the press and jeopardized Miltonic free expression (*S*[H], p. 32).[16] We much prefer the latter reading, the play of wit rather than the spelled-out distinction that Milton's opponents violated in their mistaken and misleading use of words. But if Aristotle's emphasis on representing morally significant choice in poetry as articulated thought is relevant here, the *libertas*/*licentia* antithesis appears the somewhat more probable

16. Divorce tract phraseology is interestingly ambivalent between the two senses. In close contiguity in *The Doctrine and Discipline of Divorce*, we find Milton announcing that "the draffe of men, to whom no liberty is pleasing, but unbridl'd and vagabond lust . . . , shall hence learne that honest liberty is the greatest foe to dishonest license" but also claiming that superstitious "mis-interpreting of some Scripture . . . doth . . . run us from one extreme of abused libertie into the other of unmercifull restraint" (*CPW* 2:227, 235). Milton offers the tract as instruction in the distinction between license and liberty.

sense, in view of the lines that follow. "From that mark"—the aim of becoming "wise and good"—"how far they roave we see," the speaker declares. His vocabulary resonates with associations of *telos* and *hamartia,* goal and aiming awry, terms originating in archery and taken over by Aristotle for ethical and political application. The stress on roving far from a mark promotes the licentiousness reading over the licensing one. We see "how far they roave," the speaker continues, "For all this wast of wealth, and loss of blood." In another late and abrupt move, he opens a prospect on the property damage, mismanaged funding, and human casualties of the war effort. What is its relevance to the vocabulary of goal and aim? It seems impossible to tell. If, on the one hand, the phrases introduced by "For" are predicate complements of "roave," then "For" means "for the purpose of," "with the intent of" wasting wealth and spilling blood. These, then, are ruinously wrong choices that compound the case for reading "Licence" as licentiousness.[17] But it is still utterly unclear how responsibility for these effects of war redounds on the Presbyterian opponents of the divorce tracts. If, on the other hand, "For" is taken as meaning "in spite of," the prospect on the war is somehow set over against the licentious (or licensing) criers after liberty. Such a contrast in turn suspends the expected connection between the war and the vocabulary of goal and aim; final emphasis falls on the speaker's claimed clarity of vision—nothing more. The most damaging effect of the savagery in this sonnet is that it at last engulfs the speaker, too, in the political desperation from which it springs. Belatedly acknowledging his opponents' humanity, he fails to bring their "Licence" into coherent relation with his closing prospect on the nation at war. He himself subsides into the production of sounds, scannable lines with irrecoverable meaning.

To his second sonnet on the divorce tracts in the Trinity College manuscript, Milton tried to bring a fresh outlook and some lightness of touch:

A Book was writ of late call'd *Tetrachordon;*
  And wov'n close, both matter, form and stile;
  The Subject new: it walk'd the Town a while,
  Numbring good intellects; now seldom por'd on.
Cries the stall-reader, bless us! what a word on
   A title page is this! and some in file
   Stand spelling fals, while one might walk to Mile-
   End Green. Why is it harder Sirs then Gordon,

17. The likelihood of these connotations is strengthened by a conjunctive reading of "for" as "on account of" in *Paradise Lost* 2.94–96. Satan speaks: "yet not for those [those dire Arms], / Nor what the Potent Victor in his rage / Can else inflict, do I repent or change. . . . "

Colkitto, or Macdonnel, or Galasp?
  Those rugged names to our like mouths grow sleek
  That would have made *Quintilian* stare and gasp.
Thy age, like ours, O Soul of Sir *John Cheek,*
  Hated not Learning wors then Toad or Asp;
  When thou taught'st *Cambridge,* and King *Edward* Greek.
[*S*(H), no. 12]

In his first draft Milton had begun as follows: "I writt a book of late called Tetrachordon, / And weav'd it close both matter, form, & stile, / It went off well about y[e] town a while." The substitution of impersonal passives for the first-person locutions removes the obligation to identify the speaker of the poem with the author of *Tetrachordon* and relegates to the judgment of "good intellects," rather than the author's claims, the positive qualities attributed to the work. The shift in his time reference from "of late" to "now" prompts the speaker to a candid admission couched in the sonnet's first burlesque rhyme: *Tetrachordon* is "seldom por'd on." Yet his good humor sustains both this admission and the overheard puzzlement of the bookstall browsers who try to sound out "tetrachordon," Greek for the "four-stringed" harmony Milton claimed to have made of two Old Testament and two New Testament verses on marriage and divorce. Here he proves capable of creating a moment of deliciously light social comedy by shutting off his authorial dimension and concentrating on the surface aspects of speech and behavior to which readers' reactions can, by an effort of perception, be reduced. But now comes the turn into direct address in present time that serves elsewhere as a reliable index to political significance in the political sonnets. Is it so here?

I think it is supposed to be a turn of a politically significant kind although Milton fumbles his first introduction of proper names by failing to provide independent clues to his topical drift. At best the reader recognizes four Scottish names. Annotators help by explaining that the two clans Gordon and Macdonnel[d] supplied officers for the royalist army, that "Colkitto" ("Colin the lefty") was the nickname of one of these, and that George Galaspe or Gillespie was a ranking Parliamentary preacher and a member of the Presbyterian majority in the Assembly of Divines (*S*[S], pp. 71–72; *S*[H], pp. 123–24). Addressing the London man-in-the-street, Milton's speaker in effect challenges this man's immersion in the latest war news and Parliamentary doings and also, by implication, his ready acceptance of Scots ascendancy in English affairs. This looks like a juncture which might open into some pointed criticism of busyness that excludes reflectiveness and into some Aristotelian- or Ciceronian-style counsel on the need to combine practical with theoretical considerations if one aspires to genuine political wisdom.

Instead, the "Why is it harder Sirs" question leads into a quite different remonstrance, one in which Milton took pains to preserve his speaker's geniality. "Those rugged names to our like mouths" had first read "those barbarous names" (reintroducing the red flag—"barbarous rout"—from the preceding sonnet), and then, in an intermediate stage, "those rough-hewn names." The humanist fastidiousness voiced in these lines recalls strictures drawn in *Of Education,* where it is given out that "we Englishmen being farre northerly, do not open our mouthes in the cold air" and hence inflict on "the Latin and Greek *idiom*" various "untutor'd *Anglicisms,* . . . not to be avoided without a well continu'd and judicious conversing among pure Authors" (*CPW* 2:383, 373). In the treatise Milton's stickling for pure pronunciation as he understood it enforces a serious tenet of Renaissance educational and political theory.[18] Utterance must be ruled by decorum, for speech reveals one's thought and thought reveals one's character. But in the context of this sonnet such stickling is given no relevance or rationale whatever. It seems simply fatuous. What is Quintilian to Scottish names in English mouths? What could Quintilian possibly be to this?

The lighter social tone of this sonnet is first struck by limiting attention to surfaces. This tone suggestively deepens with the prospect of subjecting surface features of speech and behavior to scrutiny as symptoms of cultural problems. But once the "Why is it harder" question has been posed, the speaker unaccountably slips away from the moment of political immediacy and human engagement to return to surface considerations that come to seem mere superficialities. He may as well be speaking to himself the two lines on rugged names, for all the sense he makes to or about the average Londoner in them. He certainly is soliloquizing when he flees back in time to invoke Sir John Cheke, first professor of Greek at Cambridge and a staunchly Protestant humanist who lived a century before Milton. Cheke lost a much publicized struggle with academic conservatives who kept his reformed system for Greek pronunciation out of the university curriculum, but the nostalgia for good old days that has overwhelmed the Miltonic speaker by this point leaves no room for recalcitrant historical facts. Acceding to the easily caricatured "O tempora! O mores!" vein of Cicero, he insures his ridiculousness by addressing Cheke in an English sentence that collapses into nonsense because it separates its adverbials "not" and "like ours" with latinate affectation: "Thy age, like ours, O

18. See further in this connection Milton's 1638 letter to a Florentine, Benedetto Buonmattei, who was writing a grammar for Tuscan. Milton there spells out his conviction that to regulate and purify the style in which one's countrymen write and speak is as great a political contribution as to rule them wisely in peace and war (*CPW* 1:328–32). What underlies such latter-day purism among humanists is, as Joshua Scodel reminds me, an endemic double consciousness: they are fully aware of linguistic change between antiquity and their own times, yet they wish the usage and values of classical times to be normative in their own.

Soul of Sir *John Cheek,* / Hated not Learning wors then Toad or Asp." What is there to deplore if, as the sentence plainly says in English, neither age hated learning? The *OED* gives no warrant for reading "like" as "likened to," an option that, if it existed, could save the sense of the sentence. There appears to be no salvaging of the speaker. Milton causes this genial but bemused and finally inconsequential rhetorician to finish by making a fool of himself: an end, we gather, befitting one who cannot sustain meaningful connections between the discourse of the city street and that of the ivory tower. How to transpose decorum from *Of Education* to contemporary politics is a challenge clearly registered in "A Book was writ," but it is just as clearly left unmet.

For Milton the author, the public record of 1645–48—three years in which he published nothing—is very different from that of 1641–45. The debacle of the divorce tracts compounded with the unhappiness of his first marriage to render politics too personal for the time being. We have seen emotional venting swamp political content in "I did but prompt the age." In the last of the divorce tracts, *Colasterion* (Greek for "an instrument of chastisement"), Milton lays animal epithets on his adversaries at much greater length. The three years' silence must be read in personal terms as recoil and self-reconstitution. But the flat rejection of his proposals for legitimating divorce and the danger of prosecution for publishing unlicensed material were at bottom political experiences that enforced responses in kind. Milton did respond politically, as shown by developments that these experiences triggered in his political thought and political perceptions.

His first, more or less instantaneous responses are addressed to the issues and the parties to be engaged on these issues. *Areopagitica* comes as an open letter to Parliament, on the heels of the unlicensed and investigated *Doctrine and Discipline of Divorce,* to argue Milton's case against the new licensing order which the Presbyterians had sponsored. His *ad hominem* defenses of the divorce tracts also reflect the policy of going after particular benighted Presbyterians for their particular views of his ideas, but not all at once giving up on Presbyterianism or Presbyterians. Their positions on church government and on church-and-state relations were ones he had defended at length in print. In the mid-1640s the Presbyterians constituted a majority in Parliament and in the special body charged with ecclesiastical reform, the Westminster Assembly of Divines.

Milton's shift in party affiliation became definite much more gradually, as he came to locate the politics of the situation not just in the issues of censorship or divorce but in a bid for powers of legislation and enforcement that would make a Presbyterian national church just as much a mechanism for compulsory religious conformity as Laudian Anglicanism had been. The slower and more oblique manifestations of this party realignment need not count against Milton's perspicacity; they can count in favor of his prudence and caution. The disparagement of Scottish names in "A

Book was writ of late" is the earliest signal of his disaffection for Presbyterians as a party, for besides the member of the Assembly of Divines, the others named are military officers who were playing a part in the emerging alliance of expediency between Presbyterians and royalists fighting the Parliamentary army.

So Milton pulled back for three years into private life, opening a school for his two nephews and several other boys in his house in London. *Of Education*'s civic concerns must have returned to his mind as he contemplated his young charges, not least because the so-called second civil war renewed hostilities in the field in 1647–48. At the same time Milton embarked upon a *History of Britain,* a project he would carry up as far as the Norman Conquest. From the outside, one might judge that these were years of political retreat for Milton, but a remarkable digression in the fourth book of the *History of Britain* shows otherwise. A remorseless series of reflections on the membership of Parliament and the Assembly of Divines in 1647–48, the passage was withheld by Milton from publication with the rest of the *History* in his lifetime. It confirms that he undertook to write the history of his country not to flee into antiquarianism, as the speaker of "A Book was writ" does, but to deepen his understanding of how men secure and use power, and to probe especially what does or does not happen when transfers of supreme authority occur by conquest or revolution.

In setting himself to this inquiry Milton implicitly judged his as well as others' earlier writings deficient in the level of penetration needed to make sound political judgments on a given society. The *History* shows him clearly differentiating between his political function as author and the role of the political leader. Previously there had been no such differentiation. As an activist, Milton the prose writer had placed himself on the same footing with the ordained minister publicly authorized to preach and with the policymakers of Parliament and the Assembly of Divines. Only in the relation of poet and officer in "Captain or Colonel" is there a foreshadowing of the differentiation that Milton now makes between holding public office and his own political function as a recorder, analyst, and counselor—a function which includes at need, however, a sharply adversarial stance. Not directly aspiring to public leadership, he could buffer his personal involvement in politics and replace acting with observing in order to trace thought in the speeches and conduct of individuals, and chart contemporary developments as patterns of choice.

Two generalizations tie the digression to the patterns of the larger *History:* first, that "the gaining or loosing of libertie is the greatest change to better or to worse that may befall a nation under civil government," and second, that a nation's success or failure in securing liberty "discovers, as nothing more, what degree of understanding, or capacitie, what disposition to justice and civilitie there is among them" (*CPW* 5:441). Milton opens discussion of the course of recent events in England by conceding that the revolutionary elements that have come to power have "had Arms, Leaders, and Successes to their wish; but to make use of so great an Advantage was not their skill." The reason for failure so far, everywhere but on the battlefield, is that the persons chosen to sit in Parliament and in the Assembly of Divines have virtually all proven void of the classical components of political virtue, the "*Wisdom* and *Integrity*" that equate the true best interests of the individual and of the state. For "when once . . . superficial Zeal and Popular Fumes . . . were cool'd, and spent in them, straight every one betook himself, setting the Common-wealth behind, his private Ends before, to do as his own profit or ambition led him." "Justice was delayed and soon after deny'd" by Parliament and its appointees for revenue collection, for the "Impositions, Taxes, Excises" voted for prosecuting the war with the king became subject to "the Ravening Seizure of innumerable Thieves in Office." Even backers of Parliament, who lent money for the war on agreed terms, found themselves unrepaid, defrauded by that "which ought to have been kept as Sacred and Inviolable as any thing holy, *The Publick Faith.*" For "that Faith . . . , after infinite Sums received, and all the Wealth of the Church not better imploy'd, but swallowed up into a private *Gulph,* was not ere long ashamed to confess Bankrupt" (*CPW* 5:441, 442, 444). Correspondingly, in the Assembly, where "a certain number of Divines were called,"

> the most part of them were such, as had Preach'd and cryed down, with great shew of Zeal, the Avarice and Pluralities of Bishops and Prelates; that one Cure of Souls was a full Employment for one Spiritual Pastour how able soever. . . . Yet these . . . men . . . wanted not boldness, to the Ignominy and Scandal of their Pastor-like Profession, and especially of their boasted Reformation, to seize into their hands . . . sometimes two or more of the best Livings . . . : by which means these great Rebukers of Non-Residence . . . were not ashamed to be seen so quickly Pluralists and Non-Residents themselves. . . . And yet the main Doctrine for which they took such pay, and insisted upon with more vehemence than Gospel, was but to tell us in effect, that . . . Spiritual Power . . . was less . . . than Bodily Compulsion; perswading the Magistrate to use it, as a stronger means to subdue and bring in Conscience, than Evangelical perswasion: . . . setting up a Spiritual Tyranny by a Secular power, to the advancing of their own Authority above the Magistrate, whom they would have made their Executioner. [*CPW* 5:446]

The political and poetic difference made by Milton's self-imposed efforts at deepening his understanding of national events and at integrating personal with public concerns in rendering judgment registers dramatically in the sonnet keyed to follow "A Book was writ" in the Trinity College manuscript (*F* 1:452–54). "On the new forcers of Conscience under the

Long PARLIAMENT" must have been written in close conjunction with the foregoing passage in the digression. This is not a standard, fourteen-line "Petrarchian stanza," but a *sonetto caudato,* a "tailed" sonnet. The form was developed by Italian poets chiefly for humorous or satiric purposes because the two-and-a-half-line tails or codas, added in any number to the initial fourteen lines, function as whips or lashes to sustain the energy of the verse in treating its subject (*S*[S], pp. 126–27). Virtually a unique English exemplar,[19] Milton's sonnet has just two tails, but they provide him with sorely needed extra room for his first attempt to bring political content to intelligible resolution in his poetry. The sestets of the three preceding political sonnets are consistent in their defective closures. Here, much more than in *Colasterion,* Milton forged an effective instrument of chastisement:

Because you have thrown of[f] your Prelate Lord,
And with stiff Vowes renounc'd his Liturgie
To seise the widdow'd whore Pluralitie
From them whose sin ye envi'd, not abhor'd,
Dare ye for this adjure the Civill Sword
To force our Consciences that Christ set free,
And ride us with a classic Hierarchy
Taught ye by meer *A. S.* and *Rotherford*?
Men whose Life, Learning, Faith and pure intent
Would have been held in high esteem with *Paul*
Must now be nam'd and printed Hereticks
By shallow *Edwards* and Scotch what d'ye call:
But we do hope to find out all your tricks,
Your plots and packing wors then those of *Trent,*
That so the Parliament
May with their wholsom and preventive Shears
Clip your Phylacteries, though bauk your Ears,
And succour our just Fears
When they shall read this clearly in your charge
New Presbyter is but *Old Priest* writ Large.

[*S*(H), no. (24)]

19. Howard Schultz, *Milton and Forbidden Knowledge* (New York, 1955), p. 205, reports that there is a caudal sonnet included in the accessory material in the 1644 edition of Samuel How's *The Sufficiencie of the Spirits Teaching,* but I could not find a poem of this form either in the first (1640) or the fifth (1653) edition—the only two to which I had access. If Schultz's find is not a ghost, Milton did not naturalize the caudal sonnet in English. Gerard Manley Hopkins gave him credit for doing so, however. Hopkins wrote to Robert Bridges that "On the New Forcers" was the model for his own "caudated" sonnet, "Tom's Garland." For the text of "Tom's Garland" and commentary, see *The Faber Book of Political Verse,* ed. Tom Paulin (London, 1986), pp. 25 and 318, which Robert von Hallberg kindly put into my hands.

Expanding the octave unit into one of twelve lines, the sonnet launches itself in a virtually flawless unfolding of its highly circumstantial content. "To seise the widdow'd whore . . . / From them whose sin ye envi'd, not abhor'd" conveys the full particulars of Milton's indictment: the charges of venality and hypocrisy as well as the underlying motives of power grabbing and profiteering from an already corrupt system. A neatly compounded ambiguity penetrates every shift of the perverse thinking that Milton discerns in his addressees' conduct: the "for this" in "Dare ye for this . . . ?" reads triply effectively as "on account of this (which you have done)" or "in spite of all this (that you have done)" or "for the sake of holding onto this (which you have)." The whore image opens the door to coarse sexual innuendo in the verb phrases "force our Consciences" and "ride us" in lines 6 and 7.

While there are technical terms—Prelate, Liturgie, Pluralitie—that may send a reader to the dictionary, no annotation is required except, perhaps, to ward off a misunderstanding of "classic"—here the adjectival form of "classis," a middle-level division in the Presbyterian system of church government. Milton is especially skillful in his handling of proper names: they are put there to pinpoint his Presbyterian objects of attack, but so presented that the men seem upstart nonentities who are not worth knowing about. In the satiric diminution beginning with "meer *A. S.*," Adam Stuart's own fashion of signing his name on his title pages, the point of zero difference is reached with "Scotch what d'ye call." The utterly assured focus on what gives particularity its significance, not on particulars as such, is compounded in the unspecific first-person plural references by which the poet, in direct address, pits himself and others against the successors to the prelates: "force our Consciences," "ride us." The reader, validly enough, takes Milton to be speaking here for all of England. This is an altogether different "we" from the plural of majesty in "I did but prompt the age." Two lines later, however, with the crucial pivot into the "now" of present time, the scope of reference to those opposing and opposed by the forcers of conscience narrows to a group under attack by "shallow *Edwards*" and Co. "Men" of apostolic "Life, Learning, Faith and pure intent"—their New Testament probity is significantly much more vital than their names—"Must now be nam'd and printed Hereticks." This generic moral description rounds out the highly accessible sense of the first twelve lines: vicious ministers are seeking to "force . . . Consciences" generally with "the Civill Sword," the mechanisms of law enforcement, and they are specifically going after some virtuous ministers in the public press (where their targets are "nam'd and printed Hereticks").

Moving from past into present time, the indictment gradates from moral to political charges: abuse of the press with the motive of religious repression. As usual in these sonnets, the resumption of direct address in present time coincides with a new access of poetic energy and political commitment. Milton announces the onset of a power struggle, meting out monosyllables with the deadly deliberation of a man pacing a duelling ground: "But we do hope to find out all your tricks / Your plots and packing wors then those of *Trent.*" Getting to countermeasures takes him to the end of line fourteen, the end of a conventional sonnet. But the unfolding of his political design is perfectly calibrated with the form of the *sonetto caudato:* a now contextually narrowed "we"—the attacked ministers and their supporters, among whom Milton numbers himself—have determined to go on the offensive. Envisaging this offensive now unleashes an energy that sustains two rounds of whips or tails, driving the sonnet toward closure with a satiric sting.

Although it falls short of the former's remarkable clarity, the poetry of the latter section registers two major developments in Milton's politics clearly enough. First, Milton signals his party realignment; he stands with the ministers attacked by Edwards and "Scotch what d'ye call." While annotators cite the works of Thomas Edwards and Robert Baillie, Scots Presbyterians who freely used the terms "heresy" and "heretic," to document the identity of the attacked ministers as members of the Independent party, it must be stressed that the verse does not require this. Milton accords total priority to freedom of conscience in matters of religion throughout this sonnet, and that priority suffices to fix the sense. In the later 1640s freedom of conscience had only one viable outlet in English politics—Independency. Religious toleration remained a major plank in this party's platform for the duration of its existence, even though Independents would never agree on how best to secure it.

The clarity about party affiliation cannot be unrelated to the second major development in these lines: the political cogency and improved specificity of the countermeasures Milton announces. They will be directed toward influencing opinion in Parliament, at the time England's sole executive as well as legislative authority. The aim is an exposé of Presbyterian machinations as being "wors then those of *Trent*"—an easily recognized allusion to the Council which, a century earlier, had codified Roman Catholic orthodoxy and launched the Inquisition in Europe. The Independents' countermeasures are, unmistakably, to take the form of a press campaign to bring out the self-serving, repressive patterns in the Presbyterians' history and discredit them with Parliament as decisively as the Laudians had been discredited before them. As in "Captain or Colonel," Milton's language lays claim to a transformative effect on power relations, but now the effect makes for political impact, not political evasiveness. This sonnet ends by vaunting the memorable formulation of its final line, representing its poetry as nothing less than the trigger to the action Parliament is sure to take "when they shall read this clearly in your charge / *New Presbyter* is but *Old Priest* writ Large." The device of re-etymologizing also reappears from "I did but prompt the age," but now it directly serves a politically and historically telling point: "priest" and "presbyter" are variant forms of one another.

What alone fails to come clear is what Milton looked to Parliament to do to control Presbyterian abuses of the press. He precludes any return to the savage Laudian measure of cutting off the ears of authors who had been convicted of publishing seditious works.[20] "Clip your Phylacteries" is the crux. Commentary has gotten as far as pointing out that phylacteries, little boxes containing quotations from the Mosaic law that are worn on the forehead by pious Jews, had been treated by Jesus (Matthew 23:5) as a badge of hypocrisy (*S*[H], p. 202). But a hitherto overlooked sarcasm in *Tenure of Kings and Magistrates* (February 1649) sheds the light we need. There Milton reprehends as a horrible misnomer the title of Herbert Palmer's book, *Scripture and Reason,* as well as the general practice of other Presbyterian authors in styling themselves "reverend and lerned Divines . . . in the Phylactery of thir own Title page" (*CPW* 3:252). Apparently Milton hoped that Parliament would order (Presbyterian) title pages containing egregious misrepresentations to be cut out of books after publication, so that unwary buyers and readers would not be taken in by fraudulent advertising in the wordy titles that were the fashion in the period. With this rather minor proviso, he stands committed to a free English press for free English consciences.

"On the new forcers of Conscience under the long PARLIAMENT" is Milton's first fully successful political poem. Locating its speaker firmly as a political being within the coordinates of government, party, and the public press, the tailed sonnet harnesses personal animus to political analysis and political objectives. As Milton's diction and imagery work through what can be said of an individual to point toward what can be said of all individuals of the type, the language of political poetry seems to rival that of political philosophy in affording access to the universals which, for Aristotle, are the objects of knowledge. But Milton's further Ciceronian insistence that knowledge must be applicable as a norm for present and ongoing choice draws his political representations back within a poetic mode, as against philosophy's concern with what holds always and timelessly. The success of the tailed sonnet as political poetry, however, was never to be replicated; its registration of the specifics of wrong and right choosing-up in the corporate framework of press, party, and Parliament in 1647–48 remains as *sui generis* as its tailed form. Why should this have been so? The last movements of thought in the digression on contemporary events in the *History of Britain* offer an answer, and it is one that bears out the continuing interdependence of Milton's poetic and political development.

20. A manuscript revision of line 17 has attracted much critical notice. Milton first wrote: "Cropp yee as close as marginall P———s eares" (*F*, p. 454). On second thought Milton must have realized the several ways in which this allusion to the popular Presbyterian author William Prynne could backfire, for Prynne's unending stream of antiestablishment polemics had cost him a horrifying double subjection to ear-cropping and ensured his status as a culture hero. For discussion, see *S*(H), pp. 202–4. Just as likely and more simply, Milton may have decided that the original line was not his considered meaning.

Milton's analysis in the digression does not exhaust itself on the venality and hypocrisy of officeholders who betray the trust of those who elected them. He gives an account of the psychology of "the People," who, at first scandalized and confused by the flagrant bad examples set by public figures around them, have now sunk into disillusionment, "some turning to Lewdness, some to flat Atheism." The sum of his judgment on Parliament and the Assembly of Divines holds that they "did not only weaken and unfit themselves to be dispensers of what Liberty they pretended, but unfitted also the People, now grown worse and more disordinate, to receive or to digest any Liberty." He laments the pattern disclosed in his *History* and reinforced in his digression: the nation has typically produced good warriors but not good statesmen. "For *Britain,* to speak a truth not often spoken, as it is a Land fruitful enough of Men stout and courageous in War, so it is naturally not over-fertile of Men able to govern justly and prudently in Peace, trusting only in their Mother-Wit." It is the national genius to be "valiant indeed, and prosperous to win a field; but to know the end and Reason of winning, unjudicious and unwise." "For the Sun which we want, ripens Wits as well as Fruits; and as Wine and Oyl are Imported to us from Abroad: so must ripe Understanding, and many civil Vertues, be imported into our minds from Forreign Writings, and examples of best Ages, we shall else miscarry still, and come short in the attempts of any great Enterp[r]ise" (*CPW* 5:448, 450).

Milton's last three political sonnets sustain the conjunction of elements that make for specifically political meaning—present-tense direct address on an issue involving the exercise of power in the public domain—but these sonnets are all directed to individuals. The contraction of discourse starkly corroborates the reassignment of political effectiveness from corporate bodies to leaders that took place in Milton's thought by the latter half of 1648.[21] Milton was personally well acquainted with two of the addressees of these sonnets, Oliver Cromwell and Sir Henry Vane the Younger, and he may also have been acquainted with Thomas, Lord Fairfax, the subject of the first. Although there is no evidence regarding the other two, Vane's sonnet is known to have been sent to him a day or two after it was composed (*S*[H], p. 157). There is some warrant, then, for conceiving of these sonnets as actual pieces of correspondence, texts whose immediacy of utterance is a taking of action on the poet's part. Speaking to an active public leader from his now-established authorial position as observer and counselor, Milton contrives to transpose the civic concerns of *Of Education* into forthright but deeply respectful man-to-man talk. As he registered in the digression, effective leadership had

21. For discussion of this development and its subsequent ramifications in Milton's prose, see Zera S. Fink, *The Classical Republicans: An Essay in the Recovery of a Pattern of Thought in Seventeenth-Century England* (Evanston, Ill., 1945), pp. 90–122.

historically been almost nonexistent among the English, so Milton determines in his own time to abet the formation of sound policy by men of sound character through the activity of poetic creation. In addressing Fairfax, Cromwell, and Vane he does not do what he represented as necessary within the conventional Renaissance didactic framework adopted in the *History*—namely, import "many civil Vertues," "ripe Understanding," and "examples of best Ages . . . from Forreign Writings" into these sonnets for their recipients' benefit.[22] Instead he offers them the example of themselves, to be understood first through the dynamic of their past public achievements and then extended to completion in a present crisis. The completion, as envisaged in poem and career, will come through a choice of action that verifies the virtue and wisdom of the leader's character all the while that it shapes the polity, after his example, toward those same ends.

Milton composed all three sonnets in the heavily suspended and enjambed syntax which Tasso promoted as a resource of the magnificent style in his *Discourses* and made a model for lofty salutation and compliment in scores of sonnets in his *Occasional or Encomiastic Verse* (*Rime d'Occasione o d'Encomio*).[23] In Tasso's handling, the encomiastic sonnet opens with a vocative, follows with a series of ascriptive clauses, and moves toward a climax in epigram or apostrophe. The themes are mainly contemplative, often retrospective—as illustrated by the number addressed to deceased worthies—and sometimes introspective, when the poet ponders the gulf between his own miseries and the exaltedness of his subject. If, as rarely, a plea is lodged, it is for personal consideration, some grace or favor. By contrast, the Miltonic variation on this model shows clearly in the sonnets to Fairfax and Cromwell: the vocative of address followed by a series of ascriptive clauses pivots back into renewed direct address in the form of an exhortation to present political action. Perhaps Milton's sonnets to individual leaders may be thought of as versified, secular collects, for their syntactic pattern closely correlates with the pattern for this kind of

22. Renaissance literary theorists placed a premium on devising examples that would be lively instances of general vices and virtues; on their directives, see John M. Steadman, *The Lion and the Elephant* (San Marino, Calif., 1974), pp. 93–96, 128–30, and 137–40. For an illuminating discussion of the then dominant, close-to-allegorizing mode from which Milton's practice diverges sharply, see John M. Wallace, "'Examples Are Best Precepts': Readers and Meanings in Seventeenth-Century Poetry," *Critical Inquiry* 1 (Dec. 1974): 273–90.

23. Angelo Solerti prepared the first critical edition of the *Rime d'Occasione o d'Encomio* as vol. 3 of *Le Rime di Torquato Tasso* (Bologna, 1900). For representative examples of the sonnet type adapted by Milton, see pp. 46, 55, 59, 108, 121, 122, 125, 166, 171, 197, 243, and for the subtype ending in a plea, pp. 251, 258, 282. The resources of the magnificent style are discussed in books 5 and 6 of Tasso's *Discourses;* see pp. 158--63, 184–88 of Cavalchini and Samuel's edition for specifics relating to the syntax of this and closely related styles.

liturgical prayer.[24] And why not? The politics of this poetry go far to intimate that men are most godlike, most virtuous and magnificent, when they use their power to execute justice in all wisdom for the state.

The first of the trio indicates a date of August 1648 in the specificity of its manuscript title, "On ye Lord Gen. Fairfax at ye seige of Colchester" (*F* 1:452). As commander-in-chief of the New Model Army, Fairfax was pressing home an offensive against English and Scots royalists. The offensive had only begun to gather momentum in May, but Fairfax was now moving against strongholds of resistance on the way to concluding the second civil war with victory for the Parliamentary war effort. Milton's lines read as follows:

Fairfax, whose name in armes through *Europe* rings
Filling each mouth with envy, or with praise,
And all her jealous monarchs with amaze,
And rumors loud, that daunt remotest kings,
Thy firm unshak'n vertue ever brings
Victory home, though new rebellions raise
Thir Hydra heads, and the fals North displaies
Her brok'n league, to impe their serpent wings,
O yet a nobler task awaites thy hand;
For what can Warr, but endless warr still breed,
Till Truth, and Right from Violence be freed,
And Public Faith cleard from the shamefull brand
Of Public Fraud. In vain doth Valour breed
While Avarice, and Rapine share the land.

[*S*(H), no. 15]

The semantic and political clarity that first distinguished the tailed sonnet recurs here in the more limited confines of conventional sonnet form. Capitalizing on the accessibility of generic description ("Life, Learning, Faith and pure intent" in "On the new forcers"), Milton steadily increases his complement of abstract nouns—"envy," "praise," "firm unshak'n vertue"—to climax in the great cluster of the sestet: "Warr," "Truth," "Right," "Violence," "Avarice, and Rapine." The cumulative force of such diction is so considerable that it can trigger semantic alteration, as shown by what happens to "Public Faith" in this context. Milton's digression in the *History* indicates that "Public Faith" was a catchword of the day. It referred to the national debt that Parliament was incurring by borrowing to meet the army's expenses, and its ironies deepened as Parliament continued to default on repayment to private lenders. In the Fairfax sonnet, Milton faces a basic difficulty entailed by his mode of

24. On Cranmer's adaptation of collect form to English in the Book of Common Prayer, see my *Native Tongue and the Word: Developments in English Prose Style, 1380–1580* (Chicago, 1984), pp. 226–43.

composition. He cannot guarantee that either the topicality or the irony in "Public Faith" will survive the generalizing of poetic and political meaning. What he does is revealing. He shores up what he can of the current senses of "Public Faith" by putting it into construction with "Public Fraud"—the latter, apparently, a phrase of his own coining. Accepting the sacrifice of topicality to his larger openwork design, he moves to assure, through the antithetical pairing of what look like sister abstractions, the survival of the irony without which vital aspects of the choice facing Fairfax would fail to find representation.

The adaptation of the entire form of a sonnet to constructive political and poetic designs first becomes fully assured in the Fairfax sonnet. Its political design pivots on the Aristotelian and Ciceronian principles that Milton assimilated as doctrine in *Of Education* but had not yet brought to coherent expression in verse. The citizen must be educated for war as well as for peace, but, as Aristotle stresses, war at best involves doing what is necessary and useful (instrumental goodness); peace is that for which war is fought: it is noble in itself (essential goodness). Whether in peace or war, virtue most broadly consists, according to Cicero, in the decorum of consistent choices and actions on behalf of the distinctively human value of a consciously created just community. To repeat from *De Officiis:* decorum "is uniform consistency in the course of our life as a whole and all its individual actions"; decorum "is that which harmonizes with man's superiority in those respects in which his nature differs from the rest of the animal creation." This decorum is effectuated by Aristotelian *proairesis* in its political application: reasoned judgment on good and evil leads to the choice of an action that defines and creates virtue in the public milieu.

Milton's corresponding poetic design works, in the ascriptive clauses of the octave, to establish Fairfax in his own eyes as a preeminent public figure in whom, as a warrior, prowess and supreme virtue converge. Europe knows that he fought first against the excesses of royal power; this is why its absolutist monarchs ("jealous" of their prerogatives like the "jealous God" of the Ten Commandments in Exodus 20:5) have taken such sharp notice of him. "The fals North" is learning why Fairfax is fighting now: to quell "new rebellions" on behalf of royal power formerly repudiated but now openly espoused (in the display of its "brok'n league"). Milton salutes Fairfax for the decorum of self-consistency in his chosen course of actions and for his synthesis of martial and moral meaning: "Thy firm unshak'n vertue ever brings / Victory home." The two senses of "vertue"—goodness and strength—come into equal play to encapsulate perfectly the core perception of Fairfax in the sonnet. The remainder of the second quatrain proceeds to emphasize the humanity of his virtue by contrast with his opponents, tenacious warriors who are nevertheless monstrous in their lack of virtue. The mixed metaphor is so precisely expressive that it must be intentional: hydra-headed rebellions "impe"—that is, feather—"their serpent wings" on the strength of the North's (peacock-like) display of its falsity.

The pivot into the sestet confronts Fairfax with a moment ripe for his exercise of *proairesis* in a public, political context: "O yet a nobler task awaites thy hand." It is an extraordinarily complex moment, at once a poetic creation, an access of philosophical insight, and the fact of the immediate English situation as focused in the poetry. Milton addresses Fairfax just at the point where it has become clear that the army he commands will win final victory over the royalists. Now what? War, the useful and necessary, is fought, as Fairfax knows, for the sake of what is noble in itself—the justice, wisely administered, that brings peace. Such peace is nowhere in prospect for England, and the sestet is admirably explicit as to why. The conditions in the civil sector manifest the same falsity and inhumanity that characterize the battlefield: "For what can Warr but endless warr still breed / Till Truth, and Right from Violence be freed." Fairfax's self-consistency of character and action, his decorum, demands that he war now against the violence of "Public Fraud," of "Avarice, and Rapine." The specific political content of Milton's last lines seems to envisage the interim use of military tribunals to try civil officials for extorting or embezzling public funds. But this is only an implication pointed by the poetry, not the level on which it conducts its political discourse. The level of explicit discourse is more philosophical both in its generality and in the rational necessity which Milton undertakes to enforce upon Fairfax. If his "vertue" is to remain "firm" and "unshak'n," he must now apply himself to securing the same in his nation. For otherwise, "In vain doth Valour bleed." The war Fairfax has waged so virtuously will redound upon his leadership in multiple political and moral contradictions. Its impact in the civil sphere will be a state of war for its own sake. More particularly, the putting down of the abuses of arbitrary royal power in which Fairfax has had so large a hand will end in perpetuating the very evils of tyranny, under which "Avarice, and Rapine share the land." Paraphrase brings out the deeply Aristotelian and Ciceronian character of the informing political conceptions, but the fineness of the poetry made of the man, the moment, and the resulting imperatives is Milton's own.

The second of this trio of sonnets was entitled in manuscript "To the Lord Generall Cromwell May 1652 On the proposalls of certaine ministers at y[e] Comm[tee] for Propagation of the Gospell." It runs as follows:

Cromwell, our cheif of men, who through a cloud
 Not of warr onely, but detractions rude,
 Guided by faith and matchless Fortitude
 To peace and truth thy glorious way hast plough'd,
And on the neck of crowned Fortune proud
 Hast reard Gods Trophies and his work pursu'd,

While *Darwen* stream with blood of Scotts imbru'd,
And *Dunbarr* feild resounds thy praises loud,
And *Worsters* laureat wreath; yet much remaines
To conquer still; peace hath her victories
No less renownd then warr, new foes arise
Threatning to bind our soules with secular chaines:
Helpe us to save free Conscience from the paw
Of hireling wolves whose Gospell is their maw.
[*S*(H), no. 16]

The similarities in the function of the ascriptive clauses in the octave of the Fairfax sonnet and the first eight-and-a-half lines of the Cromwell sonnet need no belaboring. Again the man being addressed is offered to himself in the character of a national leader through the poetic inscription of his own actions, creating a sequence that, in its poetic and political decorum, carries necessary implications for action in the present.

However, there is a major difference in the extradimensionality which Milton attributes to Cromwell's leadership. He is hailed as "our cheif of men" in both of the troubled spheres of secular society, the military and the civil ("Not . . . warr onely, but detractions rude"). The recurrence of the term "detraction" from the heading of the sonnets on the divorce tracts suggests a measure of personal identification in Milton's praise. This may well persist in the further hailing of Cromwell as an agent of the divine will, the habitual terms in which the man himself interpreted his own experience.[25] The pairing of "faith and matchless Fortitude" as Cromwell's guides traces his virtue to a sacred as well as a secular source. Reinforcement of his divine mission shows in the tribute—without parallel in the Fairfax sonnet—offered to Cromwell as one who "Hast reard Gods Trophies and his work pursu'd."

Through the abstract diction that continues to predominate in the octave, the extra dimensions attributed to Cromwell are made to translate, first, into a heightened conception of him as a leader. Another semantic alteration of a topical term serves here to exemplify Cromwell's political impact on the English scene. "Peace and truth" had been a catchword used for years by supporters of the Solemn League and Covenant (1643) to praise its aim of uniting England and Scotland in the joint establishment of a reformed national church (*S*[H], pp. 146–48). But Cromwell, seizing the initiative in changing times, has been redefining the "glorious way" to "peace and truth" by waging war on these same Scots, now manifest underminers of the solidarity sworn in the Solemn League and Covenant, invaders of English soil who sought to impose their Presbyterianism and royalism with it. Besides the diction recast to convey Cromwell's trans-

25. For copious documentation, see Christopher Hill, *God's Englishman: Oliver Cromwell and the English Revolution* (New York, 1972).

formative political impact, the imagery of opening up new terrain, of ploughing a "glorious way" to "peace and truth," carries connotations of a Cincinnatus *redivivus,* a republic's savior swept to power by popular demand.[26] This imagery compounds with that of rearing trophies "on the neck of crowned Fortune proud," evoking the gesture of a conqueror who bears his booty aloft in his hand while bearing down on the body of his vanquished adversary with his foot. A famous metaphor at the end of chapter 25 of Machiavelli's *Il Principe* had figured the bending of historical possibility to a ruler's own will as a similarly rough handling of the goddess Fortune.[27] It appears that Cromwell is being conceived as one of an exalted and rare class of political beings: a lawgiver who brings a polity into being, in contrast to a ruler who administers an already existing polity. The close notes on the *Discorsi* in Milton's *Commonplace Book* attest how thoroughly he had absorbed Machiavelli's fascination with the seemingly limitless political potential of the lawgiver figure,[28] and *Of Education* sets Lycurgus, who was supposed to be the first such Greek, at the head of figures to be studied in the "law, and legall justice" segment of Milton's curriculum (*CPW* 2:398). In the sestet of the sonnet Cromwell is exhorted to take the making of law out of Parliament's hands into his own, to strike down the "secular chaines" with which "new foes" threaten "our soules" and "free Conscience." This decisive supervention, Milton implies, is mandated by the decorum of self-consistency shown in the cited victories of the octave—Preston (1648), Dunbar (1650), and Worcester (1651)—all of them over Scots Presbyterians turned expedient royalists.

At this point, however, three-and-a-half lines from its close, an otherwise lucid and forceful sonnet sinks into murkiness and thence into cant formulations: "hireling wolves," the bathetic concluding "paw/maw" rhyme. The explanation for this radical falling-off appears once again to be the arousal of powerful personal feelings about politics that Milton could not handle poetically. We are forced back upon annotation as a crutch for deficiencies of meaning in the verse. The date supplied in the manuscript heading makes it certain that the "new foes" of May 1652 were some Independent ministers who had found in the English translation of the *Racovian Catechism,* the credo of a Continental Socinian group, more anti-Trinitarianism and other unorthodoxy than their own toleration had room for. Now a member of Cromwell's Council as the Secretary

26. Livy, Milton's favorite classical historian, relates how, in 296 B.C., Lucius Quinctius Cincinnatus was summoned from his farm work to become dictator of Rome and save the city from destruction at the hands of the beseiging Sabines (*Histories* 3.26.8).

27. Niccolò Machiavelli, *The Prince,* tr. Luigi Ricci (London, 1921), p. 102: "I certainly think that it is better to be impetuous than cautious, for fortune is a woman, and it is necessary, if you wish to master her, to conquer her by force; and it can be seen that she lets herself be overcome by these rather than by those who proceed coldly."

28. See Fink, *The Classical Republicans,* pp. 9, 98, 105–6.

for Foreign Tongues, Milton himself had approved publication of the *Catechism.* The Independent ministers in question were appealing against Milton's judgment to a panel, the Committee for the Better Propagation of the Gospel, which had been appointed to adjudicate the issue (*S*[H], pp. 145–49). A return to the sestet of the sonnet with this information discloses an "us" in line 13 that has been returned from party to national reference. Milton's probable political meaning is to urge Cromwell to be true to the nation and to his own being, to come into his own by dispensing with governmental committees for this and that, and to assure by his own fiat a genuine policy of toleration ("free Conscience") as well as a disestablished church (one rid of "hireling wolves"). But in mid-1652 both issues were tired; Milton's writing, as Wordsworth was quick to note,[29] is tired in the final couplet; and Cromwell's irresolution left both issues as stalemates.

The last of this trio of sonnets, which bears the simple manuscript title "To Sr Henry Vane the younger," was sent by Milton to his younger friend and fellow member of the Council of State on 3 July 1652, less than two months after the occasion of the Cromwell sonnet. The temporal proximity of the two sonnets is noteworthy, for Milton reaches closure in this form by at last discovering in the conjuncture of the times and the man Vane a fulfillment of political leadership in knowledge and action:

Vane, young in yeares, but in sage counsell old,
Then whome a better Senatour nere held
The helme of *Rome,* when gownes not armes repelld
The feirce *Epeirot* and the *African* bold,
Whether to settle peace or to unfold
The drift of hollow states, hard to be spelld,
Then to advise how warr may best, upheld,
Move by her two maine nerves, Iron and Gold
In all her equipage; besides to know
Both spirituall powre and civill, what each meanes
What severs each thou'hast learnt, which few have don.
The bounds of either sword to thee wee ow.
Therfore on thy firme hand religion leanes
In peace, and reck'ns thee her eldest son.

[*S*(H), no. 17]

Despite its brief compass, this sonnet is a masterly hymn to the objectives of classical political philosophy as personified and actualized in Vane.

29. Wordsworth wrote as follows in 1802 to an unknown correspondent: "The Sonnets of Milton which I like best are that to *Cyriack Skinner* [of the two, probably "*Cyriack,* this three years day"]; on his *Blindness; Captain or Colonel; Massacre of Piedmont; Cromwell,* except last two lines; *Fairfax*" (*The Early Letters of William and Dorothy Wordsworth,* ed. Ernest de Selincourt [Oxford, 1935], p. 312).

The underlying dynamic of Milton's composition derives from Aristotle's insistence on the identity of virtue and wisdom, what is noble and what is useful. Vane is introduced to himself as "young in yeares, but in sage counsell old." The greatly extended series of attributive clauses beginning in line 5 specifies diverse major areas of expertise—diplomacy for peace or for war, strategic analysis, provisioning of arms and financing for a war effort, the respective jurisdictions and separate powers of church and state—before culminating in the main predication delayed with Tassonic magnificence to line 11. It ascribes all the foregoing store of wisdom to Vane: "thou'hast learnt, which few have don." In place of an exhortation to action, what Vane has already done for England is saluted in the highest terms Milton's political conceptions afforded. He is credited with assuring the English polity the character of a mixed state, the most stable and superior type in Renaissance as in Aristotelian theory ("The bounds of either sword to thee wee ow"). Praise for Vane's wisdom culminates in the serene tableau, evocative of a seventeenth-century state portrait, of the matronly figure Religion leaning on the "firme hand" of the one whom she "reck'ns . . . her eldest son" and protector in the absence of her heavenly spouse, Christ. (By significant imagistic contrast, Fairfax was to set his hand to other military service and Cromwell was to blunt "the paw / Of hireling wolves.")

Appropriately enough, in a sonnet addressed to one of the leading exponents of republicanism in England, the more specific political content used by Milton to celebrate Vane derives from Cicero's *De Officiis*. This is signaled in lines 2–4 in an echo and a pair of allusions that would have been immediately intelligible to Vane or any other educated reader of the Renaissance although they are not to readers of our age. Milton echoes Cicero's celebrated vaunting of his own great service to the Roman republic in exposing Catiline's conspiracy (*De Officiis* 1.22.77): "Did not arms yield to the toga, when I was at the helm of state?" He then alludes to two other occasions "when gownes not armes repelld / The feirce *Epeirot* and the *African* bold"—the one, when the senator Gaius Fabricius led the whole Senate in shaming their enemy, Pyrrhus, king of Epirus, by outdoing him in an honorable gesture in time of war; the other, when the old senator and consul Marcus Atilus Regulus, a prisoner of war sent to treat with the rest of the Senate for the release of thirteen Carthaginian generals in exchange for his release, confounded King Hamilcar by arguing against the proposal at the cost of his own life (*De Officiis* 3.22.86–87, 3.26.99–101). Vane's comparable service had been performed in convincing the Council of State to go to war against the Dutch for coastal piracy that they pursued while sustaining friendly diplomatic gestures ("The drift of hollow states, hard to be spelld"). Vane had also made it practicable as well as honorable to decide for war by wholly reorganizing the British navy as Cromwell's Secretary of the Navy. Milton sent his sonnet upon the breaking of diplomatic relations with the States-General of Holland.

Despite the toll taken by intervening time from accessible meaning in the specific allusions to *De Officiis,* the Vane sonnet shows Milton in other respects mediating his indebtedness to Aristotle's *Politics* by way of Cicero's equation of decorum with supreme wisdom in a political context. These had been the key pronouncements on decorum in *De Officiis:* "Such is its essential nature, that it is inseparable from moral goodness; for what is proper is morally right, and what is morally right is proper. . . . For to employ reason and speech rationally, to do with careful consideration whatever one does, and to uphold it—that is proper" (1.27.94). And these, the defining characteristics of decorum in Cicero's general sense, are precisely the qualities ascribed by Milton to Vane's political virtue. What is more, Milton follows Cicero in assimilating to Vane's decorum all of the other primary virtues: courage ("how war may best . . . / Move"), wisdom ("to know / Both spirituall powre and civil, what each means"), and justice ("The bounds of either sword to thee we ow"). The construct, Vane as mainstay of the English church and state in July 1652, was no exercise in verisimilitude; it was as true—poetically, historically, and philosophically—as Milton knew how to make it.

But within a year of this particular conjunction of persons, occasion, and an issue of power on which Milton's creation of political poetry always depended, the construct would prove both ideal and dated. Although he had witnessed Fairfax's abrupt retirement from public life after the trial and execution of Charles, Milton could not have foreseen that Cromwell would break irrevocably with Vane when Vane challenged Cromwell's dissolution of the Rump Parliament in 1653, the next-to-last step in the launching of his one-man rule as Lord Protector at the end of that same year. The break drove Vane out of public life and made him the continuing victim of Cromwell's harassment. Milton's final sonnet to manifest the crucial conjunction for his creation of political poetry came in 1655. But the terms of "Avenge O Lord thy slaughter'd Saints" are explicitly post-political; now Milton exhorts God to action as the guarantor of the justice and wisdom without which history is meaningless and politics nonexistent.

Having examined the political sonnets as a group and as a phase in Milton's poetic career, we return to reflect on his answers to the questions about political poetry which we began by asking. Such poetry, we find, does not only not falsify historical fact but may even help to shape it if it locates representation in an impending choice, as Milton does, where events as well as character are in the making. His practice in these sonnets also shows how, by instantiating names and catchwords in a framework of generic terms, political poetry can work through particularity toward a generality that remains grounded in the coordinates uniquely determining a given moment. The location of representation in an impending choice likewise allows political poetry to stand, for the time being, on a footing equal with philosophy. The poetic mode, moreover, has resources for expression not usually tapped in philosophical formulation: a saliency of image, a condensation of utterance, and a memorability induced by meter and other aspects of its verse design. Poetry can contribute these strengths to the informing and confirming of a right choice. Through the powerfully integrative workings of decorum, whose mastery he cultivated in his political sonnets, Milton brings the timeless concerns of philosophy into the timebound materials of history without sacrificing either to the other and without vacating poetry's own claim to truth, as Aristotelian poetic theory predicted and ostensibly required.[30]

30. Wesley Trimpi's *Muses of One Mind: The Literary Analysis of Experience and Its Continuity* (Princeton, 1983) considers the analogous workings of decorum in literature, the mean in ethics, and equity in law. Michael Murrin's review of this study (*Classical Philology* 81 [1986]: 275) remarks on Trimpi's extension of the notion of decorum to "the attempt by writers to maintain a balance between the three intentions within literature which correspond to these three disciplines: the cognitive or philosophical, the judicative or rhetorical, and the formal or literary." Trimpi, wittingly or not, is being Miltonic.

Goldsmith as Monarchist

Donald Davie

In 1771, in his preface to *The History of England, from the Earliest Times to the Death of George II,* Oliver Goldsmith wrote:

> It is not yet decided in politics, whether the diminution of kingly power in England tends to encrease the happiness, or the freedom of the people. For my own part, from seeing the bad effects of the tyranny of the great in those republican states that pretend to be free, I cannot help wishing that our monarchs may still be allowed to enjoy the power of controlling the encroachments of the great at home. A king may easily be restrained from doing wrong, as he is but one man; but if a number of the great are permitted to divide all authority, who can punish them if they abuse it? Upon this principle, therefore, and not from any empty notion of divine or hereditary right, some may think I have leaned towards monarchy.[1]

This had indeed been consistently Goldsmith's principle. But he had not always avowed it so guardedly and suavely as he does here. Eight years before, in *The Traveller,* he had been much more vehement:

> Yes, brother, curse with me that baleful hour
> When first ambition struck at regal power;

I have anticipated some of my arguments as "Notes on Goldsmith's Politics," in *The Art of Oliver Goldsmith,* ed. Andrew Swarbrick (London, 1984).

1. Oliver Goldsmith, *Collected Works,* ed. Arthur Friedman, 5 vols. (Oxford, 1966), 5:339–40. Further references to this edition, including volume and page numbers, will be included in the text.

And thus, polluting honour in its source,
Gave wealth to sway the mind with double force.
Have we not seen, round Britain's peopled shore,
Her useful sons exchang'd for useless ore?
Seen all her triumphs but destruction haste,
Like flaring tapers brightening as they waste;
Seen opulence, her grandeur to maintain,
Lead stern depopulation in her train,
And over fields, where scatter'd hamlets rose,
In barren solitary pomp repose?
Have we not seen, at pleasure's lordly call,
The smiling long-frequented village fall?
Beheld the duteous son, the sire decay'd,
The modest matron, and the blushing maid,
Forc'd from their homes, a melancholy train,
To traverse climes beyond the western main;
Where wild Oswego spreads her swamps around,
And Niagara stuns with thund'ring sound?

[4:267–68, ll. 393–412]

This passage is generally remembered, because it contains in embryo what was to become *The Deserted Village*. But if that later treatment surpasses this one, as is usually but not universally supposed, Goldsmith (and we also) have to pay a price. For *The Deserted Village* is in important ways much less specific than *The Traveller*. Nothing in the later poem is so uncompromising as "Her useful sons exchang'd for useless ore . . ." Indeed it is notoriously unclear why in *The Deserted Village* the villagers have been expropriated. And this vagueness permits of the time-honoured debate whether the village, Auburn, is to be understood as in England or in Ireland. The debate of course is misconceived, since the poetic imagination surely transforms disparate experiences by amalgamating and compounding them, often enough. It remains true that agricultural distress in the 1760s took different forms in England and in Ireland; and our inability to determine which kingdom is meant shows how far the poem is from specifying the cause of the calamity. In both poems mercantile interests expropriate the villagers, but in reading *The Deserted Village* we notice this only if we are very attentive. Indeed, we may go further. If we identify "the man of wealth and pride" who drives the villagers out as a nouveau-riche "nabob," returned with a fortune from

---

Donald Davie is Andrew Mellon Professor of the Humanities at Vanderbilt University. His latest book of criticism is *Czeslaw Milosz and the Insufficiency of Lyric*. His *To Scorch or Freeze! Poems about the Sacred* will appear shortly.

the East or West Indies, this is only a plausible conjecture; the poem itself does not identify him in that way, nor in any other. And it is reasonable to wonder if this lack of specificity is not one of the features that have always made *The Deserted Village* more appealing than *The Traveller.* If so, that appeal is suspect. For instance:

> But a bold peasantry, their country's pride,
> When once destroyed, can never be supplied.
> [4:289, ll. 55–56]

Who would not agree? What bosom does not return an echo? Whom does the couplet put out of countenance? But in *The Traveller,* where the expropriation is emphatically and unequivocally laid at the door of commercial imperialism, the sentiment would embarrass anyone who practised, or profited from, the import of raw material ("ore") from overseas.

Moreover *The Deserted Village* prescribes no remedy for the state of affairs that it deplores, and so puts no reader under any obligation to do anything about it. *The Traveller* however does prescribe a remedy: enhanced power for George III. And that prescription is even less palatable for the modern reader than for Goldsmith's contemporaries. For it flies in the face of the Whig Interpretation of History—an interpretation which, though in theory we recognize its partiality, most of us are bound by more than we realize. It is one thing to exculpate George III from the charges thrown at him by Tom Paine and others; it is something else to believe, as Goldsmith would have us do, that in the contention between the king and demagogues like Paine or John Wilkes, the right (and also the *freedom*) was with the king. For that is undoubtedly what Goldsmith means when he calls on his brother to join him in cursing the inroads made on "regal power." *The Traveller* is a fervent apologia for the monarchical form of government, taking the time-honoured ground that, since the unprivileged need a power to appeal to above the power of local and financial privilege, the only such power conceivable is the power of the monarch, elevated above all sectional interests. *The Deserted Village* may be the more seductive poem; it is *The Traveller* that is clearer and more challenging.

However, Goldsmith's thinking about the monarchy had gone through an earlier phase before he wrote *The Traveller.* In 1759 in *The Bee* had appeared "Custom and Laws Compared." Here Goldsmith (for I follow Arthur Friedman in supposing him the author) finds Tacitus, with his *Corruptissima republica, plurimae leges,* at odds with "the great Montesquieu, who asserts that every nation is free in proportion to the number of its written laws." Forced to choose, Goldsmith plumps for Tacitus, and for "custom" against "laws," in this anticipating that other Irish political thinker of his day, Edmund Burke. Goldsmith concludes:

> From hence we see how much greater benefit it would be to the state rather to abridge than encrease its laws. We every day find them encreasing; acts and reports, which may be termed the acts of judges, are every day becoming more voluminous, and loading the subject with new penalties. [1:486]

In the next year we find him harping on the same string. This is in a charming paper in *The British Magazine,* "A Reverie at the Boar's-head-tavern in Eastcheap," where Mr. Rigmarole (Goldsmith himself) tells the ghost of Mistress Quickly: "I rather fancy, madam, that the times then were pretty much like our own; where a multiplicity of laws give a judge as much power as a want of law, since he is ever sure to find among the number some to countenance his partiality" (3:104).

And yet Goldsmith at once sets about reversing this judgment, or rather standing it on its head. According to his new argument, the plethora of legislation in eighteenth-century England, so far from being a sickness in the state, was a sign of its health—but only, he insists, because England was a monarchy. This argument appears first, so far as I can see, already in 1760, in an essay in *The Royal Magazine:*

> Examine every state in Europe, and you will find the people either enjoying a precarious freedom under monarchical government, or what is worse, actually slaves in a republic, to laws of their own contriving. What constitutes the peculiar happiness of Britain, is, that laws may be overlooked without endangering the state. In a mere republic, which pretends to equal freedom, every infringement upon law is a dissolution of government, and must consequently be punished with the most unremitting severity; but in England, laws may be sometimes overlooked without danger. A King who has it in his power to pardon, gives the government at once the strength of the oak, and the flexibility of the yew. [3:68]

However, Goldsmith's fullest exposition of this paradoxical position (which surely again anticipates in its tenor Burke's hostility to written constitutions) had appeared less than two weeks before in the important Letter L of *The Citizen of the World:*

> In all those governments, where laws derive their sanction from the *people alone,* transgressions cannot be overlooked without bringing the constitution into danger. They who transgress the law in such a case, are those who prescribe it, by which means it loses not only its influence but its sanction. In every republic the laws must be strong, because the constitution is feeble: they must resemble an Asiatic husband who is justly jealous, because he knows himself impotent. Thus in Holland, Switzerland, and Genoa, new laws are not frequently enacted, but the old ones are observed

> with unremitting severity. In such republics therefore the people are slaves to laws of their own making, little less than in unmix'd monarchies where they are slaves to the will of one subject to frailties like themselves.
>
> In England, from a variety of happy accidents, their constitution is just strong enough, or if you will, monarchical enough, to permit a relaxation of the severity of laws, and yet those laws still remain sufficiently strong to govern the people. This is the most perfect state of civil liberty, of which we can form any idea; here we see a greater number of laws than in any other country, while the people at the same time obey only such as are immediately conducive to the interests of society; several are unnoticed, many unknown; some kept to be revived and enforced upon proper occasions, others left to grow obsolete, even without the necessity of abrogation. [2:211]

And Goldsmith expatiates:

> Scarce an Englishman who does not almost every day of his life, offend with impunity against some express law, and for which in a certain conjuncture of circumstances he would not receive punishment. Gaming houses, preaching at prohibited places, assembled crowds, nocturnal amusements, public shews, and an hundred other instances are forbid and frequented. These prohibitions are useful; though it be prudent in their magistrates, and happy for their people, that they are not enforced, and none but the venal or mercenary attempt to enforce them.
>
> The law in this case, like an indulgent parent, still keeps the rod, though the child is seldom corrected. Were those pardoned offences to rise into enormity, were they likely to obstruct the happiness of society, or endanger the state, it is then that justice would resume her terrors, and punish those faults she had so often overlooked with indulgence. It is to this ductility of the laws that an Englishman owes the freedom he enjoys superior to others in a more popular government; every step therefore the constitution takes towards a Democratic form, every diminution of the regal authority is, in fact a diminution of the subjects freedom; but every attempt to render the government more popular, not only impairs natural liberty, but even will at last, dissolve the political constitution. [2:211–12]

Thus the Englishman of Goldsmith's time is persuaded that he lives under the rule of law by the assurance that the laws will be enforced only capriciously!

At first sight, this is one of those quixotic, "Irish" arguments that Goldsmith was famous for in conversation, which made it so difficult for his English friends, even his great champion Johnson, to take him seriously.

Yet in fact Goldsmith has here put his finger on an anomaly in eighteenth-century England that recent historians have found exceptionally significant: the anomaly that "the number of capital statutes grew from about 50 to over 200 between the years 1688 and 1820," and yet "the available evidence suggests that, compared to some earlier periods, the eighteenth-century criminal law claimed few lives." What has to be explained is "the coexistence of bloodier laws and increased convictions with a declining proportion of death sentences that were actually carried out."[2] I am quoting from an essay of capital importance, Douglas Hay's "Property, Authority and the Criminal Law." What Hay shows is that the commuting or pardoning of severe sentences was, at least outside the commercial centers of London and perhaps Bristol, a principal way of knitting English society together, in a way that was hierarchical indeed and inequitable, yet effective and even in a deep sense humane. As in other perspectives, what has been denounced in English eighteenth-century society as "corrupt" (and was even so denounced at the time) turns out to be the margin of humanity—of humane feelings and human relationships—that that society provided for. Intercession on behalf of inferiors and dependents was taken for granted as an essential part of the mechanism of society, alike by those who needed such help and those who (on conditions, of course) extended it. Without this "corrupt" play between the majesty of the law and the acknowledgment of special interests, the society would have been less flexible and less stable than it proved to be. And to this extent modern scholarship may be thought to vindicate Goldsmith's speculations, which thus turn out to have been remarkably astute. Moreover, in a curious and devious way Goldsmith may be thought to vindicate his earlier preference for "custom" over "laws," since the very multiplicity of laws ensured that their severity would be *customarily* alleviated.

What remains to be justified is Goldsmith's conviction that things could work out this way only under a monarchy. Readers of Hay's essay will be tempted to think that Goldsmith was wrong and starry-eyed about this (if nothing worse). For Hay shows that the system worked so as to put life and death in the hands of those local tyrants, justices of the peace and their cronies, from whom, on Goldsmith's understanding of the matter, the Crown was supposed to liberate the unprivileged. That pardons came from the king was a legal and ideological fiction, masking the fact that they were handed down as a result of interplaying interests in the ruling class. However, this fiction—that all clemency is the king's—has far more power than the more or less squalid or whimsical fact of letters written on behalf of this or that convicted person at this or that level of

2. Douglas Hay, "Property, Authority and the Criminal Law," in *Albion's Fatal Tree: Crime and Society in Eighteenth-century England,* ed. Hay et al. (London, 1975), pp. 18, 22; further references to this essay, abbreviated "P," will be included in the text.

influence. For it is of the nature of an ideology to be a tissue of fictions, that is to say in the most serious sense a *myth.* Hay abjures this word. And one can hardly blame him. For too often in these contexts "myth" seems at once facile and pretentious, pretending to explain what in effect it only consigns to the ineffable. Yet where "monarchy" is in question, though the word itself may be dispensed with, the sense of it hardly can be:

> Where authority is embodied in direct personal relationships, men will often accept power, even enormous, despotic power, when it comes from the 'good King', the father of his people, who tempers justice with mercy. A form of this powerful psychic configuration was one of the most distinctive aspects of the unreformed criminal law. Bentham could not understand it, but it was the law's greatest strength as an ideological system, especially among the poor, and in the countryside. ["P," p. 39]

"Powerful psychic configuration" is certainly a drier expression than "myth," but it surely means much the same thing. And indeed whenever Hay invokes "paternalism," as he is compelled to do, he acknowledges the same mythic dimension. For under a monarchical dispensation the fatherliness of a squire to his tenant is thought to mirror in microcosm the fatherliness of the king towards the entire realm.

It is notable moreover that Hay is forced to explain how "the criminal law, more than any other social institution, made it possible to govern eighteenth-century England without a police force and without a large army" ("P," p. 56), by following through the same logic which, when we first encountered it in Letter L of *The Citizen of the World,* struck us as quixotic:

> An ideology endures not by being wholly enforced and rigidly defined. Its effectiveness lies first in its very elasticity, the fact that men are not required to make it a credo, that it seems to them the product of their own minds and their own experience. And the law did not enforce uniform obedience, did not seek total control; indeed, it sacrificed punishment when necessary to preserve the belief in justice. ["P," p. 55]

This is the same logic that governs the policy of the English monarch even today. The monarch has powers which he or she retains on the tacit understanding that except in barely conceivable circumstances he or she will never exercise them. According to this understanding, the theory of monarchism is analogous to what naval strategists understand by the principle of "the fleet in being." So long as the fleet is never hazarded in combat (but only detached units or squadrons), it remains, as a menacing potency, an important pawn in grand strategy and in diplomacy. So too with the unreformed criminal law, as both Hay and Goldsmith understand it.

None of this intricate and perhaps special pleading enters into *The Traveller*. For this poem Goldsmith reverts to the not unconnected but bolder argument of "The Revolution in Low Life" (*Lloyd's Evening Post*, 1762):

> Wherever we turn we shall find those governments that have pursued foreign commerce with too much assiduity at length becoming Aristocratical; and the immense property, thus necessarily acquired by some, has swallowed up the liberties of all. Venice, Genoa, and Holland, are little better at present than retreats for tyrants and prisons for slaves. The Great, indeed, boast of their liberties there, and they have liberty. The poor boast of liberty too; but, alas, they groan under the most rigorous oppression. [3:197–98]

Goldsmith protested—and coming from Samuel Johnson's very insular England, the protestation should be attended to—that when he spoke in this lordly fashion of Venice, Genoa, Holland, he drew on the experience of one who had travelled, needy and on foot, through their territories. What poetic capital Goldsmith could make of these experiences appears in a passage where he makes a smooth and yet momentous transition from considering the Netherlands to considering Great Britain:

> Heavens! how unlike their Belgic sires of old!
> Rough, poor, content, ungovernably bold;
> War in each breast, and freedom on each brow;
> How much unlike the sons of Britain now!
>
> Fir'd at the sound, my genius spreads her wing,
> And flies where Britain courts the western spring;
> Where laws extend that scorn Arcadian pride,
> And brighter streams than fam'd Hydaspis glide.
> There all around the gentlest breezes stray,
> There gentle music melts on every spray;
> Creation's mildest charms are there combin'd,
> Extremes are only in the master's mind;
> Stern o'er each bosom reason holds her state.
> With daring aims, irregularly great,
> Pride in their port, defiance in their eye,
> I see the lords of human kind pass by
> Intent on high designs, a thoughtful band,
> By forms unfashion'd, fresh from Nature's hand:
> Fierce in their native hardiness of soul,
> True to imagin'd right above controul,

While even the peasant boasts these rights to scan,
And learns to venerate himself as man.
[4:262–63, ll. 313–34]

The diction is very stilted. Modern prejudices in favour of the colloquial will prompt us to say that the language is at no point in touch with spoken usage. But this is plainly untrue: "I see the lords of human kind pass by" could certainly be *said* (sarcastically). And that drop in the level of the diction has a force that depends on the level in the preceding lines having been pitched so high. A more "natural" idiom could not make the point with such economy. The panegyric is keyed so high, and the diction is so fulsome ("courts the western spring" . . . "Arcadian pride" . . . "fam'd Hydaspis"), precisely so that the sentiment conveyed can be undermined so soon, and so insidiously. The effect is that when this florid oratorical voice begins to drop into its discourse words like "extremes" and "irregularly" and "pride," our first reaction is to ask ourselves: "Does he understand what he is *saying?*" We begin to think that he does when we reach "the lords of human kind," but we are not wholly sure of it until "True to imagin'd right above controul." We see the claims of English complacency advanced, acceded to, and then denied, all inside twenty lines. The elevated diction is crucial for the achievement of masterly economy.

The verses that bite and drive most fiercely are yet to come:

That independence Britons prize too high
Keeps man from man, and breaks the social tie;
The self dependent lordlings stand alone,
All claims that bind and sweeten life unknown;
Here by the bond of nature feebly held,
Minds combat minds, repelling and repell'd;
Ferments arise, imprison'd factions roar,
Represt ambition struggles round her shore,
Till over-wrought, the general system feels
Its motions stopt, or phrenzy fire the wheels.
[4:263–64, ll. 339–48]

The metaphors that flame in the last two couplets—from chemistry, from the sea, from medicine, from mechanics—seem "mixed" only because in a positively Shakespearean way the imagination is whirling so rapidly from one analogy to the next. And "factions" here means something more inclusive than power-blocs vying and shouldering at court, in parliament, or in Whitehall offices. It is *minds* that are factious, and more than minds; personalities and sensibilities, human beings, are locked into this prison of unending combat, "repelling and repell'd." We have here in fact what may be the earliest and also the most caustic indictment of the world of "free enterprise," unstructured and unrestricted competitiveness, the morality of the marketplace—in ideas, in status, and in feelings, as well as commodities. Nothing can save us from this, or alleviate it, except—Goldsmith insists—the institution of monarchy. Why is a passage so memorable seldom remembered or extolled? It is easy to see why. For most of us the indictment is launched from the wrong end of what we conceive of as the political spectrum. These sentiments and insights are thought to be the monopoly of the liberal democratic left, and we refuse to acknowledge them when they come to us from conservative monarchists like Goldsmith and Johnson. The Whig Interpretation is at work once again.

At least once more, before he submerged his analysis in the indulgent haze of *The Deserted Village,* Goldsmith restated it. This was in chapter 19 of *The Vicar of Wakefield* (1766):

> "No, Sir," replied I, "I am for liberty, that attribute of Gods! Glorious liberty! that theme of modern declamation. I would have all men kings. I would be a king myself. We have all naturally an equal right to the throne: we are all originally equal. This is my opinion, and was once the opinion of a set of honest men who were called Levellers. They tried to erect themselves into a community, where all should be equally free. But, alas! it would never answer; for there were some among them stronger, and some more cunning than others, and these became masters of the rest; for as sure as your groom rides your horses, because he is a cunninger animal than they, so surely will the animal that is cunninger or stronger than he, sit upon his shoulders in turn." [4:99]

The speaker is Dr. Primrose, the vicar, who here shows that he knows about primitive communism and anticipates George Orwell's *Animal Farm* in discrediting it by way of a bestial fable. The vicar goes on:

> "Since then it is entailed upon humanity to submit, and some are born to command, and others to obey, the question is, as there must be tyrants, whether it is better to have them in the same house with us, or in the same village, or still farther off, in the metropolis. Now, Sir, for my own part, as I naturally hate the face of a tyrant, the farther off he is removed from me, the better pleased am I. The generality of mankind also are of my way of thinking, and have unanimously created one king, whose election at once diminishes the number of tyrants, and puts tyranny at the greatest distance from the greatest number of people. Now the great who were tyrants themselves before the election of one tyrant, are naturally averse to a power raised over them, and whose weight must ever lean heaviest on the subordinate orders. It is the interest of the great, therefore, to diminish kingly power as much as possible; because whatever they take from that is naturally restored to themselves; and all they have to do in the state, is to undermine

the single tyrant, by which they resume their primaeval authority." [4:99–100]

Dr. Primrose may here seem to be more tough-minded than Dr. Goldsmith, since he asserts that the power of the king is of its nature tyrannical; however, we may suppose that both the learned doctors know, and rely on their hearers to know, that *tyrannos* in ancient Greek is a term morally neutral, as "tyrant" in English is not.

Since wealth is power (thus the argument develops), and since "an accumulation of wealth . . . must necessarily be the consequence, when as at present more riches flow in from external commerce, than arise from internal industry" (4:100), it follows that in proportion as fortunes are made by international trading more and more attempts will be made to abridge the power of the monarch. The speaker, whom we may as well call Goldsmith as Primrose, accordingly declares his allegiance to "people without the sphere of the opulent man's influence," a "middle order of mankind" in whom "are generally to be found all the arts, wisdom, and virtues of society" (4:101, 102). Indeed, he does not scruple to say, "This order alone is known to be the true preserver of freedom, and may be called the People" (4:102). Here, it might reasonably be proposed, we see the sharp-sightedness of the Irishman, the outsider, detecting what now we take for granted though for observers at the time it was obscured by the conspicuousness of the landed grandees: the truth that eighteenth-century England was essentially a *bourgeois* civilization.

If the historical circumstances are such as he has described, what then, the speaker asks, is in the interest of that "middle order" with which he has declared himself in sympathy? And he answers, " 'to preserve the prerogative and privileges of the one principal governor with the most sacred circumspection. For he divides the power of the rich, and calls off the great from falling with tenfold weight on the middle order placed beneath them' " (4:102). But what began as protestation and proceeded as exposition has by this time become, as the speaker apologetically recognizes, a *harangue.* Accordingly it ends with a peroration:

> "I am then for, and would die for, monarchy, sacred monarchy; for if there be any thing sacred amongst men, it must be the anointed sovereign of his people, and every diminution of his power in war, or in peace, is an infringement upon the real liberties of the subject. The sounds of liberty, patriotism, and Britons, have already done *much,* it is to be hoped that the true sons of freedom will prevent their ever doing more. I have known many of those pretended champions for liberty in my time, yet do I not remember one that was not in his heart and in his family a tyrant." [4:102–3]

But it is plain that the alleged sacredness and anointedness of the monarch belong in a quite different dimension of discourse from the hard-nosed calculations of interest that have made the case for monarchy up to this point. That extra dimension can only be called "mythological."

Dr. Primrose, the vicar, is of course a ninny; an endearingly foolish and unworldly man—as was, so we are assured by numerous but always controvertible witnesses, Oliver Goldsmith himself. But at no point are we invited to make fun of him in his capacity as priest and pastor, spiritual guide to his flock. Nor do we see him as easily deluded by catchphrases—on the contrary his unworldliness often consists in his taking seriously and literally what other people say only as a matter of form. Accordingly, when he speaks of "the *anointed* sovereign," we are in duty bound to suppose him in earnest. And indeed to a Christian nation like the eighteenth-century English (not nominally but deeply Christian), the figure of David, shepherd-king and warrior-psalmist of ancient Israel, could not fail to loom behind, and to transfigure, the image of any king whom they knew or knew about. The myth of kingship was for them underpinned by scriptural reading and religious observance. This is surely a main part of that "powerful psychic configuration" which Hay postulates.

It has been argued that, in creating Dr. Primrose, Goldsmith miscalculated. When the Whig Addison had created the lovable but foolish Tory figure of Sir Roger de Coverley, he had taken care not to put in Sir Roger's mouth any arguments that he, Addison, could take seriously; whereas Goldsmith took no such precautions. I now think this is wrong. Addison's Coverley papers are remarkably inventive and insidious political polemic, whereas *The Vicar of Wakefield* is, as Goethe admiringly and astutely recognized, an *idyll.* Within the conventions of the idyll—and the myth of kingship is itself, one might well argue, idyllic—Goldsmith could safely expound doctrines that he took in all seriousness. Accordingly Donald Greene was surely right to quote from this chapter 19 and to present it as "the view of Goldsmith . . . one of the most vigorous rebuttals of the Whig contention that what was good for Russells and Cavendishes was good for England."[3] About politics this Irish zany was more levelheaded and penetrating than has ever been acknowledged.

3. Donald J. Greene, *The Politics of Samuel Johnson* (New Haven, Conn., 1960), p. 185.

Clare and the Place of the Peasant Poet

Elizabeth Helsinger

John Clare is one of England's best poets of place. He writes of a profound attachment to a particular rural locality, and he writes of the pain of displacement, attributed to and figured as enclosure. Both these sentiments—attachment to place and the pain of displacement—speak to middle-class fantasies and anxieties addressed, in the art and literature of the 1820s and 1830s, in the repetitious production of rural scenes of social stability and harmony.[1] But unlike the work of middle-class writers and artists, of course, Clare's poetry is of interest because of his own position within that scene. In their lifetimes, the countryside that nourished the poetry of Wordsworth and the landscapes of Constable became identified with their names, yet neither man was—in his own or others' eyes—himself fixed in one place, except by choice. Their supposed mobility is a gift of class, creating a presumption of distance between themselves, as observers, and the scenes they depicted. Clare—like Burns or Bloomfield before him—was identified with the social as well as the geographical place that was his subject. For readers both then and now, he is the "Northamptonshire peasant," whose mobility, social or geographical, would deny the stability his rural scenes are understood to recall.

1. Such scenes are perhaps best exemplified in the very popular prose sketches of rural life by Mary Russell Mitford collected as *Our Village: Sketches of Rural Character and Scenery* (published in five volumes between 1824 and 1832), some of which were reworked by Tennyson in his "English Idylls" of the 1830s. See also the landscape illustrations to collected editions of the eighteenth-century English authors like Crabbe, Cowper, Collins, and Goldsmith, or to the biographies of many other English poets; such illustrated books were especially popular from the late twenties through the early forties.

One might say that Clare is almost by virtue of that label alone a political poet. "Peasant poet" is a contradiction in terms from the perspective of English literary history, or of the longer history of the literary pastoral. The phrase must refer to two different social locations, and as such makes social place an explicit, problematic concern for the middle-class readers of that poet's work. To Clare's publisher and patrons in the 1820s, as to his editors in the 1980s, the language, the forms, the sentiments, and even the punctuation of his poetry are further markers of class difference for an audience invited to read him as a peasant poet. In recent collections concerned to recover the politics of English poetry these signs of difference are highly valued.[2] They seem to mark Clare's work as what Fredric Jameson terms "strong" political art, that is, "authentic cultural creation . . . dependent for its existence on authentic collective life, on the vitality of the 'organic' social group."[3]

At the time his poems were published class difference in English rural life was a political issue sufficiently charged to make publisher and patrons wish to minimize (though not obliterate) its marks in Clare's poetry. On the one hand, a clearly understood hierarchy was the form of social stability that rural scenes staged for their urban middle-class audiences. Evidence of class difference confirmed the survival of this hierarchy and the reader's position in it. Clare's poetry of place affirmed a system of social as well as geographical differences felt as a traditional—and essential—aspect of English national identity. On the other hand, however, the countryside was precisely where the erosion of the hierarchical relations of deference and responsibility was particularly noticeable, and disturbing, in the years after 1815. Sporadic outbreaks of protest against low wages and unemployment in 1816, 1822, and 1830 realized dramatically for the middle and upper classes what one might call a rural version of the process Marx was later to term alienation: the known and familiar inhabitants of the rural scene—laborers, village artisans—were suddenly made strange to their middle- and upper-class

2. Both *A Book of English Pastoral Verse,* ed. John Barrell and John Bull (New York, 1975) and *The Faber Book of Political Verse,* ed. Tom Paulin (London, 1986) restore Clare's original orthography and lack of punctuation to support the label "peasant poet."

3. Fredric Jameson, "Reification and Utopia in Mass Culture," *Social Text* 1 (Winter 1979): 140.

Elizabeth Helsinger is associate professor of English and general studies at the University of Chicago and a coeditor of *Critical Inquiry.* Her *Ruskin and the Art of the Beholder* was published in 1982. The present essay is part of a book in progress on representations of the rural scene in Victorian England.

neighbors, so much so that many observers were convinced that they must be strangers, intruders from another place (and another class).[4] The elements of difference, or strangeness, in Clare's poetry—the marks of his identity as rural laborer—thus also risked awaking specific anxieties among his early readers. Clare's editor and publisher, John Taylor, punctuated, regularized meter, and replaced some (though not all) of Clare's unfamiliar local vocabulary. Nonetheless, his two most important early patrons, the evangelical aristocrat Lord Radstock and the middle-class Mrs. Emmerson, objected to some lines as "radical slang" and others as "vulgar." The language of class risked rejection as politically (and sexually) subversive. Especially in an already politicized rural scene, the peasant poet could not be a neutral figure.

The signs of difference in Clare's poetry of place may explain why it has been perceived as political. They do not, however, tell us very much either about Clare's consciousness of a politics of the rural scene or about the role of that consciousness in the production of his best poetry. Clare in fact wrote very few poems explicitly political in subject and intent. One of these is the early poem "Helpstone" (before 1819) to which Lord Radstock objected; two others (later but undated), "The Mores" and "[The Lament of Swordy Well]," were not published in his lifetime. Clare's understanding of his place in the rural scene changed radically between "Helpstone" and "Swordy Well," however. The politics of the later poem shape the poetics of Clare's best work, especially the poems for *The Midsummer Cushion* that celebrate the "green language" of a new pastoral poetry.[5] I would like to explore that connection between politics and poetics as it evolved for Clare over the painful decade when he tried to gain recognition as a poet of the rural scene.

Perhaps the greatest change from "Helpstone" to a later poem about enclosure like "The Mores" comes in the way the poet locates himself with respect to the power of sight. Taylor's introduction to Clare's first volume of poetry follows Burns' 1786 introduction to his *Poems* in stressing

4. Although this term is usually associated with Marx's description of the relation of the worker to work and the product of his work, Marx indicates that it also describes the relation of the nonworker to the worker. See "Estranged Labour," *Economic and Philosophic Manuscripts of 1844,* in *The Marx-Engels Reader,* ed. Robert C. Tucker (New York, 1978), p. 81. Mitford provides a good description of the experience of defamiliarization or making strange of laborers to their middle-class neighbors in her story, "The Incendiary," about the events of 1830 (see *Our Village,* vol. 5 [1832]).

5. The manuscript of *The Midsummer Cushion* was completed by Clare before 1833, but subsequently reedited by Mrs. Emmerson and published in greatly shortened form as *The Rural Muse: Poems* in 1835. *The Midsummer Cushion* was first published in its original form in 1979 (ed. Anne Tibble and R. K. R. Thornton, The Mid Northumberland Arts Group, in assoc. with Carcanet Press).

the peasant poet's obscurity. Each of these first volumes is introduced with a request that the peasant poet, an artless singer and a child of nature invisible to the audience the book addresses, may be granted recognition—may be heeded.[6] For both Burns and Taylor, the request is hedged with apology; it carefully lays no claims to power on the part of the poet (who is inspired by Nature's powers, not his own), and it promises that if recognition is denied, the poet will be content to remain in obscurity. Clare's earliest letter to a patron (1817) sounds the same note: he thanks his correspondent for "his *Condesension* & notice" and describes himself as "a *Clown* who as yet *Slumbers* in *Obscurity* and perhaps whose *merits* deserves no better *Fate*."[7] "Helpstone" echoes those sentiments (with none of the irony at work in Burns' sophisticated self-presentation).

> Hail humble Helpstone where thy valies spread
> And thy mean village lifts its lowly head
> Unknown to grandeur and unknown to fame
> No minstrel boasting to advance thy name
> . . . .
> Unknown nor heeded where low genius trys
> Above the vulgar and the vain to rise[8]

The "scenes obscure" (l. 47) of the village and the obscure poet himself are nearly identified. Both are "unknown nor heeded," "Courting in vain each gazer's heedless view" (l. 102). Although the conventions of descriptive poetry should make the poet the primary viewer of these scenes, the poem's insistent identification of the obscure village with the unnoticed peasant poet effectively transfers the power of sight from poet to reader.

Both village and poet are in fact doubly removed from the reader's knowledge; they are not only obscure, they are also "vanished" (ll. 55, 73, 95). Village scenes are the poet's scenes of infancy (l. 53); unnoticed by any recognized (that is to say, middle-class) poet, his past, together with the village's, has left no trace in the memories of his readers.

> But now alas those scenes exist no more
> The pride of life with thee (like mine) is oer
> Thy pleasing spots to which fond memory clings
> Sweet cooling shades and soft refreshing springs

6. See Robert Burns, preface to *Poems, Chiefly in the Scottish Dialect* (Kilmarnock, 1786); and [John Taylor], introduction to *Poems Descriptive of Rural Life and Scenery* by John Clare, A Northamptonshire Peasant (London, 1820).

7. Clare to Isaiah Knowles Holland [1817], *The Letters of John Clare,* ed. J. W. Tibble and Anne Tibble (London, 1951), p. 23.

8. Clare, "Helpstone," *John Clare,* ed. Eric Robinson and David Powell, Oxford Authors series (Oxford, 1984), ll. 1–4, 9–10; unless otherwise noted, all further quotations of Clare's poetry will be to this work. This edition restores Clare's original orthography and (lack of) punctuation, in addition to publishing from manuscript a number of previously unpublished poems.

And though fate's pleas'd to lay their beauties by
In a dark corner of obscurity
As fair and sweet they blo[o]m'd thy plains among
As blooms those Edens by the poets sung
Now all laid waste by desolations hand
Whose cursed weapon levels half the land
[ll. 115–23]

Like Goldsmith, whose "Deserted Village" Clare had in mind, Clare blames not time but enclosure for the disappearance of these scenes.[9] (Following his model, Clare's poem remains general rather than specific; enclosure is never explicitly named as the problem.) But unlike Goldsmith, Clare writes not as a returning observer but as the obscure peasant who cannot leave. The poem assumes that the power to rescue both village and poet from obscurity rests with the reader. "Helpstone" is both a plea for recognition and a condemnation of heedless gazing, the privilege of the "few" who still know "Peace and Plenty" (l. 137), less benignly termed "Accursed wealth" a few lines earlier.

Accursed wealth o'er bounding human laws
Of every evil thou remainst the cause
Victims of want those wretches such as me
Too truly lay their wretchedness to thee
Thou art the bar that keeps from being fed
And thine our loss of labour and of bread
Thou art the cause that levels every tree
And woods bow down to clear a way for thee
[ll. 127–34]

The request and the condemnation are awkwardly conjoined in these lines, the object of Lord Radstock's particular censure. They represent Clare's impossible desire to win an audience for his poetry and economic support for his poetic career from those whom his poem can barely avoid identifying as the authors of his distress. But the real difficulty in the poem—underlined by its choice of a conventional form, the heroic couplet—is its reluctance to make any claims to its own authority. Clare's desire to be heeded exacted from him a high price: the implicit denial of his own powers of sight.

9. See *John Clare's Autobiographical Writings,* ed. Robinson (Oxford, 1983), p. 102. The land around Helpstone was worked on the open field system (villagers shared use-rights) through Clare's childhood. Between 1809 and 1820, the common lands were enclosed (divided into private farms, physically separated by hedges and fences). The rationale for enclosure was a more economic use of the land. Though enclosure was not alone responsible for the poor conditions of rural laborers in the 1810s and 1820s, it increased their dependence on wages in a time of falling wages, rising prices, and unemployment.

The later poem "The Mores" no longer appeals to the reader's sight at the expense of the poet's. It is concerned neither with the "gazer's heedless view" nor with the vanished scenes of a personal and communal past that the heedless gaze has allowed to disappear, but with a power of seeing claimed as one of "labour's rights" that enclosure has abrogated.

> Now this sweet vision of my boyish hours
> Free as spring clouds and wild as summer flowers
> Is faded all—a hope that blossomed free
> And hath been once no more shall ever be
> Inclosure came and trampled on the grave
> Of labours rights and left the poor a slave
> And memorys pride ere want to wealth did bow
> Is both the shadow and the substance now
>
> [ll. 15–22]

Both what is destroyed and what has destroyed it are particularized in this poem as they were not in "Helpstone" or its model, "The Deserted Village." Enclosure threatens the peculiar kind of vision that the peasant poet memorializes. From its opening line ("Far spread the moorey ground a level scene . . .") Clare's poem celebrates (and mourns) the unchecked sight of a landscape without fences as part of the "unbounded freedom" of those who work in that landscape.

"The Mores" is as confident in its appropriation of language as in its appropriation of the power of sight. Before enclosure, the moors were what the poet saw

> Still meeting plains that stretched them far away
> In uncheckt shadows of green brown and grey
>
> [ll. 5–6]

The lines play on the two meanings of "still" as both "without motion" and "continuing," to underline the timeless presence embodied in a landscape where moors and plains meet in a perpetual but imperceptible action unobstructed by any "fence of ownership." The conventional checkering of light and shade, corn and pasture, is here remembered but rewritten: where plains meet in "unbounded freedom" those "shadows of green brown and grey" are the "uncheckt" extensions of a single prospect. Clare's syntax makes the freedom of the prospect indistinguishable from the freedom of its viewer.

> Unbounded freedom ruled the wandering scene
> Nor fence of ownership crept in between
> To hide the prospect of the following eye
> Its only bondage was the circling sky
>
> [ll. 7–10]

The ambiguous reference of "its" allows both eye and prospect to escape all bounds but those of the horizon.

Where "Helpstone" may articulate the position of the peasant (obscure, unheeded), "The Mores" articulates that of the peasant poet. Clare describes and enacts an extensive power of vision different from the heedless gaze of the middle-class picturesque viewer, concerned with framing rural scenes and placing rural inhabitants firmly within those definite limits.[10] He protests enclosure experienced as a deprivation at once aesthetic and political. He couches that protest in the language of the middle-class viewer. The closing lines of the poem boldly apply to the enclosers the very terms by which his first patrons attempted to keep him in his place. By the criteria of Clare's different aesthetic, it is the enclosers whose taste is "vulgar."

> On paths to freedom and to childhood dear
> A board sticks up to notice "no road here"
> And on the tree with ivy overhung
> The hated sign by vulgar taste is hung
> [ll. 69–72]

These marks of the vulgar middle and upper classes divide the peasant's extensive landscape into "little parcels little minds to please" (l. 49), stopping up the paths of vision as of free movement.

> These paths are stopt—the rude philistines thrall
> Is laid upon them and destroyed them all!
> Each little tyrant with his little sign
> Shows where man claims earth glows no more divine
> . . . .
> And birds and trees and flowers without a name
> All sighed when lawless laws enclosure came
> [ll. 65–68, 77–78]

The enclosers are the radicals, little tyrants who advocate "lawless laws" and "rebel schemes" (l. 79) in anarchic violation not only of "labours rights" but of the integrity of the land itself, realized in the unchecked extension of an unenclosed landscape.

The liberty Clare claims is not, he insists, lawlessness. "The Mores" demonstrates the freedom within bounds that characterizes labor's way of seeing and of living—according to laws of place traditionally understood in the countryside. Visually, this means that extensive sight is always bounded by the horizon ("Its only bondage was the circling sky"). For

10. Barrell elaborates Clare's different perception of landscape in his valuable study, *The Idea of Landscape and the Sense of Place, 1730–1840: An Approach to the Poetry of John Clare* (Cambridge, 1972).

Clare those boundaries were felt as physically real, as both his poems and his prose attest. (In his autobiography, for example, he tells of wandering as a child beyond the horizons visible from his village; he became completely disoriented, a deeply disturbing experience repeated in his adult life when he moved from Helpstone to Northborough, three miles away.[11])

Formally "The Mores" suggests the same preference for an extensive freedom within the horizon of the known, though here the aesthetic results are more problematic. Clare's heroic couplets mimic the unenclosed landscapes the poem celebrates: he almost always observes the boundary of the line (marked by rhyme and coincident with syntactical breaks) but rarely counterpoints these strictly regular pauses with any internal ones. No fences divide his lines into smaller parcels. The result, to an ear trained on Pope—or any of the masters of blank verse—is a certain monotony, an absence of tension between metrical and syntactic patterns. It would be easy to put this down to lack of metrical skill; alternatively, it might be the unfortunate consequence of a literate poet's decision not to punctuate in order to appear unlettered.[12] Without punctuation, enjambed lines and strong caesuras are almost impossible to write (on the rare occasions when Clare does write them in this poem, he uses a dash to mark the internal syntactic break). The explanation seems to be both simpler (he never mastered punctuation)[13] and more interesting. His practice of testing his poems by reading them aloud to his family, who were themselves illiterate, suggests that his poetry may in fact have been shaped by the demands of primarily oral forms for stricter observance of line boundaries.[14] At the same time, the parallel between visual aesthetics and poetic form in "The Mores" makes the absence of punctuation there look like conscious choice—not to appear illiterate (Clare still wanted to be accepted as a literate poet, and did not object to Taylor's punctuating his published poems) but to express formally the poem's politics of sight. Using a metrical line perfected by literate poets, "The Mores" translates a visual concept of extensive freedom within bounds into poetic form. This seems to be one more way in which Clare tries to appropriate eighteenth-century descriptive verse to the purposes of the peasant poet. Though his surrender of poetic freedom (to enjamb) is costly, "The

11. See *John Clare's Autobiographical Writings,* pp. 33–34, and "The Flitting."

12. Robert von Hallberg pointed out to me the connection between Clare's lack of punctuation and his limited use of caesuras.

13. See *Letters,* p. 122. Robinson and Powell note that some of Clare's early manuscripts are absurdly over-punctuated while most use no punctuation (introduction to *John Clare,* p. xxi). By 1822, Clare had evidently given up trying to learn the rules of grammar and punctuation. See also a prose fragment on his impatience with such rules, reprinted in *John Clare,* ed. Robinson and Powell, p. 481. Many of Clare's later poems do use internal syntactic breaks unmarked even by dashes. Clare seems to have believed that pauses can be heard or felt without the pointers literate readers have come to rely on.

14. See *John Clare's Autobiographical Writings,* pp. 12 and 82.

Mores" is significantly more original than Clare's first poem on enclosure. Its claims to revise the vision and rewrite the language and forms of descriptive landscape poetry derive from a political consciousness that Clare did not possess when he wrote "Helpstone."

The effects of continuous and mounting disappointments to his ambitions can be traced in Clare's letters and other prose fragments.[15] But it is in a handful of poems, political in a stronger sense than what Jameson has in mind, that those disappointments produce an explicit attempt to understand what it means to be both peasant and poet.[16] These poems explore the intertwined issues of property, identity, and language. The most important is another poem about enclosure, "[The Lament of Swordy Well]."

The lament or complaint traditionally relies on a strong sense of voice; it is not surprising that Clare abandons the heroic couplet for a song form.[17] In this case, however, the lament is spoken by a piece of land. The accents and tones are those of the laborer:

> Though Im no man yet any wrong
> Some sort of right may seek
> And I am glad if een a song
> Gives me the room to speak
>
> [ll. 41–44]

15. Because the prose fragments are usually undated, the letters are the best source, and the new edition of these just published (ed. Mark Storey [Oxford, 1985]) should make it possible to establish a better chronology for the development of Clare's political opinions. The letters collected by the Tibbles suggest that Clare's disillusionment began as early as 1821; his comments become especially pointed and linked to the situation of rural labor generally beginning about 1826 (when Clare spent much of the year doing field labor). Between 1829, when Clare received from Taylor a statement of his accounts that made it clear how little he had ever earned from his poems, and 1832, when Clare moved to Northborough to try to establish financial independence as a small cottage farmer with a house and garden, his letters often touch on the themes of the political prose fragments published by Robinson and Powell in the Oxford Authors *Clare*. The undated autobiographical fragments provide another prose source for a study of Clare's developing political awareness.

16. Another explicitly political poem from this period is "The Fallen Elm," the only such poem in *The Midsummer Cushion.* I do not consider Clare's satire "The Parish" here, though it is certainly a political poem, because it does not address the same issues of property, identity, and poetic voice or language. "The Parish" has a great deal to say about class relations in the village, particularly about the growing distance between farmers and laborers. Of all Clare's political poems, it is closest to Cobbett, whose prose Clare much admired—though its early date (1823) puts it before the publication of most of Cobbett's *Rural Rides.*

17. Clare's associations for the song form were probably popular rather than pious. Though he may have owned a collection of Wesley's hymns (*John Clare's Autobiographical Writings,* p. 14 and pp. 166–67 n. 21), Methodism does not figure importantly in his background, whereas oral song traditions do (his father was a local ballad singer).

Where Wordsworth naturalizes the human poor, Clare humanizes nature. The device is not that of pathetic fallacy (where human speakers, projecting their feelings on nature, express only their own states of mind). Clare's lament voices the complaints of both land and laborer. The trope is closer to Marx ("Could commodities themselves speak, they would say . . .")[18] than to Wordsworth:

Alas dependance thou'rt a brute
Want only understands
His feelings wither branch and root
That falls in parish hands
The muck that clouts the ploughmans shoe
The moss that hides the stone
Now Im become the parish due
Is more then I can own

[ll. 33–40]

By forcing us to see how the words put in the mouth of the land describe equally well the condition of the laborer, Clare offers a different understanding of the relationship between the two. The subject of the lament is dispossession—a change in the status of both land and laborer, as of the relations between them, that for Clare is epitomized in enclosure.

The burden of the lament turns on the double meanings of two repeated terms, "own" and "keep." These meanings are developed not merely as alternatives but as active oppositions. Land and labor understand owning as claiming or confessing an attribute or name essential to defining identity ("I own Im poor like many more" [l. 153]). Their use of the word constantly undercuts owning as the enclosers mean it, possessing something outside the self as private property. When Swordy Well complains

The silver springs grown naked dykes
Scarce own a bunch of rushes

[ll. 57–58]

it is hard to read "own" in the sense of private property, as the analogy with a human voice initially suggests. The play upon "keep" is still more pointed. When Swordy Well first declares, "I hold no hat to beg a mite / . . . / But pray to keep my own" (ll. 9–12), "keeping" suggests retaining exclusive possession. But a few stanzas later it becomes clear that land and laborers employ the term in the different sense of supporting:

These things that claim my own as theirs
Where born but yesterday

18. Marx, *Capital,* vol. 1, in *The Marx-Engels Reader,* p. 328.

But ere I fell to town affairs
I were as proud as they
I kept my horses cows and sheep
And built the town below
Ere they had cat or dog to keep
And then to use me so

[ll. 65–72]

By contrast the parish, "Had it the earth to keep / Would even pine the bees to dead / To save an extra keep" (ll. 74–76). The claims to possession put forward by enclosure reject the responsibility of "keeping" laborers, gypsies, horses, cows, sheep, or the wild bees, which the stones and springs and rushes of Swordy Well once supported. The land's protests are founded on a different concept of possession in which ownership is demonstrated through use as a power for (rather than over) life. To be stripped of one's "own" is to be deprived of the power to give and enjoy life. For Swordy Well, as for the laborers whose position is articulated in the land's lament, this loss is the loss of self. When trees banks and bushes, sand and grit and stones have been carted away (ll. 60–64), what is left?

Of all the fields I am the last
That my own face can tell
Yet what with stone pits delving holes
And strife to buy and sell
My name will quickly be the whole
Thats left of swordy well

[ll. 203–8]

The "own" that Swordy Well should keep, and toil enjoy (l. 55) are not external possessions but intrinsic attributes that constitute identity. Without them, the land is faceless. And if the land is faceless, the laborer loses a sense of self inseparable from his use of the land. In this enlarged sense, enclosure, by driving out mutual relations of "keeping" with the exclusive claims of private property, deprives toil of its "own." But that threatened sense of self is implicitly maintained in the form of Clare's protesting poem. By giving an individualizing human voice to the land, the poem reclaims identity and the power of speech for the laborer. The peasant becomes a poet, whose chosen form is notably here not the heroic couplet of bourgeois literary tradition.

"[The Lament of Swordy Well]" articulates the meaning of social location to Clare's poetry of place. It is also a key to the poetics of his most characteristic poems, those written in what he called the "green language" of the pastoral poet. These poems imagine a peasant poetry written from the secure relations of owning and keeping whose loss is the subject of "[The Lament of Swordy Well]." They are in a sense generated by the pessimistic conclusion of that poem. There private property, owning and keeping in the now usual sense, creates the land itself as alienated, both from its own identity (all but the name) and from the laborer who might use and enjoy it. The stripping and impoverishment of Swordy Well, enclosed as private property, is an image of the impoverishment of human life that it causes. The green language poems, by contrast, celebrate the sensory richness of human life lived in a relation to place outside or beyond the constricting ties of exclusive ownership. Clare's utopian imagination is very close to Marx's.

> Just as *private property* is only the sensuous expression of the fact that man becomes *objective* for himself and at the same time becomes to himself a strange and inhuman object; just as it expresses the fact that the assertion of his life is the alienation of his life, that his realization is his loss of reality, is an *alien* reality: conversely, the positive transcendence of private property—i.e., the *sensuous* appropriation for and by man of the human essence and of human life, of objective man, of human *achievements*—is not to be conceived merely in the sense of *direct,* one-sided *gratification*—merely in the sense of *possessing,* of *having.* Man appropriates his total essence in a total manner, that is to say, as a whole man. . . .
>
> The transcendence of private property is therefore the complete *emancipation* of all human sense and attributes.[19]

Like Marx little more than a decade later, Clare conceives the effect of privatizing land as a reduction in the possible human relations with place to the single sense of "having." In the conventions of descriptive literature and painting established in eighteenth-century England, the sense that expresses possession is that of sight. Clare's utopian project, especially in the poems of *The Midsummer Cushion,* is to imagine a language of relation that transcends the limitations of a middle-class poetics of the rural scene.

Such language is not easily conceived or written. Clare chose to remain a poet of the obscure, of what is hidden and of what is commonplace and so unnoticed. His poems attempt to convey the rich texture of relations between the land and its obscure wild and human tenants, but these poems too risk reducing their subjects to sights to be possessed, an experience Clare had known firsthand. (In the brief months of his fame, he was constantly summoned to satisfy the gaze of the curious. He discovered that he, not his poems, was the rural scene they believed they had purchased.)[20] Some of Clare's best poems circumvent the problem

19. Marx, "Private Property and Communism," *Economic and Philosophic Manuscripts of 1844,* in *The Marx-Engels Reader,* p. 87.

20. See *John Clare's Autobiographical Writings,* pp. 118–23.

of a possessive viewer by merging the voices of the poet and his subject (as in "Swordy Well" or "The Fallen Elm"); elsewhere in *The Midsummer Cushion* the dangers of poetic seeing and the problems of finding a language outside the literature of the rural scene become an explicit thematic concern.

One group of poems narrates quests for the hidden—walks in search of birds' nests. In patches of woods, heath, or even the corners of fields, Clare finds remnants of unowned land in an enclosed landscape. These offer the sensory richness, if not the extensive vision, that he associates with labor's freedom before enclosure. Clare loves these secret places that take him out of sight, too; in the rural scenes produced for the middle-class public (including those he writes himself) these hidden spots are not in view. He is the only intruder (as he knows himself) on a scene which does not yet know what it is to be seen.

> For nature here in self delight
> Bestows her richest gifts—the green
> Luxuriance all around—the light
> Seems more then any common scene
> And yet appears no looker on
> Left to herself and solitude
> I seem myself the only one
> Intruding on her happy mood
> ["The Meadow Grass," ll. 41–48]

To be unseen, in these poems, is to remain "unknown to wrong" ("The Nightingales Nest," l. 92)—where "wrong" is equated with the reduction to a possession that seeing can symbolize. Thus the woodland birds he meets are insistently presented as "tenants" only, still innocent of the different relations established by private property:

> these feathered heirs of solitude
> Remain the tennants of this quiet wood
> And live in melody and make their home
> ["The Robins Nest," ll. 88–90]

Their relation to the land is like that of laborers, before enclosure. They are perpetual tenants, whose rights to keep and be kept by the land are implicitly recognized by landowners who have not enclosed or improved.

> Where old neglect lives patron and befriends
> Their homes with safetys wildness—where nought lends
> A hand to injure—root up or disturb
> The things of this old place—there is no curb
> Of interest industry or slavish gain
> To war with nature so the weeds remain

And wear an ancient passion that arrays
Ones feelings with the shadows of old days
["The Robins Nest," ll. 50–57]

The parallel between human and wild tenants, as in "Swordy Well," constantly informs the language of these poems. Where "Swordy Well" laments the loss of labor's "own"—identity and enjoyment of the land—Clare's woods poems seek to realize rights of sensory possession quite different from the rights of property expressed by sight in bourgeois culture. The tenants inherit more with their leases than the use of a land that will support them. They "live in melody"; they (and through them, Clare) inherit "the old woodlands legacy of song" ("The Nightingales Nest," l. 93). The rights of these tenants have their basis in tradition: they are both "ancient" and continuing. Where they remain in force (in the woods) the "moss grows old and keeps an evergreen" ("The Robins Nest," l. 60).

In this old ancient solitude we might
Come ten years hence of trouble dreaming ill
And find them like old tennants peaceful still
["The Robins Nest," ll. 65–67]

Clare would like to imagine that he can leave undisturbed the "tennants of this woodland privacy" ("The Robins Nest," l. 101). "Well leave it as we found it—safetys guard / Of pathless solitude shall keep it still / . . . / We will not plunder music of its dower / Nor turn this spot of happiness to thrall" ("The Nightingales Nest," ll. 62–63, 69–70). But he is not the unobserved listener, the poet of imagination, of Keats' poem: he is a descriptive poet. Wishing to see and yet avoid the consequences of possessive sight (plundering, enslaving), Clare is led to the hidden, the remote, the secret, where he can momentarily imagine—in what is perhaps an understandable indulgence—that he too can disappear ("Buried in green delights," "Lost in such extacys"): the first, last, and only viewer ("The Robins Nest," ll. 15, 23).

These poems of hidden places reveal another difficulty in Clare's position. In "Swordy Well" he can merge the voice of the rural poet with that of the rural laborer; in the name of the land, he speaks for ties of place and people that are local and known only to the unpropertied classes. In the bird nest poems the poet is set apart—from his audience, by his care to protect the places he seeks from their unheeding gaze, but also from rural laborers, by his identity as one who sees. Clare's protective concern for nightingales' nests indicts his intrusion as well, as he half recognizes. But his relation to the human inhabitants of the rural scene, whom he does not protect, is more troubling. Labor's toil is here associated with the "gain" that destroys that different relation to the land and its nonhuman inhabitants which only the seeing poet appears to value.

I hate the plough that comes to dissaray
Her holiday delights—and labours toil
Seems vulgar curses on the sunny soil
And man the only object that distrains
Earths garden into deserts for his gains
["The Moorehens Nest," ll. 32–36]

In part this is the protest against the burden of work that forms the background to all Clare's celebrations of rural pleasures. Unlike Marx (or his English contemporaries, Ruskin and Morris), Clare never, even in his most utopian moments, imagines that physical labor might be happiness, the natural expression of human capacities. Perhaps this represents a more genuinely working-class perspective than Ruskin's or Morris' or Marx's; probably it also reflects Clare's debt to a georgic tradition stretching back to Hesiod and to Genesis. But Clare's resentment of toil extends here to the laborer as well. As he became increasingly conscious of the differences that divided him from the middle-class audience he once hoped to approach as a professional poet, he remained no less conscious of the differences that had long set him apart in his rural community. The decade of disappointments Clare experienced after 1821 politicized his sense of place,[21] but it also brought home to him his own placelessness—long before his devastating move from Helpstone to Northborough in 1832.

In writing of the commonplace Clare apparently avoids the politically awkward position of the hidden observer, but the contradictory locations of "peasant" and "poet" continue to complicate his relation to sight and to poetic language. A second group of poems (including "Summer Images," "Pastoral Poesy," "The Voice of Nature," "The Eternity of Nature") attempts to formulate a poetics of the commonplace in which seeing is reconceived as heeding, or paying attention: a nonpossessive form of perception. Directed toward what is both ordinary and shared, it is imagined as a response of the individual to the particular that is claimed as play or pastime, in opposition to toil for gain. "Summer Images," one of Clare's more ambitious efforts, articulates this conception of seeing and

21. Clare's books no longer sold, and his publishers delayed promised publications interminably and stopped answering his letters. His efforts to sell poems to the literary annuals or to interest his publishers in prose projects were not successful. The income from a fund collected by his early patrons proved inadequate to support his growing family, and their expectation that he could combine poetry with agricultural labor bitterly unrealistic—especially during a period of falling wages and scarce employment in the fields. Clare was not able either to make himself economically independent by his pen, or—for social and psychological as well as economic reasons—to write poetry as an amateur while he lived the life of a laborer. In 1832, in a last try for independence, he moved to a cottage with a small plot of land in a neighboring village, a move that disastrously ruptured the ties of place on which he had depended. Within five years, Clare entered the first of several insane asylums where he was to spend the rest of his life.

inadvertently illustrates its saving power for Clare. The poem's early stanzas use elevated but conventional diction, awkwardly manipulating grammatical function and word order.

Me not the noise of brawling pleasures cheer
In nightly revels or in city streets
But joys which sooth and not distract mine ear
    That one at leisure meets
In the green woods and meadows summer shorn
    Or fields where bee flye greets
    Ones ear with mellow horn

[ll. 22–28]

As an attempt to write an ode in the manner of Gray, "Summer Images" is not a success. The labored elevation of its form and language, moreover, underlines the paradox of Clare's desire to protect his rural "images" from possessive desires: these are clearly marked as pictures composed for sale to a middle-class audience. But partway through, a series of active verbs of perception (mark, trace, thread, see, note, heed, espy, list, hark, hear) take control of the poem, straightening out its distorted syntax and redirecting it from the general to the particular. Shifting his attention from poetic meadows to his own fields, Clare practices a different kind of seeing, closer to what had been earlier in the poem figured as a human encounter: a meeting and exchange of greetings (joys "that one at leisure meets" in "fields where bee flye greets / Ones ear"). As in any human meeting, the particularity of what is met is crucial. The images that the poem now offers (the leaping frog scattering dew, the homebound hedger whose swishing leather doublet scares the sheep [ll. 99–102, 169–73]) are more like those of the bird nest poems, where perceiving is distinguishing the telling marks of identity—the "five brun-coloured eggs" of the robin ("The Robins Nest," l. 99), the "dead oaken leaves" and "velvet moss" of the nightingale's nest ("How curious is the nest no other bird / Uses such loose materials" ["The Nightingales Nest," ll. 76–79]), or the rhythms of bird songs, carefully studied and adapted as the forms of Clare's own songs—as is the blue cap's in "Songs Eternity":

Dreamers list the honey be[e]
Mark the tree
Where the blue cap tootle tee
Sings a glee

[ll. 31–34]

Such acts of "heeding" affirm that neither the land nor its inhabitants are faceless.

No—pasture molehills used to lie
And talk to me of sunny days

And then the glad sheep listing bye
And still in ruminating praise
Of summer and the pleasant place
And every weed and blossom too
Was looking upward in my face
With friendships welcome "how do ye do"
["The Flitting," ll. 121–28]

Observer and observed are alike redeemed from facelessness by this reciprocal act of greeting: "All tennants of an ancient place / And heirs of noble heritage" ("The Flitting," ll. 129–30).

The human figures that the poet encounters in the later stanzas of "Summer Images" are similarly noticed and implicitly "greeted," without the uneasy note of condescension that elsewhere separates poet from peasants. They are laborers—but laborers at rest. They exemplify a less conscious version of the kind of reciprocity between poet and place that Clare's poems celebrate as play. "They greet joy unawares" (l. 14), and nature, who loves to "meet vibrating joys" (l. 193), contributes her images to their unconscious creativity. The "cow tending boy to toil unreconsiled / Absorbed as in some vagrant summer dream" is dancing to his shadow, the "pausing boy / Listens the mellow sounds / And hums in vacant joy" (ll. 85–91, 166–68). These ghosts of the poet's younger self bridge the uncomfortable gap between him and his neighbors visible in "The Moorehens Nest." The laborers at leisure respond to the images the poet heeds, the common sights and sounds of rural summer. And like the poet's, theirs is a protest against alienating work. Their dreaming, listening, dancing, and humming, is play: "Pastimes the muse employs" ("Summer Images," l. 195). Walking through the fields, the poet recovers, with the aid of these mediating figures, the nonpossessive enjoyment of place whose loss is mourned in "Swordy Well."

Play pastime—all times blotting pen conseals
Come like a new born joy
To greet me in the fields
[ll. 187–89]

Perception is only part of what Clare must figure differently in these poems. The language that embodies those perceptions is equally problematic for the peasant poet. "True poesy is not in words" begins the poem that he chose to close the central section of *The Midsummer Cushion* ("Summer Images" opens it).[22] Sometimes Clare thinks of this poetic language as visual: "images that thoughts express" ("Pastoral Poesy," l. 2), or "pictures round the fields that lie / In my minds heart like things that cannot die" ("The Moorehens Nest," ll. 11–12). More often it is

22. The text of "Pastoral Poesy" is taken from Tibble and Thornton's edition of *The Midsummer Cushion,* p. 291.

aural: "Melodys of earth and sky" ("Songs Eternity," l. 13), the "rich music" that "breaths in summers every sound" and in her "varied greens" ("Summer Images," ll. 134–35) to make a harmony for both ear and eye. Often this language is simply imagined as silence: "A silence that discourses more / Then any tongue can do" ("Pastoral Poesy," ll. 39–40), or a song to be heard in what others call silence—the equivalent of beauty to be discovered in the commonplace:

> The many look for sound—'tis silence speaks,
> And song like sunshine from her rapture breaks[23]

Turning his back on the language of literary tradition, the peasant poet heeds these melodies of earth and sky, "Natures universal tongue" ("Songs Eternity," l. 53), and tunes his own song to theirs:

> And so I worship them in bushy spots
> And sing with them when all else notice not
> And feel the music of their mirth agree
> With that sooth quiet that bestirreth me
> And if I touch aright that quiet tone
> That soothing truth that shadows forth their own
> Then many a year shall grow in after days
> And still find hearts to love my quiet lays
> ["The Eternity of Nature," ll. 51–58]

Nature's language has a life that words can approximate only if they echo her tones and images. These are perpetually renewed, and therefore eternal. The child "with pleasure in his eye" will continue to "cry the daisy a familiar cry"—as Eve did ("The Eternity of Nature," ll. 13–22). The robin "Sings unto time a pastoral and gives / A music that lives on and ever lives" ("The Eternity of Nature," ll. 45–46).

> And little brooks that hum a simple lay
> In green unnoticed spots from praise away
> Shall sing—when poets in times darkness hid
> Shall lie like memory in a pyramid
> ["The Eternity of Nature," ll. 33–36]

The distinctive character of nature's language, and of the pastoral poetry tuned to its "quiet tone," is touched for Clare in the varied resonance of "green." It is a peculiarly English phenomenon—understandable to anyone who has tried to paint or photograph English countryside—that the features of its landscape constantly collapse into a monotony of green.

23. Clare, "The Voice of Nature," *John Clare: Selected Poems,* ed. Tibble and Tibble (London, 1965), ll. 29–30; see also "Meadow Grass," ll. 65–66.

From Marvell's description of the creative power of mind transcending nature's variety in "The Garden" ("Annihilating all that's made / To a green thought in a green shade") to Wordsworth's enactment of it in "Tintern Abbey" (where orchards, woods, hedgerows, and farms "lose themselves" in "one green hue" before the sign of the poet's presence, the rising smoke of a hermit's fire), this phenomenon has a rich poetic history. Clare's use of it defines his different relation to a poetic tradition. For Clare the business of mind is never to exercise power over nature by annihilating distinctions; nature's green is not monotony but a harmony "of varied greens / Woods meadows hedgrows cornfields all around" ("Summer Images," ll. 135–36), to which he tunes his poetry. It is a term that has value for Clare from its association with the relations to place that make his poetry possible. Green is the color of that most commonplace of living things, the grass of fields and meadows, as it is the name of the common place of every village. Because for Clare what is common permits a sensory richness of enjoyment excluded by possession, "green" is not a reductive but an expansive adjective, as in the "green delights" and "green luxuriance" that are nature's "richest gifts" in "The Robins Nest" and "Meadow Grass." And green is the sign of the peculiar eternity of life in nature, where all are tenants whose ancient rights of use will be perpetually renewed: the grass, the moss, the nightingale's joys, are "ever green" ("Songs Eternity," l. 57; "The Robins Nest," l. 60; "The Nightingales Nest," l. 41). All these valued meanings—ordinariness, shared use, sensory richness, perennial life—cohere in Clare's famous description of his own pastoral poetry as "a language that is ever green" ("Pastoral Poesy," l. 13).[24]

To imagine different relations of perception and a new language is not, of course, equivalent to creating them. The pastoral poesy of *The Midsummer Cushion* remains a utopian project. The poems retreat from the extensive freedom of an unenclosed landscape to the "sooth quiet" of marginal spaces, but even so they and their poet bring not only the language and forms but also the economic and perceptual relations of bourgeois culture with them. To the extent that Clare was read at all, his poems were received as rural scenes, illustrations of the stable community that he and his audience wanted to believe in. This was a consequence both of Clare's own ambiguous relations to rural labor and bourgeois culture and of the conditions of production and exchange into which his poetry entered. Clare's title illustrates the dilemma of the peasant poet, which he could sometimes recognize but never completely overcome. Unlike his earlier titles, chosen for him by Taylor, *The Midsummer Cushion* does not announce itself as part of the existing pastoral tradition

24. The phrase "green language" has been made famous in part by Raymond Williams' sensitive use of it in his chapter on Clare in *The Country and the City* (London, 1973), pp. 127–41.

(as do *Poems Descriptive of Rural Life, The Village Minstrel,* or *The Shepherd's Calendar*). As Clare explains in a prefatory note, the phrase belongs to a popular and rural culture:

> It is a very old custom among villagers in summer time to stick a piece of greensward full of field flowers & place it as an ornament in their cottages which ornaments are called Midsummer Cushions And as these trifles are field flowers of humble pretentions & of various hues I thought the above cottage custom gave me an oppertunity to select a title that was not inapplicable to the contents of the Volume[25]

Like even the cushions found in cottages, however, Clare's book, though it speaks of the life of the fields, thrusts that life into alien contexts: the forms of a different verbal culture, the literary marketplace, and finally middle- and upper-class homes. Clare was himself aware of the dangers of this uprooting:

> But take these several beings from their homes
> Each beautious thing a withered thought becomes
> Association fades and like a dream
> They are but shadows of the things they seem
> Torn from their homes and happiness they stand
> The poor dull captives of a foreign land
> ["Shadows of Taste," ll. 147–52]

In heeding the obscure, Clare risked the death that representation demands (his field flowers wither as ornaments), but he also risked the loss of vitality that translation can mean. His birds, Clare evidently feared, enter poetry only by giving up something of the vivid uniqueness of the singular and literal. Poetry remains, in this sense, a foreign land and a foreign language for Clare, and he, like his birds, experienced the fate of the alienated—poor dull captives of a foreign land—even as he imagined a language where the dispossessed, as ancient tenants, might be at home.

The "green language" poems of *The Midsummer Cushion,* though determined by a politicized sense of place (and so understood at the time) are themselves not poems of direct political criticism but of an imagination both nostalgic and utopian. "The Fallen Elm" is the only poem of protest in a volume which otherwise generalizes loss to a human rather than a political condition. The problem of giving voice to his increasingly political consciousness remained acute for Clare. His most outspokenly critical poem, "The Parish" (1823), protesting the increasingly self-interested

25. Clare, *The Midsummer Cushion,* n.p.

treatment of labor by farmers, proved unpublishable, though formally it remained within an eighteenth-century tradition of satiric rural poetry. "The Mores" and "Swordy Well" also stayed in manuscript. A number of prose fragments, probably from around 1830, are equally outspoken but were neither completed nor published. Part of Clare's difficulty in speaking out is clear in these fragments, however: he distrusts not only the political rhetoric of middle-class reformers and their representations of the rural scene, but also the political expression of rural labor: mob action.[26] The Swing riots of 1830, some of which came as close to Clare as Market Deeping, a few miles from Helpstone, produced almost no literate political protest beyond the cryptic threats to local farmers and parsons signed "Captain Swing."[27]

Clare's solution to this dilemma—finding a political voice outside a middle-class rhetoric, in the absence of any audience for a political poetry of rural labor—was expressed as a formal choice. His poetry increasingly empowers a countering term, "song," and the cultural tradition it represents. Like Burns, Clare had always written songs, and like the earlier poet, he too discovered that his publisher and patrons considered these efforts unworthy of a seriously ambitious poet. Yet as his incomplete autobiography makes clear, he recognized that his own poetic roots were divided between a popular culture of rural song and story, and descriptive poetry of the rural scene.[28] His father was a well-known local ballad singer, and Clare himself became a collector of ballads and of fiddle tunes. His interest in rural song was both professional and archaeological: he seems to have understood his collecting as historical preservation of a disappearing locality and as a source of stories and rhythmic material for his own writing.[29] His interest extended to literary songs as well—not only Burns', but the collections of Scott and Bishop Percy and, increasingly in the mid-twenties, miscellanies of Elizabethan and seventeenth-century songs, which inspired a number of experiments in their manner. This evidence that Clare, despite the responses of his publisher and patrons, pursued rural song and its connections with local and popular culture as an alternative to poetry of the rural scene is borne out by the way in which "song" is used as an explicit subject in a number of poems. Perhaps the most striking of these is "Songs Eternity"—itself a particularly successful song—which ascribes all the characteristics of Clare's "green

26. See, for example, *The Prose of John Clare,* ed. Tibble and Tibble (London, 1951), p. 225.

27. See Eric J. Hobsbawm and George Rudé, *Captain Swing* (New York, 1968) for the best account of the Swing disturbances. Their charts indicate three instances of arson at Deeping in December 1830.

28. See *John Clare's Autobiographical Writings,* pp. 9–10 and 82.

29. George Deacon gives a full account of Clare's collecting activities, together with transcriptions of the tunes and words he collected, in *John Clare and the Folk Tradition* (London, 1983).

language" poems specifically to an oral tradition at once natural and popular. "Songs like the grass are evergreen" (l. 57):

> Songs once sung to adams ears
> Can it be
> —Ballads of six thousand years
> Thrive thrive
> Songs awakened with the spheres
> Alive
>
> [ll. 15–20]

"The Voice of Nature" makes a similar identification of Clare's poetry of place with song, though there the simultaneous theme of nature as a book tends to produce metaphoric confusion. Clare's most specific identification with song as the voice of rural labor, however, occurs in the introductory lines to his "Child Harold" (a long poem very loosely modeled on Byron's, but more than half composed of songs). "Many are poets—though they use no pen," he begins,

> —The life of labour is a rural song
> That hurts no cause—nor warfare tries to wage
> Toil like the brook in music wears along—
>
> [ll. 1, 6–8]

Ironically, Clare's "Child Harold" and its politically caustic, sometimes obscene companion, "Don Juan," were conceived not as Clare's own voice but as Byron's, after Clare had been sent to the insane asylum at High Beech in Epping Forest with delusions that he was, among other people, that poet. It is as if Clare could only speak his politically (and sexually) suspect words with Byron's aristocratic license. And even then, of course, the poem is careful to dissociate "rural song" from class "warfare."

Clare lost the rural laborer's special relation to common places that, as memory or utopian projection, had shaped the "green language" of his best poetry. With it he lost a sense of personal identity, as "[The Lament of Swordy Well]" foresees—even his name. The "I Am" poems of his later asylum days, with their bleak refrain, "I only know, I am," fulfill with stunning completeness the fears expressed in an earlier essay on "Self-Identity": "Forget thyself & the world will willingly forget thee till thou art nothing but a living-dead man dwelling among shadows & falsehood. . . . A person who denies himself must either be a madman or a coward."[30] Yet though the poet of the "I am" poems no longer knows who or what he is, Clare continued to write poems, and these

30. *Prose,* p. 239.

were almost all, now, songs. Perhaps as the act of writing asserted him a poet, so that of writing songs continued to assert a political identity. That identity was hard won, and it rarely allowed him to write political poetry, yet the sense of social place that Clare's commitment to rural song came to express is inseparable from the achievements of his finest poems. Writing songs in Northampton Asylum, Clare might reassume the place of the peasant poet,

> And be my self in memory once again
> ["The Robins Nest," l. 41].

He the Compeller

Turner Cassity

It is possible to speak of internal exile; of internal politics, no. One is tempted to say that Rudyard Kipling became a political poet because he preferred writing in the second or third person to writing in the first person. In the 834 pages of the collected poems there is exactly one lyric written *in propria persona,*[1] and that is the final one:

> If I have given you delight
>   By aught that I have done
> Let me lie quiet in that night
>   Which shall be yours anon.
>   ["The Appeal"][2]

Criticism, apart from the Kipling Society, has let him lie only too quiet, but he has not returned us the courtesy. The poems give delight frequently, but they also raise disquiet. To read them (as to read Crabbe) is to suspect that meditation and the first person have rather paupered English poetry. The hermetic lyric of personal emotion and its sloppier successor, the psychological self-search, account for an appalling percentage of all verse. The leftovers of imagism have done little to make up the deficit.

Any writer who, as a matter of ritual, dined annually on Empire Day with Alfred Milner was not precisely objective, but from the first Kipling was inclined to swathe himself in alienation effects: to disappear

1. I go on the assumption that the "Dedication" to *Soldiers Three* is written in the persona of a persona.

2. All of the Kipling quotations are from *Rudyard Kipling's Verse, Definitive Edition* (Garden City, N.Y., 1940).

in narrative and dialogue and rhetorical structure. As we should now say, he concealed himself behind mouthpieces. Let us honor his appeal and not speculate as to his reasons for reticence. Any fool who has the facts of his life should be able to figure them out, and in any case they were shared by many of his class and his generation. As a double blind, like other political poets, he availed himself of the politician's privilege of speaking out of both sides of his mouth.

To be honest, we must admit that his artistic decisions may have been influenced by the laws of libel, but it is also possible that his respect for privacy extended even to that of his enemies. The determination to name names has caused the topical poems of Alexander Pope to date in a way that those of Kipling do not, although in every other respect Kipling is the more direct. In his anxiety that no one miss the point he was capable of writing the same poem twice and then interleaving the two. One might use a term of current chic and say each is an intertext of the other. Depending on the values you wish to apply, you may regard the method as overkill or as making assurance doubly sure.

If we had only the descriptive passages in "The Dykes"—and they are extraordinary; again, Crabbe comes to mind—if we had only the description (I have italicized it), the meaning would be fully conveyed. In another writer we should call the manner post-symbolist.

We have no heart for the fishing—we have no hand for the oar—
All that our fathers taught us of old pleases us now no more.
All that our own hearts bid us believe we doubt where we do not deny—
There is no proof in the bread we eat nor rest in the toil we ply.

Look you, our foreshore stretches far through sea-gate, dyke, and groin—
Made land all, that our fathers made, where the flats and the fairway join.
They forced the sea a sea-league back. They died, and their work stood fast.
We were born to peace in the lee of the dykes, but the time of our peace is past.

Far off, the full tide clambers and slips, mouthing and testing all,
Nipping the flanks of the water-gates, baying along the wall;
Turning the shingle, returning the shingle, changing the set of the sand . . .
We are too far from the beach, men say, to know how our outworks stand.

Turner Cassity is the author of *Hurricane Lamp,* published in 1986. Among other things, he is an old Caribbean hand, and a former employee of the South African Civil Service. He knows the Transvaal, including Lichtenberg, well.

So we come down, uneasy, to look; uneasily pacing the beach.
These are the dykes our fathers made: we have never known a
breach.
Time and again has the gale blown by and we were not afraid;
Now we come only to look at the dykes—at the dykes our fathers
made.

O'er the marsh where the homesteads cower apart the harried sunlight flies,
Shifts and considers, wanes and recovers, scatters and sickens and dies—
An evil ember bedded in ash—a spark blown west by the wind . . .
We are surrendered to night and the sea—the gale and the tide
behind!

At the bridge of the lower saltings the cattle gather and blare,
Roused by the feet of running men, dazed by the lantern-glare.
Unbar and let them away for their lives—the levels drown as they stand,
Where the flood-wash forces the sluices aback and the ditches deliver inland.

Ninefold deep to the top of the dykes the galloping breakers stride,
And their overcarried spray is a sea—a sea on the landward side.
Coming, like stallions they paw with their hooves, going
they snatch with their teeth,
Till the bents and the furze and the sand are dragged out,
and the old-time hurdles beneath.

Bid men gather fuel for fire, the tar, the oil, and the tow—
Flame we shall need, not smoke, in the dark if the riddled
sea-banks go.
Bid the ringers watch in the tower (who knows how the dawn shall prove?)
Each with his rope between his feet and the trembling bells above.

Now we can only wait till the day, wait and apportion our shame.
These are the dykes our fathers left, but we would not look to the
same.
Time and again we were warned of the dykes, time and again we
delayed.
Now, it may fall, we have slain our sons, as our fathers we have
betrayed.

Walking along the wreck of the dykes, watching the work of the sea!
These were the dykes our fathers made to our great profit and ease.
But the peace is gone and the profit is gone, with the old sure
days withdrawn . . .
That our own houses show as strange when we come back in the
dawn!

In theory we should disapprove of "evil" as applied to "ember," but in the event it is perfect, as is "deliver" for the ditches. "Considers," for the sunlight, is a stroke of genius. It is like an enharmonic change: unjustifiable, but striking in a way nothing else can be. Nothing could say more than "overcarried spray is a sea—a sea on the landward side." If we had only these, however, we should miss the equally extraordinary power of

These were the dykes our fathers made to our great profit and ease.
But the peace is gone and the profit is gone, with the old sure
    days withdrawn . . .

One has to admire the honesty of "profit." It is we who are the euphemists. If you want to hear a spade called a spade, go to the Victorians.

Incidentally, why did a writer who wrote so often for the narrow columns of newspapers write in such enormously long lines? As a journalist himself he must have known that the typesetters and the copy editors would render his formats unrecognizable. One might even speculate that his insistent rhythm is a device to hold his structures together in defiance of cut-and-paste.

The speakers in "The Dykes" are generic. The speaker in "Lichtenberg" is so effectively characterized that one insults him to call him a mouthpiece.

Smells are surer than sounds or sights
    To make your heart-strings crack—
They start those awful voices o' nights
    That whisper, "Old man, come back!"
That must be why the big things pass
    And the little things remain,
Like the smell of the wattle by Lichtenberg,
    Riding in, in the rain.

There was some silly fire on the flank
    And the small wet drizzling down—
There were the sold-out shops and the bank
    And the wet, wide-open town;
And we were doing escort-duty
    To somebody's baggage-train,
And I smelt wattle by Lichtenberg—
    Riding in, in the rain.

It was all Australia to me—
    All I had found or missed:
Every face I was crazy to see,
    And every woman I'd kissed:
All that I shouldn't ha' done, God knows!
    (As He knows I'll do it again),
That smell of the wattle round Lichtenberg,
    Riding in, in the rain.

And I saw Sydney the same as ever,
    The picnics and brass-bands;

And my little homestead on Hunter River
    And my new vines joining hands.
It all came over me in one act
  Quick as a shot through the brain—
With the smell of the wattle round Lichtenberg,
    Riding in, in the rain.

I have forgotten a hundred fights,
  But one I shall not forget—
With the raindrops bunging up my sights
    And my eyes bunged up with wet;
And through the crack and the stink of the cordite,
    (Ah, Christ! My country again!)
The smell of the wattle by Lichtenberg,
    Riding in, in the rain!

The Australian with the Proustian insights is one of the most engaging characters in all poetry, and to say so is to recognize at once that characterization has not been a strong suit of the English lyric. If you omit the Renaissance tailor's dummies in Browning you are left with the right jolly old elf and that is about it. I am not quite persuaded that this particular Aussie would ever be willing to settle down by his uninterestingly described Hunter River (or anywhere else), but otherwise I cannot fault the poem. The application of the refrain to the repetitious drizzle is a fine example of turning weakness into strength.

I should like to compare the poem with Yeats' "An Irish Airman Foresees His Death," mildly to the detriment of the latter, which has been overpraised, although, for Yeats, it is refreshingly without claptrap.

I know that I shall meet my fate
Somewhere among the clouds above;
Those that I fight I do not hate,
Those that I guard I do not love;
My country is Kiltartan Cross,
My countrymen Kiltartan's poor,
No likely end could bring them loss
Or leave them happier than before.
Nor law, nor duty bid me fight,
Nor public men, nor cheering crowds,
A lonely impulse of delight
Drove to tumult in the clouds;
I balanced all, brought all to mind,

The years to come seemed waste of breath,
A waste of breath the years behind
In balance with this life, this death.

The punctuation is Yeats', not mine. I cannot resist pointing out that even in a country of ground fogs, "clouds above" is a tautology. Further, I doubt that many of the really poor made it into the Royal Flying Corps. Perhaps in calling Kiltartan's poor his countrymen the airman is speaking as southerners used to speak of "our Negroes." In other words, the poem is either inaccurate or patronizing. I am aware of the argument that any representation in dialect necessarily patronizes. If it is true, then by extension it is true of all written speech, which leaves us with the tape recorder as an ultimate reminder that the best way to condemn people is out of their own mouths. I am not sure that Kipling's sales figures refute the argument, but they at least indicate that many of his readers were unaware they were being patronized. The poem ends in a great wash of existential despair, for which, in all fairness, Perfidious Albion can hardly be held responsible. The Australian may be war-weary but he is certainly not world-weary, and one is simply not sure that Yeats would have been aware of the distinction. Not a creature of the 1890s for nothing. If you are writing about "those that I fight I do not hate" there is another way to do it.

I do not love my Empire's foes,
Nor call 'em angels; still,
What *is* the sense of 'atin those
'Oom you are paid to kill?
So, barrin' all that foreign lot
Which only joined for spite,
Myself, I'd just as soon as not
Respect the man I fight.
Ah, there, Piet!—'is trousies to 'is knees,
'Is coat-tails lyin' level in the bullet-sprinkled breeze;
'E does not lose 'is rifle an' 'e does not lose 'is seat.
I've known a lot o' people ride a dam' sight worse than Piet.

I've 'eard 'im cryin' from the ground
Like Abel's blood of old,
An' skirmished out to look, an' found
The beggar nearly cold.
I've waited on till 'e was dead
(Which couldn't 'elp 'im much),
But many grateful things 'e's said
To me for doin' such.
Ah, there, Piet! whose time 'as come to die,
'Is carcase past rebellion, but 'is eyes inquirin' why.
Though dressed in stolen uniform with badge o' rank complete,
I've known a lot o' fellers go a dam' sight worse than Piet.

. . . .

From Plewman's to Marabastad,
From Ookiep to De Aar,

Me an' my trusty friend 'ave 'ad,
  As you might say, a war;
But seein' what both parties done
  Before 'e owned defeat,
I ain't more proud of 'avin won
  Than I am pleased with Piet.
    Ah, there, Piet!—picked up be'ind the drive!
    The wonder wasn't 'ow 'e fought, but 'ow 'e kep' alive,
    With nothin' in 'is belly, on 'is back, or to 'is feet—
    I've known a lot o' men behave a dam' sight worse than Piet.
["Piet"]

"Oom" may or may not be a pun, and the double meaning of "lose 'is seat" will be lost on the generations of the automobile, but "the bullet-sprinkled breeze" is on a level with that most compelling of all antiwar passages:

The flying bullet down the Pass,
That whistles clear: "All flesh is grass."
["Arithmetic on the Frontier"]

The refrain, without the justification of that in the poem previously quoted, simply impedes things, as refrains usually do. "Abel" is a trifle too ingenious to be really moving. We shall never know in exactly what sense Kipling meant "rebellion," and he did not intend that we should; it is the ambiguity that moves us. The narrator would say that the word is as appropriate to the second Anglo-Boer War as to the first ("suzerainty" and all that); Piet would argue otherwise.

For American writers, their military service is frequently their one excursion outside alienation, or is at minimum a venture from one kind of estrangement into another. In any decade the number of competent novels about the military is high. The number of poems is not high, but the number of competent civilian poems is not high either. For novelists, the shared experience and the expectation of a knowledgeable audience seem to bring out the best. The best poems of combat have been written by those who experienced it (was Homer blind or blinded?), but the best poems of military life, the best in English, at any rate, were written by a war correspondent. We must be cautious, however, in assuming that Kipling was motivated by the assurance of commonality. In the first place, Queen Victoria's was not a mass army. Individual regiments with county constituencies and highly idiosyncratic traditions fought splendid little wars. If, like the Irish Guards, a regiment was without a long history, Kipling helpfully created traditions for them, just as he attempted to seduce the disaffected into patriotism. When the Boer War broadened the army's base, far from celebrating democracy, he approached his subject as an amalgam of trade guilds, each with its own arcana: sappers, artillery, "jollies," mounted infantry. He understood the degree to which exclusion attracts us and was at his very best in dealing with hangers-on. His water carrier has become his signature figure, and his bureaucrats, animal handlers, medics, musicians, barmaids, publicans, and officers-club whores convince as individuals and as types. One feels he would have had a deep understanding of that ultimately most successful and most excluded of officers-club professionals, Wallis Warfield Spencer.

Further, in one overriding sense he was impeccably democratic. He did not believe that perceptions are limited by education or by class or by genius. He endows his privates and non-coms with his own dazzling gifts. The "time-expired soldier-man" who en route home observes "Old Aden, like a barrick-stove / That no one's lit for years an' years" can make entire legions of lyricists disappear. If the device, and it is a device, strikes you as unconvincing, bear in mind that the following are the documented perceptions of an eighteen-year-old dogface:

> The night air was cooling now and a small sea wind stirred and only a few clouds high up moved slowly east hiding a swatch of stars as they went. . . . He led them around a not old banyan tree, the gnarled above ground roots making them stumble in the darkness, the pencil-thin branch roots not grown into the earth yet and dangling free from the branches slapping them repeatedly in the face.

The young soldier was James Jones.

In all of the *Barrack-room Ballads* and their successors in kind there is only one detail that rings false to me. It is in " 'Back to the Army Again.' "

I carried my slops to the tailor; I sez to 'im, "None o' your lip!
You tight 'em over the shoulders, an' loose 'em over the 'ip,
For the set o' the tunic's 'orrid." An' 'e sez to me, "Strike me dead,
But I thought you was used to the business!" an' so 'e done what I said.

I think those instructions to the tailor would have been reversed. In my own military service, and I spent it on the eighteenth parallel of latitude, I never knew humidity or heat to triumph over vanity.

Critics of three generations have distrusted Kipling because he does not say that war is hell. He said what Homer says: some of war is hell. Either might have agreed that civil strife is total hell.

If Ireland is notorious for its excess of patriotism, Canada is notorious for a lack of it. I of course except Quebec. As a frequent visitor at Groote Schuur the poet had to strain to be impartial about the Afrikaners, and the strain occasionally shows. French Canadians he did not even attempt to deal with, although during his residence in Vermont he must have encountered more than a few. In "The Prairie" we find him endeavoring to create a Canadian patriotism as it were from scratch; a patriotism for the English-speaking, that is.

"I see the grass shake in the sun for leagues on either hand,
I see a river loop and run about a treeless land—
An empty plain, a steely pond, a distance diamond clear,
And low blue naked hills beyond. And what is that to fear?"

"Go softly by that river-side or, when you would depart,
You'll find its every winding tied and knotted round your heart.
Be wary as the seasons pass, or you may ne'er outrun
The wind that sets that yellowed grass a-shiver 'neath the sun."

"I hear the summer storm outblown—the drip of the grateful wheat.
I hear the hard trail telephone a far-off horse's feet.
I hear the horns of Autumn blow to the wild-fowl overhead;
And I hear the hush before the snow. And what is that to dread?"

"Take heed what spell the lightning weaves—what charm
the echoes shape—
Or, bound among a million sheaves, your soul shall not escape,
Bar home the door of summer nights lest those high planets drown
The memory of near delights in all the longed-for town."

"What need have I to long or fear? Now, friendly, I behold
My faithful seasons robe the year in silver and in gold.
Now I possess and am possessed of the land where I would be,
And the curve of half Earth's generous breast shall soothe and
ravish me!"

In spite of some mesmerizing details, and a much more subtle and varied rhythm than is common for its author, the poem fails in that it confines itself wholly to landscape. The couplet at the end of the fourth stanza is majestic, scenically and rhythmically, but as a matter of fact it is the near delights of the longed-for town that the poem needs. There was a time when the Klondike was as prominent on feature pages as, say, El Salvador or Nicaragua today—writers know a gold rush when they see one—and what strikes us about writing from the Yukon is how seldom it looks away from the card table, the potbellied stove, and the mirror behind the bar, just as, a decade ago, itinerant revolutionaries never lifted their eyes from *The Thoughts of Chairman Mao.* Even among ecologists it is not landscape but the idea of landscape that commands loyalty. In brief, like the Canadian north, the poem is underpopulated, in spite of the alternative speakers and all those quotation marks. I would further point out that although it extends over a great many degrees of latitude, the Canadian Shield is not exactly generous. Granite never is. Few who read hunt, so I had better add that the horns of Autumn are actual, not metaphorical.

The danger in writing patriotic poems is that they will be taken seriously, and we can be confident that "Ulster" is quoted today.

> The dark eleventh hour
> Draws on and sees us sold
> To every evil power
> We fought against of old.
> Rebellion, rapine, hate,
> Oppression, wrong and greed
> Are loosed to rule our fate
> By England's act and dead.
>
> . . . .
>
> We know the wars prepared
> On every peaceful home,
> We know the hells declared
> For such as serve not Rome—
> The terror, threats, and dread
> In market, hearth, and field—
> We know, when all is said,
> We perish if we yield.

The poem ought to be printed in orange ink. Without a blush of shame he inverts the social order, representing Rome on top and Geneva underneath, whereas throughout the history of the Protestant Plantation the exact opposite has been true. One cannot even call it sleight of hand; it is too brazen. It is, of course, brazenly effective. No more efficacious incitement to mutiny exists, and at Curragh it in fact incited mutiny.

Unless, like the Orangemen, they were creatures of his inversion lens, Kipling had no empathy for underdogs. As Americans we too seldom have the frisson of seeing a man hit when he is down. We have our own version of that old lie the public school ethos. Kipling does not hesitate to hit below the belt. It is one of the great pleasures of reading him. Anyone who does not enjoy the following lines is guilty of self-deception.

> Because he served a master
> Before his Kingship came,
> And hid in all disaster
> Behind his master's name,
> So, when his Folly opens
> The unnecessary hells,
> A Servant when He Reigneth
> Throws the blame on someone else.
>
> His vows are lightly spoken,
> His faith is hard to bind,
> His trust is easy broken,

He fears his fellow-kind.
The nearest mob will move him
To break the pledge he gave—
Oh, a Servant when He Reigneth
Is more than ever slave!
["'A Servant When He Reigneth'"]

Kipling's position was simple: society is by definition a structure; a structure by definition has a top and a bottom.

I am no authority on Anglo-Indian society, whose hierarchies make the Faubourg Saint Germain seem democratic, but I am prepared to guess that so indifferently confessional a writer as Kipling lets us see his parents' stratum of it infrequently. At this distance, we cannot know whether the young genius of the short story regarded himself as social climbing or as slumming. He was an Englishman; it had to be one or the other. Certainly we glimpse the elder Kiplings in "The Exiles' Line" (the Pacific and Orient), but the gentle parody of *The Rubáiyát of Omar Khayyám* prevents too close an identification or too heady a dose of nostalgia.

Yea, heedless of the shuttle through the loom
The flying keels fulfil the web of doom.
   Sorrow or shouting—what is that to them?
Make out the cheque that pays for cabin-room!

And how so many score of times ye flit
With wife and babe and caravan of kit,
   Not all thy travels past shall lower one fare,
Not all thy tears abate one pound of it.

. . . .

Indeed, indeed from that same line we swear
Off for all time, and mean it when we swear;
   And then, and then we meet the Quartered Flag,
And, surely for the last time, pay the fare.

. . . .

But we, the gipsies of the East, but we—
Waifs of the land and wastrels of the sea—
   Come nearer home beneath the Quartered Flag
Than ever home shall come to such as we.

The camp is struck, the bungalow decays,
Dead friends and houses desert mark our ways,
   Till sickness send us down to Prince's Dock
To meet the changeless use of many days.

Bound in the wheel of Empire, one by one,
The chain-gangs of the East from sire to son,
    The Exiles' Line takes out the exiles' line
And ships them homeward when their work is done.

How runs the old indictment? "Dear and slow,"
So much and twice so much. We gird, but go.
    For all the soul of our sad East is there,
Beneath the house-flag of the P. & O.

His final degree of contempt, at "home," he reserves for the Picts, who, one assumes, are reporters of the Liberal fortnightlies as distinguished from right-thinking newspaper journalists, of whom, till the end, Kipling regarded himself as one.

Rome never looks where she treads.
    Always her heavy hooves fall
On our stomachs, our hearts or our heads;
    And Rome never heeds when we bawl.
Her sentries pass on—that is all,
    And we gather behind them in hordes,
And plot to reconquer the Wall,
    With only our tongues for our swords.

We are the Little Folk—we!
    Too little to love or to hate.
Leave us alone and you'll see
    How we can drag down the State!
We are the worm in the wood!
    We are the rot at the root!
We are the taint in the blood!
    We are the thorn in the foot!

Mistletoe killing an oak—
    Rats gnawing cables in two—
Moth making holes in a cloak—
    How they much love what they do!
Yes—and we Little Folk too,
    We are busy as they—
Working our works out of view—
    Watch, and you'll see it some day!

No indeed! We are not strong,
    But we know Peoples that are.
Yes, and we'll guide them along
    To smash and destroy you in War!
We shall be slaves just the same?
    Yes, we have always been slaves,

But you—you will die of the shame,
And then we shall dance on your graves!
["A Pict Song"]

The distinction is one he makes himself.

Who once has stood through the loaded hour
Ere, roaring like the gale,
The Harrild and the Hoe devour
Their league-long paper-bale,
And has lit his pipe in the morning calm
That follows the midnight stress—
He hath sold his heart to the old Black Art
We call the daily Press.

. . . .

The Pope may launch his Interdict,
The Union its decree,
But the bubble is blown and bubble is pricked
By Us and such as We.
Remember the battle and stand aside
While Thrones and Powers confess
That King over all the children of pride
Is the Press—the Press—the Press!
["The Press"]

Nevertheless in confronting his inventions of a patriotism for the England to which he came as a stranger you cannot put down a suspicion that the person he is struggling hardest to convince is himself. *Songs Written for C. R. L. Fletcher's "A History of England"* are just that, poems of the schoolroom, although the hatcheting of James I is justly famous ("A shifty mother's shiftless son") and "The Roman Centurion's Song" is one to which any regular can respond ("I've served in Britain forty years. What should I do in Rome?"). The poems in which he uses Rome as a convenient if transparent metaphor are without exception more successful than those in which he speaks of England without intervention. His poems on the countryside are full of flowers, and might have been written by a garden-club lady. A very talented garden-club lady, of course. One hint of the tropics can wipe them out. The thoughts of the reader, and the writer, turn "To the night, to the palms in the moonlight, / And the fire-fly in the cane" ("The Native-Born"). It is the poems from the other side of his mouth that carry a lively conviction.

. . . awful old England again,
And 'ouses both sides of the street,

And 'edges two sides of the lane,
And the parson an' gentry between,
. . . the sunshine of England is pale,
And the breezes of England are stale,
An' there's somethin' gone small with the lot.
["Chant-Pagan"]

Nor does he always speak through and of the lower orders.

For undemocratic reasons and for motives not of State.
They arrive at their conclusions—largely inarticulate.
Being void of self-expression they confide their views to none;
But sometimes in a smoking-room, one learns why things were done.

Yes, sometimes in the smoking-room, through clouds of "Ers" and "Ums,"
Obliquely and by inference, illumination comes,
On some step that they have taken, or some action they approve,
Embellished with the *argot* of the Upper Fourth Remove.

In telegraphic sentences, half nodded to their friends,
They hint a matter's inwardness—and there the matter ends.
["The Puzzler"]

I have objected to Kipling's over-obvious rhythm, of which the quotation just above is an extreme example. In his defense I have to say if he used it the reason has to be that he liked it. He was capable of rhythm as subtle and as forceful as any poet who ever wrote. A stanza from "'Late Came the God'" is as finished as anything in Dryden and not nearly so empty.

Late came the God, having sent his forerunners who were
  not regarded—
 Late, but in wrath;
Saying: "The wrong shall be paid, the contempt be rewarded
 On all that she hath."
He poisoned the blade and struck home, the full bosom receiving
The wound and the venom in one, past cure or relieving.

The beginning of "A British-Roman Song" is equally accomplished.

My father's father saw it not,
  And I, belike, shall never come
To look on that so-holy spot—
    The very Rome—

Crowned by all Time, all Art, all Might,
  The equal work of Gods and Man,

City beneath whose oldest height—
The Race began!

Kipling, who was not a university man, could make the classics work for him more vividly than Housman, who was no doubt inhibited by professional considerations. The line in "The Prairie," with its strict adherence to the root meaning of the Greek in "telephone" instead of the onomatopoetic but inaccurate "telegraph" (for the sound of the horse's hooves), is beyond praise. The double take it provokes in the reader endows the line with a winning freshness.

I have no intention of venturing into the abyss of sexual politics, except to remind you that "The Vampire" is not about women. It is about a woman (you do remember the years we waste and the tears we waste? The rag, the bone, and the hank of hair?). To compensate, there is "The First Chantey." The effect is somewhat as if one of those overpowering but underoccupied women in the paintings of Arnold Böcklin had gone into action.

Mine was the woman to me, darkling I found her:
Haling her dumb from the camp, held her and bound her.
Hot rose her tribe on our track ere I had proved her;
Hearing her laugh in the gloom, greatly I loved her.

Swift through the forest we ran, none stood to guard us,
Few were my people and far; then the flood barred us—
Him whom we call Son of the Sea, sullen and swollen.
Panting we waited the death, stealer and stolen.

Yet ere they came to my lance laid for the slaughter,
Lightly she leaped to a log lapped in the water;
Holding on high and apart skins that arrayed her,
Called she the God of the Wind that He should aid her.

Life had the tree at that word (Praise we the Giver!),
Otter-like left he the bank for the full river.
Far fell their axes behind, flashing and ringing,
Wonder was on me and fear—yet she was singing!

Low lay the land we had left. Now the blue bound us,
Even the floor of the Gods level around us.
Whisper there was not, nor word, shadow nor showing,
Till the light stirred on the deep, glowing and growing.

Then did He leap to his place flaring from under,
He the Compeller, the Sun, bared to our wonder.
Nay, not a league from our eyes blinded with gazing,
Cleared He the Gate of the World, huge and amazing!

This we beheld (and we live)—the Pit of the Burning!
Then the God spoke to the tree for our returning;
Back to the beach of our flight, fearless and slowly,
Back to our slayers went he; but we were holy.

Men that were hot in that hunt, women that followed,
Babes that were promised our bones, trembled and wallowed!
Over the necks of the Tribe crouching and fawning—
Prophet and priestess we came back from the dawning!

"Holding on high and apart from the skins that arrayed her" reduces the poem momentarily to a period piece—after all, it is 1896, and a matron cannot be running around naked—but the stanza on the sunrise is very twentieth-century indeed. "He the Compeller, the Sun" might be distilled—and clarified—from Valéry. The Aristotelian Prime Mover has not often made so dramatic an entrance: Zarathustra goes to sea. The notion of woman as the vessel of natural wisdom is present but not insisted upon. Notice that the Prophet, like the House of Peers in *Iolanthe,* has done nothing in particular. He is altogether satellite to the Priestess. Very few poets before Kipling or after could so deftly have reinforced the straightforward narrative with the symbolic or the symbolic with the straightforward, or prevented the quasi-archaic idiom from bringing the forward motion to a halt. Imagine the prepositional-phrase inflation to which the dactylic meter would have reduced Byron or Swinburne. Kipling's concision here is a rebuke to both, and, for that matter, to Tennyson.

The poem is one which Carl Jung and R. S. Baden-Powell could have enjoyed equally, and you can read as much or as little into it as you wish. Is it, Herr Doktor, a rewrite of the Tree of Knowledge with a happy ending? Do not tell us that the entire poem can be read as a metaphor of the sex act. We are perfectly aware of it, and so was the least perceptive Edwardian Boy Scout. Knowing Kipling's enthusiasm for machines, we can also inscribe it as a triumph of technology, although the trampling down of the crouching and fawning by the scientific elite will no doubt make some of us more ill at ease than it made the author. Then there are journeys of rebirth, and *ewige Wiederkehr* . . .

Kipling's most telling comment on sexual politics is stated much more briefly.

'E was warned agin 'er—
  That's what made 'im look;
She was warned agin 'im—
  That is why she took.
["The Sergeant's Weddin' "]

Without the Jungian cargo, the boat is reinvented in "The Junk and the Dhow."

One-piecee stick-pidgen—two-piecee man.
Straddle-um—paddle-um—push-um off to sea.
That way Foleign Debbil-boat began.
But before, and before, and ever so long before
Any shape of sailing-craft was known,
The Junk and the Dhow had a stern and a bow,
And a mast and a sail of their own—ahoy! alone!
As they crashed across the oceans on their own!

. . . .

The Junk and the Dhow, though they look like anyhow,
Had rudders reaching deep below their keel—ahoy! akeel!
As they laid the Eastern Seas beneath their keel!

As a text, it is the discourse of the margins versified. Pidgins and creoles are highly political, having been wrangled, no more decisively than anything else, on the floor of the U.N. It is the wrangle over dialect (see above) carried to its logical or, if you prefer, illogical conclusion. Here we presumably have a creole, since it is in the nature of a pidgin that it has no native speakers, and we are in the speaker's stream (Equatorial Current?) of consciousness. Before you take irreversible offense, consider that what the poem actually says is the precise opposite of what one expects of an ethnocentrist. I shall not defend the appearance of the junk—in matters of naval design I am mostly ethnocentric—but I cannot believe that so perceptive an observer as Kipling found the dhow anything but beautiful. I must tell you, however, that its only other appearance in the oeuvre is as a slave ship, in "The Rhyme of the Three Captains": "He is lazar within and lime without; ye can nose him far enow, / For he carries the taint of a musky ship—the reek of the slaver's dhow." Smells are surer than sights or sounds, and Kipling, unlike Burton, had as little enthusiasm for Arabs as for Africans.

Whatever our own opinion, we must defer to Kipling's in matters of ships and the sea. He wrote more poems about seafaring life than he wrote about India. I have made an actual count. The figures, if you are interested, are seventy-one for the Raj and eighty-two for the Jolly Roger. Besides steamers, junks, and dhows, he covered cattle boats, freighters, galleys, galleons, full riggers, sealers, and Viking long ships. Nor is this mention in passing. Each has its separate poem. Among modern warships he treated cruisers, destroyers, mine-layers, mine-sweepers, and submarines. I do not mention canoes, kayaks, paddle wheelers, gunboats, Nile steamers, and other riverine craft. "The Three-Decker" is a ruefully amusing, affectionate poem in which the high-Victorian three-volume novel and the full-rigged ship are equated. It tells us as much about the genre as the Michael Sadleir bibliography does, and in a single line it fixes the tall ship forever: "You'll see her tiering canvas in sheeted silver spread." The treatment in "The Derelict" owes nothing to "The Rime of the Ancient Mariner."

> Blind in the hot blue ring
> Through all my points I swing—
> Swing and return to shift the sun anew.
> Blind in my well-known sky
> I hear the stars go by,
> Mocking the prow that cannot hold one true.

Kipling's sailors, like Conrad's, are at their most memorable on shore.

> . . . was there ever sailor free to choose
> That didn't settle somewhere near the sea?
>
> . . . .
>
> He knows he's never going on no cruise—
> He knows he's done and finished with the sea;
> And yet he likes to feel she's there to use—
> If he should ask her—as she used to be.
>
> Even though she cost him all he had to lose,
> Even though she made him sick to hear or see,
> Still, what she left of him will mostly choose
> Her skirts to sit by. How comes such to be?
>
> ["The Virginity"]

For the answer we do not have to look far.

> I was not four and twenty then—Ye wadna judge a child?
> I'd seen the Tropics first that run—new fruit, new smells, new air—
> How could I tell—blind-fou wi' sun—the Deil was lurkin' there?
> By day like playhouse-scenes the shore slid past our sleepy eyes;
> By night those soft, lasceevious stars leered from those velvet skies,
> In port (we used no cargo-steam) I'd daunder down the streets—
> An ijjit grinnin' in a dream—for shells an' parrakeets,
> An' walkin'-sticks o' carved bamboo an' blowfish stuffed an' dried—
> Fillin my bunk wi' rubbishry the Chief put overside.
>
> ["McAndrew's Hymn"][3]

Later in "McAndrew's Hymn" Kipling introduces one of his great inspirations: a siren song sung in a Scots burr. It could have occurred to no one else; no one else could have brought it off. It is funny and moving

3. One might mention in connection with shore leave that Kipling is the supreme poet of hangover. He treats it at length in "La Nuit Blanche," "The Shut-Eye Sentry," and "Cells."

and seductive together; and, I might add, it advances the action. As for his sea itself, "the old gray widow-maker" has entered the language; his southern sea ought to: "The orderly clouds of the Trades, the ridged, roaring sapphire thereunder" ("The Sea and the Hills"). Why had none of his sea poems the popularity of his writing from the subcontinent? The technical content in them can be high, but the military vocabulary and the Hindi in *Barrack-room Ballads* were not common knowledge either. Probably readers are more at ease with out and out exotica than with something they feel they ought to know but don't.

Nothing is more difficult to describe than description, but since it is the basis of all writing, and since Kipling's sets a standard, we must make an effort. We can say at once that the best description is brief. In poetry as in prose, the moment it overstays its welcome we begin to skip. Extended Homeric similes are the least evocative. I privately suspect these are interpolations, or extensions, from other hands. Homer himself did not need them. The essentially Homeric is not in the great set-pieces that halt the action but in the brilliantly efficient single lines that move it along, hitting off description as they go.

> . . . the wind caught, booming in the sail,
> And a flushing wave sang backward from the bow.
> [*Odyssey*]

> And the savor curled in crooked smoke toward heaven
> [*Iliad*][4]

Communication is perfectly possible; across four thousand years, Homer speaks to us more clearly than the deconstructionists. All nineteenth-century poets read Homer; only Kipling learned from him. Or learned the right things from him. If *Sohrab and Rustum* were in Greek we should not mistake it, nor any line of it, for Homer.

Obviously, a great deal of our pleasure in description depends on the thing being described. We can neither see nor describe things that now exist chiefly to be looked at. Venice and Yosemite are good examples. If we are reasonably lucky Venice will sink and glaciers will return to Yosemite. Until then nothing can be done. It is a pity the floodlights at Niagara Falls have become so tasteful. When they were in the colors of a rotating lamp the falls were worth visiting, which is to say that Kipling's engineers are more useful, visually, than Henry James' artists. By their aid Homer's line is updated, in "The Long Trail": "And the steady fore-foot snores through the planet-powdered floors." Of course, like artists, they have their failures. Pollution is not new: "The cooking-smoke of even rose and weltered and hung low" ("With Scindia to Delhi").

4. Both lines are quoted in the translations of Robert Fitzgerald.

The injunction of the creative writing class—that description should appeal to as many senses as possible—can backfire. The warmèd jewels in "The Eve of St. Agnes" bring to mind the twitch and the gooseflesh that must have risen as the chilly necklace was placed. Nor must description always be concrete. Abstraction works if it works. Pound's "bewildering Spring" puts profusion in front of us in a way that no enumeration of forsythia and dogwood could, just as "orderly" spaces the clouds for us without the necessity of a meteorological chart. Having said unflattering things about Yeats, I am pleased to say that in "the waters' drowsy blaze" he does not need flattering. Those who have the gift can articulate the same observation not identically but equally well.

> Dawn off the Foreland—the young flood making
>   Jumbled and short and steep—
> Black in the hollows and bright where it's breaking—
> ["Mine Sweepers"]

> . . . a calm darkens among water lights . . .
> [Wallace Stevens, "Sunday Morning"]

The least infusion of the sublime into description will cause us not only to skip but to skip eight and ten pages at a time. Goethe and Shelley are barely readable; or rather, instantly readable. The absolute absence of the sublime undoubtedly gave Kipling his original boost. Perhaps good description is like the art of the fugue. There are no rules, only examples.

For a writer there is one advantage in identifying with the political right: critics do not search in your work for folk sources. Nothing panics criticism like an original, and Kipling was utterly that. Grasping at straws, his early critics seized at the possibility that his verses had affinities with music-hall songs. Do not believe it for a moment. What opportunity would the child in the House of Desolation or the young man in Lahore have had to go to music halls? The songs he might have learned from were too racy to have much sale as sheet music, besides which, the most popular performers preferred to keep their material in manuscript. It was their livelihood. There is also internal evidence. Kipling did not count his syllables. When Arthur Sullivan got ready to set "The Absent-Minded Beggar" he must have longed for you know who. "Mandalay" did not become a parlor song until 1907, and Oley Speaks, through no coincidence, set only the stanzas in which the syllable placement *is* identical. That euphoric idyll "Danny Deever" would, as the elder O'Neill feared of his son's plays, send the audience home to commit suicide. It belongs where it has its survival, as an encore in the concert hall. After an evening of Hugo Wolf it can seem comforting. Kipling may have wished to crack the music halls by aping their manner, but that is quite a different thing from owing to them. "Soldiers of the Queen" is imitated from Kipling, not vice versa. Kipling in fact owed to the most productive and ingenious half-century in the history of English light verse, that which immediately preceded his own birth. I for one am ready to concede that he made the distinction between verse and poetry meaningless (it may have been anyway), although T. S. Eliot got hideously hung up on this nonissue in trying to deal with it. But then, hang-ups were Eliot's thing. On the occasions, and they are not few, when Edwin Arlington Robinson tried to imitate Kipling's quasi-theatrical manner, you see how much surer Kipling's touch in this respect was. His masterpiece in unequivocally light verse is "The Prodigal Son."

My father glooms and advises me,
My brother sulks and despises me,
And my Mother catechises me.
Till I want to go out and swear.
And, in spite of the butler's gravity,
I know that the servants have it I
Am a monster of moral depravity
And I'm damned if I think it's fair!

. . . .

So I was a mark for plunder at once,
And lost my cash (can you wonder?) at once,
But I didn't give up and knock under at once.
I worked in the Yards, for a spell,
Where I spent my nights and my days with hogs,
And shared their milk and maize with hogs
Till, I guess, I have learned what pays with hogs
And—I have that knowledge to sell!

So back I go to my job again,
Not so easy to rob again,
Or quite so ready to sob again
On any neck that's around.
I'm leaving, Pater. Good-bye to you!
God bless, you, Mater! I'll write to you . . .
I wouldn't be impolite to you,
But, Brother, you *are* a hound!

Inevitably, there is a politics of poetry. To his credit, Kipling took no part in it. Had he wished to, he was formidably armed, but he was too famous, too rich, and too talented to care. As if to prove he could, he wrote two poems in free verse, and they are among his best. "The Runes on Weland's Sword" is in the manner we associate with H. D. and the imagists of the 1920s. It differs from them in sticking to a straightforward serial syntax, and in saying something. It may be an argument for increased naval appropriations.

To gather Gold
At the world's end
I am sent.

The Gold I gather
Comes into England
Out of deep Water.

Like a shining Fish
Then it descends
Into deep Water.

. . . .

The Gold I gather
Is drawn up
Out of deep Water.

Like a shining Fish
Then it descends
Into deep Water.

One is surprised to see a Teutonophobe capitalizing so many of his nouns. His other experiment, and it is wholly successful, is in the extended line of Walt Whitman. As he covered himself in the first example by openly describing it as runic, he covers himself this time by presenting the poem as the work of an unlettered youth. It is from the short story "The Finest Story in the World," in which it is dictated from the beyond. So Whitman would have been wise to leave himself an out. One would say Mrs. Yeats learned from it, except she did not learn enough. Again, Kipling writes in complete sentences, one of the last practitioners of *vers libre* to do so.

We fainted with our chins on the oars and you did not see that
we were idle, for we still swung to and fro.
Will you never let us go?
The salt made the oar-handles like shark-skin; our knees were
cut to the bone with salt-cracks; our hair was stuck to
our foreheads; and our lips were cut to the gums, and you
whipped us because we could not row.
Will you never let us go?
But, in a little time, we shall run out of the port-holes as the water
runs along the oar-blade, and though you tell the others

to row after us you will never catch us till you catch the
oar-thresh and tie up the winds in the belly of the sail.
Aho!
Will you never let us go?

["Song of the Galley-Slaves"]

On the evidence here, the beyond has no more interest in the sublime than we have, although the soul escaping "as the water runs along the oar-blade" oddly foreshadows Ezra Pound and "The Tomb at Akr Çaar"; perhaps even the Pound of the *Cantos*.

I cannot prove that "The Bees and the Flies" was written to make the Georgians look ridiculous—it predates the first of their anthologies by four years—but it has that happy result. I read it annually as a corrective to Sturge Moore. It is paraphrased from Virgil's *Georgics*.

A farmer of the Augustan Age
Perused in Virgil's golden page
The story of the secret won
From Proteus by Cyrene's son—
How the dank sea-god showed the swain
Means to restore his hives again.
More briefly, how a slaughtered bull
Breeds honey by the bellyful.

The egregious rustic put to death
A bull by stopping of its breath,
Disposed the carcass in a shed
With fragrant herbs and branches spread,
And having well performed the charm,
Sat down to wait the promised swarm.

Nor waited long. The God of Day
Impartial, quickening with his ray
Evil and good alike, beheld
The carcass—and the carcass swelled.
Big with new birth the belly heaves.
Beneath its screen of scented leaves.
Past any doubt, the bull conceives!

The farmer bids men bring more hives
To house the profit that arrives;
Prepares on pan, and key and kettle,
Sweet music that shall make 'em settle.
But when to crown the work he goes,
Gods! What a stink salutes his nose!

Where are the honest toilers? Where
The gravid mistress of their care?

A busy scene, indeed, he sees,
But not a sign or sound of bees.
Worms of the riper grave unhid
By any kindly coffin-lid,

Obscene and shameless to the light,
Seethe in insatiate appetite,
Through putrid offal, while above
The hissing blow-fly seeks his love,
Whose offspring, supping where they supt,
Consume corruption twice corrupt.

The couplets are as skillfully handled as any from the eighteenth century, the eighteenth century of Jonathan Swift, and one's admiration is increased by the fact that the effects are made and the material treated in four feet, not five. "The God of Day / Impartial, quickening with his ray / Evil and good alike" is He the Compeller compelling. The unexpected runover from "day" to "impartial" and the inversion of the foot with "evil" demonstrate an imagination and poise, a self-confidence that should again force anyone, including this writer, to rethink the stereotype of Kipling as a metrist of the rough and ready. The rough and ready, the crudity, if you like, is in his moral perceptions. The phrase was not available to him, but the lack did not prevent him from depending on situational ethics: what philosophy has for the two sides of its mouth. However, morality in any form obtrudes less often into his poems than into his fiction, where it can hardly be avoided.

Rudyard Kipling was one of those fewest writers as much at home in poetry as in prose, and, as you care to look at it, the most ambivalent or the most ambidextrous among them. The usual dichotomy is that one medium will show us only the writer's workshop; to glimpse his psyche we have to go to the other. Even in so balanced a poet-novelist as Thomas Hardy, anyone concludes early on that, for him, poetry was the more intimate utterance, just as, for Melville, it was prose. For Kipling it is not possible to say. Many of his best poems were printed as chapter headings to some of his best stories ("Late Came the God" heads "Wish House") without compromising the independence of either. Each can stand absolutely alone; they do not even especially illuminate each other, nor is there any suggestion of using up leftovers; and from the first moment of Kipling's fame there was no need to use the prose to give the poetry wider exposure. Toward the end of his career the opposite may have been true. Many have written of him as a deeply divided man, and he was—so was Leo Tolstoy—but one cannot speak of things done with his right hand or his left hand, and no one did more to break down the artificial division between "poetic" and "prosaic" subject matter. I should hazard a guess, and no more than a guess, that he wrote poetry or prose depending on which he had a commission for.

Neither talent deserted him. His late work is in no sense a falling off, although, in the poems, it is not a deepening either. The response to the physical world in the "Brazilian Verses" of 1927 is as ready, and the expression of it as fresh, as in the colonial ballads of forty years earlier. "A Song of Bananas" has one of the miraculous images in the whole of poetry.

> Little birds inhabit there, simple townsmen all—
>   Jewelled things no bigger than a bee;
> And the opal butterflies plane and settle, flare and rise,
>   Through the low-arched greenery,
>   (That is malachite and jade of the sea.)

He works the miracle by his old technique of overkill: the description in the third line of the stanza applies both to the swarm and to the individual butterfly. At this latest date he does not resort to that weariest of lyric formulas, I saw *x* and I thought *y*. He creates a structure; that is, he externalizes.

> "Poison of asps is under our lips"?
>   Why do you wrench them apart?
> To learn how the venom makes and drips
>   And works its way to the heart?
>
> It is unjust that when we have done
>   All that a serpent should,
> You gather our poisons, one by one,
>   And thin them out to your good.
>
> ["'Poison of Asps'"]

If the old self and the young self of the Beerbohm cartoon had each a muse hovering overhead, Max would have had to make those muses identical.

Kipling, like Scripture, can be quoted to any purpose. To infuriate those who objected to TV's *Amerika:*

> When the Cambrian Measures were forming, They promised
>   perpetual peace.
> They swore, if we gave them our weapons, that the wars of the
>   tribes would cease.
> But when we disarmed They sold us and delivered us bound to
>   our foe,
> And the Gods of the Copybook Headings said: "*Stick to the*
>   *Devil you know.*"
>
> ["The Gods of the Copybook Headings"]

Or to reinforce those—the same media, possibly the same persons—who become exercised over the slaughter of baby seals.

> I meet my mates in the morning, a broken, scattered band.
> Men shoot us in the water and club us on the land;
> Men drive us to the Salt House like silly sheep and tame,
> And still we sing Lukannon—before the sealers came.
>
> ["'Lukannon'"]

Like Wagner, he will be an embarrassment if you think artists should hold exemplary views. If you are willing to take him in his variety you will enjoy him as the astounding creative phenomenon he was. Should his politics, fifty years after his death, be an obstacle for you still, I can tell you—it is no secret—that he was a direct influence on a phenomenon of very different persuasion, Bertolt Brecht.[5] We need not pretend that either was an especially attractive personality. It may always be a secret that Kipling, however, in very unlikely company, was the greatest imagist of them all.

5. Just how direct has not been remarked. The influence is not confined to use of the vernacular, nor to the vaguely Indian setting of *Mann ist Mann.* "Das Lied von der Unzulanglichkeit" is lifted from "The Wishing-Caps."

> If I don't run after Fortune,
> Fortune must run after me.

Both the "Abschiedslied" from the second act of *Dreigroschenoper* and "Surabaya Johnny" (from *Happy End*) are from "Mary, Pity Women."

> You call yourself a man
> For all you used to swear,
> An' leave me, as you can,
> My certain shame to bear?
> I 'ear! You do not care—
> You done the worst you know.
> I 'ate you, grinnin' there. . . .
> Ah, Gawd, I love you so!
>
> *Nice while it lasted, an' now it is over—*
> *Tear out your 'eart an' good-bye to your lover!*
> *What's the use o' grievin', when the mother that bore you*
> *(Mary, pity women?) knew it all before you?*

I have quoted the lines without omission, in the exact format in which they appear in the poem.

Writing War Poetry Like a Woman

Susan Schweik

Like the military itself, traditionally the most overtly male of preserves, the canon of the poetry of war presented in recent bibliographies or anthologies is especially and intensely androcentric. In the modern war poem as it is usually defined, the experience of the masculine soldier and the voice of the masculine author predominate. A reader of didactic discussions of war poetry written during the Second World War might therefore be surprised at the frequency with which American literary critics held up a text written by a woman as the single, paradigmatic, exemplary war poem: Marianne Moore's "In Distrust of Merits." W. H. Auden, for instance, called "In Distrust" "the best of . . . all" war poems of World War II.[1] Moore was so lionized on the American home front, her poem so praised, that Randall Jarrell began his famous critical answer to "In Distrust" with a mock-apologetic "Miss Moore is reviewed not as a poet but as an institution," going on to cite, acerbically, a reviewer who had called Moore "the greatest living poet" and then demanded that she be "placed in Fort Knox for the duration."[2]

The uses of Moore as institution, for the duration, deserve closer study than Jarrell's ironies might suggest; they shed light on assumptions prevalent in both the 1940s and the 1980s about what "war" means, what

1. W. H. Auden, review of *Nevertheless,* by Marianne Moore, *New York Times,* 15 Oct. 1944, p. 20.

2. Randall Jarrell, "Poetry in War and Peace," *Partisan Review* (Winter 1945); reprinted in *Kipling, Auden and Co.: Essays and Reviews, 1935–1964* (New York, 1980), p. 127. All further references to this essay, abbreviated "PWP," will be included in the text.

"war poetry" means, and where "woman" stands in relation to both. In the following pages, I shall be concerned specifically with how Moore's work invokes and attempts to revoke traditional formulations of sexual difference in wartime, and with how Jarrell's responses undertake a related task. I shall also be concerned, more broadly, with constructions of gender in theoretical controversies during the early forties over the criteria by which war poetry should be judged, particularly over standards of authorial credibility. These arguments matter because they set terms which still tend to define the parameters of current aesthetic and political evaluations of the war poem—values shared by texts as magisterial as the recent *Oxford Book of War Poetry* and as adversarial as collections of poems by Vietnam War protesters or veterans. But a look back to the volatile home-front debates about the decorum of the growing subgenre of war poetry reveals not only what most contemporary anthologists and critics of war literature have inherited from the Second World War period but also what they have attempted to discard or repress: the active presence of women *as subjects* in the discourse of war.

In the forties, many critics seized on "In Distrust of Merits" as a way of reforming the canon of war poetry, a canon till then largely shaped by the masculine "soldier poems" of British Great War poets such as Wilfred Owen and Siegfried Sassoon. First World War soldier poetry had, of course, never been a stable commodity; it could never be guaranteed to be written by a genuine soldier from a genuine trench, as Robert Graves' pointed summary of the tradition, written in 1948, makes clear:

> When war poetry became a fashion in 1915, a good deal of it was written imitatively by civilians who regretted that age or unfitness prevented them from also 'making the supreme sacrifice.' . . . Also, many soldiers wrote as though they had seen more of the war than they really had. Robert Nichols, for instance, whose brief service in France . . . was ended by sickness . . . scored a great success . . . as a crippled warrior, reading . . . to University and women's club audiences.[3]

These falsehoods only go to prove, rather than render suspicious, the power of the standards for war poems which became normative in the university and the women's club during and after the Great War. Within the developing tradition of war poetry, those poems were privileged

3. Robert Graves, "The Poets of World War II," *The Common Asphodel: Collected Essays on Poetry 1922–1949* (London, 1949), p. 308.

Susan Schweik is assistant professor of English at the University of California, Berkeley. She is at work on a book manuscript entitled *A Word No Man Can Say for Us: American Women Poets and the Second World War.*

which were, or seemed to be, rooted in the original ground of men's literal combat experience. War poems should be backed, as Sassoon described Owen's work, by the authority of experience of the infantry soldier.[4]

In World War II, however, that lonely masculine authority of experience—the bitter authority derived from direct exposure to violence, injury, and mechanized terror—was rapidly dispersing among general populations. Graves notes, with some discomfort, that the Second World War soldier "cannot even feel that his rendezvous with death is more certain than that of his Aunt Fanny, the firewatcher."[5] American culture was, obviously, characterized by far greater disjunctions between male and female "experience" of war than the British blitz society Graves describes, and the modern tradition of soldier poetry, with its ironic emphasis on unmendable gaps between the soldier author and the civilian reader, retained its strong influence. Still, public discussions of war and literature in the United States dwell frequently on the new conjunctions between civilians and soldiers, front and home front, and men and women, focusing on their shared morale or effort as well as on their common deprivation and vulnerability.

In a war newly perceived as "total," Moore's work could exemplify the power of a representative civilian voice. It could also represent modernism provisionally embracing realist and didactic functions, coming round to correcting earlier trends toward self-referentiality. Thus Richard Eberhart, arguing in his introduction to a well-known anthology of war poetry that "the spectator, the contemplator, the opposer of war have their hours with the enemy no less than uniformed combatants," praises Moore for abandoning the "complacencies of the peignoir" to write "In Distrust of Merits."[6] His phrasing links Moore with another civilian war poet, Wallace Stevens; by dressing Moore in Stevens' peignoir in order to show her doffing it, he represents her as a formerly feminine object of desire who has emerged from the coquetries of her sex into a new, superior, gender-free authority. Now, Eberhart argues, "the bloodshed of which she writes has caused her to break through the decorative surface of her verse" to a "different kind of utterance." For Eberhart, the poem's value lies in its violation of Moore's usual mannered aestheticism. She "breaks through" a feminine surface, as if puncturing skin, but the result is not a wound but a mouth: a "different kind of utterance," in which "the meaning has dictated the sincerity."[7] Oscar Williams, in the preface to a comparable anthology, also reads the poem as a model of

4. See Siegfried Sassoon, introduction to Wilfred Owen, *Poems* (London, 1920).

5. Graves, "The Poets of World War II," p. 310.

6. Richard Eberhart, "Preface: Attitudes to War," in *War and the Poet: An Anthology of Poetry Expressing Man's Attitudes to War from Ancient Times to the Present,* ed. Eberhart and Selden Rodman (New York, 1945), pp. xv, xiii.

7. Ibid., p. xiii.

transparent earnestness, offering it as a solution to the problem of Edna St. Vincent Millay, the "bad" woman war poet who is excoriated in these discussions as often as Moore is extolled. Describing one of Millay's war poems as "a sentimental piece of verse written by an American civilian, designed to be read by . . . people themselves out of danger because they are protected by a wall of living young flesh, much of which will be mangled," Williams contrasts Moore's "In Distrust of Merits":

> But with true poets the poetry is in the pity . . .
>
> I ask the reader to study closely a war poem peculiarly fitted to illustrate my present thesis. It is also written by a woman, a civilian. "In Distrust of Merits," by Marianne Moore, is the direct communication of honest feeling by one ready to search her own heart to discover the causes of war and accept her full share of responsibility for its effects.[8]

Moore's poem was indeed "peculiarly fitted to illustrate" Williams' anxious argument for a civilian war poetry, a pure "heart" which could express the "pity" of war—Owen's famous dictum—with no more false sentiment and no more indirection than a soldier poet would bring to the subject. As peculiarly fitted for illustration as the poem was, however, it could not transcend the intensities of the debates in which it was held up as an example, and it could not render the disputations over literary representation of war any less likely or necessary. "In Distrust of Merits" is no less didactic, no less overtly ideological, and no less a marked product of its own time than the patriotic poetry Millay wrote under the guidance of the Writers' War Board. Later readers, in fact, may well be more struck by what Moore's and Millay's war poems have in common than by the ways in which they diverge. Contemporary critics of Moore's work tend to dismiss "In Distrust" if they do not ignore it entirely; one of Moore's most sympathetic readers, Bonnie Costello, expresses her distaste in terms which might be used to define Millay's war work: the poem's conventional pronouncements "show too much the pressure of news."[9] This "too much," the offhand signal of shared evaluative norms, adumbrates for Costello's contemporary audience—one composed, presumably, largely of literary critics—a familiar set of postwar aesthetic values. A good poem—that is, a poem unpressured, or pressured just enough—will be cleanly universal and timeless, where "In Distrust" bears too obviously the imprints of an immediate historical and cultural context; it will be neutral, where "In Distrust" is polemical; it will enact poetically, where

8. Oscar Williams, ed., *The War Poets: An Anthology of the War Poetry of the Twentieth Century* (New York, 1945), p. 6.

9. Bonnie Costello, *Marianne Moore: Imaginary Possessions* (Cambridge, Mass., 1981), p. 110.

"In Distrust" spouts off oratorically; it will address an elite readership, where "In Distrust" invites the same kind of attention as the *Saturday Evening Post.*

But in another context—that, for instance, of forums organized during World War II to express and to prove American high culture's commitment to the war effort—a poem may be more likely to be judged uncompelling if it lacks ideological commitment and fails to appeal to a mass audience, if it shows too little "the pressure of news." We can sense the force of the strong demand during the war years for a literature which was overtly topical and politically engaged in Elizabeth Bishop's anxious words to the publisher of her first book of poems in 1945: "The fact that none of these poems deal directly with the war . . . will, I am afraid, leave me open to reproach."[10] Open to reproach then and now, either for its overt political commitment or for its lack of it, an obvious reminder of shifting standards of literary value and of the ideological constitution of poetry, the war poem of the forties often proves embarrassing. It is no surprise that Moore herself, in 1961, dismisses "In Distrust of Merits": "It is sincere but I wouldn't call it a poem. . . . As form, what has it? It is just a protest."[11]

During the forties, critics and anthologists like Williams and Eberhart encouraged their readers to understand Moore's poem as a firm resolution of wartime aesthetic crises. But we need not look later than the war period itself for evidence of "pressure" on and in the poem. Moore's private worksheets point to her own engagement with "In Distrust" as a field of dynamic and unresolved tensions, not to the poem's status as the one calm eye at the core of a storm. And Randall Jarrell's public critique of "In Distrust of Merits" declares a crisis of representation which, Jarrell argues, Moore's poem not only fails to assuage but also exacerbates. For both Moore and Jarrell, the conflicts of writing and reading about war which "In Distrust" provokes arise, particularly, around notions of sexual difference; for both of them, not least of the pressures the poem showed too much was the pressure of gender.

By Moore's own account, "In Distrust" did indeed originate out of the "pressure of the news": she once said that her incentive for writing the poem was a newspaper photograph of a dead soldier.[12] That image remains in the finished poem, flickering at its center: "O / quiet form

10. Elizabeth Bishop to Houghton Mifflin, 22 Jan. 1945, in *Elizabeth Bishop: A Bibliography, 1927–1979,* ed. Candace W. MacMahon (Charlottesville, Va., 1980), p. 8.

11. Marianne Moore, "Interview with Donald Hall," in *A Marianne Moore Reader* (New York, 1961), p. 261.

12. See Laurence Stapleton, *Marianne Moore: The Poet's Advance* (Princeton, N.J., 1978), p. 134.

upon the dust, I cannot / look and yet I must."[13] Like another battlefield image in another Moore war poem, "Keeping Their World Large"—"That forest of white crosses! My eyes won't close to it"—the scene of the dead soldier both repels and compels attention (*CP*, p. 145). These images draw the eye with hypnotic, irrational power and hold it there, trapped in its helpless, frightened gaze at the nightmare facts the pictures represent. Unlike other cultural artifacts represented in dozens of other Moore poems, these printed battle scenes elicit a strong resistance or an inability to attend to them carefully; the eyes try unsuccessfully to close, the face to swerve away.[14] In general, as Costello notes, Moore "is always observing while she is making observations."[15] But this poem seems to represent the process by which its author works as a constant struggle against evasion: here, it suggests, I am always fighting against the desire *not* to observe while I make measured assertions about the meaning of warfare.

Moore's letters and workbooks in the years preceding the publication of "In Distrust of Merits" reveal the force and shape of that struggle. Several developing ideas about war laid the groundwork for the poem's arguments. In 1939, Moore wrote to her brother, who was a naval chaplain on a ship in the Pacific, that in the process of reading Reinhold Niebuhr she had come to the conclusion that "intolerance is at work in us all *in all* countries,—that we ourselves 'persecute' Jews and Negroes & submit to wrongful tyranny. Or at least feel 'superior' in sundry ways."[16] Earlier, in her conversation notebook in June of 1938, Moore had observed: "In ancient times, people (barbarous) razed cities and murdered the innocent. One is faint before it and these people are with us now. One does not feel detached by one's horror—even if they are not of our country. They are *we*. They are of our kind."[17] This sense of war as a self-reflecting fight against personal intolerance shows up in the decisive ending, borrowed from a sermon, of an earlier poem, "The Labors of Hercules," in which one of the almost impossible labors is "to convince snake-charming controversialists / that one keeps on knowing . . . that the German is not a

13. Moore, "In Distrust of Merits," *The Complete Poems of Marianne Moore* (New York, 1967), pp. 136–38. Page references for other poems in this collection, abbreviated *CP*, will be included in the text.

14. Costello describes extensively how the emblems in Moore's poems of "a world already represented" draw "descriptions of the world into a private setting where the world might be brought under imaginary control," epitomizing Moore's method of "imaginary possession" (Costello, *Imaginary Possessions*, p. 6).

15. Costello, *Imaginary Possessions*, p. 38.

16. Quoted in Stapleton, *The Poet's Advance*, p. 130.

17. The quotations from Moore's unpublished material which follow are taken from conversation and reading notebooks in the Moore collection of the Philip H. and A. S. W. Rosenbach Foundation, Philadelphia, Pennsylvania. Excerpts will be cited hereafter as "Rosenbach," followed by their file numbers. This entry is from Rosenbach 1251/1 (conversation notes 1938–1957), dated 10 June 1938.

Hun" (*CP,* p. 53). It appears, too, in the "promise we make to the fighting" in "In Distrust of Merits": "We'll / never hate black, white, red, yellow, Jew, / Gentile, Untouchable."

We can trace in the notebooks the ongoing development of an idea of "inwardness" which becomes the central principle of "In Distrust"; much of this idea, as Laurence Stapleton has determined, derives from and revises conversations Moore had with her mother. On 23 July 1942, she notes down in her reading diary the crucial phrase, "There never was a war that was not inward"; in the same entry, the climactic end of the poem is worked out: "I inwardly did nothing. / O Iscariot-like crime! / Beauty is everlasting / and dust is for a time"; and an entry on 22 March 1943 explains the crime more explicitly than it is defined in the published version of the poem: "Black white red yellow mixed Jew gentile and untouchable—they're begging and I inwardly did nothing. . . ." On a later page, in an undated entry, Moore further explores the value of inward action and inwardness, setting down the following: "Outstanding. Futile word. No indwelling."[18] This comment may be read as a partial gloss on the title of the poem: "merits," which are to be distrusted, are external, static signs of what a culture determines to be "outstanding"; successful "indwelling" struggle, in contrast, secret, dynamic and uncategorizable, cannot be signified in fixed medals or badges. Outward wars, in which men urged to be outstanding try to outstand each other, are caused, so the major argument of "In Distrust" goes, by a failure of each of us to exercise a continual inward struggle against the imperious and aggressive aspects of our own selves. Only by vigilantly practicing a form of inward warfare can we avoid external catastrophe.[19] "It is a violence from within that protects us from a violence without": Moore quotes Stevens approvingly in a wartime review of his work she entitled "There Is a War That Never Ends," adding that Stevens "and the soldier are one."[20] If Stevens was a soldier poet, Moore might be one too, fighting in an ongoing conflict which was no less vital for being intellectual, spiritual, and figurative rather than bodily and literal.

Stevens' concept of inward war offers the imagination and its supreme fictions alone as a way of understanding, transcending, and solving world conflict. Moore's offers more orthodox Christian consolations as well and incorporates ideas of Christian spiritual warfare, as expressed in such conversation notes as the following: "It is not that we fear to have the body struck down from the soul that we hate war, but because man is not complete unless he has the power of peace in his soul" (14 August

18. Rosenbach 1251/12 (reading diary 1942–58), three entries: 23 July 1943; 22 Mar. 1943; undated.

19. For an excellent discussion of "images of sweetened combat" in Moore's work, see Costello, *Imaginary Possessions,* pp. 108–32.

20. Moore, "There Is a War That Never Ends," *Predilections* (New York, 1955), p. 41.

1937); "The one good of war is that it brings people in their helplessness to pray. It keeps people from being satisfied with an indolent peace . . ." (2 November 1935).[21] In "In Distrust," Moore will develop this idea of sacred and inward spiritual warfare in language which openly declares its ties to the authoritative rhetoric of Scripture ("O / Star of David, star of Bethlehem . . .").

But for every self-confident aphorism which generates a legitimate meaning for the war or imposes some kind of order upon it, we can locate others in the notebooks which demonstrate Moore's hesitation and anxiety. Moore can speak emphatically about the symbolic war within, but when she turns to the particular manifestations of the war without—its battles and body counts, the daily events which filled the pages of the newspapers—her voice assumes a deferent and nervous tone. "I:?" reads a mysterious note in the conversation diary for August 1937, continuing, "was the nobly fought for nothing. If they aren't killed they come back maimed or ["considerably weakened" is crossed out here] and disabled prospectively." In September 1940: "May those who fight in squadrons have a vision. We are sending them to their death." In the spring of 1943, amid several pages of scattered notes for the poem, the war within is first figured positively—"how does one resist invasion / but by resistance inwardly?"—but then loses its power, becoming a trap or cage: "Prisoner of inwardness."[22]

A nearby passage exemplifies the difficulty of Moore's struggle to authorize her own voice as representative and universal: "(may) humbly but with—confidence (may as one.) Say OUR."[23] Moore, I believe, is exploring here, amid considerable self-doubt and self-interrogation, the possibility of assuming the voice of a collective "we," a pronoun which would function, as John Ellis has suggested it does in wartime film documentaries, to articulate a nation, or the whole world, "as both actor and observer, enunciator and addressee."[24] "Say our," she orders herself—or recalls someone else's order—after speaking in muted parentheses. But for Moore, who is well aware of distinctions which cannot be entirely erased between herself as American civilian and the young male soldiers whose anonymous forms filled news photographs, the urge to "say our" may be a difficult, dangerous, and even reprehensible ambition. The line which begins, in a preliminary version of "In Distrust of Merits," "*we* are fighting fighting fighting" becomes, in the chastened final version, "they are fighting fighting fighting."[25] "All too literally," goes the epigraph

21. Both entries are taken from Rosenbach 1251/1. On the Christian tradition of spiritual warfare narrative, see Sue Mansfield, *The Gestalts of War: An Inquiry into Its Origins and Meanings as a Social Institution* (New York, 1982), pp. 127–33.

22. Rosenbach 1251/1, dated 9 Aug. 1937; 1251/1, dated 23 Sept. 1940; 1251/12, undated.

23. Rosenbach 1251/12, dated 22 Mar. 1943.

24. John Ellis, "Victory of the Voice?" *Screen* 22, no. 2 (1981): 69.

25. Rosenbach 1251/2, dated 23 July 1942.

of her "Keeping Their World Large," "their flesh and their spirit are our shield" (*CP*, p. 145). The "our" here is a limited, indebted pronoun. The poet who is a civilian and a woman can write of figurative war with aplomb, but of all too literal warfare she is wary and unsure, and she feels herself all too literally to be speaking passively, helplessly. In the context of the war, can a protected American woman "say our"?

"The difficulty is one of language," Moore wrote in one of her reading notebooks, copying a passage from Alexander G. Clifford's *Conquest of North Africa, 1940–1943.* "The facts of modern warfare are outside normal human experience and strictly speaking only the facts of normal human experience are reproductive in words."[26] She went on to write out sections of a review of the book by Colonel Joseph I. Greene: "He shows the highly observant [*sic*] of details that have a special meaning in war: Few things have a smaller comparative secondhand value than battle." These passages, taken together, allow us to differentiate between two kinds of difficulty which, Moore felt, complicated and vexed the representations of war in her poems. One is a universal difficulty inherent in all language, which shapes its vocabulary, according to Clifford's argument, out of an everyday human consensus; it therefore can never "reproduce" modern warfare because modern warfare, by definition, renders the "known" world abnormal and unknowable, completely resistant to mimesis. The other is a difficulty specific to the protected American, who can bring to her war poem no telling details derived from her own experience and who can only describe battle "secondhand," in inadequate comparisons. If the difficulty is one of language, it is also one of gender, of age, of all other specific cultural, psychological, and biographical contexts which determine the exact place of a civilian woman writer.

Women, of course, acted and suffered in the most direct ways in the war of 1939–1945, many American women among them. At the same time, many American men, even many American soldiers, experienced the war no more directly than their average female counterparts.[27] Several well-known soldier poets of the Second World War—Randall Jarrell and Richard Eberhart, for instance—did not actively participate in combat. In the end, though, Jarrell's actual distance from the "front lines" matters very little, while Moore's matters very much. Jarrell and Eberhart were "men as men," speaking for men, and therefore had imaginative right to the voice of the soldier, the terrain of the "front."

26. Rosenbach 1251/12, undated.

27. The feminist historian Susan M. Hartmann notes, "The global scope of American involvement, the increasing complexity of modern war, and the development of military technology had reduced the proportion of military personnel directly engaged in battle. During World War II 25 percent of military personnel never left the United States, and only about one in eight actually saw combat" (Hartmann, *The Home Front and Beyond: American Women in the 1940s,* American Women in the Twentieth Century [Boston, 1982], p. 34).

Cynthia Enloe has described how "society's bastion of male identity," the military, "believes it must categorise women as peripheral, as serving safely at the 'rear' on the 'home front.' Women *as women* must be denied access to 'the front,' to 'combat.' . . . The military has to constantly redefine 'the front' and 'combat' as wherever 'women' are not."[28] Marianne Moore, writing from where women were, wrote inevitably about war within a situation of lack and absence, within a sense of herself as peripheral rather than central. Williams, Eberhart, and Auden might tout "In Distrust" as a universal war poem, but it, and all Moore's writing on war, show marked evidence of the specific stresses which result when an American woman writes a Second World War poem *as a woman.*

In "In Distrust of Merits," the tension between moral self-confidence on the one hand and felt or feared inadequacy on the other is pronounced and strenuous. Half in distrust of merits, half in defense of them, suspicious of herself but awed and moved by Allied soldiers, speaking in a voice half subdued and half like the gyroscope's fall in another Moore poem, "trued by regnant certainty" (*CP,* p. 134), Moore engages in what Geoffrey Hartman has called her "dialogue of one, an ironic crossfire of statement that continually denies and reasserts the possibility of a selfless assertion of the self":[29]

> Strengthened to live, strengthened to die for
> medals and positioned victories?
> They're fighting, fighting, fighting the blind
> man who thinks he sees—
> who cannot see that the enslaver is
> enslaved; the hater, harmed. O shining O
> firm star, O tumultuous
> ocean lashed till small things go
> as they will, the mountainous
> wave makes us who look, know
>
> depth. Lost at sea before they fought! O
> star of David, star of Bethlehem,
> O black imperial lion
> of the Lord—emblem
> of a risen world—be joined at last, be
> joined. There is hate's crown beneath which all is
> death; there's love's without which none
> is king; the blessed deeds bless

28. Cynthia Enloe, *Does Khaki Become You? The Militarization of Women's Lives* (Boston, 1983), p. 15.

29. Geoffrey Hartman, "Six Women Poets," *Easy Pieces* (New York, 1985), p. 111.

the halo. As contagion
    of sickness makes sickness,

contagion of trust can make trust. They're
    fighting in deserts and caves, one by
one, in battalions and squadrons;
    they're fighting that I
may yet recover from the disease, My
Self; some have it lightly; some will die. "Man's
        wolf to man" and we devour
            ourselves. The enemy could not
        have made a greater breach in our
            defenses. . . .

Who is the subject of the first two lines of the poem? An "I"? a "she" or a "he"? an "us"? ("Say our.") Only after some uncertainty are we brought to a decisive distance from the active third-person subjects of the poem. The strengthened ones turn out to be "they" alone, the "they" of the professional army in distant places, surveyed as if by telescopic lens, "lost at sea before they fought," or "fighting in deserts and caves, one by / one, in battalions and squadrons," "Some / in snow, some on crags, some in quicksands."

These stylized summations of the various landscapes of combat are the poem's most "literal" moments. Moore strives here to represent the intractable, actual conditions of Second World warfare but does so in the language of the newsreel. More often, however, the war represented in "In Distrust" is entirely disengaged from history, becoming a figurative or archetypal war of wars rather than a specific historical event labeled "Second" and "World." The enemy has both a relatively literal status and a more predominantly allegorical one within this poem. For instance, the "blind / man who thinks he sees— / who cannot see that the enslaver is / enslaved" and who later is described as "small dust of the earth / that walks so arrogantly" may refer to Hitler or Mussolini or Hirohito, or to any men who live in and fight for a nation-state whose dominant ideologies are "fascist" or "militarist," but he also stands for an archetypal Everyman and Everywoman. Very much like Orgoglio or Archimago in *The Faerie Queene,* he represents an interior spiritual danger, Blindness and Aggression and Pride, while the speaking "I" and the "we" that the "I" addresses stand, like Spenserian allegorical heroes, for the self which must struggle with its own inward enemies in order to achieve and maintain a patient self-knowledge. Moore's narrative of spiritual trial recounts an essential, universal struggle within all selves for perfection of the soul and accounts for warfare as both a part of that struggle and the result of its lapses: "I must / fight till I have conquered in myself what / causes war." The poem's world is a world of inward emblems in which all selves have the opportunity to choose, and continually work toward, the archetypal qualities they wish to incorporate and embody: "There is hate's crown beneath which all is / death; there's love's without which none / is king; the blessed deeds bless / the halo."

At several crucial points in "In Distrust of Merits," however, the speaker's emblematic certainty dissolves, and the voice becomes edgy and mistrustful of itself and its surroundings. The formless force of the tidal wave which, apparently, has sunk a military ship near the start of the poem "makes us who look, know / depth," Moore writes—but whether the depth we discover is a new inward, spiritual dimension of ourselves or simply the terrifying flux of an uncontrolled and uncontrollable world ("O tumultuous / ocean lashed till small things go / as they will") we cannot be sure. At other moments, the speaker's voice more openly undermines and disables itself. Earlier I quoted one of the poem's most determined liberal morals: "We'll / never hate black, white, red, yellow, Jew, / Gentile, Untouchable." In context, this message, set off by quotation marks, retains its power, but the speaker severely undercuts her own authority:

We
vow, we make this promise

to the fighting—it's a promise—"We'll
never hate black, white, red, yellow, Jew,
Gentile, Untouchable." We are
not competent to
make our vows. With set jaw they are fighting,
fighting, fighting . . .

Here the promise is first subtly questioned in Moore's use of the pat phrase, "it's a promise," a colloquial form of emphasis which, like "without a doubt" or "really," subverts its own assurances by being overly reassuring. A more open interrogation follows, as the speaker's voice entirely discredits itself and its collective audience: "we are not competent." Inability to vow, in a world which demands strong action and speech, constitutes a desperate handicap; moreover, this vision of the self as unstable and ineffective is inimical to the vision of the ultimately capable self which must be implicit in the "spiritual warfare" narrative in other parts of "In Distrust of Merits." Although the self in any "inward warfare" plot must have serious weaknesses to combat, it must as well have access to competence—an access in serious question here.

Other moments of high moral certitude in the poem are followed by other instances of equally radical self-distrust. The assertion that "there never was a war that was / not inward" ends "I must / fight till I have conquered in myself what / causes war, *but I would not believe it*" (my italics). Moore asserts her moral and then withdraws, anxiously, painfully.

The next lines—"I inwardly did nothing. / O Iscariot-like crime!"—suggest a reading which aligns itself with the tradition of spiritual warfare narrative: "I would not believe it," in the past imperfect tense, can be read as a statement of self-castigation following a confession of a crime which can only now be atoned for ("I would not believe it then"). But it can also be interpreted as "I refuse to believe it now—I continue to be recalcitrant"; here, again, doubt and resistance threaten to replace confidence and preclude continuation of the redemptive spiritual warfare plot. "They are fighting," Moore writes in stanza five, ". . . that / hearts may feel and not be numb. / It cures me; or am I what / I can't believe in?" The extremity of personal doubt here, which goes beyond the requisite moral self-suspicion of the spiritual warrior, calls into question the veracity and validity of the war poem which it interrupts.

Or am I what I can't believe in? This kind of self-questioning may certainly be an attempt to put into literary practice the kind of humility Moore advocates in "In Distrust of Merits." But it also seems to be a response to her distance from the violence of which she is attempting to make sense. "If these great patient / dyings," she writes, "—all these agonies / and wound-bearings and bloodshed— / can teach us how to live, these / dyings were not wasted." *If* they can teach us, she says, not "they can teach us." The affirmations of meaning and purgations of suffering here are conditional, fragile, subject to denial from within the poem itself—a poem with "distrust" in its very title. We can feel the language straining in this passage, with its overblown "wound-bearings," an abstract euphemism atypical of Moore's style. When Americans safe on our own continent attempt to write about war, Cary Nelson has argued, "our own physical security makes the language flat and unconvincing. We have no historical ground for sympathetic identification; such words will not come to us."[30] In "In Distrust of Merits," Moore calls for such words to come to her, but she also, at key points, dramatizes her own failure to find them.

The poem is interspersed throughout with wholehearted, ringing assertions of piety that are likely to annoy modern critics trained to value ironies and complexities. It ends with a credo particularly trite by most contemporary standards: "Beauty is everlasting / and dust is for a time." But this confident declaration is prefaced immediately by three notably self-suspicious lines: "I would not believe it. / I inwardly did nothing. / O Iscariot-like crime!" Even this last apostrophe, the figure Jonathan Culler calls the most "pretentious and mystificatory in the lyric," cannot entirely dispel the humbling and demystifying force of the comparison of the self to Judas.[31] Before simply dismissing the final couplet, which

30. Cary Nelson, *Our Last First Poets: Vision and History in Contemporary Poetry* (Urbana, Ill., 1981), p. 17.

31. Jonathan Culler, "Apostrophe," *Diacritics* 7 (Winter 1977): 60.

reverts suddenly to traditional accentual meter instead of the pure syllabic verse Moore usually preferred, as sentimental and clichéd, we would do well to remember Jane Tompkins' warnings about the politics of those labels when they are applied to nineteenth-century popular novels, works whose function is "heuristic and didactic rather than mimetic" and which "do not attempt to transcribe in detail a parabola of events as they 'actually happen' in society": "What the word *sentimental* really means in this context is that the arena of human action . . . has been defined not as the world, but as the human soul. [Such works develop] a theory of power that stipulates that all true action is not material, but spiritual."[32] In "In Distrust," however, the spiritual cannot, except with difficulty and momentarily, supersede other theories of power; definitions of "the arena of human action" waver. In a variety of ways familiar to readers of modern poetry, the poem undercuts its own apparent anti-ironic commitment to the war well fought. Part of its force for its contemporary audience surely lay in its expression and partial resolution of conflicts between Christian typology and modernist suspicion.

The poem's shaky mixture of tempered heroic assertion and strong ironic contradiction guaranteed its great appeal for forties critics and anthologists, who, with the harsh memory inscribed in the antiwar soldier poetry of the last war behind them, faced the difficult task of reshaping a canon which could at once convey the war's brutality and represent its necessity, recognize both its justice and its meaninglessness. "In Distrust," which could be read as either an inconclusive or a conclusive "just war" plot, as patriotic or antipatriotic, satisfied their needs precisely. But Moore's most appreciative respondents tended to mute the conflicts in the poem in their public reviews, subsuming its self-fragmentations into a clear, single, reassuring spiritual quest narrative. Her own later description of the writing of the poem shares these critics' emphasis on authenticity of feeling—"It is sincere. . . . Emotion overpowered me"—but her account emphasizes, much more than theirs, the presence of contradictory drives and inward disjunctions: "Haphazard; as form, what has it? It is just a protest—disjointed, exclamatory. Emotion overpowered me. First this thought and then that."[33] For Moore, as she looks back on "In Distrust," the major effect of the poem is that of breaks and outbreaks, a sense of unresolvable conflict.

In a 1945 issue of *Partisan Review,* shortly after "In Distrust" was published in the volume *Nevertheless* to wide acclaim, Randall Jarrell

32. Jane Tompkins, *Sensational Designs: The Cultural Work of American Fiction 1790–1860* (New York, 1985), pp. xvii, 151. Paul Fussell discusses the metrical shift at the end of the poem in his *Poetic Meter and Poetic Form* (New York, 1965), pp. 8–9.

33. Moore, "Interview," p. 261.

undertook a dissenting opinion. His review's opening lines manage at once to acknowledge and gently mock Moore's privileged position in the new canon of war poetry. Its closing lines, too, bow to Moore with respect, affection, and a trace of condescension. In between, Jarrell constructs an impassioned argument, one which forces its readers to grapple with some of the most powerful and intractable cruxes in the interpretation of modern war literature. At the same time, like the male reviewers with whom he argues over Marianne Moore, he systematically misreads her war poems, ignoring their dynamic processes, overemphasizing the static quality of images within them, and presenting Moore as exaggeratedly sanguine, stolid, and simpleminded.

From the start, his review of "In Distrust" introduces Moore's entire poetic project as a fussy exercise in formal tedium. Moore operates with "static particulars . . . at the farthest level of abstraction from the automatically dynamic generalizations of the child or animal"; her lines merely fix "specimens on their slides"; her rhymes are the opposite of the kinesthesia of common English rhyme; "everything combines to make the poem's structure . . . a state rather than a process" ("PWP," pp. 127–28). Jarrell's emphasis, however disapproving, on the visual aspects of Moore's poetics, on the defamiliarizing textuality of her poetry, provides a useful corrective to readings such as Williams' or Eberhart's which treat the war poems as direct utterances from the heart. But his insistence on the sterile calm of the poems precludes assessment of the kind of flux and tension I have been describing in "In Distrust."

This initial suppression of the agonistic elements in Moore's entire body of work prepares for a more particular erasure of struggle in her war poems. With a fierce wit which suggests that there is a great deal at stake for him in this argument, Jarrell objects to Moore's *Nevertheless* on several grounds. She writes too much about inanimate or nonhuman characters (referring to the poem "Nevertheless," a parable which involves a regenerating strawberry, he asks dryly, "how can anything bad happen to a plant?" ["PWP," p. 128]). Her fables concerning things and animals evade the complexities of the human, of consciousness, and they evade hard facts of social and political relationship; what's more, they evade the presence of inexplicable violence in the world, as Jarrell illustrates with a fable of his own:

> The way of the little jerboa on the sands—at once True, Beautiful, and Good—she understands; but . . . the little larvae feeding on the still-living caterpillar their mother has paralyzed for them? We are surprised to find Nature, in Miss Moore's poll of it, so strongly in favor of Morality. . . . To us, as we look skyward to the bombers, . . . [she] calls *Culture and morals and Nature still have truth, seek shelter there,* and this is true; but we forget it beside the cultured, moral, and natural corpse . . . At Maidanek the mice had holes, but a million and a half people had none. ["PWP," p. 128]

It is worth noting the obvious, in the face of Jarrell's impressive appeal to the hard facts about real nature (as opposed to what he defines as Moore's weak, selective version): this is an unresolvable ideological quarrel. The slim grape tendril in Moore's "Nevertheless," which represents how "the weak overcomes its / menace" (*CP,* p. 126), bears no less and no more essential and immediate a relation to human experience than Jarrell's caterpillar unable to escape from the sinister larvae-mother, or than the mice at Maidanek who, serving a different rhetorical purpose, *can* escape into a hole. Whether or not a reader can return to "Nevertheless" after hearing Jarrell's case out and find the poem of equal value will depend on—among other things—the reader's assumptions about the efficacy or the futility of individual human action, beliefs about what constitutes the self, and, not least, predilections for or aversions to traditional forms of Christian verse such as allegory or parable.

For at issue here are hard questions not only about what human nature "is," but also about how it should be represented. Should war and can war be depicted by emblems, fables, moral allegories? Or is it incomparable, unrepeatable, irreducible, like each individual person lost to torture, or to genocide, or to battle, or lost for no reason those who survive will ever know? Should this war, and can it, be depicted at all, or does Maidanek, as Elie Wiesel has argued, negate "all literature as it negates all theories and doctrines?"[34]

In the presence of the silent object of the corpse, Jarrell argues, linguistic and symbolic orders collapse; the adjectives "cultured" and "moral" cannot adhere in any meaningful way to a dead and tortured body which remains "natural" only in the most literal sense we have for that word. Moore has made a similar point, in her reading notes: "The difficulty is one of language." Yet Jarrell's corpse, whose presence temporarily erases the memory of all reassuring symbolic order, is itself a symbolic construction, placed "beside" us through a linguistic act, within a cultural artifact which is also a moral argument about the truth of nature. Jarrell does not elaborate on Maidanek's possible undoing of all poetry, his own as well as Moore's. He seeks, provisionally, to affirm a notion of aesthetic decorum: that the war demands literary treatment which, though always overtly acknowledging language's difficulties, still represents itself as relatively literal, relatively rooted in the external world of actual Second World War experience, in contrast to Moore's obviously stylized and overtly figurative fables of inward warfare.

Underlying this aesthetic dictum is an implicit political aim. War is, in a word which crops up repeatedly in Jarrell's reviews of this period, "incommensurable"; its dark realities resist easy simile or analogy; to openly imagine metaphors for what happens to people in war—unless those metaphors refer eventually, emphatically, back to the suffering

34. Elie Wiesel, *A Jew Today,* trans. Marion Wiesel (New York, 1978); cited in Annette Insdorf, *Indelible Shadows: Film and the Holocaust* (New York, 1983), p. xi.

body—is, therefore, to participate directly in war's perpetuation by falsifying the truth. Jarrell implies that traditional literary techniques such as allegory or fable, which fail to satisfy strict standards of verisimilitude in their depiction of human pain and violence, carry with them a proclivity for, if not a necessary relationship to, warmongering since they do not show sufficiently the pressure of the literal. For Moore, as for Jarrell, a good war poem is an antiwar poem, but Moore assumes, with a strong tradition of Christian rhetoric and ethics behind her, that parables have special power, not only to comfort sufferers but to change behavior. Writing, however ironically, within that tradition, she is primarily interested in war's relation to the states of the cultured, moral, and supernatural *soul.* And indeed there is no clear evidence that Moore's work impressed her wide audience with the wrongness of war any less or any more than Jarrell's, or that the difficulty which was one of language was any less or more apparent to her readers.

Although gender seems to be of no concern in this discussion of the relation between literary technique and political values, Jarrell makes use of conventional formulations of sexual difference throughout as he shapes his terms and rhetorical strategies. He employs, for instance, an underlying image of an oblivious woman, "timid" and "private spirited" in her patterned garden while war rages around her, a figure whose presence pervades literature about women's role in wartime.[35] In order to carry off this reading of Moore, which demands that she be inert and impervious, Jarrell ignores moments in the war poems, such as those I have traced in "In Distrust," which suggest a troubled, conscious relation to her distance from direct conflict and suffering. In "In Distrust of Merits," for instance, he ignores most notably the moment of resistance to looking at the photograph of the dead soldier ("I cannot / look and yet I must"), a point at which Moore's poem itself enacts the fear which precedes the moment of forgetting all ethical consolations "beside the cultured, moral, and natural corpse."[36] Moore seems to demonstrate

35. Perhaps the most famous text in the long tradition in which an overprotected, feminine *hortus conclusus* is opposed to masculine engagement in historical crisis is Ruskin's "Of Queen's Gardens," *Sesame and Lilies: Three Lectures* (Chicago, 1890), pp. 72–101. In the Second World War period, see Arthur Koestler's Sylvia in "The Artist and Politics," *Saturday Review of Literature* 25 (31 Jan. 1942), pp. 3–4, 14–15; the attack on American women for failing to prevent war in Philip Wylie's *Generation of Vipers* (New York, 1942); Pearl Buck's chapter on women, domesticity, and war in *Of Men and Women* (New York, 1941); and Williams' image of American civilians protected by a wall of flesh, quoted earlier in this essay.

36. Costello argues persuasively, in her discussion of Jarrell's review, that Moore's work not only is part of a tradition of domestic "feminine realism . . . which links observation to ethical generalization" in American women's poetry but also constitutes a transformation of that tradition: "All the poems follow a dictum of resistance even while they move through an apparent structure of observation-moral, for they continually propose definitions only to unravel them" (Costello, "The 'Feminine' Language of Marianne Moore," in *Women and*

here, in fact, the very qualities Jarrell praises in Ernie Pyle, the legendary Second World War correspondent, who, Jarrell says, "knew to what degree experience . . . is 'seeing only faintly and not wanting to see at all.' "[37]

What distinguishes Pyle's sight and aversion to sight from Moore's is, of course, his eyewitness status; he, unlike Moore, has the right to claim the words from Whitman which Jarrell cites often: "I was the man, I suffered, I was there."[38] Jarrell's eulogy for Pyle, written a few months before his review of *Nevertheless,* provides an instructive contrast to his treatment of Moore's war poetry. Paradoxically, Pyle's open recognition of his inability to "see" or know war in some primary, unmediated way functions, for Jarrell, only to reconfirm the credibility of his testimony, to further authenticate his eye. In the Pyle piece, Jarrell shifts repeatedly, sometimes even instantaneously, between tributes to two contradictory principles, both part of the aesthetic which Second World War poets inherit from modernism: that authentic experience, felt beyond cliché, is vital ground for the work of art, and yet that all language is nonreferential and all experience is inseparable from already determined cultural and linguistic systems.[39] Or as Gertrude Stein writes in her *Wars I Have Seen,* a predictably playful critique of referentiality in war literature, "However near a war is it is not very near. Perhaps if one were a boy it would be different, but I do not think so."[40] Praising Ernie Pyle, Jarrell negotiates with great care between mythologizing and demythologizing the idea of transparent representation of direct experience. He begins a statement about Pyle, "What he cared about was the facts" but then adds "But facts are only facts as we see them, as we feel them"; he places "real and imaginary" in close proximity, following his phrase "the real war" with "that is, the people in it, all those private wars the imaginary sum of which is the public war" ("EP," p. 112). Still, despite the repeated, cautious moments in Jarrell's treatment of Pyle which emphasize the mediated and mediating aspects of Pyle's writing, it is Pyle's *nearness* to war—the nearness of what Stein calls "boys," a close masculine contact with literal combat—which finally, for Jarrell, renders his work of value.[41]

Language in Literature and Society, ed. Sally McConnell-Ginet, Ruth Borker, and Nelly Furman [New York, 1980], p. 235). Costello follows Emily Stipes Watt's work in *The Poetry of American Women from 1932 to 1945* (Austin, Tex., 1977).

37. Jarrell, "Ernie Pyle," *Kipling, Auden and Co.,* p. 112; all further references to this essay, abbreviated "EP," will be included in the text.

38. See, for instance, Jarrell's repeated quotations from Whitman in "These Are Not Psalms," *Kipling, Auden and Co.,* pp. 122–26.

39. I owe to conversation with Catherine Gallagher my formulation of this point.

40. Gertrude Stein, *Wars I Have Seen* (New York, 1945), p. 9.

41. A similar complex conflation of "real" and "imaginary" occurs in Jarrell's description of Owen as "a poet in the true sense of the word, someone who has shown to us one of those worlds which, after we have been shown it, we call the real world" (Jarrell, "The Profession of Poetry," *Kipling, Auden and Co.,* p. 169). Ernest Hemingway's introduction

When Jarrell turns in his review of Moore to an angry, eloquent reading of "In Distrust of Merits," he once again identifies his own stance, with some careful qualification, as less mediated in relation to the real war than Moore's. Here again he partially misreads Moore, and does so eloquently, imaginatively, in the service of a landmark modern protest against war. Objecting to Moore's representation of warfare as heroic ("fighting," he writes, "is the major theme of the poem"), he chides her for her failure to understand and remember

> that [soldiers] are heroes in the sense that the chimney sweeps, the factory children in the blue books, were heroes: routine loss in the routine business of the world . . . that most of the people in a war never fight for even a minute—though they bear for years and die forever. They do not fight, but only starve, only suffer, only die: the sum of all this passive misery is that great activity, War. . . .
>
> Who is "taught to live" by cruelty, suffering, stupidity, and that occupational disease of soldiers, death? The moral equivalent of war! ["PWP," p. 129]

The sudden, sputtered interpolation of the famous title phrase of William James' "Moral Equivalent of War" points to implicit concerns which are at the heart of Jarrell's argument with "In Distrust of Merits." Jarrell rightly finds traces of James' influence on Moore's representations of war. Those echoes are complex enough to merit a detailed study in themselves, but what matter here are simpler questions: how does Jarrell read James' essay, and why does he cite it with such sardonic emphasis here?

James functions as a shorthand representative of several political and aesthetic evils with which Jarrell wishes to connect Moore's war work and from which he wishes to strongly differentiate his own. He objects, as I have said, to any process of image-making which attempts to find overt "equivalences" for war. He objects as strenuously to an idea of human nature which emphasizes what James calls "energies and hardihoods," or human intentionality, at the expense of ignoring or minimizing human dependence, powerlessness, and suffering. James proposes systems for developing, as a substitute for war, "toughness without callousness,

---

to his anthology of writing about war, *Men at War,* reveals identical ambivalence. On the one hand Hemingway, paying tribute to Stephen Crane's *Red Badge of Courage,* argues that the writer's imagination "should produce a truer account than anything factual can be. For facts can be observed badly." On the other hand, he praises Crane's depiction of a boy "facing *that thing which no one knows about who has not done it*" (Hemingway, intro., *Men at War: The Best War Stories of All Time* [New York, 1942], pp. xv, xviii; my italics). See also the strained arguments about experience in Williams' collection of prose statements by poets on poetry and war, part of his *War Poets.*

authority with as little criminal cruelty as possible";[42] Jarrell would argue that there is no toughness without callousness, no authority without cruelty, and that most people are the subservient victims of both. Finally, and most radically, Jarrell objects to James' explicit and Moore's implicit constructions of the idea of masculinity in their arguments for positive and peaceful modes of combat. James' main argument—that military conflict will persist until antimilitarists find an adequate substitute (the "moral equivalent") for the central function of war, "preserving manliness of type"—is energized by a pervasive anxiety about constitutions of masculinity, a fear that martial experience alone can make a man.[43] Linking Moore's images of inward war to James' manly equivalents, Jarrell articulates his difference from both writers: where they see only the exemplary heroism of stalwart foot soldiers, he sees pernicious, exploitive myths of manhood, and his critique of "In Distrust" gathers force and turns to outrage as he seeks to undo what he perceives as deadly codes of masculine style.

Jarrell's challenge to social constructions of masculinity points to a paradox: how can his review, which Bonnie Costello describes as upholding "in clear sexual categories" a brutal "male vision of amoral nature," be written by the pacifist writer whom Sara Ruddick, the feminist pacifist, has cited as a " 'maternal' man" whose war work exemplifies the kind of "preservative love" generally taught to and practiced by women?[44] Why does Jarrell simultaneously *refer* to rigid distinctions of sexual difference, in his reading of Moore as a woman in a garden and in his own claim to the authority of a soldier, and *refuse* to accept conventional scripts for masculine soldierly behavior? How can he write at once like a man and like a woman, and at the same time criticize Moore both for writing like a woman (timidly, privately, obliviously) and writing like a man (glorifying intention, and Truth, and cause, and war)?

Ways of "writing like a woman" or "writing like a man," as J. Hillis Miller has suggested, often "tend to change places or values in the moment of being defined and enacted": "The male thinks he is writing constatively, but in fact his affirmations are groundless performatives. The woman writer knows there is no truth, no rhythm but the drumbeat of death, but this means that her broken, hesitant rhythms are in resonance with the truth that there is no truth."[45] In Jarrell's argument with Moore, it is the woman poet who is placed in the position of the "constative,"

42. William James, "The Moral Equivalent of War," *Memories and Studies* (Westport, Conn., 1941), pp. 291–92.

43. Ibid., p. 292.

44. Costello, "The 'Feminine' Language," p. 234; see Sara Ruddick, "Pacifying the Forces: Drafting Women in the Interests of Peace," *Signs* 8 (Spring 1983): 479.

45. J. Hillis Miller, "Mr. Carmichael and Lily Briscoe: The Rhythm of Creativity in *To the Lighthouse*," in *Modernism Reconsidered*, ed. Robert Kiely (Cambridge, Mass., 1983), p. 188.

"masculine" writer who actually produces "groundless performatives," and it is the male critic who places himself in the role of the feminine writer who knows no rhythm but the drumbeats of death. But if Moore and Jarrell do exchange "places and values" of masculinity and femininity, they do not do so randomly or idiosyncratically. Their shifting reenactments and redefinitions of selfhood have strong political motives and implications within the specific social context of the American Second World War home front.

"Dividing the protector from the protected, defender from defended, is the linchpin of masculinist as well as military ideology," Ruddick writes.[46] Both Moore's distrustful text and Jarrell's even more distrustful review of that text seem to circle around the same linchpin, at once overdetermined by structures of sexual difference in wartime and desperately evasive of those structures. Evasive and exaggerated in opposite directions: where Moore, the female civilian, attempts to imagine a world where everyone could be a soldier, Jarrell, the male soldier, attempts to imagine a world where everyone could be an innocent. We might say that Moore writes "In Distrust of Merits" as if to argue that everyone can act "like a man," and Jarrell his review as if to argue that everyone is passive "as a woman."

The tradition of ironic soldier poetry which has dominated critical discussion of war poems for most of this century encourages sensitive readings of Jarrell's project but not of Moore's. Another look at Jarrell's critique of Moore's images of war may help to explain this situation. "Most of the people in a war," Jarrell writes, "never fight for even a minute—though they bear for years and die forever" ("PWP," p. 129). "Bear for years" is a peculiar phrase—oddly abstract in the midst of a relatively concretizing series of passive verbs—and an apt one. The word "bear," though it does not necessarily signify a feminine condition (people of both genders bear burdens and bear pain), carries nonetheless a strong association with the female body. In our culture generally, as Margaret Homans has argued in her *Bearing the Word,* "the literal is associated with the feminine, the more highly valued figurative . . . with the masculine," and this "complex and troubling tradition" originates in a simple actuality: "that women bear children and men do not."[47] Jarrell's "bear" invokes an image of childbirth to redescribe war not just because childbearing is linked to pain or because it is associated with submission to the brunt of things, but because it represents a prolonged encounter with unmitigated, unmediated fact. Childbirth, in Homans' words, is inherently a structure of literalization, in which "something becomes real that did not exist before—or that existed as a word, a theory, or a 'conception' " and by which "the relatively figurative becomes the relatively literal."[48] Throughout

46. Ruddick, "Pacifying the Forces," p. 472.

47. Margaret Homans, *Bearing the Word: Language and Female Experience in Nineteenth-Century Women's Writing* (Chicago, 1986), pp. 5, 88.

48. Ibid., p. 26.

his career, but particularly in the early forties, Jarrell strove to define a poetics of war which could adequately recognize that warfare itself is a "structure of literalization": "what in peace struggles below consciousness in the mind of an economist," he writes, "in war wipes out a division" ("EP," p. 113).

Valuing a war poetry which is rooted, as nearly as possible, in the concrete, the material, the "borne," Jarrell writes within a strong tradition of masculine antiwar protest in which the soldier becomes responsible for transcribing the literal. The more "literal" the representation of men's experience within this tradition of soldier poetry, the more feminized those men will appear, as their function shifts from "fighting" to "bearing." Thus, in Owen's classic, inaugural war poem "Dulce et Decorum Est," the depiction of gas warfare, which represents iself as starkly realistic in opposition to earlier clichés, begins with a description of the men as bent "like hags."[49] "Dulce" was originally titled "To A Certain Poetess" and written in angry response to Jessie Pope's metaphors of war as, among other things, football. In this tradition of soldier poetry which has dominated critical discussion of war poems for most of this century, men come to occupy the place of the literal *as well as women,* or to displace women entirely; the figurative, in turn, is associated especially with the feminine, with the abstract allegories and stylized banalities of "certain poetesses." And in this case, the text's commitment to "literal" representation, its firm alliance with an authority of male experience, makes it *especially* highly valued and qualifies it for inclusion in the ranks of canonical war poetry.[50]

I do not want to deny the importance, the potential efficacy, or the polemical brilliance of the appeal to literal experience in the modern tradition of war literature.[51] But when experience is privileged or even required as an aesthetic, political, and moral criterion for the proper war

49. See Owen, "Dulce et Decorum Est," *Collected Poems,* ed. C. Day Lewis (London, 1963), p. 55. For the Jessie Pope connection, see Day Lewis' notes on the manuscript variations on the same page. On the persistent analogy in Western culture between warmaking and childbearing, see Nancy Huston, "The Matrix of War: Mothers and Heroes," in *The Female Body in Western Culture,* ed. Susan Rubin Suleiman (Cambridge, Mass., 1986).

50. Many of the essays in the "American Representations of Vietnam" issue of *Cultural Critique* 3 (Spring 1986) explore American culture's continuing myths of the special value of the soldier/veteran's experience. See especially Michael Clark, "Remembering Vietnam," pp. 46–78; Rick Berg, "Losing Vietnam: Covering the War in an Age of Technology," pp. 92–125; John Carlos Rowe, "Eye-Witness: Documentary Styles in the American Representation of Vietnam," pp. 126–50; Philip Francis Kuberski, "Genres of Vietnam," pp. 168–88.

51. Nor do I mean to imply that women in American culture cannot and do not employ strategies of literalization in their representations of war. Elaine Scarry's recent, powerful treatment of "injury and the structure of war" in *The Body in Pain: The Making and Unmaking of the World* (New York, 1985), for instance, is very much within the tradition advocated and represented by Jarrell here.

poem, the attendant dangers are several. Overvaluation of the concrete and particular may prevent recognition of war poems which have overtly given expression to significant ideological principles and conflicts—even when those poems, like Moore's "In Distrust," clearly speak in abstract terms which large audiences of contemporaries found compelling.[52] Where obviously stylized and didactic literary techniques such as Moore's allegory signal from the start both their literariness and their political and philosophical stakes, a more narrative war poem which refers more openly to real experience may not recognize the limits of what constitutes the "real" within it.[53] In American forties war poetry, for instance, "experience of war" was generally taken to comprehend the experience of the soldier but not generally, during the war itself, the experience of the Holocaust victim, the Japanese American in an internment camp, or a woman working in a defense plant. Finally, reading war poetry as we have so often been taught to read it—as a register of difference between and within men over the affairs of manhood, in which, say, the euphemisms of generals are broken open by the literalizing story of the soldier—we may once again be complicit in rendering women (who have also, always, had our say about war) silent and invisible and static, suppressing our own dynamic and complex relations to systems of warmaking. Rereading "In Distrust" in the context of a different set of texts—the body of highly abstract works by women which enact inward wars rooted in spiritual traditions, from Emily Dickinson's Civil War meditations to two of the most influential poems of the Second World War, Edith Sitwell's "Still Falls the Rain" and H. D.'s *Trilogy*—we may begin to understand not only the potential power of figurative models of representation and protest in war literature, but also how thoroughly and insistently Moore writes her war poems "like a woman."

In his *Complete Poems,* Jarrell's "Eighth Air Force" appears as the first poem of a section called "Bombers," a classic collection of soldier

52. Tompkins discusses related problems in the evaluation of popular nineteenth-century works with "designs upon their audiences" in her introduction and throughout *Sensational Designs.*

53. Homans notes this danger in myths of female experience (see *Bearing the Word,* p. 15), citing Jane Gallop on the inherently conservative nature of a "politics of experience." In her discussion of Irigaray's work on the female body, Gallop goes on, however, to warn at the same time against unproblematic *denials* of experience: "the gesture of a troubled but nonetheless insistent referentiality is essential" if one's aim is "a *poiésis* of experience, that attempts to reconstruct experience itself, to produce a remetaphorization . . . a salutary jolt out of the compulsive repetition of the same" (Gallop, "*Quand nos lèvres s'écrivent:* Irigaray's Body Politic," *Romanic Review* 74 [Jan. 1983]: 83). The most powerful "soldier poems" in the present canon of war poetry—Owen's "Dulce," for instance, or Jarrell's "Death of the Ball Turret Gunner"—certainly attempt to produce such salutary jolts, strongly revising the metaphors which formerly applied to the male body in war.

poems of the modern ironic type. Beginning with a detailed, mimetic representation of a tangible scene of soldiers' encampment—what tune the drunk sergeant whistles, what ordinary card games three soldiers play between missions—"Eighth Air Force" shifts quickly back and forth from literal narrative to tense, abstract meditation, till its original representational mode is replaced entirely by a lyric soliloquy spoken by Pilate at Christ's trial, or, more accurately, by a voice which sounds partly Pilate-like.

The poem is almost obsessively concerned not just with humanity but with masculinity—the speaker explicitly identifies himself as "a man, I," and the word "man" occurs, with heavy stress, at the end of over a third of the poem's lines and repeatedly within them. It therefore seems a culmination of and a self-reflexive commentary on the androcentric traditions of war poetry and warmaking. "Eighth Air Force" is, we might say, a poem about how a man looks at other men, and how he struggles to come to terms with what "manhood" means for himself in a culture at war. Yet the poem's first turn away from literal description and toward the abstract question of manhood, accomplished through an allusion to Plautus, suggests a more pressing intertextual relation to an influential contemporary text by a woman. "'Man's wolf to man,'" Moore quotes Plautus' words in "In Distrust," "and we devour / ourselves." Jarrell writes: "shall I say that man / Is not as men have said: a wolf to man?"[54]

Other insistent connections between the two texts suggest that despite Jarrell's distaste for "In Distrust" in his review, the power of the poem was not so easily dismissed. The struggle with the meaning of manhood in "Eighth Air Force" may be read as energized not by the fellow soldier's sight of real men but by the fellow poet's reading of a civilian woman's work. Jarrell's poem, in a number of ways, deliberately retraverses Moore's terrain. Both poets, for instance, employ the traditional device of representing the soldier as Christ (a strategy used by patriotic and antiwar poets alike throughout this century); both poems focus inward, on the dilemma of the observer of the crucifixion. When placed within the context of the American literary culture which lauded Moore's war poetry during and immediately after the Second World War, Jarrell's portrayal of the Pilate-like observer, which might otherwise seem a meditation on enduring, universal questions about guilt, justice, and forgiveness, can now be understood as a specific, topical revision of Moore's influential representation of the self as Iscariot-like. His soldiers, half innocents and half murderers, bear, too, a direct revisionary relation to Moore's heroic, patient fighters.

Although Moore's uses of Plautus and New Testament narrative appear at first to be far more dogmatic than Jarrell's, in the context of "In Distrust" they are undercut as dramatically. It seems to me likely

54. Jarrell, "Eighth Air Force," *The Complete Poems* (New York, 1969), p. 143.

that whether Jarrell consciously recognized it or not, he found a model for the self-questioning, "disjointed, exclamatory" voice of "Eighth Air Force," one of the most significant "soldier poems" to come out of the Second World War, in the searching voice of "In Distrust of Merits." Jarrell comes to sound most like Moore in a poem which, more than any other of his war works, acknowledges that no poetic text can say with unequivocal, literal meaning, "I was the man, I suffered, I was there," and that all poetic representation must also take place, in part, from the position of Pilate, the implicated observer who says, "Behold the man!" If we are to better understand the relation of suffering to observing, "there" to "not there," front to sidelines in twentieth-century war and twentieth-century war poetry, present-day critics and anthologists must recognize that the discourse of war consists not just of "what men have said" but also of what women like Marianne Moore have written.

Caribbean and African Appropriations of *The Tempest*

Rob Nixon

> Remember
> First to possess his books.
> —*The Tempest*

The era from the late fifties to the early seventies was marked in Africa and the Caribbean by a rush of newly articulated anticolonial sentiment that was associated with the burgeoning of both international black consciousness and more localized nationalist movements. Between 1957 and 1973 the vast majority of African and the larger Caribbean colonies won their independence; the same period witnessed the Cuban and Algerian revolutions, the latter phase of the Kenyan "Mau Mau" revolt, the Katanga crisis in the Congo, the Trinidadian Black Power uprising and, equally important for the atmosphere of militant defiance, the civil rights movement in the United States, the student revolts of 1968, and the humbling of the United States during the Vietnam War. This period was distinguished, among Caribbean and African intellectuals, by a pervasive mood of optimistic outrage. Frequently graduates of British or French universities, they were the first generation from their regions self-assured and numerous enough to call collectively for a renunciation of Western standards as the political revolts found their cultural counterparts in insurrections against the bequeathed values of the colonial powers.

In the context of such challenges to an increasingly discredited European colonialism, a series of dissenting intellectuals chose to utilize a

European text as a strategy for (in George Lamming's words) getting "out from under this ancient mausoleum of [Western] historic achievement."[1] They seized upon *The Tempest* as a way of amplifying their calls for decolonization within the bounds of the dominant cultures. But at the same time these Caribbeans and Africans adopted the play as a founding text in an oppositional lineage which issued from a geopolitically and historically specific set of cultural ambitions. They perceived that the play could contribute to their self-definition during a period of great flux. So, through repeated, reinforcing, transgressive appropriations of *The Tempest,* a once silenced group generated its own tradition of "error" which in turn served as one component of the grander counterhegemonic nationalist and black internationalist endeavors of the period. Because that era of Caribbean and African history was marked by such extensive, open contestation of cultural values, the destiny of *The Tempest* at that time throws into uncommonly stark relief the status of value as an unstable social process rather than a static and, in literary terms, merely textual attribute.

Some Caribbean and African intellectuals anticipated that their efforts to unearth from *The Tempest* a suppressed narrative of their historical abuse and to extend that narrative in the direction of liberation would be interpreted as philistine. But Lamming, for one, wryly resisted being intimidated by any dominant consensus: "I shall reply that my mistake, lived and deeply felt by millions of men like me—proves the positive value of error" (*PE,* p. 13). Lamming's assertion that his unorthodoxy is collectively grounded is crucial: those who defend a text's universal value can easily discount a solitary dissenting voice as uncultured or quirky, but it is more difficult to ignore entirely a cluster of allied counterjudgments, even if the group can still be stigmatized. Either way, the notion of universal value is paradoxically predicated on a limited inclusiveness, on the assumption that certain people will fail to appreciate absolute worth. As Pierre Bourdieu, Barbara Herrnstein Smith, and Tony Bennett have all shown, a dominant class or culture's power to declare certain objects or activities self-evidently valuable is an essential measure

1. George Lamming, *The Pleasures of Exile* (New York, 1984), p. 27; all further references to this work, abbreviated *PE,* will be included in the text.

Rob Nixon is a Ph.D. candidate in English at Columbia University. He is working on the topics of exile and Third World-metropolitan relations in the writing of V. S. and Shiva Naipaul.

for reproducing social differentiation.[2] But resistance to the hegemony of such hierarchies is still possible. In this context, Lamming's statement exudes the fresh confidence of the high era of decolonization, in which a "philistinism" arose that was sufficiently powerful and broadly based to generate an alternative orthodoxy responsive to indigenous interests and needs.

For Frantz Fanon, decolonization was the period when the peoples of the oppressed regions, force-fed for so long on foreign values, could stomach them no longer: "In the colonial context the settler only ends his work of breaking in the native when the latter admits loudly and intelligibly the supremacy of the white man's values. In the period of decolonization, the colonized masses mock at these very values, insult them, and vomit them up."[3] From the late fifties onward, there was a growing resistance in African and Caribbean colonies to remote-controlled anything, from administrative structures to school curricula, and the phase of "nauseating mimicry" (in Fanon's phrase) gave way to a phase in which colonized cultures sought to define their own cultures reactively and aggressively from within.[4] In short, decolonization was the period when "the machine [went] into reverse."[5] This about-face entailed that indigenous cultural forms be substituted for alien ones—inevitably a hybrid process of retrieving suppressed traditions and inventing new ones. Both approaches were present in the newfound preoccupation with *The Tempest:* hints of New World culture and history were dragged to the surface, while at other moments the play was unabashedly refashioned to meet contemporary political and cultural needs.[6]

2. See Pierre Bourdieu and Jean-Claude Passeron, *La Reproduction: Eléments pour une théorie du système d'enseignement* (Paris, 1970), and Bourdieu, *La Distinction: Critique sociale du jugement* (Paris, 1979); Barbara Herrnstein Smith, "Contingencies of Value," *Critical Inquiry* 10 (Sept. 1983): 1–35; Tony Bennett, *Formalism and Marxism* (London, 1979), "*Formalism and Marxism* Revisited," *Southern Review* 16 (1982): 3–21, and "Really Useless 'Knowledge': A Political Critique of Aesthetics," *Thesis 11* 12 (1985): 28–52.

3. Frantz Fanon, *The Wretched of the Earth,* trans. Constance Farrington (New York, 1968), p. 43.

4. Jean-Paul Sartre, preface, ibid., p. 9.

5. Ibid., p. 16.

6. Shakespeare's debt to the Bermuda pamphlets and other Elizabethan accounts of the New World has been extensively analyzed, often in relation to the evolution of British colonial discourse in the seventeenth century. See especially Frank Kermode, introduction to *The Tempest* (New York, 1954), pp. xxv–xxxiv; Stephen J. Greenblatt, "Learning to Curse: Aspects of Linguistic Colonialism in the Sixteenth Century," in *First Images of America: The Impact of the New World on the Old,* ed. Fredi Chiappelli, 2 vols. (Berkeley and Los Angeles, 1976), 2:561–80; Leslie A. Fiedler, "The New World Savage as Stranger: Or, ''Tis new to thee,'" *The Stranger in Shakespeare* (New York, 1972), pp. 199–253; Peter Hulme, "Hurricanes in the Caribbees: The Constitution of the Discourse of English Colonialism," in *1642: Literature and Power in the Seventeenth Century: Proceedings of the Essex Conference on the Sociology of Literature, July 1980,* ed. Francis Barker et al. (Colchester, 1981), pp. 55–83; Barker and Hulme, "Nymphs and Reapers Heavily Vanish: The Discursive

Given the forcefulness of the reaction against the values of the colonial powers, it may appear incongruous that Caribbean and African intellectuals should have integrated a canonical European text like *The Tempest* into their struggle; it made for, in Roberto Fernández Retamar's words, "an alien elaboration."[7] And this response may seem doubly incongruous given Shakespeare's distinctive position as a measure of the relative achievements of European and non-European civilizations. In discussions of value, Shakespeare is, of course, invariably treated as a special case, having come to serve as something like the gold standard of literature. For the English he is as much an institution and an industry as a corpus of texts: a touchstone of national identity, a lure for tourists, an exportable commodity, and one of the securest forms of cultural capital around. But the weight of Shakespeare's ascribed authority was felt differently in the colonies. What for the English and, more generally, Europeans, could be a source of pride and a confirmation of their civilization, for colonial subjects often became a chastening yardstick of their "backwardness." The exhortation to master Shakespeare was instrumental in showing up non-European "inferiority," for theirs would be the flawed mastery of those culturally remote from Shakespeare's stock. A schooled resemblance could become the basis for a more precise discrimination, for, to recall Homi Bhabha's analysis of mimicry in colonial discourse, "to be Anglicized is *emphatically* not to be English."[8] And so, in colonial circumstances, the bard could become symptomatic and symbolic of the education of Africans and Caribbeans into a passive, subservient relationship to dominant colonial culture.

One aspect of this passive orientation toward Europe is touched on by Lamming, the Barbadian novelist who was to appropriate *The Tempest* so actively for his own ends. Discussing his schooling during the early 1940s, Lamming recalls how the teacher "followed the curriculum as it was. He did what he had to do: Jane Austen, some Shakespeare, Wells's novel *Kipps,* and so on. What happened was that they were teaching exactly whatever the Cambridge Syndicate demanded. That was the point of it. These things were directly connected. Papers were set in Cambridge

---

Con-texts of *The Tempest,*" in *Alternative Shakespeares,* ed. John Drakakis (London, 1985), pp. 191–205; and Paul Brown, " 'This thing of darkness I acknowledge mine': *The Tempest* and the Discourse of Colonialism," in *Political Shakespeare: New Essays in Cultural Materialism,* ed. Jonathan Dollimore and Alan Sinfield (Ithaca, N.Y., 1985), pp. 48–71.

7. Roberto Fernández Retamar, "Caliban: Notes Toward a Discussion of Culture in Our America," trans. Lynn Garafola, David Arthur McMurray, and Robert Marquez, *Massachusetts Review* 15 (Winter/Spring 1974): 27; all further references to this work, abbreviated "C," will be included in the text.

8. Homi Bhabha, "Of Mimicry and Man: The Ambivalence of Colonial Discourse," *October* 28 (Spring 1984): 128.

and our answers were sent back there to be corrected. We had to wait three to four months. Nobody knew what was happening till they were returned."[9] Given the resistance during decolonization to this kind of cultural dependency, those writers who took up *The Tempest* from the standpoint of the colonial subject did so in a manner that was fraught with complexity. On the one hand, they hailed Caliban and identified themselves with him; on the other, they were intolerant of received colonial definitions of Shakespeare's value. They found the European play compelling but insisted on engaging with it on their own terms.

The newfound interest in *The Tempest* during decolonization was, in terms of the play's history, unprecedentedly sudden and concentrated. However, in the late nineteenth and early twentieth century, *The Tempest*'s value had been augmented by a prevalent perception of it as a likely vehicle first for Social Darwinian and later for imperial ideas. This tendency, which Trevor Griffiths has thoroughly documented, was evident in both performances and critical responses to the play.[10] A notable instance was *Caliban: The Missing Link* (1873), wherein Daniel Wilson contended that Shakespeare had preempted some of Darwin's best insights by creating "a novel anthropoid of a high type."[11] Amassing evidence from the play, Wilson deduced that Caliban would have been black, had prognathous jaws, and manifested a low stage of cultural advancement. Wilson's text shuttles between *The Tempest,* Darwin, and Linnaeus and is interlarded with detailed brain measurements of gibbons, baboons, chimpanzees, and a range of ethnic groupings.

Ironically, it was Beerbohm Tree's unabashedly jingoistic production of *The Tempest* in 1904 that elicited the first recorded response to the play in anti-imperial terms, as one member of the audience assimilated the action to events surrounding the Matabele uprising in Rhodesia:

9. Ian Munro and Reinhard Sander, eds., *Kas-Kas: Interviews with Three Caribbean Writers in Texas: George Lamming, C. L. R. James, Wilson Harris* (Austin, Tex., 1972), p. 6. For kindred treatments of the way British-centered curricula generated mimicry and cultural dependency in the former British West Indies, see Austin Clarke, *Growing Up Stupid Under the Union Jack: A Memoir* (Toronto, 1980), and Chris Searle, *The Forsaken Lover: White Words and Black People* (London, 1972).

10. Trevor R. Griffiths, " 'This Island's Mine': Caliban and Colonialism," *Yearbook of English Studies* 13 (1983): 159–80. Although Griffiths does not tackle the question of value directly, his essay complements mine insofar as it focuses on how *The Tempest* was appropriated not in the colonies but in Britain. Griffiths' analysis treats both the heyday of imperialism and the subsequent retreat from empire. For discussion of how *The Tempest* was taken up from the seventeenth century onward, see Ruby Cohn, *Modern Shakespeare Offshoots* (Princeton, N.J., 1976), pp. 267–309. Cohn's account of the two adaptations of the play by the nineteenth-century French historian and philosopher Ernest Renan is especially comprehensive.

11. Daniel Wilson, *Caliban: The Missing Link* (London, 1873), p. 79.

> When the man-monster, brutalised by long continued torture, begins, 'This island's mine, by Sycorax my mother, which thou takest from me', we have the whole case of the aboriginal against aggressive civilisation dramatised before us. I confess I felt a sting of conscience—vicariously suffered for my Rhodesian friends, notably Dr. Jameson—when Caliban proceeded to unfold a similar case to that of the Matebele. It might have been the double of old King Lobengula rehearsing the blandishments which led to his doom: 'When thou camest first / Thou strok'dst me, and mad'st much of me; would'st give me'—all that was promised by the Chartered Company to secure the charter.[12]

Just as the Matabele uprising was a distant, premonitory sign of the anticolonial struggles to come, so, too, W. T. Stead's unorthodox response to *The Tempest* anticipated a time when the play would be widely mobilized and esteemed as an expression of "the whole case of the 'aboriginal' against aggressive civilisation."

But it was another forty-four years before any text provided a sustained reassessment of *The Tempest* in light of the immediate circumstances leading up to decolonization. That text was *Psychologie de la colonisation,* written by the French social scientist, Octave Mannoni. However much Third World intellectuals have subsequently quarreled with his manner of mobilizing the play, Mannoni's inaugural gesture helped to shape the trajectory of those associated appropriations which lay ahead and, concomitantly, to bring about the reestimation of *The Tempest* in Africa and the Caribbean. Mannoni's novel response enabled him to evolve a theory of colonialism with Prospero and Caliban as prototypes; conversely, his hypotheses about colonial relations, arising from his experiences in Madagascar, made it possible for him to rethink the play. This reciprocal process was not gratuitous but prompted by an early stirring of African nationalism: Mannoni is insistent that his theory only fell into place through his exposure to one of the twilight moments of French colonialism—the Madagascan uprising of 1947–48 in which sixty thousand Madagascans, one thousand colonial soldiers, and several hundred settlers were killed. In 1947 his ideas began to take shape, and, by the time the revolt had been suppressed a year later, the manuscript was complete. The occasional character of *Psychologie de la colonisation* is foregrounded in the introduction, which Mannoni closes by marking the coincidence of his ideas with "a certain moment in history, a crisis in the evolution of politics, when many things that had been hidden were brought into the light of day; but it was only a moment, and time will soon have passed

12. W. T. Stead, "First Impressions of the Theatre," *Review of Reviews* 30 (Oct. 1904); quoted in Griffiths, " 'This Island's Mine,' " p. 170.

it by."[13] The pressing horrors of the Madagascan crisis prompted Mannoni to find a new significance for *The Tempest,* encouraging him to weave a reading of Shakespeare's poetic drama through his reading of the incipient drama of decolonization.

Mannoni's account of the psychological climate of colonialism is advanced through an opposition between the Prospero (or inferiority) complex and the Caliban (or dependence) complex. On this view, Europeans in Madagascar typically displayed the need, common among people from a competitive society, to feel highly regarded by others. However, the Prospero-type is not just any white man, but specifically the sort whose "grave lack of sociability combined with a pathological urge to dominate" drives him to seek out uncompetitive situations where, among a subservient people, his power is amplified and his least skills assume the aspect of superior magic (*PC,* p. 102). Whether a French settler in Africa or Shakespeare's duke, he is loath to depart his adopted island, knowing full well that back home his standing will shrink to mundane dimensions. Mannoni found the Madagascans, on the other hand, to be marked by a Caliban complex, a dependence on authority purportedly characteristic of a people forced out of a secure "tribal" society and into the less stable, competitively edged hierarchies of a semi-Westernized existence. According to this theory, colonialism introduced a situation where the Madagascan was exposed for the first time to the notion and possibility of abandonment. Crucially, the colonist failed to comprehend the Madagascan's capacity to feel "neither inferior nor superior but yet wholly dependent," an unthinkable state of mind for someone from a competitive society (*PC,* p. 157). So, in Mannoni's terms, the Madagascan revolt was fueled less by a desire to sunder an oppressive master-servant bond than by the people's resentment of the colonizers' failure to uphold that bond more rigorously and provide them with the security they craved. What the colonial subjects sought was the paradoxical freedom of secure dependence rather than any autonomous, self-determining freedom. This assumption clearly shaped Mannoni's skepticism about the Madagascans' desire, let alone their capacity, to achieve national independence.

Mannoni values *The Tempest* most highly for what he takes to be Shakespeare's dramatization of two cultures' mutual sense of a trust betrayed: Prospero is a fickle dissembler, Caliban an ingrate. The nodal lines here, and those that draw Mannoni's densest commentary, are spoken by Caliban in the play's second scene. They should be quoted at length,

13. [Dominique] O. Mannoni, *Prospero and Caliban: The Psychology of Colonization,* trans. Pamela Powesland (New York, 1964), p. 34; all further references to this work, abbreviated *PC,* will be included in the text. The centrality of *The Tempest* to Mannoni's theory was given added emphasis by the extended title of the English translation.

for they are taken up repeatedly by subsequent Caribbean and African appropriators of *The Tempest.*

> When thou cam'st first,
> Thou strok'st me, and made much of me, wouldst give me
> Water with berries in't, and teach me how
> To name the bigger light, and how the less,
> That burn by day and night, and then I lov'd thee
> And show'd thee all the qualities o' th' isle,
> The fresh springs, brine-pits, barren place and fertile:
> Curs'd be I that did so! All the charms
> Of Sycorax, toads, beetles, bats, light on you!
> For I am all the subjects that you have,
> Which first was mine own king; and here you sty me
> In this hard rock, whiles you do keep from me
> The rest o' th' island.[14]

To Mannoni, it appears evident that "Caliban does not complain of being exploited; he complains of being betrayed." He "has fallen prey to the resentment which succeeds the breakdown of dependence" (*PC,* p. 106). This view is buttressed by an analogous interpretation of Caliban's revolt in league with Trinculo as an action launched "not to win his freedom, for he could not support freedom, but to have a new master whose 'foot-licker' he can become. He is delighted at the prospect. It would be hard to find a better example of the dependence complex in its pure state" (*PC,* pp. 106–7).

Such statements rankled badly with Caribbean and African intellectuals who, in the fifties, for the first time sensed the imminence of large-scale decolonization in their regions. In such circumstances, the insinuation that Caliban was incapable of surviving on his own and did not even aspire to such independence in the first place caused considerable affront and helped spur Third Worlders to mount adversarial interpretations of the play which rehabilitated Caliban into a heroic figure, inspired by noble rage to oust the interloping Prospero from his island. Fanon and Aimé Césaire, two of Mannoni's most vehement critics, found the "ethno-psychologist's" disregard for economic exploitation especially jarring and accused him of reducing colonialism to an encounter between two psychological types with complementary predispositions who, for a time at least, find their needs dovetailing tidily.[15] *Psychologie de la colonisation,* these critics charged, made Caliban out to be an eager partner in his

14. William Shakespeare, *The Tempest,* act 1, sc. 2, ll. 332–44; all further references to the play will be included in the text.

15. See Fanon, *Peau noire, masques blancs* (Paris, 1952), and Aimé Césaire, *Discours sur le colonialisme,* 3d ed. (Paris, 1955). See also the section, "Caliban on the Couch," in O. Onoge, "Revolutionary Imperatives in African Sociology," in *African Social Studies: A Radical Reader,* ed. Peter C. W. Gutkind and Peter Waterman (New York, 1977), pp. 32–43.

own colonization. Mannoni, in a statement like "wherever Europeans have founded colonies of the type we are considering, it can safely be said that their coming was unconsciously expected—even desired—by the future subject peoples," seemed to discount any possibility of Europe being culpable for the exploitation of the colonies (*PC*, p. 86). Mannoni's critics foresaw, moreover, just how readily his paradigm could be harnessed by Europeans seeking to thwart the efforts for self-determination that were gathering impetus in the fifties.

Fanon and Césaire's fears about the implications of Mannoni's thesis were vindicated by the appearance in 1962 of *Prospero's Magic: Some Thoughts on Class and Race* by Philip Mason, an English colonial who sought to give credence to Mannoni's ideas by using them to rationalize resistance to colonialism in Kenya ("Mau Mau"), India, and Southern Rhodesia. The upshot of this effort was Mason's conclusion that "a colonial rebellion may be a protest not against repression but against progress, not against the firm hand but against its withdrawal" and that (for such is every "tribal" society's craving for firm authority) "countries newly released from colonialism . . . [will experience] a reduction of personal freedom."[16]

Prospero's Magic is an intensely autobiographical and occasional work. Its author, in siding with Mannoni, was also seeking to counteract the first fully fledged Caribbean appropriation of *The Tempest,* Lamming's recently published *Pleasures of Exile* (1960). The lectures comprising *Prospero's Magic* were delivered at the University College of the West Indies on the eve of Jamaica's independence and are based on Mason's more than twenty years as a colonial employee in India, Nigeria, and Rhodesia, where he witnessed the death throes—or as he terms it, the fulfillment—of British imperialism. Rereading *The Tempest* in the political atmosphere of 1962, he was discomfited by his recognition of the Prospero in himself. Circumstances had altered: "While many of us today find we dislike in Prospero things we dislike in ourselves, our fathers admired him without question and so indeed did my generation until lately" (*PM*, p. 92).[17] Mason tried to square his awareness that colonialism was becoming increasingly discredited with his personal need to salvage some value and self-respect from his decades of colonial "service." So he was at once a member of the first generation to acknowledge distaste for Prospero and personally taken aback by his own sudden redundancy: "With what deep reluctance does the true Prospero put aside his book and staff, the magic of power and office, and go to live in Cheltenham!" (*PM*, p. 96).

16. Philip Mason, *Prospero's Magic: Some Thoughts on Class and Race* (London, 1962), p. 80; all further references to this work, abbreviated *PM,* will be included in the text.

17. Though it is underscored by a different politics, Sartre makes a related remark in his preface to *The Wretched of the Earth:* "We in Europe too are being decolonized: that is to say that the settler which is in every one of us is being savagely rooted out" (Sartre, preface, p. 24).

Mason, for one, conceived of himself as writing at the very moment when the colonial master was called upon to break and bury his staff.

By the time Caribbeans and Africans took up *The Tempest,* that is, from 1959 onward, widespread national liberation seemed not only feasible but imminent, and the play was mobilized in defense of Caliban's right to the land and to cultural autonomy. "This island's mine by Sycorax my mother / Which thou tak'st from me" (1.2.333–34) are the lines that underlie much of the work that was produced by African and Caribbean intellectuals in the 1960s and early 1970s.[18] Those same two lines introduce Caliban's extended complaint (quoted at length above), the nodal speech Mannoni had cited as evidence that Shakespeare was dramatizing a relation of dependence, not one of exploitation. But, significantly, and in keeping with his very different motives for engaging with the play, Mannoni had lopped off those two lines when working the passage into his argument. On this score, Third World responses consistently broke with Mannoni: Caliban, the decolonizer, was enraged not at being orphaned by colonial paternalism but at being insufficiently abandoned by it.

The first Caribbean writer to champion Caliban was Lamming. His nonfictional *Pleasures of Exile* can be read as an effort to redeem from the past, as well as to stimulate, an indigenous Antillean line of creativity to rival the European traditions which seemed bent on arrogating to themselves all notions of culture. Lamming's melange of a text—part essay on the cultural politics of relations between colonizer and colonized, part autobiography, and part textual criticism of, in particular, *The Tempest* and C. L. R. James' *The Black Jacobins* (1938)—was sparked by two events, one personal, the other more broadly historical.[19] Lamming began his text in 1959, shortly after disembarking in Southampton as part of the great wave of West Indian immigrants settling in Britain in the fifties. But his circumstances differed from those of most of his compatriots, for he was immigrating as an aspirant writer. As such he was keenly aware of taking up residence in the headquarters of the English language and culture and, concomitantly, of being only ambiguously party to that language and culture, even though a dialect of English was his native tongue and even though—for such was his colonial schooling—he was more intimate with Shakespeare and the English Revolution than with the writings and history of his own region.

Lamming's reflections on the personal circumstances which occasioned *The Pleasures of Exile* are suffused with his sense of the book's historical

18. For a thematic rather than a historical survey of the figure of Caliban in Third World writing, see Charlotte H. Bruner, "The Meaning of Caliban in Black Literature Today," *Comparative Literature Studies* 13 (Sept. 1976): 240–53.

19. See C. L. R. James, *The Black Jacobins: Toussaint Louverture and the San Domingo Revolution* (New York, 1963).

moment. Writing on the brink of the sixties, he was highly conscious that colonial Africa and the Caribbean were entering a new phase. The political mood of the book is expectant ("Caliban's history . . . belongs entirely to the future" [*PE,* p. 107]), most evidently in his account of an envious visit to Ghana, the first of the newly independent African states. That trip sharpened his anguished sense of the British West Indies' failure as yet to achieve comparable autonomy. He recalls the intensity of that feeling in his introduction to the 1984 edition: "There were no independent countries in the English-speaking Caribbean when I started to write *The Pleasures of Exile* in 1959. With the old exceptions of Ethiopia and Liberia, there was only one in Black Africa, and that was Ghana. Twenty years later almost every rock and pebble in the Caribbean had acquired this status" (*PE,* p. 7). While looking ahead to Caribbean self-determination, Lamming was also writing self-consciously in the aftermath of an action one year back that had quickened nationalist ambitions throughout the area: "Fidel Castro and the Cuban revolution reordered our history. . . . The Cuban revolution was a Caribbean response to that imperial menace which Prospero conceived as a civilising mission" (*PE,* p. 7).

Lamming's relationship to decolonization is markedly distinct from Mannoni's. The Frenchman was in Madagascar as a social scientist observing and systematizing the psychological impulses behind an incipient struggle for national autonomy, while the Barbadian's reflections on decolonization are less distanced and more personal, as he declares himself to be Caliban's heir. Lamming's and Mannoni's different tacks are most conspicuous in their treatment of Caliban's pronouncement: "You taught me language; and my profit on't / Is, I know how to curse" (1.2.363–64). From that quotation Mannoni launches an analysis of the role in 1947–48 of the westernized Malagasies, some of whom had become so acculturated during study abroad that they could no longer engage with their countryfellows. The cross-cultural status of yet others who were less thoroughly assimilated but had become fluent in acrimony facilitated their rise to positions of leadership in the national resistance. Lamming, by contrast, takes up Caliban's remarks on language as one who is himself a substantially Europeanized Third Worlder, a West Indian nationalist living in England, and someone reluctant to segregate his theoretical from his autobiographical insights.[20] Much of the personal urgency of Lamming's text

20. Given the antipathy between Trinidadian-born V. S. Naipaul and the more radical Lamming, and given Lamming's identification with Caliban, it is probable that Naipaul had the Barbadian in mind in his fictional *A Flag on the Island,* where the narrator parodies Caribbean celebrations of Caliban by citing a local autobiography, *I Hate You: One Man's Search for Identity,* which opens: " 'I am a man without identity. Hate has consumed my identity. My personality has been distorted by hate. My hymns have not been hymns of praise, but of hate. How terrible to be Caliban, you say. But I say, how tremendous. Tremendousness is therefore my unlikely subject' " (Naipaul, *A Flag on the Island* [London, 1967], p. 154).

stems from his assimilation of Caliban's linguistic predicament to his own. As a writer by vocation, he is especially alert to the way colonialism has generated linguistic discrimination, to how, as a West Indian born into English, he is branded a second-class speaker of his first language.

Though Lamming addresses the question of the unlanded Caliban who declares "This island's mine," he dwells most obsessively on the educational inheritance which he finds enunciated in the speech "You taught me language." While the nationalist struggle provides a shaping context for *The Pleasures of Exile,* Lamming's Caliban is not just any colonial subject but specifically the colonized writer-intellectual, the marginal person of letters. Lamming's root frustration is the ostensible lack of parity between the possibilities for political and for cultural freedom. Come formal independence, the people may establish their own laws and governments, but won't Caribbean writers still lag behind, permanently shackled to the colonizer's language—whether English, French, or Spanish—since it is the only one they have? "Prospero lives in the absolute certainty that Language which is his gift to Caliban is the very prison in which Caliban's achievements will be realised and restricted. Caliban can never reach perfection, not even the perfection implicit in Miranda's privileged ignorance" (*PE,* p. 110).[21] That is, as long as Caliban is still bound to his former master's language, he is still partly condemned to live the life of a servant.

What holds for language holds equally for culture in general. If Caliban's accent sounds sour and deformed to the British ear, so too his knowledge of British traditions—no matter how relentlessly they have been drummed into him in Barbados—will be shown up as flawed and fragmentary. Yet on this score Lamming is unevenly pessimistic, for his very appropriation of *The Tempest* testifies to his faith in the Caribbean intellectual's capacity to scale the conventional heights of British culture. Instead of deferring slavishly to a British norm, Lamming manages—with Caliban's lines at the ready—to treat that norm as a pretext for and object of abuse. To write about Shakespeare is a strategy for commanding a hearing in the West, but he values this audibility primarily because it enables him to draw attention to his ostracism. He is only too aware of the implications of quoting Shakespeare to legitimate his "illegitimate" treatment of that same hallowed author:

> It is my intention to make use of *The Tempest* as a way of presenting a certain state of feeling which is the heritage of the exiled and colonial writer from the British Caribbean.

21. Cf. the remark by Chris Searle, another writer who reads Caribbean culture through the Prospero–Caliban dichotomy: "The ex-master's language . . . is still the currency of communication which buys out the identity of the child as soon as he begins to acquire it" (Searle, *The Forsaken Lover,* p. 29).

> Naturally, I anticipate from various quarters the obvious charge of blasphemy; yet there are occasions when blasphemy must be seen as one privilege of the excluded Caliban. [*PE,* p. 9]

Lamming seizes the outcast's prerogative to impiety in part to shake the insiders' monopoly of a text that draws and bears on Caribbean history. But this destructive impulse feeds a more positive one: the desire to mount an indigenous countertradition, with a reinterpreted Caliban from 1611 and the contemporary, about-to-be-liberated Antillean of 1959 flanking that tradition. So for all its dense, original analogies between *The Tempest* and the Caribbean of the late fifties, what is at stake in *The Pleasures of Exile* is something larger than the immediate, local value of a Shakespearean play: it is the very possibility of decolonizing the area's cultural history by replacing an imposed with an endemic line of thought and action. Within the context of this grand design, the initial gesture of annexing Shakespeare was pivotal, as it generated a Caliban who could stand as a prototype for successive Caribbean figures in whom cultural and political activism were to cohere. Lamming's reconstructed tradition runs through Toussaint Louverture, C. L. R. James, and Fidel Castro to the author himself who, like many of his generation of West Indian writers, immigrated to England to embark on a literary career but while there also pressed for his region's independence. That these particular figures should have been selected to brace the countertradition points to Lamming's conviction that—linguistic dilemmas notwithstanding—Caribbean culture and politics had been and should ideally continue to be allies in each other's decolonization.

In spirit, Lamming's dissident reassessment of one of the high texts of European culture had been matched by the Trinidadian James' reverse angle in *The Black Jacobins* on one of the most celebrated periods of European history, the French Revolution. *The Pleasures of Exile* is designed to make these two unorthodox gestures seem of a piece, through remarks such as "[there] C. L. R. James shows us Caliban as Prospero had never known him" (*PE,* p. 119). James' Caliban is Toussaint Louverture, leader of the first successful Caribbean struggle for independence, the Haitian slave revolt of 1791–1803. As the title of his book might suggest, James was concerned to dredge up a counternarrative, from a Caribbean perspective, of events which had been submerged beneath the freight of Eurocentric history. For Lamming, James' action and others like it were essential to the establishment of a Calibanic lineage; but once established, that lineage had still to be sustained, which would require one salvaging operation after another. This apprehension was borne out when, at the time of writing *The Pleasures of Exile,* Lamming discovered that James' book, out of print for twenty years, was in danger of sinking into neglect. So he set himself the task of doing in turn for James what James had done for Louverture: keeping afloat a vital, remedial tradition that was threatening to disappear.

During the era of decolonization, negritude proved to be one of the strongest components of this remedial tradition, and it was the negritudist from Martinique, Césaire, who came to renovate *The Tempest* theatrically for black cultural ends in a manner indebted to Lamming if fiercer in its defiance. These two writers' approaches coincided most explicitly in their determination to unearth an endemic lineage of cultural-cum-political activists; it is telling that within the space of two years, each man published a book resuscitating Toussaint Louverture and celebrating his example.[22]

Césaire's *Une Tempête* (1969) exemplifies the porous boundaries between European and Afro-Caribbean cultures even within the anticolonial endeavors of the period. As an influence on Césaire's response to Shakespeare, Lamming keeps company with Mannoni and the German critic, Janheinz Jahn. Mannoni had experience of French island colonies in both Africa and the Caribbean for, prior to his stint in Madagascar, he had served as an instructor in a Martinican school where Césaire had been his precocious student. More than twenty years later, in *Discours sur le colonialisme,* Césaire upbraided his former schoolmaster for not thinking through the implications of his colonial paradigm. And Césaire's subsequent, inevitably reactive adaptation of Shakespeare further demonstrated just how far he had diverged from Mannoni's motives for valuing *The Tempest.* More in keeping with the spirit of *Une Tempête* was Jahn's *Geschichte der neo-afrikanischen Literatur,* which appeared a few years before Césaire wrote his play. Jahn's pioneering study gave prominence to the Calibanesque in Mannoni and Lamming and, by designating the negritude writers (Césaire, Leopold Senghor, and Ousmane Diop) black cultural liberators à la Caliban, hinted at ideas that Césaire was to develop more amply. Notable among these was Jahn's attempt to counteract Lamming's dejected pronouncements about the confining character of Prospero's language by exhorting Caliban to free himself through cultural bilingualism—by recovering long-lost African strains and using them to offset the derivative, European components of his cultural identity. Jahn urged further that suitable elements of European culture be transformed into vehicles for black cultural values. Along these lines, negritude could be defined as "the successful revolt in which Caliban broke out of the prison of Prospero's language, by converting that language to his own needs of self-expression."[23]

Césaire has been quite explicit about his motives for reworking *The Tempest:*

22. See Lamming, *The Pleasures of Exile,* and Césaire, *Toussaint Louverture: la révolution française et le problème colonial* (Paris, 1961).

23. Janheinz Jahn, *Neo-African Literature: A History of Black Writing,* trans. Oliver Coburn and Ursula Lehrburger (New York, 1969), p. 242.

> I was trying to 'de-mythify' the tale. To me Prospero is the complete totalitarian. I am always surprised when others consider him the wise man who 'forgives'. What is most obvious, even in Shakespeare's version, is the man's absolute will to power. Prospero is the man of cold reason, the man of methodical conquest—in other words, a portrait of the 'enlightened' European. And I see the whole play in such terms: the 'civilized' European world coming face to face for the first time with the world of primitivism and magic. Let's not hide the fact that in Europe the world of reason has inevitably led to various kinds of totalitarianism . . . Caliban is the man who is still close to his beginnings, whose link with the natural world has not yet been broken. Caliban can still *participate* in a world of marvels, whereas his master can merely 'create' them through his acquired knowledge. At the same time, Caliban is also a rebel—the positive hero, in a Hegelian sense. The slave is always more important than his master—for it is the slave who makes history.[24]

Césaire's perception of Prospero as "the man of methodical conquest" and his insistence on the slave as the preeminent historical agent become the touchstones for his radically polarized adaptation of Shakespeare. Forgiveness and reconciliation give way to irreconcilable differences; the roles of Ferdinand and Miranda are whittled down to a minimum; and the play's colonial dimensions are writ large. Antonio and Alonso vie with Prospero for control over newly charted lands abroad, and Shakespeare's rightful Duke of Milan is delivered to the island not by the providence of a "happy storm" but through a confederacy rooted in imperial ambitions. Prospero is demythologized and rendered contemporary by making him altogether less white magical and a master of the technology of oppression; his far from inscrutable power is embodied in antiriot control gear and an arsenal. Violating rather than communing with life on the island, he is, in Caliban's phrase, the "*anti-Natur.*"

Une Tempête self-consciously counterpoises the materialist Prospero with an animistic slave empowered by a culture that coexists empathetically with nature. Indeed, Caliban's culture of resistance is his sole weaponry, but it is more formidable than the shallow culture Shakespeare permits him, as Césaire plumbs the depths of the slave's African past to make him a more equal adversary.[25] Caliban's defiance is expressed most strongly through the celebration of the Yoruba gods Shango and Eshu; two of his four songs of liberation fete Shango, an African figure who has

24. Césaire, quoted in S. Belhassen, "Aimé Césaire's *A Tempest,*" in *Radical Perspectives in the Arts,* ed. Lee Baxandall (Harmondsworth, 1972), p. 176.

25. For the fullest discussion concerning Césaire's Africanizing of Shakespeare, see Thomas A. Hale, "Aimé Césaire: His Literary and Political Writings with a Bio-bibliography" (Ph.D. diss., University of Rochester, 1974), and "Sur *Une tempête* d'Aimé Césaire," *Etudes Littéraires* 6 (1973): 21–34.

survived in Caribbean voodoo and Brazilian macumba. And in a critical irruption, Eshu scatters Prospero's carefully ordered classical masque, making the imported divinities seem precious, effete, and incongruous.

Césaire's Caliban also goes beyond Shakespeare's in his refusal to subscribe to the etiquette of subjugation:

> CALIBAN: Uhuru!
> PROSPERO: Qu'est-ce que tu dis?
> CALIBAN: Je dis Uhuru!
> PROSPERO: Encore une remontée de ton langage barbare. Je t'ai déjà dit que n'arrive pas ça. D'ailleurs, tu pourrais être poli, un bonjour ne te tuerait pas![26]

This opening exchange between Caliban and his colonial overlord sets the stage for Césaire's conviction that the culture of slaves need not be an enslaved culture. Here he is more optimistic than Lamming, who saw Caribbean cultures of resistance as ineluctably circumscribed by the colonizer's language; one thinks particularly of Lamming in Ghana, casting an envious eye over children chatting in their indigenous tongue, a language that "owed Prospero no debt of vocabulary" (*PE,* p. 162). Even if Césaire's Caliban cannot throw off European influences entirely, his recuperation of a residual past is sufficient to secure his relative cultural autonomy. Crucially, his first utterance is "Uhuru," the Swahili term for freedom which gained international currency through the struggles for decolonization in the late fifties and sixties. And Caliban retorts to Prospero's demand for a *bonjour* by charging that he has only been instructed in the colonial tongue so he can submit to the magisterial imperatives, and by declaring that he will no longer respond to the name Caliban, a colonial invention bound anagramatically to the degrading "cannibal." Instead, the island's captive king christens himself "X" in a Black Muslim gesture that commemorates his lost name, buried beneath layers of colonial culture. The play supposes, in sum, that Caribbean colonial subjects can best fortify their revolt by reviving, wherever possible, cultural forms dating back to before that wracking sea-change which was the Middle Passage.

Césaire's remark that the slave, as maker of history, "is always more important than his master" has both a retrospective and an anticipatory force, pointing back to Louverture, Haiti, and the only triumphant slave revolt, and forward through the present to colonialism's demise. Césaire steeps his play most explicitly in the contemporary Afro-Caribbean struggles for self-determination when he stages, via Ariel and Caliban, the debate, ubiquitous in the late fifties and sixties, between the rival strategies for

26. Césaire, *Une Tempête: D'après "la Tempête" de Shakespeare—Adaptation pour un théâtre nègre* (Paris, 1969), p. 24.

liberation advanced by proponents of evolutionary and revolutionary change. The mulatto Ariel shuns violence and holds that, faced with Prospero's stockpiled arsenal, they are more likely to win freedom through conciliation than refractoriness. But from Caliban's perspective Ariel is a colonial collaborator, a political and cultural sellout who, aspiring both to rid himself nonviolently of Prospero and to emulate his values, is reduced to negotiating for liberty from a position of powerlessness. The success of Caliban's uncompromising strategies is imminent at the end of the drama. When the other Europeans return to Italy, Prospero is unable to accompany them, for he is in the thrall of a psychological battle with his slave (shades of Mannoni here), shouting "Je défendrai la civilisation!" but intuiting that "le climat a changé." At the close, Caliban is chanting ecstatically, "La Liberté Ohé, La Liberté," and defying the orders of a master whose authority and sanity are teetering.[27]

Césaire, then, radically reassessed *The Tempest* in terms of the circumstances of his region, taking the action to the brink of colonialism's demise. He valued the play because he saw its potential as a vehicle for dramatizing the evolution of colonialism in his region and for sharpening the contemporary ideological alternatives open to would-be-liberated Antilleans. Césaire sought, from an openly interested standpoint, to amend the political acoustics of Shakespeare's play, to make the action resonate with the dangers of supine cultural assimilation, a concern since his student days that was accentuated during the high period of decolonization. This renovation of the play for black cultural ends was doubly impertinent: besides treating a classic sacrilegiously, it implicitly lampooned the educational practice, so pervasive in the colonies, of distributing only bowdlerized versions of Shakespeare, of watering him down "for the natives." *Une Tempête* can thus be read as parodying this habit by indicating how the bard might have looked were he indeed made fit reading for a subject people.

Césaire's play was published in 1969. The years 1968 through 1971 saw the cresting of Caribbean and African interest in *The Tempest* as a succession of essayists, novelists, poets, and dramatists sought to integrate the play into the cultural forces pitted against colonialism. During those four years, *The Tempest* was appropriated among the Caribbeans by Césaire, Fernández Retamar (twice), Lamming (in a novelistic reworking of some of the ideas first formulated in *The Pleasures of Exile*), and the Barbadian poet Edward Braithwaite. In Africa, the play was taken up during the same period by John Pepper Clark in Nigeria, Ngugi Wa Thiong'o in Kenya, and David Wallace in Zambia.[28] Among these, Braithwaite and

27. Ibid., p. 92.

28. See Fernández Retamar, "Cuba Hasta Fidel," *Bohemia* 61 (19 September 1969): 84–97, and "Caliban: Notes Toward a Discussion of Culture in Our America"; Lamming, *Water with Berries* (London, 1971); Edward Braithwaite, *Islands* (London, 1969), pp. 34–38; John Pepper Clark, "The Legacy of Caliban," *Black Orpheus* 2 (Feb. 1968): 16–39;

Fernández Retamar followed Lamming's lead, finding a topical, regional urgency for the play through articulating the Cuban revolution to Caliban's revolt. Braithwaite's poem, "Caliban," salutes the Cuban revolution against a backdrop of lamentation over the wrecked state of the Caribbean. The body of the poem, with its clipped calypso phrasing, knits together allusions to Caliban's song, " 'Ban, 'Ban, Ca-Caliban," Ferdinand's speech, "Where should this music be?" and Ariel's response, "Full fadom five." But it is Caliban the slave, not the royal Alonso, who suffers a sea-change, falling "through the water's / cries / down / down / down / where the music hides / him / down / down / down / where the si- / lence lies." And he is revived not by Ariel's ethereal strains and, behind them, Prospero's white magic, but by the earthy music of the carnival and the intercession of black gods.[29]

But it was Fernández Retamar, a prominent figure in the cultural renovation of postrevolutionary Cuba, whose interest in the play was most specifically sparked by that nation's experience of decolonization. He first brought *The Tempest* glancingly to bear on the circumstances of his region in "Cuba Hasta Fidel" (1969); two years later he elaborated more fully on this correspondence. The second essay, "Caliban: Notes Toward a Discussion of Culture in Our America," at once passionately chronicles the accumulative symbolic significance of Caliban and commemorates those whose deeds and utterances bodied forth the author's conception of the Calibanesque. This sixty-five-page exhortative history draws together many of the issues deliberated by earlier writers:

> Our symbol then is not Ariel . . . but rather Caliban. This is something that we, the *mestizo* inhabitants of these same isles where

---

Ngugi Wa Thiong'o, "Towards a National Culture," *Homecoming: Essays on African and Caribbean Literature, Culture, and Politics* (Westport, Conn., 1983); David Wallace, *Do You Love Me Master?* (Lusaka, 1977). In Lamming's allegorical novel, Caliban resurfaces in the form of three West Indian artists who reside in London and collectively play out the dilemmas of colonizer–colonized entanglements during the era of decolonization. Clark's reflections turn on the relation between "the colonial flag and a cosmopolitan language." Clark both follows and reroutes Lamming's insights on this subject as, unlike his Caribbean predecessor, he approaches English from an African perspective, that is, as a second language. Ngugi's essay, published in 1972, was originally delivered at a conference in 1969. In it he assails Prospero for first dismantling Caliban's heritage and then denying that such a culture ever existed. Ngugi proceeds to sketch strategies for reaffirming the value of that damaged inheritance, notably by decolonizing language and education. Wallace's play was first performed in 1971. Regional nuances aside, *Do You Love Me Master?* is much of a piece with trends already discussed: aided by rioting prisoners, Caliban, a cursing Zambian "houseboy," drives the "bossman," Prospero, out of the country. In the final scene Prospero's stick, more truncheon than wand, is broken, and the crowd encircles the master shouting "Out, out!" and waves banners proclaiming freedom. The play incorporates songs in three African languages.

29. Braithwaite, "Caliban," *Islands,* p. 36.

> Caliban lived, see with particular clarity: Prospero invaded the islands, killed our ancestors, enslaved Caliban, and taught him his language to make himself understood. What else can Caliban do but use that same language—today he has no other—to curse him, to wish that the "red plague" would fall on him? I know no other metaphor more expressive of our cultural situation, of our reality. ["C," p. 24]

Fernández Retamar proceeds to list thirty-five exemplary Calibans, among them Louverture, Castro, Césaire, and Fanon. And just as Lamming had singled out Louverture for special treatment, here José Martí, the late nineteenth-century Cuban intellectual and political activist who died in the struggle for Cuban independence, is commended at length for his fidelity to the spirit of Caliban.[30]

Fernández Retamar, as flagrantly as Lamming, makes it apparent how little interest he has in affecting any "scholarly distance" from *The Tempest.* Far from striving to efface his personality, affiliations, and the circumstances of his reading of *The Tempest,* he steeps his essay in occasion and function and speaks consistently in the first-person plural, a voice that inflects his words with a sense of collective autobiography. His interest is in the advantage to be derived from the play by a community who, from a European perspective, could possess at best an ancillary understanding of Shakespeare and, at worst, would be likely perpetrators of barbarous error.[31] Yet that very exclusion conferred on them a coherent identity: "For it is the coloniser who brings us together, who reveals the profound similarities existing above and beyond our secondary differences" ("C," p. 14). Oppositional appropriations of *The Tempest* could be enabling because "to assume our condition as Caliban implies rethinking our history from the *other* side, from the viewpoint of the *other* protagonist" ("C," p. 28). Put differently, having the nerve to push the play against the Western critical grain, marginalized Caribbeans were relieved of the struggle, unwinnable in Western terms, to gain admission to the *right* side. Their brazen unorthodoxy thus became instrumental in redefining the *wrong* as the *other* side, in opening up a space for themselves where their own cultural values need no longer be derided as savage and deformed.

Fernández Retamar's essay is synoptic yet retains a distinctively Cuban bent, illustrative of the diversity among the consistently adversarial readings

30. The strong historical presence of Martí in the essay is redoubled by Fernández Retamar's invocation, from the same era, of José Enrique Rodó's *Ariel.* Published in 1900, this Uruguayan novel was written in direct response to the 1898 American intervention in Cuba. Rodó identifies Latin America with Ariel, not Caliban.

31. The European suspicion that colonized people would treat Shakespeare with, to invoke Fernández Retamar's phrase, "presumed barbarism" was starkly evident when the Parisian critics dismissed Césaire's *Une Tempête* as a "betrayal" of the bard. See Hale, "Sur *Une Tempête* d'Aimé Césaire," p. 21.

of the play. For one thing, Cuba straddles the Caribbean and Latin America geographically and culturally, and Fernández Retamar's arguments are marked by this double affinity. His focus is hemispheric, and his Caliban, originally the victim of European conquistadors, now labors more directly under North American imperialism. And coming from a society where mulattos predominate, he instinctively defines "our America" as *mestizaje,* as culturally and ethnically mixed; the conflict between Prospero and Caliban is consequently seen in class rather than racial terms.[32] Where for the negritudist Césaire Caliban had most emphatically to be black and Ariel, the favored servant and counterrevolutionary, to be mulatto (a correspondence between race and privilege native to Martinique and much of the formerly French and British Caribbean), for Fernández Retamar, the Ariel-Caliban split is predominantly one of class. The lofty Ariel is representative of the intellectual who must choose between collaborating with Prospero and deliberately allying himself with Caliban, the exploited proletarian who is to advance revolutionary change.

Lemuel Johnson's volume of poems, *highlife for caliban* (1973), marks the decline of *The Tempest*'s value as an oppositional force in decolonizing cultures. Johnson writes out of the historical experience of Freetown, Sierra Leone's capital, a forlorn city of slaves who had been liberated by Britain and had resettled there. Their freedom is announced but scarcely felt as such. The backdrop to the poems is neocolonial: Caliban is now head of state, but his nationalist ideals have become corrupted and enfeebled by power. By the same token, he has experienced the gulf between formal independence and authentic autonomy, as his nation remains in Prospero's cultural and economic thrall and the final exorcism of the master seems improbable. This condition is psychologically dissipating, for "it is the neocolonial event that finally divests Caliban of that which had kept him whole—a dream of revenge against Prospero. But how shall he now revenge himself upon himself?"[33]

The Tempest's value for African and Caribbean intellectuals faded once the plot ran out. The play lacks a sixth act which might have been enlisted for representing relations among Caliban, Ariel, and Prospero once they entered a postcolonial era, or rather (in Harry Magdoff's phrase), an era of "imperialism without colonies."[34] Over time, Caliban's recovery of his island has proved a qualified triumph, with the autonomy

32. See Marta E. Sánchez, "Caliban: The New Latin-American Protagonist of *The Tempest*," *Diacritics* 6 (Spring 1976): 54–61.

33. Sylvia Wynter, "Afterword," in Lemuel Johnson, *highlife for caliban* (Ann Arbor, Mich., 1973), p. 137.

34. Harry Magdoff, "Imperialism without Colonies," in *Studies in the Theory of Imperialism,* ed. Roger Owen and Bob Sutcliffe (New York, 1972), pp. 144–70.

of his emergent nation far more compromised than was imagined by the generation of more optimistic nationalists—politicians and writers alike—who saw independence in. Third Worlders have found it difficult to coax from the play analogies with these new circumstances wherein Prospero, having officially relinquished authority over the island, so often continues to manage it from afar.

With the achievement of formal independence, the anticolonial spirit of insurrection has been dampened and the assertive calls to reconstruct endemic cultures attenuated. By the early seventies the generation of more idealistic (and often more literary) leaders who bridged the periods pre- and postindependence was being replaced by a cohort of Third World leaders who in power have become preoccupied, as Edward Said has noted, primarily with technocratic concerns and defense.[35] Issues of national or racial identity have largely been superseded by issues of survival. In this climate, Shakespeare's play has been drained of the immediate, urgent value it was once found to have, and the moment has passed when a man like Lamming could assert so sanguinely that "*The Tempest* was also prophetic of a political future which is our present. Moreover, the circumstances of my life, both as a colonial and exiled descendant of Caliban in the twentieth century, is an example of that prophecy" (*PE,* p. 13). The play's declining pertinence to contemporary Africa and the Caribbean has been exacerbated by the difficulty of wresting from it any role for female defiance or leadership in a period when protest is coming increasingly from that quarter. Given that Caliban is without a female counterpart in his oppression and rebellion, and given the largely autobiographical cast of African and Caribbean appropriations of the play, it follows that all the writers who quarried from *The Tempest* an expression of their lot should have been men. This assumption of heroic revolt as a preeminently male province is most palpable in Fernández Retamar's inclusion of only one woman in his list of thirty-five activists and intellectuals who exemplify the Calibanesque.

Between the late fifties and early seventies *The Tempest* was valued and competed for both by those (in the "master"-culture's terms) traditionally possessed of discrimination and those traditionally discriminated against. On the one hand, a broad evaluative agreement existed between the two sets of feuding cultures, the colonizers and the colonized both regarding the play highly. On the other hand, the two groups brought utterly different social ambitions to bear on the play. Writers and intellectuals from the colonies appropriated *The Tempest* in a way that was outlandish in the original sense of the word. They reaffirmed the play's

35. See Edward Said, "In the Shadow of the West," *Wedge* 7/8 (Winter/Spring 1985), p. 10.

importance from outside its central tradition not passively or obsequiously, but through what may best be described as a series of insurrectional endorsements. For in that turbulent and intensely reactive phase of Caribbean and African history, *The Tempest* came to serve as a Trojan horse, whereby cultures barred from the citadel of "universal" Western values could win entry and assail those global pretensions from within.

Dancing at the Devil's Party: Some Notes on Politics and Poetry

Alicia Ostriker

> If you/I hesitate to speak, isn't it because we are afraid of not speaking well? But what is "well" or "badly"? With what are we conforming if we speak "well"? What hierarchy, what subordination lurks there, waiting to break our resistance? What claim to raise ourselves up in a worthier discourse? Erection is no business of ours: we are at home on the flatlands.
>
> —Luce Irigaray, "When Our Lips Speak Together"

My education in political poetry begins with William Blake's remark about John Milton in *The Marriage of Heaven and Hell:* "The reason Milton wrote in fetters when he wrote of Angels & God, and at liberty when of Devils & Hell, is because he was a true Poet and of the Devil's party without knowing it."[1] The statement is usually taken as a charming misreading of Milton or as some sort of hyperbole. We find it lumped with other readings which supposedly view Satan as the hero of *Paradise Lost,* such as Percy Bysshe Shelley's in *A Defence of Poetry,* although neither Blake nor Shelley says anything of the kind.[2]

I consider Blake's statement simply accurate. I think it the best single thing anybody has ever said about *Paradise Lost.* If not clear as a bell,

1. William Blake, "The Marriage of Heaven and Hell," *Complete Poems,* ed. Alicia Ostriker (New York, 1977), p. 182.

2. Let one instance serve: Marjorie Hope Nicolson wonders whether the members of the "'Satanic School' of Milton criticism" (Blake, Shelley, Byron) have read past books 1 and 2 of *Paradise Lost* (*John Milton: A Reader's Guide to His Poetry* [New York, 1963], p. 186).

then at least as compressed as diamonds. The insouciant opening gesture takes for granted what to Blake (and to me) is obvious: that the poetry qua poetry is better, more exciting, more energetic in the sections dominated by Satan, worse, duller, less poetic in the sections dominated by God. As a lover of poetry Blake has evidently struck a perplexity. Why (he asks himself) does Milton's Satan excite me and his God bore me even though he plainly intends me to adore God and scorn Satan? The answer could have been that Milton "wrote in fetters" where constrained by theology and the danger of lapsing into inadvertent sacrilege, but "at liberty" otherwise. Other critics have claimed that it is impossible to make God talk successfully in a poem, but the Book of Job is enough to refute that position. Why did Milton choose to make God talk at all? Dante cleverly avoided that difficulty.

The second half of Blake's sentence not only solves the *Paradise Lost* problem but proposes a radical view of all poetry which might be summarized as follows: All art depends on opposition between God and the devil, reason and energy. The true poet (the good poet) is necessarily the partisan of energy, rebellion, and desire, and is opposed to passivity, obedience, and the authority of reason, laws, and institutions. To be a poet requires energy; energetic subjects make the best material for poems; the truer (better) the poetry, the more it will embody the truths of Desire. But the poet need not think so. He can be of the devil's party without knowing it.

The metaphoric train of Blake's sentence is as significant as its idea. "No ideas but in metaphors" might be a useful rule of thumb for poets and critics, especially when we engage in ideological discourse, where words so easily collapse into formulaic wallpaper. A metaphor gives us at least a fighting chance of saying something real. "Fetters . . . liberty . . . party" announces that the theological issue in *Paradise Lost* is inseparable from the political issue. "Are not Religion and Politics the Same Thing?" Blake asks elsewhere. "Prisons are built with stones of Law, Brothels with bricks of Religion," one of the pungently metaphorical Proverbs of Hell, draws the parallels neatly: in both cases, authoritarian systems must create something to punish. Law creates Crime, Religion creates Sin. A century and a half later, Michel Foucault rediscovers this plain truth.

But to return to *Paradise Lost:* Milton's Supreme Being, at the apex of the cosmic hierarchy, is committed to maintaining his own "glory." At the opening of book 3 he explains it all: created beings must have free will, otherwise their adoration would be unsatisfying; commands

---

Alicia Ostriker, professor of English at Rutgers University, is the author of *Stealing the Language: The Emergence of Women's Poetry in America.* Her most recent book of poetry is *Imaginary Lover.*

and prohibitions must be promulgated, otherwise men and angels would have no opportunity to demonstrate their adoration through obedience. Foreseeing that Mankind will fall, God asks as querulously as any father whose son has totaled the car, "Whose fault? / Whose but his own? Ingrate, he had of me / All he could have."[3] In making plans for man's redemption, the Father applauds himself for his own magnanimity, "so shall my glory excel" (*PL* 3:133). As William Empson long ago demonstrated, Milton's (which is to say Christianity's, in the moment of Milton's writing) God is both tyrannical and dull, in addition to being disagreeably egocentric, legalistic, and self-justifying.[4] Satan on the other hand is not at all a good fellow, but he is fascinating and complex—passionate, intelligent, eloquent, capable of introspection, responsive to experience and situation, sexually attractive (as in the scene where Eve is fascinated by the sinuous form of the serpent), and arousable. He can be haughty, humiliated, despairing, hopeful, awed, jealous, spiteful, self-deluding, generous, resolute, exhausted. He is one of us. He is interesting. Milton's God is at best a schoolmaster, at worst Blake's nasty Nobodaddy. And all this is conveyed quite magnificently by Milton's own poetry. At the same time, Milton unquestionably intended to justify God's ways to men, as a poet "enchanted" (C. S. Lewis' splendid term) by the idea of Hierarchy and the beauty of Obedience.[5] Most of his readers have unquestionably thought he was doing so successfully. Only lately do we begin to learn that *Paradise Lost* contains two contradictory belief systems within one poem, and that herein dwells its genius.[6]

Milton's God-Satan opposition demonstrates how a repressive hierarchical structure must inevitably precipitate rebellion. When we look at Adam and Eve we see a parallel inevitability attending gender stratification. "He for God only, she for God in him." Adam is supposed to (benignly) lead and guide, as he has been created with the fuller measure of Reason (*PL* 4:299). Eve is supposed to (voluntarily) follow, having been created with enough Reason to appreciate how wise and superior Adam is, but not enough to be independently trustworthy, especially

3. Milton, *Paradise Lost, Complete Poems and Major Prose,* ed. Merritt Y. Hughes (New York, 1985), 3:96–98; all further references to this work, abbreviated *PL* and with book and line numbers, will be included in the text.

4. See William Empson, *Milton's God* (London, 1965).

5. See C. S. Lewis, *A Preface to "Paradise Lost"* (London, 1961), p. 80.

6. Older writers, for example A. J. A. Waldock, have contended that if we find "a fundamental clash . . . between what the poem asserts, on the one hand, and what it compels us to feel, on the other," then it is an artistic failure (*"Paradise Lost" and Its Critics* [Cambridge, 1947], p. 145). I have argued to the contrary, regarding the "duplicity" in many women writers as well as in Milton, in *Stealing the Language: The Emergence of Women's Poetry in America* (Boston, 1986), pp. 39–42. Blake, Shelley, Empson, and—most persuasively and exhaustively to date—Jackie Di Salvo in *War of Titans: Blake's Critique of Milton and the Politics of Religion* (Pittsburgh, 1983) contend that the contradictions in Milton constitute his aesthetic and intellectual value to us.

since she has been created with something of an overdose of Passion. What Milton's God has made, in other words, is an unstable system. It has to break down, and does break down as soon as Eve realizes that she does not like being dominated. Hierarchy, in the instant that it crosses the line from description to prescription, invites defiance. From the moment we meet Adam and Eve we see the crack in the crockery. It is going to break, it is going to—ah, it has broken. Again, Eve is more interesting poetically than Adam, a well-meaning fellow but a bit of a stiff.

If the true poet is of the devil's party without knowing it, what happens when the poet sets forth with malice aforethought as a devil's advocate? Well, Byron's self-conscious satanic heroes are almost as boring as Milton's God. De Sade, that self-conscious satanist, is not boring only because he is of God's party without knowing it, the hysterical Sadean railings against priests, nuns, virtue, motherhood, and so on, indicating the presence of a particularly virulent superego which he persisted in trying to crush. Blake himself, passionately heterodox as he was, harbored an unacknowledged seed of orthodoxy in the longing for certitude and transcendence which gradually revealed itself in his late prophecies. In Blake's best work, we see the energetic struggle to defeat these seductive cravings internally as well as externally; we see a man who insists that contraries are necessary to life and art; and we see an artist who, like Milton, contains within himself both sides of a monumental cultural and psychic quarrel.

But beyond good and evil? Beyond dominance and obedience? Beyond the dualities, however excitingly charged and contradictory? Of course: plurality. All trades: their gear and tackle and trim. The Whitman catalog, which delights by its scurry and randomness as we are delighted by the spectacle of a city street. The hundred unique characters of Shakespeare, trooping in their rings of alliance and conflict, each doubtless representing a vitally debatable political position, but in bulk representing an infinite variety which ultimately dwarfs debate. What Dryden said of Chaucer: Here is God's plenty.

Dualities are human inventions which we impose on the world and on ourselves in the effort to tame and dominate whatever we conceive of as other. Meanwhile the world remains a continuum, infinite in all directions. The artist, then, defies (our, his, her) impulse to dominate by containing both halves of any argument, and by the attempt to imitate the continuum. From *The Merchant of Venice* we can argue pro and con anti-Semitism, from *Lear* pro and con patriarchal absolutism, from *Antony and Cleopatra* the claims of the state against those of eros—but *The Complete Plays of Shakespeare* argues the smallness of argument. Exuberance, says Blake, is beauty. The man who imagined the Wife of Bath, with her gat-tooth, her debater's points against clerical misogyny, and her six or seven husbands—what's he but exuberant? And when we recall that he imagined as well the pious and priggish Prioress, the high-minded Knight, the low-minded Miller, the slimy Pardoner, the innocent Troilus, the experienced Cressida, and so forth, we cannot but wonder at readings which would reduce Chaucer to a Christian or a courtier. I believe, though I cannot prove, that the plenteousness of great writers is always their most radical quality, in that it implicitly defies category and authority. In whatever age, and whatever the writer's ostensible political positions, plenitude signals the democratizing/subversive impulse, the dance of the devil's party.

In *A Defence of Poetry,* Shelley says, "The great secret of morals is love; or a going out of our own nature. . . . A man, to be greatly good, must imagine intensely and comprehensively; he must put himself in the place of another and of many others."[7] I take this to mean that we first crack the wall between ourselves and our enemy, discovering the foe within the self. Then we find that we and the world are neither single nor double but multiple. If poets are, as Shelley concludes, the "unacknowledged legislators of the world," it is because of this capacity for multiplicity.

"Trust thyself: every heart vibrates to that iron string."[8] As the creation of the poem depends on this, so does the reading of it. I mean actual reading; what we do ourselves, for pleasure.

Suspicious as I am of theory, which is always prescribing to me what I should prefer and interfering with my personal responses, I want to stress the importance of lively response to the political as to any other aspect of a poem. If a work fails to arouse me, how can I begin to understand it, much less judge it?

Yet there are different kinds of arousals. First of all, and let us be candid about this, we love what is on our side. Poems by Blake, Whitman, William Carlos Williams, Allen Ginsberg, for example, in my own case. The critic who attempts to disguise advocacy, pretending to possess literary standards without ideological implications, is not to be trusted—nor did any critic of major stature pretend to do so until the late nineteenth century. Yet we can also become excited in the presence of the enemy camp, if someone whose work runs contrary to our deep convictions is writing strongly enough to crystallize our differences. (Eliot, for example, in my own case.) A mild Albion's Angel, lost without the crutch of authority and orthodoxy, snob, anti-Semite, gynephobe—how beautifully he shows me the beauty of what I must struggle to oppose. Or, a more obvious and violent sort of foe, the LeRoi Jones of "Black Art" advocating "poems

7. Percy Bysshe Shelley, "A Defence of Poetry," *Shelley's Critical Prose,* ed. Bruce R. McElderry, Jr. (Lincoln, Neb., 1967), pp. 12–13.

8. Ralph Waldo Emerson, "Self-Reliance," *Complete Essays and Other Writings,* ed. Brooks Atkinson (New York, 1940), p. 146.

that kill" in the sleekest of jive rhythms, demonstrating the attractiveness of hate. I like to think that I love in political poetry whatever I love in poetry anyway. Language being known and used by someone who delights in the lay of words together. Wit, grace, passion, eloquence, playfulness, compression, vitality, freshness. A voice that is at once the poet's voice and the voice of a time, a nation, a gender. The many, mysteriously funneled through the one: not I, not I, but the wind that blows through me. Only I hope to be aware that "whatever I love in poetry anyway" has, if I cut into it, a political dimension.

I like the word "love" better than the word "evaluate." Bring out number, weight, and measure in a year of dearth, says Blake. I find "love" more reliable than "evaluate." First I see what I love, then I try to understand it. In this way it seems I can love one thing and another, each for different reasons, rather than the same thing over and over and smaller and smaller.

Take Elizabeth Bishop's "Brazil, January 1, 1502," with its brilliant description of a tropic landscape as if it were a tapestry or an embroidery, followed by a description of "the Christians, hard as nails, / tiny as nails, and glinting, / in a creaking armor," who arrive with a dream of "wealth . . . plus a brand-new pleasure":

> Directly after Mass, humming perhaps
> *L'Homme armé* or some such tune,
> they ripped away into the hanging fabric,
> each out to catch an Indian for himself—
> those maddening little women who kept calling,
> calling to each other (or had the birds waked up?)
> and retreating, always retreating, behind it.[9]

The women are like the female lizard Bishop has earlier pictured, "her wicked tail straight up and over, / red as a red-hot wire." The poem delicately and ironically manipulates the parallel between women and land, alike subject to ripping/raping. In its resemblance to a just-finished embroidery, the landscape has already been feminized; the goddess who by implication has stitched it would naturally madden "the Christians." At the same time, the mediation of this embroidery conceit along with Bishop's casual half-amused tone, which throughout the poem negotiates slyly between the perspective of a twentieth-century viewer and that of a sixteenth-century conquistador, frames and distances our horror at the brutality to which the poem alludes. Finally, Bishop's conclusion implies, though in an equally bemused way, that the landscape and its natives may have been, may remain, mysteriously unconquerable.

9. Elizabeth Bishop, "Brazil, January 1, 1502," *The Complete Poems* (New York, 1969), p. 106.

Given the historical realities of conquest, rape, the slave trade, and genocide in Brazil and elsewhere, this conclusion is itself a bit maddening to me as reader. I instinctively look for more bitterness, more denunciation, some recognition that although Nature may be unconquerable, individual lives and cultures are not. Withholding these gratifications to my (perhaps correct) opinions, Bishop instead reminds me that a conqueror's rapacity may be insatiable precisely because it can never feel it has truly possessed what it has conquered—and this is a still more distressing thought. As a consequence of Bishop's artistry, whenever I reread "Brazil, January 1, 1502," I am seduced anew by its fascinatingly elusive mix of calm and anger, disturbed anew by the sense of how profoundly rooted in the erotic and the sacred is the will toward empire.

Here is a part of another poem on the theme of conquest, using the same idea that the conquerors justify their acts by perceiving the conquered as animals. Untitled, it is by Lydia Yellowbird:

> When you came
> you found a people
> with red skin
> they were one
> with all living things
>
> But you did not see this
> beauty
> instead you saw them
> as animals, primitive
> savage.[10]

Compared to the Bishop poem, this is embarrassingly naive. It lacks irony and distance, its language is banal and abstract, it fails to imagine (as against stating) what the enemy "saw," and so it has no poetic interests beyond its message. Any poetry which is merely political—and nothing else—is shallow poetry, although it may serve a valuable temporary purpose. Or so I think. Yet if I heard this poem performed, let's say, in Santa Fe to the right audience, I might well be more stirred by it than by the Bishop poem. As Jerome Rothenberg and others have reminded us, Native American poetry is traditionally oral and functional, not literary, and one of its proper functions is to maintain a spirit of tribal community. Do I contradict myself? Very well, then, I contradict myself. Another example: after a Ginsberg reading at Rutgers, I asked a graduate student of radical bent how she liked him. Well, he had been singing Blake's "Tyger," and she had been sitting there in the front row under his knees while he bounced his harmonium up and down and wagged his body

10. Lydia Yellowbird, untitled poem, in Lynda Koolish, *A Whole New Poetry Beginning Here: Contemporary American Women Poets,* 2 vols. (Ann Arbor, Mich., 1981), p. 179.

around, for what seemed like forever. It was embarrassing. And had she not read Bakhtin, I asked; and did she not notice that Ginsberg's performance was *carnivalesque?* Oh, that's right, she said; it's so different when it's real life.

The poetry I know best, just now, is American women's poetry since 1960. When I began reading this body of work in the mid-seventies, it was speaking to me as woman and as poet in ways no other poetry ever had. Repeatedly I found myself lifted by some stroke of brilliant analysis or bold metaphor, frightened and spurred by acts of courage I could scarcely hope to duplicate in my life or my art. For "what oft was thought but ne'er so well expressed," in women's poetry, evidently meant what had long been locked under the censor's trapdoor and was now for the first time rushing forth into the light of consciousness and language. Gradually I became aware that I was living in the midst of a literary movement which I wanted not only to experience but to describe as a critic. The love, then, came first; the effort to comprehend followed.

What I had to work from, in writing *Stealing the Language,* was eventually something over two hundred individual volumes of poetry by women and a dozen or so anthologies. From these emerged a large but indistinct picture of the women's poetry movement in America since 1960, which slowly assumed focus. I was trying to define what was new, what was altering and expanding "poetry," "woman," those terms we so foolishly think we already know the meaning of. I needed to demonstrate how the advent of this writing was causing the past history of literature subtly, lightly, irretrievably to change. For as Eliot in "Tradition and the Individual Talent" so finely explains that the order of art rearranges itself whenever a genuinely original work appears, so it must shift for larger scale literary movements.[11] The women's poetry movement, it

11. See T. S. Eliot, "Tradition and the Individual Talent," *Selected Prose of T. S. Eliot,* ed. Frank Kermode (New York, 1975), pp. 38–39. See my *Stealing the Language,* pp. 1–13, on the relation of women's poetry to "tradition." Also see *Shakespeare's Sisters: Feminist Essays on Women Poets,* ed. Sandra M. Gilbert and Susan Gubar (Bloomington, Ind., 1979), and *Coming to Light: American Women Poets in the Twentieth Century,* ed. Diane Wood Middlebrook and Marilyn Yalom (Ann Arbor, Mich., 1985). Virtually all feminist criticism locates women's writing in terms of its cultural marginality. The discovery that marginality may be a strength is a recent one. For an excellent discussion of women poets writing on politics, history, and the self in the context of cultural patterns they hope to transform, see Rachel Blau DuPlessis, " 'Perceiving the Other-side of Everything': Tactics of Revisionary Mythopoesis," and "The Critique of Consciousness and Myth in Levertov, Rich, and Rukeyser," chaps. 7 and 8 of *Writing beyond the Ending: Narrative Strategies of Twentieth-Century Women Writers* (Bloomington, Ind., 1985), pp. 105–22 and 123–41. For a study of contemporary women's poetry which focuses on its political dimensions, see *A Whole New Poetry.* Volume 2 of this work is a collection of essays by women poets on their art; almost all perceive themselves as engaged in the radical transformation of self and society. Jan Clausen's *A Movement of Poets: Thoughts on Poetry and Feminism* (Brooklyn, N.Y., 1982) offers a thoughtful insider's

seemed to me, was on the order of romanticism or modernism, destined to produce substantial rearrangements. But of course one senses this in one's bones long before one can say precisely what has happened.

What then is important in contemporary women's poetry? Some linked motifs announce themselves: self-definition, the body, the eruption of anger, the equal and opposite eruption of eros, the need for revisionist mythmaking. What Adrienne Rich has called "the oppressor's language" comes into perpetual question in this poetry, along with the language's rooted dualisms: male vs. female, sacred vs. profane, mind vs. body, public vs. private, logos vs. eros, self vs. other, subject vs. object, art vs. life. Not surprisingly, the strongest women poets tend to oppose hierarchy; they like boundary-breaking, duality-dissolving, and authority-needling.

Formally and stylistically, too, there are interesting developments. I want here to sketch three of these, all of which derive from and relate to particular political issues and are, I feel, designed to subvert and transform the oppressor's language into something a little closer to the heart's desire. They are the exoskeletal style, Black English, and the feminist-communal ritual. I stress the matter of style because a new music in poetry always signals a new meaning. When the music changes, the walls of the city tremble, says Plato. It is by a tuned listening, prior to thought and reflection, that we instinctively locate the dance of the devil's party.

Presumably in response to our culture's identification of femininity with pliability, many of the best women poets use what I call an exoskeletal style: hard, steely, implacably ironic. This is a multipurpose device. It makes the condescending label "poetess" impossible, as it is conspicuously and exaggeratedly antisentimental. It is useful for satire and parody. It is a kind of formal shell like the armor on so many of Marianne Moore's beasts, a sign of the need for self-protection on the part of the vulnerable. Unlike Moore, however, these poets do not pretend to be charming eccentrics. Often this style is used to challenge the neutrality of the reader, addressing a "you" who is perceived as an antagonist or lover-antagonist and whose role the reader is forced to play. Usually at the same time the style implicates the poet in the oppressive scenarios she delineates. Among the finest deployers of this style are Diane Wakoski, Cynthia Macdonald, Margaret Atwood, and Sylvia Plath. In Plath's "Lady Lazarus," for example, the suicidal poet addresses the doctor who has restored her to life:

> I am your opus,
> I am your valuable,
> The pure gold baby

---

account of the problems of politicization and the expectations of political correctness for poets within the feminist community. From these and other writers on women's poetry I have learned immeasurably.

That melts to a shriek.
I turn and burn.
Do not think I underestimate your great concern.[12]

Note the language-play by which "opus" mocks the world of art, "valuable" the world of commerce and commodity, and "pure gold baby" reduces both to the level of vulgar hype. Note too the rhyme, in the service of contempt and self-contempt. Plath is, as women are trained to be, a commodity, an act, an exhibitionist doing "the big strip tease." She is perhaps the female object in a male poem—perhaps one of those poems like the *Divine Comedy* or Wordsworth's Lucy poems in which she has to die first. Was it Poe who said that the most poetical subject imaginable is the death of a beautiful woman? She is perhaps Galatea in the shaping hands of Pygmalion. She is passive and compliant as someone who is truly feminine should be. The "you" of "Lady Lazarus" is in the first instance a kind of sleazy sideshow manager, then becomes "Herr Doktor . . . Herr Enemy," and finally that ultimate source and rationale for male cultural authority and control, "Herr God, Herr Lucifer." As Blake's Urizen compounded the qualities of Milton's rationality-obsessed God and Milton's heaven-exiled Satan, so Plath's supreme being is perfectly evil because he is perfectly good. Plath has begun "Lady Lazarus" by describing her skin as a Nazi lampshade and her face as a "featureless, fine / Jew linen." Critics who dismiss the holocaust imagery of this poem as childish self-aggrandizement or self-pity[13] fail to notice its identification of a historical and political evil with ahistorical and cosmic masculine authority, and the uncomfortable collapsing of good and evil into each other.

The "you" is also ourselves. Plath's portrait of the female artist as self-destroyer locks us inside a universe of concentric spheres of victimization in which we are invited if not compelled to recognize our complicity. To read is to occupy a position not unlike that of Milton's God. We are superior, remote, omniscient, judgmental, able to call the poet into life

12. Sylvia Plath, "Lady Lazarus," *The Collected Poems,* ed. Ted Hughes (New York, 1981), p. 246.

13. See, for example, Marjorie Perloff, "Sylvia Plath's 'Sivvy' Poems: A Portrait of the Poet as Daughter," in *Sylvia Plath: New Views on the Poetry,* ed. Gary Lane (Baltimore, 1979): "In the demonic *Ariel* poems, she could finally vent her anger, her hatred of men, her disappointment in life." "She had really only one subject: her own anguish and longing for death. To a degree, she camouflaged this narrowness by introducing political and religious images. . . . But since the woman who speaks throughout *Ariel* hates all human beings just as she hates herself, her identification with the Jews who suffered at Auschwitz has a hollow ring" (pp. 163, 173). I would argue to the contrary that the combination of anger and self-hatred within victimized individuals and classes is probably a universal human pattern of precisely the sort we need poets to explore. Note: When we wish to ignore the political dimension of a woman poet's work, the usual strategy is to assert that the work is "really" purely personal.

by picking up her book, able to "peel off" her disguises by critical examination. But of course Plath shares our complicity. For if this poem is a critique of control—who is more controlled than this artist? Plath's style, here and in much of her late work, brilliantly represents precisely what it despises; that is its genius, and it is the genius in a great deal of angry women's poetry.

Plath's status as representative feminist martyr invites a question: is such poetry politically useful? This is not a literary question, but it is still answerable. No, if we are looking for a correct position which cleanly distinguishes Us from Them, the good girls from the bad guys. Yes, if we are convinced that such distinctions are false, and that accurate diagnosis must precede effective cure.

Women's poems are not of course necessarily written from within the dominant literary language. A powerful resource for poets lucky enough to have access to it is Black English, with its rich body of cadences and phrases lifted from field hollers, spirituals, gospel, and blues on its musical side, as well as the King James Bible, high-energy preaching, and verbal rituals like rapping and the dozens on its oratorical side.[14] The artful mimesis of "uneducated" speech has been a strategy of social criticism since Huckleberry Finn, first because it lets us enjoy the pleasure of breaking school rules (and we all know in our hearts that rules are in the service of the rulers; to obey them is to accede to social structures for which grammatical structures are the gateway), second because it pits lively imagery against dry abstraction, humor against precept, the play of improvisation and the body's rhythms against the strictures of prior form.

Compare, for example, both Elizabeth Bishop and Lydia Yellowbird with the dry wit of June Jordan in "Poem About My Rights." Jordan is angry that she can't "go out without changing my clothes my shoes / my body posture my gender identity my age," recalls that in France "if the guy penetrates / but does not ejaculate then he did not rape me," and "if even after smashing / a hammer to his head if even after that if he / and his buddies fuck me after that / then I consented," and proceeds to elaborate the connection between rape and imperialism:

> they fucked me over because I was wrong
> . . . .
> which is exactly like South Africa
> penetrating into Namibia
> . . . .

14. See Stephen Henderson, *Understanding the New Black Poetry: Black Speech and Black Music as Poetic References* (New York, 1973); June Jordan, "White English/Black English: The Politics of Translation," *Civil Wars* (Boston, 1981), pp. 59–73; and the discussions of gender, class, race, and language in *This Bridge Called My Back: Writings by Radical Women of Color,* ed. Cherríe Moraga and Gloria Anzaldúa (Watertown, Mass., 1981).

and if
after Namibia and if after Angola and if after Zimbabwe
and if after all of my kinsmen and women resist even to
self-immolation of the villages and if after that
we lose nevertheless what will the big boys say will they
claim my consent?[15]

Without the unpunctuated rhythm, the combination of street-talk and authority-speak, without the legal-military "penetrate" next to the idiomatic "big boys," we would have a weaker poem. Again, in "The Rationale, or, She Drove Me Crazy," Jordan composes a bravura piece with a surprise ending. The speaker in this poem is telling it to the judge:

"suddenly there she was
alone
by herself
gleamin under the street lamp. I thought
'Whoa. Check this out? Hey, Baby! What's
happenin?' I said under my breath.
And I tried to walk past but she was lookin
so good and
the gleam and the shine and
the beautiful lines of her
body sittin out there
alone
by herself
made me wild. I went wild. But
I looked all around to see where her
owner / where the man in her life could
probably be. But no show. She was out.
By herself. On the street:
As fine, as ready to go as anythin you could
ever possibly want to see so
I checked out myself: what's this?
Then I lost my control; I couldn't resist.
What did she expect? She looked foreign
besides and small and sexy
and fast
by the curb. So I lost my control and
I forced her open and I entered
her body and I poured myself
into her
pumpin for all I was worth
wild as I was
when you caught me

15. Jordan, "Poem About My Rights," *Passion: New Poems, 1977–1980* (Boston, 1980), p. 87.

third time apprehended
for the theft of a Porsche."[16]

Surprised? The obvious moral here is that a woman out alone is no more "asking for it" than a car asks to be stolen. A deeper point is that the poem's joke works as well as it does because our history leads us to think of women as property. As they used to say in the Gothics, he was burning to possess her, his dark-eyed beauty. But this point couldn't be made without Jordan's tuned ear for attractive jive talk. For the fact is that these are highly seductive rhythms, and that the real secret of the poem is the poet's Shelleyan ability to put herself in the place of a bad black dude, in order to let us put ourselves there, hearing that voice of self-justification in our own heads.

And what else can it mean to be an outlaw, in language and ideology? For a less violent but no less incandescent effect, here is Lucille Clifton's "Admonitions," quoted in full:

boys
i don't promise you nothing
but this
what you pawn
i will redeem
what you steal
i will conceal
my private silence to
your public guilt
is all i got

girls
first time a white man
opens his fly
like a good thing
we'll just laugh
laugh real loud my
black women

children
when they ask you
why is your mama so funny
say
she is a poet
she don't have no sense[17]

The radical quality of such a poem will not be fully apparent to readers for whom gender and race are political issues but maternity is not. But

16. Jordan, "The Rationale, or, She Drove Me Crazy," *Passion*, pp. 11–12.
17. Lucille Clifton, "Admonitions," *Good Times* (New York, 1969).

as feminist theory has for some time noticed, ours is a culture in which "mother" is object not speaking subject, for our psychology and literature alike represent maternity not from the maternal but from the child's perspective. Maternal autonomy, sexuality, and conflict are consequently suspect; mother is "good" insofar as she selflessly devotes herself to her offspring. A second consequence is that maturation of both male and female children in our culture is supposed to depend on rejection of the mother, identification with the father. A third, so pervasive that we scarcely realize its absurdity, is the privatization of maternity: the mother's role in our culture is a domestic not a public one. She is a being whose love for her children must in no way impinge on society's power to dispose of these children as it chooses.[18]

Contemporary women poets writing as mothers have come to challenge our social assumptions regarding maternity. Additionally, they tend in describing mother-child relationships to propose a profoundly antihierarchical view of human power and need.[19] What if we did not assume that to be powerful means to require worship and obedience? What if we imagined that it might mean the ability to participate in pain and joy? What if Milton's God, and the authorities modeled on his parental design, looked a bit more like Lucille Clifton? She tutors her children in defiance instead of obedience; is unafraid of her sons' lawlessness, her daughters' sexuality, and her own lack of conventional dignity. Her first two stanzas connect class war, gender war, and racism in the framing context of an opposed principle of maternal affection. Her final stanza connects maternity to poetry,[20] and both to play, with a casual impropriety that suggests a contest already won. "Noble" has been changed to "no bull," as Williams promised; but the charm and unpretentiousness of such a poem increases its radicalism. Clifton's insouciance is of a similar

18. The major feminist texts on the issue of motherhood as it intersects with history and political life are Adrienne Rich, *Of Woman Born: Motherhood as Experience and Institution* (New York, 1976); Dorothy Dinnerstein, *The Mermaid and the Minotaur: Sexual Arrangements and Human Malaise* (New York, 1976); and Nancy Chodorow, *The Reproduction of Mothering: Psychoanalysis and the Sociology of Gender* (Berkeley and Los Angeles, 1978). See also Susan Suleiman, "Writing and Motherhood," in *The (M)other Tongue: Essays in Feminist Psychoanalytic Interpretation*, ed. Shirley Nelson Garner, Claire Kahane, and Madelon Sprengnether (Ithaca, N.Y., 1985), pp. 352–77; and Julia Kristeva, "Stabat Mater," and Nancy Huston, "The Matrix of War: Mothers and Heroes," in *The Female Body in Western Culture: Contemporary Perspectives*, ed. Suleiman (Cambridge, Mass., 1986), pp. 99–118 and 119–138.

19. Contemporary poets concerned with "maternal politics" include Alta, Susan Griffin, Adrienne Rich, Audre Lorde, Marilyn Krysl, Sharon Olds, Robin Morgan, Marie Ponsot (to name a few). Griffin's widely anthologized "I Like to Think of Harriet Tubman" is probably the best-known single poem in this field. My book *The Mother/Child Papers* (1980; Boston, 1986) was conceived as an attempt to explore interlacings between maternal experience, violence, and war in the domestic microcosm and the global macrocosm.

20. The creativity/procreativity metaphor as a topos in women's writing is discussed by Susan Friedman, "Creativity and the Childbirth Metaphor: A Case Study for Gender Difference in Literary Discourse," *Feminist Studies* (forthcoming).

order to Blake's, born of anger, love, and the confidence of ultimate victory. Or, as Ida Cox used to sing, "Wild women don't worry, / Wild women don't have the blues."[21]

All these poems operate in a sense by being bilingual, negotiating between the dominant language and a marginal one, employing particularly provocative versions of what Nancy Miller calls "the irreducibly complicated relationship women have historically had to the language of the dominant culture," and what Rachel Blau DuPlessis calls the "both/and vision" of women's writing.[22]

The poems I have cited (and feminist poems as a rule) have in common an "I" which readers will find intensely engaged and engaging, aligned with the feminist conviction that the personal is the political. The poems defy divisions between public and private life because they recognize that such divisions promote oppression; a corollary is that neither poet nor reader can occupy a neutral literary space like Bishop's in "Brazil, January 1, 1502." To render a centuries-old pattern of political violence with the clarity of a tapestry but without an appearance of personal engagement is one legitimate poetic strategy; to pursue transformation through the poetic implication of the self is another.

Some such logic lies behind the phenomenon of the ritual poem in feminist spiritual circles—that is to say, a poem intended to be performed, or to invoke an imagined performance, in a ceremonial setting. The primary intention of such poetry is to strengthen a sense of group, communal, or collective identity and commitment; it may or may not simultaneously critique the dominant culture and its rituals. The poet in ritual poetry enacts a bardic, shamaness' or priestess' role; she may or may not also play the part of the self-examining individual we expect literary poets to be. For poet and reader-participant alike, ritual poetry implies the possibility of healing alternatives to dominance-submission scenarios. It suggests nonoppressive models of the conjunction between religion and politics, usually by re-imaging the sacred as immanent rather than transcendent, by defining its audience as members of a potentially strong community rather than as helplessly lonely individual victims, and by turning to nature (seen as sacred and female) as a source of power rather than passivity. The language of ritual poetry, as it approximates chant, foregrounds recurrent sounds and rhythms, the sensuous qualities of words as against their referential qualities—or, as Julia Kristeva would have it, the semiotic above the symbolic. In this way too it withdraws from the logocentricity we associate with the oppressor's language and

21. Ida Cox, "Wild Women Blues," in *The World Split Open: Four Centuries of Women Poets in England and America, 1552–1950,* ed. Louise Bernikow (New York, 1974), p. 279.

22. Nancy K. Miller, "Emphasis Added: Plots and Plausibilities in Women's Fiction," in *Feminist Criticism: Essays on Women, Literature, and Theory,* ed. Elaine Showalter (New York, 1985), pp. 342–43; DuPlessis, "For the Etruscans," in *Feminist Criticism,* p. 276.

approaches the pleasurable condition of the mother tongue. "Transformation," observes Paula Gunn Allen, "is the oldest tribal ceremonial theme . . . common to ancient Europe, Britain, and America." As Deena Metzger writes in the collage-essay "Affiliations Toward the End of Dying of Silence," exemplifying the faith of many women poets for whom the notion of the isolated artist is a tired cliché, "breaking silence" for a woman writer "has the same meaning as breaking bread. / It is an act of community."[23]

At the present moment the writers of ritual poetry include Black poets like Audre Lorde and Ntozake Shange, Native American poets like Paula Gunn Allen, Wendy Rose, Carole Lee Sanchez, Joy Harjo, and Chrystos, Third World women like Sylvia Gonzalez and Jessica Hagedorn.[24] African goddesses, voodoo, Spider Woman, and other emblematic spiritual beings already figure widely in these poems much as Zen eminences inhabit the writing of an earlier generation of white males who needed to find or invent a sacred space from which to critique both sacred and secular institutions of the dominant American majority. Unsurprisingly, ritual poetry has received little attention from feminist academic circles, which are not themselves exempt from either racism or logocentricity, although this neglect may diminish as the excellence of "minority" women's poetry in America makes itself increasingly felt.[25]

23. Paula Gunn Allen, "Answering the Deer: Genocide and Continuance in American Indian Women's Poetry," in *Coming to Light,* p. 230; Deena Metzger, "Affiliations Toward the End of Dying of Silence," in *A Whole New Poetry,* 2:313. Much of the ritual poetry written by women is not designed to be "literary," having arisen in the context of the women's spirituality movement. See Gloria Z. Greenfield, Judith Antares, and Charlene Spretnak, "The Politics of Women's Spirituality," *Chrysalis: A Magazine of Women's Culture* 6 (1978): 9–15; Z. Budapest, *The Feminist Book of Lights and Shadows* (Los Angeles, 1976) and *The Holy Book of Women's Mysteries* (Los Angeles, 1979); *Womanspirit Rising: A Feminist Reader in Religion,* ed. Carol P. Christ and Judith Plaskow (San Francisco, 1979); Starhawk, *The Spiral Dance: A Rebirth of the Ancient Religion of the Great Goddess* (San Francisco, 1979). My own interest, however, is primarily in the writing of those women who locate themselves deliberately at the intersection of literature, religion, and politics, and see their work as part of an effort to transform all three.

24. Important anthologies containing some of this material are Carole A. Simone, ed., *Networks: An Anthology of San Francisco Bay Area Women Poets* (Palo Alto, Calif., 1979); *This Bridge Called My Back;* and *That's What She Said: Contemporary Poetry and Fiction by Native American Women,* ed. Rayna Green (Bloomington, Ind., 1984).

25. The difficulty of the task is made clear in Adrienne Rich's essay "Disloyal to Civilization: Feminism, Racism, Gynephobia," *On Lies, Secrets, and Silence: Selected Prose, 1966–1978* (New York, 1979), pp. 275–310. A progressive (in my opinion) sign is the acknowledgment within the academy of Black and Native American women writers of experimental fiction such as Zora Neale Hurston, Toni Morrison, Alice Walker, Toni Cade Bambara, Leslie Silko, and Joy Harjo, whose stylistic "difference" emerges from a strong sense of community and communal voice. It remains, however, to be argued that such writers (rather than the "postmoderns" who are so much more easily assimilated by the theoretician) compose the true avant-garde of our time.

The imagination of female sacredness coincides with the critique of language, and both are seen as necessary conditions for political change in Judy Grahn's "She Who," a poem sequence written in 1971–72 which has subsequently become a lesbian-feminist classic. The opening section of "She Who" reads like glossolalia; a polyrhythmic set of repetitions imitates the noise of liturgical question and response, the noise of a congregation or the wind, and the naming of a goddess who might be anywoman:

> She, she SHE, she SHE, she WHO?
> she-she WHO she-WHO she WHO-SHE?
> She, she who? she WHO? she, WHO SHE?
> . . . .
> She SHE who, She, she SHE
> she SHE, she SHE who.
> SHEEE WHOOOOOO[26]

If we compare this with, say, "Who is the king of glory? . . . The Lord of Hosts, He is the king of glory," at least one crucial distinction is Grahn's funniness. As in Blake's *Marriage,* fun is a method of resisting the culture's identification of the sacred with hierarchy and command. More important, the passage cannot be read solely with the eye. It requires the voice, the participation of the body, at which point we find that Grahn's sounds and rhythms (try it, reader) are both difficult and catchy. Succeeding sections of "She Who" cover much familiar (and some unfamiliar) feminist territory—the life cycle of a woman's body, her powerlessness as an object in society and culture, her potential for power and pleasure—in a succession of formal experiments full of wordplay, teasingly disrupted syntax and narrative line and, above all, hand-clapping and foot-tapping rhythms:

> a fishwife a cunt a harlot a harlot a pussy
> a doxie a tail a fishwife a whore a hole a slit
> ["SW," "The enemies of She Who call her various names," p. 84]

> am I not crinkled cranky poison
> am I not glinty-eyed and frozen
> . . . .
> are you not shamed to treat me meanly
> when you discover you become me?
> ["SW," "plainsong from an older woman to a younger woman," pp. 104, 106]

26. Judy Grahn, "She Who," *The Work of a Common Woman: The Collected Poetry of Judy Grahn, 1964–1977* (New York, 1978), p. 77; all further references to this work, abbreviated "SW," will be included in the text.

Most of "She Who," like most feminist writing, is preoccupied with struggle. Its final section, a catalog of sixty-one women, shifts from the defensively dual to the expansively plural as in Whitmanesque fashion it invites us to be large and contain multitudes:

> the woman who carries laundry on her head
> the woman who is part horse
> the woman who asks so many questions
> the women who cut somebody's throat
> . . . .
> the woman who eats cocaine
> the woman who thinks about everything
> the woman who has the tatoo of a bird
> the woman who puts things together
> the woman who squats on her haunches
> the woman whose children are all different colors
> . . . .
>
> when She-Who-moves-the-earth will turn over
> when She Who moves, the earth will turn over.
> ["SW," p. 108]

This move toward a litany—a chant of possible selves, a vision of multiplicity as revolutionary—at present remains a marginal gesture within a marginal literature. Women inclined toward mysticism tend to make such gestures more easily than women inclined toward social realism; those who write outside the literary and academic establishments more readily than those inside. Marginality perhaps helps to free the imagination; Grahn's "She Who" is sister to Blake's devil.

I like the gesture, the opening. My students enjoy performing "She Who" at the close of a semester. I believe that, as Luce Irigaray says in "When Our Lips Speak Together," to recognize the claims of plurality is to make hierarchy defunct: "You/I: we are always several at once. And how could one dominate the other?"[27] At its most radical, contemporary women's poetry begins to ask that question.

27. Luce Irigaray, *This Sex Which Is Not One,* trans. Catherine Porter with Carolyn Burke (Ithaca, N.Y., 1985), p. 209.

"Azikwelwa" (We Will Not Ride): Politics and Value in Black South African Poetry

Anne McClintock

> In the colonial context the settler only ends his work of breaking in the native when the latter admits loudly and intelligibly the supremacy of the white man's values. In the period of decolonization, the colonized masses mock at these very values, insult them and vomit them up.
>
> —FRANTZ FANON, *The Wretched of the Earth*

On the winter morning of 16 June 1976, fifteen thousand black children marched on Orlando Stadium in Soweto, carrying slogans dashed on the backs of exercise books. The children were stopped by armed police who opened fire, and thirteen-year-old Hector Peterson became the first of hundreds of schoolchildren to be shot down by police in the months that followed. If, a decade later, the meaning of Soweto's "year of fire" is still contested,[1] it began in this way with a symbolic display of contempt for the unpalatable values of Bantu education, a public rejection of the "culture of malnutrition" with which blacks had been fed.[2] The local

"Azikwelwa," we will not ride, is a slogan expressing the people's refusal to ride on state transport during the bus and train boycotts.

1. At least three general analyses of the Soweto uprising have emerged: deeper African National Congress involvement in the community; strains on the educational system, unemployment and recession, with greater industrial militancy stemming from the strikes in the early seventies; and the emergence of Black Consciousness ideology. See Tom Lodge, *Black Politics in South Africa Since 1945* (Johannesburg, 1983), pp. 321–62.

2. See M. K. Malefane, " 'The Sun Will Rise': Review of the Allahpoets at the Market Theatre, Johannesburg," *Staffrider* (June/July 1980); reprinted in *Soweto Poetry*, ed. Michael Chapman, South African Literature Series, no. 2 (Johannesburg, 1982), p. 91. *Soweto Poetry* will hereafter be cited as *SP*.

provocation for the Orlando march was a ruling that black children be taught arithmetic and social studies in Afrikaans—the language of the white cabinet minister, soldier, and pass official, prison guard, and policeman. But the Soweto march sprang from deeper grievances than instruction in Afrikaans, and the calamitous year that passed not only gave rise to a rekindling of black political resistance but visibly illuminated the cultural aspects of coercion and revolt.

The children's defacement of exercise books and the breaking of school ranks presaged a nationwide rebellion of uncommon proportion. The revolt spread across the country from community to community, in strikes, boycotts, and street barricades. It represented in part the climax of a long struggle *between* the British and Afrikaans interlopers for control over an unwilling black populace and was at the same time a flagrant sign of the contestation of culture, an open declaration by blacks that cultural value, far from shimmering out of reach in the transcendent beyond, would now be fought for with barricades of tires, empty classrooms, and precocious organization.

After Soweto, new forms of artistic creation appeared across the country. Poetry groups burgeoned in the black townships, creating poetic forms which by received standards were "unliterary" and incendiary, written in "murdered" English, formally inelegant and politically indiscreet. Yet, as it turned out, the poetry reached a far wider audience in South Africa than ever before, posing an unsettling threat to the legitimacy of white settler aesthetics on South African soil and giving rise to an unusually intense debate on the nature of aesthetic value and its relation to what might broadly be termed politics.

The most visible sign of the new Soweto poetry was the launching of *Staffrider* magazine in 1978 by Ravan Press. A "staffrider" is the township name for one who—in mimicry of railway staff—boards at the last minute the dangerous trains hurtling workers to the white city, snatching free rides by clambering onto the roofs of the overcrowded coaches or by hanging from the sides. A staffrider poet, as the editorial of the first issue explained, is thus a "*skelm* of sorts," a miscreant hanging at an acute angle to official law and convention.[3] Tenacious and precarious, at odds with state decree, a black poet becomes a "mobile, disreputable bearer

3. "About Staffrider" (editorial), *Staffrider* 1 (May/June 1978); reprinted in *SP*, p. 125.

Anne McClintock is a Ph.D. candidate in English at Columbia University. She is the author of a monograph on Simone de Beauvoir and is working on a dissertation on race and gender in British imperial culture.

of tidings."[4] More than anything else, the *Staffrider* poet is figured as part of a group in motion, destined to arrive suddenly in the midst of white urban centers.

From the outset, *Staffrider* flouted almost every decorum of sacerdotal authority. A fierce rebuttal of white poetic standards, the magazine paraded an aesthetics of calculated defiance and collectivity. Not only did its literary contents and format—a generic mosaic of poems, photography, articles, graphics, oral history, and short stories—effectively challenge the prestige of the "literary," but its methods of creation and distribution revolutionized periodical publishing in South Africa.

Staffrider was literature in a hurry. Partly because of the nervous post-Soweto climate of surveillance and bannings, it named no editors and placed responsibility for speedy distribution in the hands of township groups and small shops. *Staffrider* had to be a magazine "that would move very quickly without drawing too much attention to itself . . . a contradiction in normal publishing terms."[5] Carefully egalitarian from the outset, the magazine was intended to air the growing number of poets around the country who were writing collectively, and to do so in a way that allowed the art groups themselves to choose the poems to be published. In other words, editorial policy and content lay very much in the hands of readers and writers beyond the publishing house. As Mike Kirkwood, director of Ravan Press, explained, "Nobody wanted the kind of editorial policy that comes from the top: 'We've got a policy. We've got standards. If you fit in with this policy, come up to these standards, we'll publish you.' "[6]

Not surprisingly, the state took immediate umbrage, and the first issue was banned—the Publications Directorate justifying its actions on the grounds that some of the poems undermined "the authority and image of the police."[7] Nor was the state alone in its displeasure. Members of the white literary establishment were piqued by the appearance of a magazine which could brazenly announce: "Standards are not golden or quintessential: they are made according to the demands different societies make on writers, and according to the responses writers make to those demands."[8] Soweto poetry became as a result the locus of a fierce debate

4. Michael Kirkwood, quoted in Ursula A. Barnett, *A Vision of Order: A Study of Black South African Literature in English, 1914–1980* (Amherst, Mass., 1983), p. 37.

5. Nick Visser, " '*Staffrider:* An Informal Discussion': Interview with Michael Kirkwood," *English in Africa* 7 (Sept. 1980); reprinted in *SP,* p. 129. *Staffrider* was conceived in 1977 during discussions with groups such as the Mpumulanga Arts Group. One of the best known of these groups, the Medupe Writers, with a membership of over two hundred, had taken poetry readings to the schools and communities, and was promptly banned in October 1977, along with the South African Students' Organization, the Black People's Convention, and other Black Consciousness organizations.

6. Ibid.

7. *Staffrider* (May/June 1978); quoted in Barnett, *A Vision of Order,* p. 38.

8. *Staffrider* (July/Aug. 1978); quoted ibid.

over the value of black culture and the politics of black aesthetics, not only in the white academy and white publishing houses but also in black classrooms and universities, community halls, poetry groups, and private homes. At stake was whether aesthetic value could any longer credibly be seen to emanate from the text itself, a transcendental immanence somehow detached from the squalor of politics and "the shame of the ideological." In South Africa, as elsewhere, though perhaps more flagrantly, the question of value became entangled with the history of state and institutional power; the history of publishing houses and journals; the private and public histories of the black and white intellectuals, teachers, writers, and evangelists; and the changing relation between this black intermediate class and the worker and oral poets—the Xhosa *iimbongi*, or the migrant Sotho *likheleke*, "the people of eloquence."[9] Questions of education, constituency, and audience were evoked and therewith the possibility that value is not an essential property of a text but a social relation between a work and its audience, constituted rather than revealed, and endorsed or outstripped by successive orders of power.

> It was a joy to recite and listen to the grandeur of Shakespeare on campus. . . . The spoken word or phrase or line was the thing, damn the dialectic.
>
> —ES'KIA MPHAHLELE

The first full generation of black writers in English were the Sophiatown writers of the fifties, years Lewis Nkosi dubbed the "fabulous decade."[10] Sophiatown was a freehold suburb close to the heartland of white Johannesburg where blacks could still own land. Poor and very violent, a jumble of potholed streets and shacks, Sophiatown was at the same time a genuine community where the loyal neighborliness of social life and the huge street armies allowed the police only a precarious foothold. Crowded with varied social groupings, it was hospitable both to militant defiance and middle-class dreams, attracting the elite of the black entertainment and political underworld to its *shebeens* and jazz clubs,[11] and becoming, as the poet Nat Nakasa put it, "the only place where African writers and aspirant writers ever lived in close proximity, almost as a community."[12] From exile Miriam Tlali would voice a common

9. See David B. Coplan, *In Township Tonight: South Africa's Black City Music and Theatre* (London, 1985), and "Interpretive Consciousness: The Reintegration of Self and Society in Sotho Oral Poetry," *American Ethnologist*, forthcoming.

10. Lewis Nkosi, *"Home and Exile" and Other Selections* (London, 1983), p. 3; all further references to this work, abbreviated *HE*, will be included in the text.

11. A *shebeen* is an illegal house of entertainment usually run by a woman, selling beer and liquor to black people.

12. Nat Nakasa, *The World of Nat Nakasa: Selected Writings of the Late Nat Nakasa*, ed. Essop Patel (Johannesburg, 1975), p. 80; all further references to this work, abbreviated *NN*, will be included in the text.

nostalgia for the lost Sophiatown that would survive only a few more years before the Nationalists moved in to destroy it: "Sophiatown. That beloved Sophiatown. As students we used to refer to it proudly as 'the center of the metropolis' . . . The best musicians, scholars, educationists, singers, artists, doctors, lawyers, clergymen" came from there.[13]

In the fifties Sophiatown became the center for a vital and jazzy generation of black writers. In 1951, a few years after the Nationalists rose to power, *Drum,* the first journal for black writing in English, was launched with funds from Jim Bailey, son of Sir Abe Bailey, the Rand gold and racehorse millionaire. Alongside the mimeographed broadsheet, the *Orlando Voice, Drum* became the mouthpiece of writers such as Nkosi, Nakasa, Can Themba, Todd Matshikiza, Es'kia Mphahlele, Casey Motsisi, Henry Nxumalo, and Bloke Modisane, who produced a spate of fiction, autobiography, poetry, and journalism. With this came a new aesthetic and a new politics of value. *Drum* "was coming into a real literary renaissance. . . . People were really writing furiously . . . There was . . . a new kind of English being written. Significantly, it was the black man writing for the black man. Not addressing himself to the whites. Talking a language that would be understood by his own people."[14] Nonetheless, if the Sophiatown writing paraded a "new kind of English," it was one riven with ambivalence toward the august relics of a white European tradition still lingering in the schools. Educated for the most part in the English-run church schools and uneasily straddling the worlds of black and white culture, the black writer and intellectual at this time could still rub shoulders, despite official opprobrium, with some mostly liberal and mostly English whites. This ambiguous situation, which sets these writers entirely apart from the later Soweto generation, left a mark on their writing and on their notions of aesthetic value. The governing paradox of their situation was that the aesthetic which they fashioned with passion and difficulty was shaped not only by their own desires but also by the fact that the Sophiatown intelligentsia became at that time the last real battlefield on which the English and the Afrikaners fought for sway over the cultural values of the black intermediate class.

Violence in colonized cultures is not always unlettered. If, in the colonies, as Frantz Fanon knew, the policeman and soldier by their immediate presence "maintain contact with the native and advise him by means of rifle butts and napalm not to budge,"[15] these same colonies also need the tactful squadrons of moral teachers, advisors, and bewilderers to coax those who are ruled into admitting the legitimacy and "universality" of the ruler's values. Rule by gunpowder and whip is blended with forms

13. Miriam Tlali, *Muriel at Metropolitan* (Johannesburg, 1975), p. 70.

14. N. Chabani Manganyi, "'The Early Years': Interview with Es'kia Mphahlele," *Staffrider* (Sept./Oct. 1980); reprinted in *SP,* p. 42.

15. Frantz Fanon, *The Wretched of the Earth,* trans. Constance Farrington (New York, 1968), p. 38.

of cultural cajolement which create an atmosphere of deference and complicity immeasurably easing the burden of policing. As a result a divided complicity springs up between the lords of humankind and the colonized "elite." The colonized intellectual, "dusted over by colonial culture,"[16] therefore comes to play a checkered role in the life of the people.

In South Africa the persuasive culture during the colonial period was that of the British settlers, who, after the freeing of the slaves in 1834, began in the new mission schools and churches to groom a tiny black elite to walk abroad as the evangelists, catechists, and peddlers of European ways of life.[17] The Afrikaners were forced by their rout during the Boer War to genuflect to this same British culture, but they soon began their long refusal in a nationalist crusade which they won politically in 1948 and continued to wrestle for culturally throughout the fifties. The situation of the black intellectual and artist became as a result unusually pinched, as the British and the Afrikaners, in their long slow tussle over land and labor, also vied jealously with each other for different methods of control over black culture.

Over the years the British and Afrikaans struggle for sway over black lives and values would take different but related shapes, in a tango of mutual embrace and recoil. As a result the situation of the black intellectual was anomalous. Unclassed by whites, born of black parents but schooled and salaried by the English, steeped in white culture but barred at the door, contemptuous of Afrikaners, respectful of white English capital, often knowing Shakespeare but not the languages of the people, in love with the township but identifying with the world of the mind, the Western-educated black writer learned to live at more than one social level at a time, and, standing in perpetual imbalance, created a form of writing that was divided against itself.

The politics of value that emerged was torn and contradictory. Nakasa, journalist for *Drum* and *Golden City Post,* the first black journalist on the *Rand Daily Mail,* and one of the first of the "wasted people" to leave the country into exile, called himself ironically "a native from nowhere" and asked, "Who am I? Where do I belong in the South African scheme of things? Who are my people?" (*NN,* p. 77). Son of a Pondo, he did not know the tongue of his father's people. Brought up speaking Zulu, he cast off his mother's language as unfit for the times. Mphahlele, educated before the Bantu Education Act of 1953 depredated an already ravaged black schooling, bears similar witness to the paradox of that generation's position. The library of the Johannesburg boarding school he attended in 1935 offered him the shimmering promise of a world of white culture

16. Ibid., p. 47.

17. See Baruch Hirson, *Year of Fire, Year of Ash: The Soweto Revolt, Roots of a Revolution?* (London, 1979), chap. 1.

magically protected from "the vulgarity, the squalor, the muck and smell of slum life" of Marabastad, his black Pretoria location.[18] Poetry, which his English teachers had taught him "must be about trees, birds, the elements," offered him a "refuge in the workshop of mind" from the rusted tin shacks and streets filthy with children's stools, and, since there was no one a fledgling black writer could go to for advice, he learnt to "[write] verse out of a book as it were," a white book ("E," p. 76).

Writing in the heady atmosphere of postwar liberal humanism, before Sharpeville made such values untenable, the Sophiatown writers attempted to wed the aesthetic values of these two incongruent worlds: the vitality of township life and the glamorous, if niggardly, allure of a white culture they could glimpse but not grasp: "the location shebeen and the Houghton soiree."[19] For Nakasa the cult of the illegal black *shebeen* gave writing its dash and substance, but he longed for the "techniques of Houghton" to grace black writing with the formal "discipline" it lacked (*NN,* p. 37). Yet this distinction between the Dionysian pulse of black life and the Apollonian discipline of white form was a familiar one, imbibed from a ready European tradition. Probably more than any other black writer of that time, Nkosi's taste for black writing was soured by his fidelity to European literary standards; measured by these, the black scene, as he saw it, quite desperately lacked "any significant and complex talent" (*HE,* p. 131). He scoffed at the "bottomless confusion" of attempts by African intellectuals to refashion an image of themselves from their ravaged cultures.[20] Most lamentable, as far as he was concerned, was the unnatural African proclivity for breeding art with politics, which produced sorry generic hybrids: "the journalistic fact parading outrageously as imaginative literature."[21]

18. Mphahlele, "My Experience as a Writer," in *Momentum: On Recent South African Writing,* ed. M. J. Daymond, J. U. Jacobs, and Margaret Lenta (Pietermaritzburg, 1984), p. 75; all further references to this article, abbreviated "E," will be included in the text.

19. Chapman, introduction, *SP,* p. 16. Houghton is one of Johannesburg's lavish white suburbs. In *Blame Me on History* (London, 1963), Bloke Modisane admitted that he had wanted acceptance "in the country of my birth; and in some corner of the darkened room I whisper the real desire: I want to be accepted into white society. I want to listen to Rachmaninov, to Beethoven, Bartok and Stravinsky" (p. 35).

20. Nkosi, "White on Black," *Observer,* 1 April 1962, p. 46.

21. See Mbulelo Mzamane in *Momentum,* p. 302. The silky taboo of white Johannesburg women became, for Nkosi at least, the promised loot of collaboration with white liberals in league against the Nationalist state, and when he at last came "subtly to despise white South Africans" (*HE,* p. 23), it was the renunciation of white women that smarted most: "The image of the white female beauty is one that rings most frequently the cash register of the Negro psyche. In any case, we all know how notoriously alluring women of the ruling class have always proved to be for aspiring revolutionaries, black or white" (*HE,* p. 150). In the cash nexus of Nkosi's psyche, aspiring revolutionaries were apparently strictly male, and revolution a manichean struggle between male races over the spoils of white female beauty—the untiring and magnificent role of black women in resistance found no place.

Plagued in these ways by conflicts of allegiance and aesthetic value, theoretically obedient to the cleavage of art and politics yet hopeful that the multiracial courtship of white and black liberal artists "might yet crack the wall of apartheid,"[22] disparaging traditional culture yet equivocally fascinated by township life, the early *Drum* writers couched their exposures of farm atrocities, township dissent, and prison life in a style that was often flamboyant with "the grand Shakespearean image" ("E," p. 79). Sporting a studied sardonic detachment, these writers for the most part regarded the African nationalist movements with a certain amusement and were regarded in turn with misgivings. Intimate with English mining capital and courted by English liberals, lacing their politics with "cheese-cake, crime, animals, babies,"[23] at no time, as David Rabkin points out, did the *Drum* writers bring their scrutiny to bear on the migrant labor system or the conditions of the African mine workers.[24]

If Mphahlele could call *Drum* "a real proletarian paper," this was only in part true, for the aesthetic of the Sophiatown writers was by all appearances the style of individual heroics.[25] In *Home and Exile* Nkosi recalls with nostalgia that in both one's personal and aesthetic life "one was supposed to exhibit a unique intellectual style" (*HE*, p. 9). For Nkosi, as for Nakasa, it was the liberal promise of gradual admission into the "new and exciting Bohemia" of the multiracial suburban parties of Johannesburg that gave life and writing much of its savor (*HE*, p. 17). Nakasa hankered for a "common" or universal rather than black experience, for an uncolored aesthetic unity of vision and for a culture that emanated "from a central point in the social structure."[26] But the alluring Bohemia of Houghton as the radiating point of a central and "universal" artistic vision was a dream of cultural glamour which the state began to legislate further and further out of reach.

At about this time the Nationalists began to prize open the handclasp of the black and white liberals, wagging "a finger of cold war at white patrons"[27] of multiracial poetry readings, music, and theater and barring writers such as Nkosi, Nakasa, and Modisane from the palaces of white

22. See Robert Kavanagh, *Theatre and Cultural Struggle in South Africa* (London, 1985), p. 62.

23. See ibid., p. 60.

24. See David Rabkin, "*Drum* Magazine (1951–1961) and the Works of Black South African Writers Associated with It" (diss., University of Leeds, 1975), p. 57.

25. Manganyi, "Interview with Es'kia Mphahlele," p. 42.

26. Nakasa, "Writing in South Africa," *The Classic* 1, no. 1 (1963); reprinted in *SP*, p. 37.

27. Mphahlele, *Down Second Avenue* (London, 1959), p. 182; quoted in Kavanagh, *Theatre and Cultural Struggle*, p. 51.

entertainment. In *Blame Me on History* Modisane voiced his despair that as his white friends gradually stopped inviting him to their homes or visiting him in Sophiatown, South Africa "began to die" for him.[28] The state increasingly made the fata morgana of a "universal" artistic vision a mockery, but Nakasa, for one, could not throw off the inherited cultural cringe that "virtually everything South African was always synonymous with mediocrity" (*NN,* p. 36). In 1964 he joined a steady trickle of writers into exile, where he later surrendered to the unlivable contradictions of his position and threw himself from a skyscraper window in New York.

Beyond the reach of the mission schools and the English-owned newspapers and journals, however, a rich and polyphonic black culture—of oral art, township musicals and theater, South African jazz and jive, *marabi, kwela,* and *mbaqanga*—was sustaining and renewing itself under conditions of considerable difficulty. David Coplan's pathbreaking *In Township Tonight* pays brilliant tribute to the musicians, poets, dancers, actors, and comedians who, in the churches, *shebeens,* dance halls, and mine compounds of urban South Africa, fashioned the nascent shape of a national culture. Drawing on performance traditions from all over the subcontinent, Africans had carried with them to the cities of diamonds and gold—*eDiamini,* Kimberley, and *eGoli,* Johannesburg—a heritage of intricate rural cultures from which a proletarian populace, living "by their wits in the shadows and shanties of the mushrooming locations," created as time passed "hybrid styles of cultural survival."[29]

Sotho migrant workers, for example, walking or riding in buses hundreds of miles to the cities and mines, drew on traditional forms of Sotho praise poetry (*lithoko*) to fashion a modern genre of oral performance *sefela* (pl. *lifela*) which could somehow negotiate the intractable contradictions between home and mine.[30] An anomalous, threshold oral poetry, one foot in the *shebeens* of the city and one in the villages, *sefela* gives rise, perhaps unavoidably, to the governing narrative theme of travel and to such elaborate liminal images as the train:

Hlanya le mabanta a litsepe,
Hanong ho eona ho le ho fubelu,
Ihloana la tollo ha le bonoe

28. Modisane, *Blame Me on History;* quoted ibid., p. 60.

29. See Coplan, *In Township Tonight.*

30. The *lifela* performance is a public competition during which two or more poets (*likheleke,* "eloquent persons" [Coplan, *In Township Tonight,* p. 17]) display the desired criteria of their craft: sustained extemporary eloquence, originality of figure and metaphor, musical patterning, the aptness of donated or borrowed formulaic elements, and the refashioning of shared experience into aesthetic form.

Liporo li otla maloanloahla
Mahlephisi a lla likoto-koto
Poncho tsa bina,
"Ielele-ielele!"
Ea phulesa eaka e ea re lahla
Terene ea chesetsa maqaqa naha,
Ha 'metlenyana ha chela lilaong . . .

Madman with iron belts,
Inside its mouth [furnace], such fiery redness,
Its eye [lamp] is blinding,
Trainrails beat rattling, [cars] coupled together,
The rattling railjoints sang,
"Ielele-ielele!"
It pulled out as if it would throw us off-board
The train set aflame the humble country Boers' fields,
Rabbits roasted alive in their holes . . . [31]

The exclusion and denigration of these forms of emergent urban culture within both black and white communities is itself an act of political exclusion and a crucial part of the politics of evaluation. It fosters a misleading sense of the representativeness of the Sophiatown writing in its most self-consciously "literary" manifestations as well as critical indifference to the scantily understood traffic of influence not only between traditional and contemporary oral poetry but also between these forms and poems composed for print. One might usefully compare, for example, two poems published by Sol Plaatje in 1920 which indicate the tugging of two incommensurate traditions that would gradually infuse and influence each other over the years:

Speak not to me of the comforts of home,
Tell me of the Valleys where the antelopes roam;
Give me my hunting sticks and snares
In the gloaming of the wilderness;
Give back the palmy days of our early felicity
Away from the hurly-burly of your city,
And we'll be young again—aye:
Sweet Mhudi and I.[32]

31. Molefi Motsoahae ("Madman with iron belts"). I am very much indebted here to Coplan's "Interpretive Consciousness." The quotation is from his translation.

32. Solomon Tshekisho Plaatje, "Sweet Mhudi and I," *Mhudi: An Epic of South African Native Life a Hundred Years Ago* (Lovedale, 1933); reprinted in *The Return of the Amasi Bird: Black South African Poetry, 1891–1981*, ed. Tim Couzens and Essop Patel (Johannesburg, 1982), pp. 49–50.

The poem's self-consciously literary eloquence, uneasy submission to imported metrical and rhyming patterns, and implausible literary cliché offer a curious contrast with the following invocation to an alternative oral lyric source, which draws, if incompletely, on oral patterns of repetition and parallelism, incantation and interjection:

> Yes, keep and feed the sprite,
> Especially the hairy sprite;
>   Yebo! yebo!
> He'll show us how to crack magic out of poles
> So that we'll scatter and slay our enemies,
> Then nobody will do us harm
> While we use this wonderful charm;
>   Yebo! yebo!
> Let the hairy spirit live
> Let him live, let him live.
>   Yebo! yebo!
>   Yebo! yebo![33]

Nevertheless, if the glamour of Sophiatown as "the place of 'sophisticated gangsters, brave politicians and intellectuals'" chiefly satisfied a small and relatively privileged coterie of intellectuals and writers (*NN*, p. 5), this glamour cast its radiance and influence over an entire generation, and it was this group of writers which the state would soon turn to destroy.[34]

The political climate of the fifties was unruly. The National party had triumphed in 1948 and now set about the dogged implementation of modern apartheid. Black resistance to the Suppression of Communism Act of 1950, to racial classification under the Population Registration Act, to petty apartheid on trains, to the passes, to the manifold indignities and scourges, flared in the Defiance Campaign in 1952, the most successful organized resistance the African National Congress (ANC) was ever to stage, and this resistance met in turn the unswerving brunt of Nationalist wrath.

The Nationalist policy of "tribal" segregation in the "bantustans" was by now under way, and, partly to prevent urban blacks from identifying too intimately with the urban environment and its values, partly to uproot what they not inaccurately felt were the seedbeds of resistance in the freehold suburbs, and partly to place the heel of state control more firmly on migrant labor, the Nationalists began the razing of the black freehold townships. The first and most famous of those to be destroyed was Sophiatown.

33. Plaatje, "Song"; reprinted ibid., p. 45.
34. See Lodge, *Black Politics*, p. 95.

At night you see another dream
White and monstrous;
Dropping from earth's heaven,
Whitewashing your own black dream.
—MAFIKA GWALA

On 9 February 1955 eight trucks and two thousand armed police rolled into Sophiatown to begin the forced evictions to Soweto which would, despite fragile and futile resistance, last six years.[35] Over the next decade the demolition across the country of "black spots" and the removal of the people to dreary, gridded townships would satisfy the state's cold dream of utterly rational control. White architects were notified that the layout of black townships should obey principles ensuring the utmost surveillance and control: roads had to be wide enough to allow a Saracen tank to turn; houses had to be lined up so that firing between them would not be impeded.[36] At the same time the houses and highways of black art began to be policed as vigilantly and the situation of the black artist began subtly to change.

In 1953 black education was taken from provincial and largely English control and placed in the hands of the national Department of Native Affairs. In a speech before the senate in June 1954, H. F. Verwoerd, architect of these cultural removals and graphic designer of the new layout of the artistic life of black South Africa, was quite frank about the aims of the Bantu Education Act: "The Natives will be taught from childhood to realise that equality with Europeans is not for them. . . . There is no place for him [the Bantu] above the level of certain forms of labour."[37] Henceforth blacks would have "ethnically" separate schools, syllabi, teachers, languages, and values. In 1959 the Extension of University Education Act parceled out the "different" ethnic groups to different universities. The Bantu Education Act, like the destruction of Sophiatown, was a crucial event in the history of black culture not simply because it began the transfer of black education from hegemonic English control to more flagrantly coercive Afrikaner Nationalist hands but also because it threatened the alliance between the black and white liberals and drove the white-educated black artists back into their communities. More blacks would now receive a deliberately impoverished schooling, with the effect of leveling out some of the differences between the tiny educated elite and the vast illiterate populace that had existed before. From then onward, blacks would be subjected more efficiently than ever to what Malefane

35. See ibid., chap. 4.

36. See Hirson, *Year of Fire,* p. 184.

37. Hendrik F. Verwoerd, Policy of the Minister of Native Affairs, 7 June 1954, *Verwoerd Speaks: Speeches 1948–1966,* ed. A. N. Pelzer (Johannesburg, 1966); quoted in Hirson, *Year of Fire,* p. 45.

calls a calculated policy of "cultural malnutrition." This would have a marked effect on black literature and would bring about significant changes in notions of aesthetic value.

In 1960 the Pan-Africanist Congress (PAC) anti-pass-law campaign ended calamitously at Sharpeville. The ANC and PAC were banned, and both resistance movements went underground and into exile. The destruction of Sophiatown foretold the almost total erasure of *public* black writing in the sixties as the state flexed the full measure of its muscle in a decade of bannings, detentions, and torture, crushing the last illusions of liberal reform. Bannings, exile, and death throttled an entire generation of writers, and the "long silence" of the sixties began. This silence was in some ways more apparent than real, for it has been pointed out that in terms of sheer volume more poetry was written during the sixties than the fifties, though it was published later.[38] The Publications and Entertainment Act (1963) extended legal state censorship to cultural affairs within the country, and in 1966 most of the black writers who had already gone into exile were listed under the Suppression of Communism Act, even though most of them were liberals of one cast or another: Matshikiza, Themba, Modisane, Mphahlele, Nkosi, Cosmo Pieterse, and Mazisi Kunene. Forty-six authors were gagged by the Government Gazette Extraordinary of 1 April 1966 which forbade the reading, reproduction, printing, publication, or dissemination of any speech, utterance, writing, or statement of the banned. In exile both Themba and Arthur Nortje followed Nakasa in suicide.

Nevertheless, the effect on black writing was not solely deleterious. In 1963, the same year that Nelson Mandela was banished to Robben Island, a black literary journal called *The Classic* opened in Johannesburg. It was named not in honor of a patrimony of excellence enshrined in the white canonical classic but ironically and anticanonically, after *The Classic* laundromat behind which the journal began in an illegal *shebeen*. *The Classic,* edited by Nakasa before he went into voluntary exile, began to publish the first of the Soweto poets.

Sharpeville and its aftermath ushered in a period of calculated refusal of canonized white norms and standards. The South African liberal aesthetic, itself never whole or complete and already strained by its distance from the European tradition, began to fray and unravel. Most white English poets, increasingly edged from cultural power, comforted themselves in their unclassed solitude with the contradictory faith that the lonely poetic voice was also the eloquent mouthpiece of universal truth—a faith that became increasingly untenable for educated black writers not only barred from the white "universal" but also standing, at this point, somewhat uneasily within their own communities. During this

38. See Couzens and Patel, eds., *The Return of the Amasi Bird,* p. 10.

period a marked change in aesthetic values took place as black literature became steadily more radical and polarized.

The poets of the generation after the Bantu Education Act had to begin from scratch. Their predecessors were in exile and their work silenced. As Tlali wrote in "In Search of Books," "They say writers learn from their predecessors. When I searched frantically for mine there was nothing but a void. What had happened to all the writings my mother had talked about?"[39] Nevertheless, the Bantu Education Act, zealously shielding blacks from the blandishments of European culture, had done black writing an unwitting service, for the Soweto writers of the seventies sidestepped many of the conflicts of cultural fealty that had plagued the Sophiatown generation. Carlos Fuentes has spoken of the problem for the North American writer of warding off the ghosts of the European tradition, "hanging from the chandeliers and rattling the dishes."[40] Similarly, white South African poets, unhoused by history, spent decades knitting their brows over their vexed relation to a European tradition that both was and was not theirs. The Soweto poets, bereft of Donne, Milton, Wordsworth, Eliot, had no such ghosts to lay to rest.

The pre-Soweto generation, nurtured on what now seemed an artificially "literary" eloquence, had suffered a different form of cultural malnutrition. Sipho Sepamla, for one, "brought up on Shakespeare, Dickens, Lawrence, Keats and other English greats," envies the Soweto poets' ignorance of Western tradition: "I would have liked to have been fed on Mphahlele, La Guma, Themba, Nkosi. I would have liked to have laid my hands on the 'unrewarding rage' of Richard Wright, James Baldwin, LeRoi Jones. . . . It would seem my emptiness, my rootlessness, my blindness is all that is supposed to keep me in my place."[41] At the same time, within the country, the Black Consciousness movement had begun to shatter the long quiescence of the sixties.

Soweto poetry was born in the cradle of Black Consciousness and has to be seen within this milieu. Black Consciousness began largely as a black campus movement in 1968 and spanned almost a decade until the banning, after Soweto, of all Black Consciousness organizations in October 1977. Mobilizing black students around the rallying cry of color and the slogan, "Blackman, you are on your own," Black Consciousness was at this stage, however, the dream of the elite black urban petite bourgeoisie, a movement of students, professionals, intellectuals, artists, and a few clergy.[42] In 1972 the South African Student Organization (SASO) tried to breach the gulf between the intellectual elite and the people of the ordinary black community and in 1972 formed the Black

39. Tlali, "In Search of Books," *Star,* 30 July 1980; reprinted in *SP,* p. 45.

40. Carlos Fuentes, "The Art of Fiction LXVIII," *Paris Review* 23 (Winter 1981): 149.

41. Sipho Sepamla, "The Black Writer in South Africa Today: Problems and Dilemmas," *New Classic* 3 (1976); reprinted in *SP,* p. 116.

42. See Hirson, *Year of Fire,* pp. 60–114; Lodge, *Black Politics,* pp. 321–62.

People's Convention in an effort to give Black Consciousness nationwide clout. But the appeal to the community was uncertain and contradictory, and, partly because the tendrils it extended to organized workers were always slender, it never grew into a mass organization.

The question of cultural values took center stage as literacy campaigns, black theater, and poetry readings were fostered in the belief that cultural nationalism was the road to political nationalism. Since shedding canonized white norms and values was imperative, whites had to be barred and all white values challenged and replaced. As Steve Biko put it, "Black culture . . . implies freedom on our part to innovate without recourse to white values."[43] Politically, early Black Consciousness was reformist rather than radical, a blend of moderates, Christian anticommunists, liberals, and black entrepreneurs. It was chronically masculine in orientation (calling for "the restoration of black manhood"), without an analysis of class or gender, and strongly anti-Marxist: "We are not a movement of confrontation but a movement of introspection."[44]

The Black Consciousness movement has as a result been rebuked for being politically naive and theoretically inconsistent, for placing its faith in a timeless black soul and the personal growth of the individual. But at the same time, as the poet Mafika Gwala put it: "Everywhere it was surveillance. It seemed that reading and cultural topics were the only things to sustain one."[45] At a time when so many political organizations and people were being scotched, black poetry helped revive and sustain resistance to white culture. "The brooding was replaced by an understanding of hope" ("CW," p. 40). Moreover, as the Nationalists drove wedge after wedge between the so-called different ethnic groups, Black Consciousness and the resurgence of black cultural values embraced all embattled groups, Coloreds, Indians, and Asians, within the term "black." For all its undoubted political shortcomings, which became most telling and costly during the Soweto revolt, Black Consciousness provided a rallying cry, a powerful and necessary incitement. As the writer Essop Patel put it, "Black Consciousness provided the initial impetus in the rejection of art as an aesthetic indulgence. Once the black poet freed himself from Eurocentric literary conventions, then he was *free* to create within the context of a national consciousness. The black poet's starting point was the articulation of the black experience."[46]

43. Steve Biko, "Black Consciousness and the Quest for a True Humanity," in *Black Theology: The South African Voice,* ed. Basil Moore (London, 1973), p. 45. See also his *I Write What I Like,* ed. Aelred Stubbs (New York, 1978), and "White Racism and Black Consciousness," in *Student Perspectives on South Africa,* ed. Hendrik W. van der Merwe and David Welsh (Cape Town, 1972), pp. 190–202.

44. Drake Koka, quoted in "Inside South Africa: A New Black Movement Is Formed," *Sechaba* 7 (March 1973): 5.

45. Mafika Gwala, "Writing as a Cultural Weapon," in *Momentum,* p. 37; all further references to this article, abbreviated "CW," will be included in the text.

46. Patel, "Towards Revolutionary Poetry," in *Momentum,* p. 85.

and when I'm supposed to sing
I croak curses.
—ZINJIVA WINSTON NKONDO

Black poetry flourished at this time, becoming what Gwala called a "jaunt in search of identity" ("CW," p. 38). Not surprisingly, the first Soweto poetry shared many of the dilemmas of the Black Consciousness movement. Not the least of its problems was that it was written, even though in protest, in English, with a privileged white audience in mind, and thus bore the subtle onus of having to curtail itself for the liberal press.

The English literary establishment was beginning to listen to black poets with half an ear. White poets had trickled back from their lonely jaunts into the veld looking for roots and were now writing a little uneasily about black men honing their pangas in the woodshed. In 1971 Lionel Abrahams took a publishing gamble and printed Oswald Mtshali's phenomenally successful *Sounds of a Cowhide Drum,* sparking at the same time an agitated debate on the value of black poetry and provoking a number of white critics to fits of discriminating judgment bordering on incivility.[47]

Until the seventies, the white and almost exclusively male British canon was troubled only by mild internal differences over value in the English-speaking universities, remaining squarely within an imported Leavisite tradition. In 1959 the Oxford University Press could publish *A Book of South African Verse* that featured thirty-two white male and four white female poets, yet not one black writer of either sex. Until the seventies, the presiding liberal aesthetic faith—in individual creativity, immanent and "universal" literary values, unity of vision, wholeness of experience, complexity of form, refined moral discrimination untainted by political platitude, irony, taste, cultivated sensibility, and the formal completion of the work of art—had for the most part been artificially cordoned off from black experience by segregated education, severe censorship of texts, bannings of writers, and blocking of distribution.

From the seventies onward, however, white liberals began to court black poets while simultaneously having for the first time to defend the presiding liberal tenets within the English-speaking universities at the level of ideology, in an unprecedented flurry of reviews, debates, articles, conferences, and so on. In other words, if some black poetry was to be

47. Some of the reasons for the cultural shift and for the success of Mtshali's book—the first book of poems by anyone, black or white, ever to make a commercial profit—lay in the external interest taken in Africa as one African nation after another won independence. But it is one of the stubborn quirks of decolonization that as Europe decamped from African soil, the literary scramble for Africa began—with Western publishing houses vying for black writers. Inside South Africa, some white liberals, increasingly inched into inconsequence, also saw fit to throw in their lot with black protest.

selectively ushered into the canon, it was only if it could be shown to exhibit at the door certain requisite values which, in turn, had to be vociferously announced without betraying the selective and interested nature of these values. The first phase of reforming the canon thus began with its circumspect expansion to include some black texts previously ignored but now revealed to exhibit certain features shared with the already existing white tradition.

Mtshali's seminal *Sounds of a Cowhide Drum,* for example, was met with a hearty round of applause for his deployment of some of the familiar favorites of the Leavisite tradition. Mtshali was commended for his ironic and individual voice in lines such as:

> Glorious is this world,
> the world that sustains man
> like a maggot in a carcass.

He was praised for his strength of feeling, moral energy, liberation of imagination, and the originality of his concrete images in a poem such as "Sunset":

> The sun spun like
> a tossed coin.
> It whirled on the azure sky,
> it clattered into the horizon,
> it clicked in the slot,
> and neon-lights popped
> and blinked "Time expired",
> as on a parking meter

or in:

> A newly-born calf
> is like oven-baked bread
> steaming under a cellophane cover.[48]

Nadine Gordimer's rapturous preface to the first edition invoked Blake and Auden. When Mtshali was reproved for falling short, however, it was for his lack of formal and intellectual complexity, his failure to meld form and content, and for his paeans to the African past, which cost him "universality."

Mtshali stood at that contested moment when English hegemony was yielding reluctantly to Nationalist coercion. His parents were teachers at a Catholic mission school where he had received a thoroughly English

48. Oswald Mtshali, "High and Low," "Sunset," "A Newly-Born Calf," *Sounds of a Cowhide Drum* (New York, 1972), pp. 28, 24, 13.

schooling. But the Bantu Education Act denied him entry to a white university, and, refusing to go to the black one allocated him, he was working as a scooter-messenger when *Sounds of a Cowhide Drum* was published. Lodged in this way between the intellectual elite and the community, Mtshali shared as a result many of the ambiguities of the black intermediate class and the Black Consciousness milieu in general. He has, for example, been taken to task by more radical black poets of the later Soweto generation for bathing in romantic reverence for the "timeless relics" of his past, as in the titular poem of his collection:

> I am the drum on your dormant soul,
> cut from the black hide of a sacrificial cow.
>
> I am the spirit of your ancestors . . .
>
> [*S*, p. 78]

For Mtshali the task of the poet was to immortalize the "debris of my shattered culture" and to reclaim the "timeless existence and civilization" of precolonial South Africa, a timeless idyll which others have argued never existed.[49] At the same time, his outraged images of the bloodied baby torn by township curs, the calloused washerwoman, the drunk with mouth dripping vomit, were tempered with a rural yearning and—as critics noted with some relief—with a critical but essentially Christian message. Mtshali's liberal audience was well disposed to criticism of the Nationalist state onto which it displaced its own impotency and doubts, but, firmly situated within the state's institutions and lacking any authentic hope for the future, it was not ready to overthrow it.

In a period of record unemployment and a steady barrage of work stoppages, there began a spate of cultural forums and conferences—the Theatre Council of Natal (TECON), the SASO conference on Creativity and Black Development (1972), the Black Renaissance Convention at Hammanskraal (1974). A flurry of black poetry collections appeared, and most were summarily banned: Kunene's *Zulu Poems* (1970), Keorapetse Kgositsile's *My Name Is Afrika* (1971), *Seven South African Poets* (1971), James Matthews' and Gladys Thomas' *Cry Rage* (1972), Mongane Serote's *Yakhal'inkomo* (1972), and *To Whom It May Concern: An Anthology of Black South African Poetry* (1973). Hostile, impassioned, and well beyond the pale of accepted aesthetic standards, the new Soweto poetry was an intemperate, jangling, often hallucinatory depiction of "the terrible canopy of nightmares" that shadowed ghetto life:

> THEY stole the baritone
> Wifey eats her own head-bone

49. Mtshali, "Black Poetry in Southern Africa: What It Means," *Issue: A Quarterly Journal of Africanist Opinion* 6 (Spring 1976); reprinted in *SP*, p. 107.

She squeezes a stony brow into the spoon
Children may nibble the pap-like moon . . . [50]

Most significantly, as the new poetry poached liberally on jazz and jive rhythms, black Americanisms, township vernacular, and the gestural, musical, and performative aspects of oral traditions, notions such as the integrity of the text and the test of time came to be rendered increasingly irrelevant. Much of this transitional poetry was still written for print but was beginning to evince signs of an imminent abandonment and destruction of the text:

I leave in stealth
    and return in Black anger
O---m! Ohhhhmmmm! O-hhhhhhmmmmmmm!!![51]

and:

You've trapped me whitey! Meem wanna ge aot Fuc
Pschwee e ep booboodubooboodu blllll
Black books,
    Flesh blood words shitrrr Haai,
        Amen.[52]

The Soweto poets' refusal to see poetry in the Coleridgean sense as that which contains "within itself" the reason why it is so and not otherwise was, moreover, resonant with the powerful, if embattled, traditions of oral poetry within black culture.[53] In African oral poetry the

> focus is on the performance in its social context, on the function of the performance in society, almost to the exclusion of transmission of the text over time.
>
> The poet serves as a mediator between the ruler and the ruled, as an inciter, a molder of opinion, a social critic. He is not only concerned to chronicle the deeds and qualities of the ancestors of his contemporaries, he also responds poetically to the social and political circumstances confronting him at the time of his performance.[54]

50. Anonymous, "They Took Him Away," *Staffrider* (Mar. 1978).

51. Gwala, *Jol'iinkomo* (Johannesburg, 1977), p. 68.

52. Mongane Serote, "Black Bells," *Yakhal'inkomo* (Johannesburg, 1972), p. 52.

53. See S. T. Coleridge, *Biographia Literaria* (New York, 1834), chap. 14.

54. Jeff Opland, "The Isolation of the Xhosa Oral Poet," in *Literature and Society in South Africa*, ed. Landeg White and Couzens (New York, 1984), pp. 175, 176–77.

Not only did the yardsticks of immanent value brandished by white critics bear scant resemblance to the traditions of the Xhosa *izibongo* and *Ntsomi,* the Sotho *lithoko,* and *sefela,* but white critics' failure to recognize the presence within contemporary poetry of such oral infusions left them ill-equipped to pass judgment either on the poems themselves or on their social roles and contexts.[55] Ignorant of the intricate traditions of repetition and parallelism that hold in oral poetry, white critics disparaged black poetry on more than one occasion for falling into cliché and repetitious image. Moreover, as Ursula Barnett and others have shown, "often we find in the imagery of black poetry a complicated system of symbols which works on several levels and requires a knowledge of history, myth and legend."[56] Drawing on powerful oral traditions of communality of theme and performance, energetic audience participation, conceptions of the poet as lyric historian and political commentator, black poetry was making the case, as Tony Emmett has put it, for its study "on its own terms, and it is in the light of the oral, political and communal facets of black poetry that the most penetrating criticism is likely to be made."[57]

Serote's "Hell, well, Heaven," for example, resembles the pulse of *marabi* music's segmental repetition of basic riffs, sharing its "predisposition for the merciless two or three cord vamp":

> I do not know where I have been,
> But Brother,
> I know I'm coming.
> I do not know where I have been,
> But Brother,
> I know I heard the call.[58]

The lines reveal as well the influence of gospel and *makwaya,* choral music developed by mission-educated Africans from American popular song and European and traditional African elements.[59] The musical influence

55. See Ruth Finnegan, *Oral Literature in Africa* (Oxford, 1970); Harold Scheub, *The Xhosa Ntsomi* (Oxford, 1975); Elizabeth Gunner, "Songs of Innocence and Experience: Women as Composers and Performers of *Izibongo,* Zulu Praise Poetry," *Research in African Literatures* 10 (Fall 1979): 239–67; Mbulelo Mzamane, "The Uses of Traditional Oral Forms in Black South African Literature," in *Literature and Society in South Africa,* pp. 147–60; Coplan, *In Township Tonight* and "Interpretive Consciousness."

56. Barnett, *A Vision of Order,* p. 43.

57. Tony Emmett, "Oral, Political and Communal Aspects of Township Poetry in the Mid-Seventies," *English in Africa* 6 (Mar. 1979); reprinted in *SP,* p. 183.

58. Serote, "Hell, well, Heaven," *Yakhal'inkomo,* p. 16.

59. D. K. Rycroft, "Melodic Imports and Exports: A Byproduct of Recording in South Africa," *Bulletin of the British Institute of Recorded Sound* (1956); quoted in Coplan, *In Township Tonight,* p. 106.

of township jazz is both thematically and rhythmically fundamental to a great deal of Soweto poetry:

> Mother,
> my listening to jazz isn't leisure
> It's a soul operation[60]

These musical traces evoked the defiant and restorative worlds of the *marabi* dances, jazz clubs, *shebeens,* and music halls, and heralded the increasingly performative and communal nature of black poetry:

> Up and up
> on a wild horse of jazz
> we galloped on a network
> of blue notes
> delivering the message:
> Men, Brothers, Giants![61]

A defiant celebration of the bitter bane of color, Soweto poetry awoke in the state an exact revenge. If the English poet Douglas Livingstone was confident that poetry is "certainly not going to change the world," the state was not about to take chances.[62] The Minister of Justice, Jimmy Kruger, spoke ominously of poems "that kill" and responded in turn.[63] Many of the collections were suppressed, and not a few of the poets were detained. Mthuli Shezi, playwright and vice chairman of the Black People's Convention in 1972, died after being pushed under a train in a trumped-up dispute with a railway official.

In 1974 Portuguese colonial rule in Africa collapsed. In South Africa a rally in support of Mozambique's victorious Frelimo was banned and nine leaders were given long sentences. Gwala recalls that in the same year the University of Cape Town hosted a conference on the New Black Poetry, inviting him and some other black poets to take "black poetry to Whitey's territory" ("CW," p. 43). Debating on the phone with Onkgopotse Tiro whether or not to accept the invitation, Gwala had joked that all of southern Africa was now "terry country." That same day Tiro was blown up in Botswana by a parcel bomb sent by the South Africans, and when Gwala heard the news he decided not to attend. This personal gesture

60. Gwala, "Words to a Mother," *Staffrider* (May/June 1978).

61. Mtshali, "Riding on the Rainbow," *Sounds of a Cowhide Drum,* p. 26.

62. Douglas Livingstone, "The Poetry of Mtshali, Serote, Sepamla and Others in English: Notes Towards a Critical Evaluation," *New Classic* 3 (1976); reprinted in *SP,* p. 160. All further references to this essay, abbreviated "PM," will be included in the text.

63. Jimmy Kruger, *The Star,* 14 Sept. 1977; quoted in Emmett, "Aspects of Township Poetry," p. 176.

expressed a general direction being taken, as Black Consciousness turned a cold shoulder on white liberalism. The frayed threads in South African culture began to give, as black poetry and Black Consciousness tugged far more insistently than before. As Mtshali voiced this change of heart: "I once thought I could evangelise and convert whites. . . . But . . . I have now turned to inspire my fellow blacks . . . to seek their true identity as a single solid group."[64]

The search for identity as a solid group faced black intellectuals with a choice akin to that sketched out by Antonio Gramsci: at critical moments the traditional intellectuals, indirectly tied to the establishment yet considering themselves independent, have to choose whether to cast in their lot with the ascendant revolutionary class, as organic intellectuals. In Gwala's words,

> The purpose here today is to see to it that the intellectual decides whether to uphold superior status or is ready to phase himself out of the role of being carrier of a white official culture. It is here that we have to accept and promote the truth that we cannot talk of Black Solidarity outside of class identity. Because as our black brother has put it, it is only the elite that are plagued by the problem of identity. Not the mass of the black people. The common black people have had no reason to worry about blackness. They never in the first place found themselves outside or above their context of being black. But the student, the intellectual, the theologian, are the ones who have to go through foreign education and assimilate foreign ethical values. Later when weighed against the reality of the black situation, this alienates them from their people.[65]

At the same time, the question of group identity is bedeviled by more than the problem of class relations between the educated writer and the "mass of the black people," for it is already apparent that the overwhelming underrepresentation of women (as Gwala's drift of pronoun betrays) in the poetry and debates raises serious questions about education, community attitudes, access to publishing channels, public status and mobility in the communities, gendered conflicts of interests and power, and so on, as issues that have as crucial a bearing on the question of value as might any "aesthetic" question alone.[66]

64. Barnett, "Interview with Oswald Mtshali," *World Literature Written in English* 12 (1973); reprinted in *SP*, p. 100.

65. Gwala, "Towards the Practical Manifestation of Black Consciousness," in *Black Renaissance: Papers from the Black Renaissance Convention*, ed. T. Thoahlane (Johannesburg, 1975), p. 31.

66. There is little work on the specific position of black female poets. See Gunner, "Songs of Innocence and Experience," and Coplan, *In Township Tonight.*

Let them cough their dry little academic coughs.
—RICHARD RIVE

When James Matthews and Gladys Thomas brought out *Cry Rage,* "critics hyena-howled. It was not poetry, they exclaimed."[67] The profusion of black poetry could not, however, be ignored; neither could it any longer be pinched and squeezed to meet canonical requirements. It began to pose a discomforting threat not only to some of the most cherished values of the established aesthetic but also to the very idea of the canon itself. Critics became more vocal in their complaints: black poets were trampling on every propriety of the English language, sacrificing formal decorum for the "red haze of revenge lust"[68] and the "'rat-tat-tat' of machine guns" of protest ("PM," p. 160). As Alan Paton would have it, "a writer is, more often than not, a private creature,"[69] whereas black writers, seduced by "the portentously-conceived category 'Black,'" tended chronically to "group-thinking."[70] Livingstone felt that blacks would face considerable difficulty surviving "the harsh glacier of time" and would have trouble qualifying for "the toughest definition of a poet . . . a man who has been dead for 100 years, and one of his works is still read" ("PM," p. 157), a tough definition indeed for black female poets. These were the four general charges leveled against black writing in the seventies: sacrifice of the intrinsic rules of the craft for political ends, formal ineptitude, loss of individual expression and originality, and hence sacrifice of longevity.

In return Gwala asked, "Questions crop up. Questions such as: what moral right does the academic have to judge my style of writing? What guidelines outside the culture of domination has he applied?" ("CW," p. 48). Unwilling to give ground in the struggle for "command" over the English language, white critics peppered their reviews of black poetry with quibbles over formal lapses, "bad" grammar, and decline of standards. Black poets rejoined that "there has never been such a thing as pure language" ("CW," p. 43), and Sepamla urged, "If the situation requires broken or 'murdered' English, then for God's sake one must do just that."[71] The critical skirmishes over grammatical niceties concealed in this way the much more serious question of who had the right to police township culture. Black poetry was in fact a very conscious flouting of received notions of formal elegance: poets were forging their own precepts out of forms of township speech unfamiliar, and therefore unnerving,

67. James Matthews, in *Momentum,* p. 73.

68. Lionel Abrahams, "Political Vision of a Poet," *Rand Daily Mail,* 17 June 1974; reprinted in *SP,* p. 74.

69. Alan Paton, in *Momentum,* p. 90.

70. Abrahams, "Black Experience into English Verse: A Survey of Local African Poetry, 1960–70," *New Nation* 3 (Feb. 1970); reprinted in *SP,* pp. 138–39.

71. Sepamla, "The Black Writer," p. 117.

to white critics. Black poetry was often a hybrid medley of English, *tsotsitaal,*[72] and black Americanisms, with blends of black South African languages:

> Once upon a bundu-era
> there was *mlungu* discrimination
> as a result of separate *masemba* . . . [73]

The language of white officialdom was mocked, insulted, and inverted: "Your dompas is dom to pass you / Your X-mas gift: 72 hours . . . "[74]

Black poets were equally suspicious of Paton's claim that politics destroyed the sovereignty of the intrinsic "rules of the craft."[75] Frankie Ntsu kaDitshego/Dube's poem "The Ghettoes" argues figuratively that the apolitical stance is itself a political act:

> Those who claim to be non-smokers are wrong
> The place is polluted with smoke from
> Chimneys
> Trucks
> Hippos
> Gun-excited camouflage
> dagga-smokers
> and burning tyres
> Non-smokers are smokers too![76]

In more ways than one, black poetry posed a serious challenge to notions of the poem as a freestanding creation, judged excellent if obedient to immanent rules radiating from within the craft. For black poets, the canon as the patrimony of excellence, bequeathed from generation to generation by the finest of minds and borne unscathed through history, was rendered indefensible by the very circumstances in which they were living. In his poem "The Marble Eye" Mtshali parodied the formal completion of the work of art housed in tradition's mausoleum:

> The marble eye
> is an ornament
> coldly carved by a craftsman

72. *Tsotsitaal* is an urban African dialect spoken by all African proletarians, especially by young members of street gangs or possible criminals. Coplan argues that *tsotsi* is a corruption of the American term "zoot suit" (see *In Township Tonight,* p. 271).

73. Mothobi Mutloatse, "Bundu Bulldozers," quoted in *SP,* p. 170. *Mlungu* means "white man"; *masemba* means "shit."

74. Anonymous, "It's Paati to Be Black," *Staffrider* (Mar. 1978). *Dompas* refers to the hated passes; *dom* is Afrikaans for "stupid."

75. Paton, in *Momentum,* p. 89.

76. Frankie Ntsu kaDitshego/Dube, "The Ghettoes," *Staffrider* (July/Aug. 1979).

to fill an empty socket
as a corpse fills a coffin.
[*S*, p. 71]

Given the conditions of township life, the poem could no longer pretend to mimic the burnished completion of a well-wrought urn or the jeweled finish of an icon. Gwala for one called for "an art of the unattractive,"[77] and N. Chabani Manganyi argued that the "unified image" sanctioned by literary tradition was an unforgivable indulgence.[78] Against Paton's commonplace claim that protest would damage the fine formal filigree of the artwork, these poets charged that the paramount value of their poetry was neither ontological nor formal but strategic. Strategic change rather than the test of time became the reiterated principle. "In our ghetto language there can be no fixity. The words we use belong to certain periods of our history. They come, they assume new meanings, they step aside" ("CW," p. 48). Gwala was equally unimpressed by the lure of immortality. Publication was not the sole aim: "What mattered would be the spoken word. Whether it lay hidden under mats or got eaten by the rats would be a different story" ("CW," p. 37).

Most significantly, the performative, gestural, and dramatic traces in much of the poetry evinced its gradual transformation from a printed "literary" phenomenon to a social performance, from text to event, replete with theatrical, gestural, and oral traces:

Soon they are back again
Arriving as bigger black battalions
    with brows biceps brains
    trudging the 'white' soil: phara-phara-phara!
And the kwela-kwela cop:
'These Bantus are like cheeky flies:
    You ffr-ffr-ffrrr with Doom!'
And see them again![79]

In this way, much of the new Soweto poetry bore witness to what Raymond Williams has described as "the true crisis in cultural theory" in our time, that is, the conflict "between [the] view of the work of art as object and the alternative view of art as a practice."[80] For most black

77. Gwala, "Towards a National Theatre," *South African Outlook* (Aug. 1973); quoted in Chapman, intro., *SP*, p. 21.

78. See Chapman, intro., *SP*, p. 21.

79. Anonymous, "It's Paati to Be Black." *Kwela-kwela* is the township name for the large police pickup vans. See Coplan, *In Township Tonight*, pp. 157–60, for the origins of the term. *Doom* is a spray insecticide.

80. Raymond Williams, *Problems in Materialism and Culture* (London, 1980), pp. 47–48.

poets, and there *are* exceptions, aesthetic value is neither immanent nor genetic but rather what Terry Eagleton has called "transitive," that is, "value for somebody in a particular situation. . . . It is always culturally and historically specific."[81] Supporting, albeit independently, many of the theoretical arguments on value in the work of Western critics such as Eagleton, Catherine Belsey, Tony Bennett, Stuart Hall, Paul Lauter, Francis Mulhern, Barbara Herrnstein Smith, and Jane Tompkins,[82] the Soweto poets claimed that the literary canon is less a mausoleum of enduring truths, less a *thing,* than it is an uneven, somersaulting social practice scored by contestation, dissension, and the interests of power.

Beset by censorship, by strictly curtailed access to commercial publishing channels, by the dangers of identification and subsequent harassment, and inheriting to boot powerful traditions of communal performance, black Soweto poetry began to evince the calculated destruction of the text.[83] More and more, black poetry is composed for a black listening audience rather than an overseas readership in ways that create poetic forms less vulnerable to censorship and easier to memorize, the spoken word spreading more quickly, more widely, and more elusively than printed texts. Poetry has taken flight from the literary magazines and has been performed increasingly at mass readings, United Democratic Front rallies, funerals, memorial services, garage parties, community meetings, and musical concerts, sometimes to the accompaniment of flutes and drums, drawing on oral traditions and miming customs.

Mbulelo Mzamane points out that many black poets, while quite unknown to white South Africans, have vast followings in Soweto, Tembisa, Kwa-Thema.[84] Flouting the prestige of the "literary," this "poetry turned

81. Terry Eagleton and Peter Fuller, "The Question of Value: A Discussion," *New Left Review* 142 (Nov./Dec. 1983): 77.

82. See, for instance, Eagleton, "Aesthetics and Politics," *New Left Review* 107 (Jan./Feb. 1978): 21–34; *Criticism and Ideology: A Study in Marxist Literary Theory* (London, 1978); and "Criticism and Politics: The Work of Raymond Williams," *New Left Review* 95 (Jan./Feb. 1976): 3–23; Catherine Belsey, *Critical Practice* (London, 1980); Tony Bennett, *Formalism and Marxism* (London, 1979), and "Marxism and Popular Fiction," *Literature and Popular History* 7 (Fall 1981): 138–65; Stuart Hall, "Cultural Studies: Two Paradigms," in *Culture, Ideology and Social Process: A Reader,* ed. Bennett et al. (London, 1981), pp. 19–37; Barbara Herrnstein Smith, "Contingencies of Value," *Critical Inquiry* 10 (Sept. 1983): 1–36, and "Fixed Marks and Variable Constancies: A Parable of Literary Value," *Poetics Today* 1 (Autumn 1979): 7–31; Paul Lauter, "History and the Canon," *Social Text* 12 (Fall 1985): 94–101; Francis Mulhern, "Marxism in Literary Criticism," *New Left Review* 108 (Mar./Apr. 1979): 77–87; Jane Tompkins, *Sensational Designs: The Cultural Work of American Fiction, 1790–1860* (New York, 1985); Peter Widdowson, " 'Literary Value' and the Reconstruction of Criticism," *Literature and History* 6 (Fall 1980): 139–50.

83. The performative and popular aspects of this poetry mark it off from the Western modernist destruction of the text.

84. See Mbulelo Mzamane, "Literature and Politics among Blacks in South Africa," *New Classic* 5 (1978); reprinted in *SP,* p. 156.

theater," transient, immediate, and strategic, beloved and popular, overturns the essentialist question of "what constitutes good literature" and insists that it be recast in terms of what is good for whom, and when it is good, and why. Tenacious in the face of great distress, wary of some of the more moderate demands of early Black Consciousness, politically more radical in its demands yet relentlessly plagued by problems of gender, engaging at every moment the difficulties and bounty of its multiple traditions, this transitional black South African poetry faces considerable formal and social challenges. Black poets are no longer solely intent on desecrating those Western norms they feel to be invalid, vomiting them up and insulting them; they are now also engaged in the necessarily more difficult yet more positive endeavor of fashioning poetic values defensible in terms *other* than those simply of opposition and resistance to white values. Forcing poetry and criticism to step outside the magic circle of immanent value, into history and politics where criteria of judgment remain perpetually to be resolved, black poets are no longer content to snatch impudent rides on the dangerous trains of white tradition. Instead they are expressing increasingly a collective refusal to ride at all until the trains are theirs: "azikwelwa," we will not ride.

Contemporary Poetry, Alternate Routes

Jerome J. McGann

> Opposition is true friendship.
> —WILLIAM BLAKE, *The Marriage of Heaven and Hell*

> that the vanishing point might be on every word.
> —LYN HEJINIAN, "Grammar and Landscape"

What is the significance of that loose collective enterprise, sprung up in the aftermath of the sixties, known as L=A=N=G=U=A=G=E Writing? To answer this question I will be taking, initially, a somewhat oblique route. And I shall assume an agreement on several important social and political matters: first, that the United States, following the Second World War, assumed definitive leadership of a capitalist empire; second, that its position of leadership generated a network of internal social contradictions which persist to this day (the collision of imperialist demands with the isolationist and revolutionary nationalism of American ideology); third, that this postwar period has been characterized, at the international level, by an extended cold war shadowed by the threat of a global catastrophe, whether deliberate or accidental. Whatever one's political allegiances, these truths, surely, we hold as self-evident.

Postwar American poetry is deployed within that general arena, and to the degree that it is "political" at all, it reflects and responds to that set of overriding circumstances.[1] In my view the period ought to be seen

1. Black and feminist writing in the United States often confines the focus of the political engagement to a more restricted national theater. Nevertheless, even in these cases engagement is necessarily carried out within the global framework I have sketched above.

as falling into two phases. The first phase stretches from about 1946 (when Robert Lowell's *Lord Weary's Castle* appeared) to 1973 (when Lowell capped his career with the publication of *History*). This period is dominated by a conflict between various lines of traditional poetry, on one hand, and the countering urgencies of the "New American Poetry" on the other. In the diversity of this last group Donald Allen argued for a unifying "characteristic": "a total rejection of all those qualities typical of academic verse."[2]

Of course, this representation of the conflict between "tradition" and "innovation" obscures nearly as much as it clarifies. The New American poets were, in general, much more inclined to experimentalism than were writers like Richard Wilbur, Anthony Hecht, Louis Simpson, or Donald Justice. But Allen's declaration can easily conceal the academic and literary characteristics of the innovators. Robert Duncan and Charles Olson, for example, key figures in the New American Poetry, can hardly *not* be called "literary" or even "academic" poets. If they opened certain new areas in the field of poetic style, no less could and has been said of Lowell, even in his early work. And if Frank O'Hara seems the antithesis of academic work, John Ashbery is, in his own way, its epitome. Yet both appear in Allen's *New American Poetry* anthology. Moreover, who can say, between O'Hara and Ashbery, which is the more innovative of the two—so different are their styles of experimentation?

The issue here is not stylistic, however, but ideological and ultimately political. We can see this more clearly if we recall the "political style" of American writing between 1946 and 1973. It is unmistakably liberal-left. This is as true, in general, for the traditionalists as it is for the innovators.

If we turn to compare the period 1946–73 with the years since, many of the same literary conflicts persist. Nevertheless, this most recent period is sharply distinguished by one momentous difference: the dramatic shift to the political right which has taken place following the Vietnam War. Like every other part of society, the literary world registered these new social circumstances. Specifically, two new lines of work began to make their presence felt. The first of these might be called personal (not confessional) or localized verse, though Robert von Hallberg has called

2. *The New American Poetry: 1945–1960,* ed. Donald M. Allen (New York, 1960), p. xi.

Jerome J. McGann is Commonwealth Professor of English, University of Virginia. His most recent critical work, *Buildings of Loss: The Knowledge of Imaginative Texts,* will appear late in 1987.

it the poetry of the suburbs. It is marked, stylistically, by a moderated surface urbanity and, substantively, by an attempt to define "social" and "political" within a limited, even a personal, horizon. Furthermore, one observes in this work a renewed interest in narrative forms—a significant stylistic inclination, as we shall see more clearly in a moment. Robert Pinsky is perhaps the most conspicuous practitioner, and promoter, of this poetic mode, but it includes a large and heteronomous group of other, chiefly academic poets. Its spokesmen are Richard Howard, Helen Vendler, and—most recently—von Hallberg. "The poetry I admire [from the last forty years]," von Hallberg says, "is fairly spoken of as one of accommodation rather than opposition."[3]

The other line is L=A=N=G=U=A=G=E Writing. Here a conscious attempt has been made to marry the work of the fifties' New American Poetry with the post-structural work of the late sixties and seventies. As Frost, Yeats, Auden, and Stevens are the "precursors" of the poets of accommodation, Pound, Stein, and especially Zukofsky stand behind the L=A=N=G=U=A=G=E writers. Oppositional politics are a paramount concern, and the work stands in the sharpest relief, stylistically, to the poetry of accommodation.[4]

In a sense, the period from 1973 to the present appears to repeat the central struggle of 1946–73 between the "academics" and the "New American Writers." L=A=N=G=U=A=G=E Writing is distinctively experimental, while poets like Pinsky, Louise Glück, and John Hollander are traditionalists; and whereas the L=A=N=G=U=A=G=E writers

3. Robert von Hallberg, *American Poetry and Culture, 1945–1980* (Cambridge, Mass., 1985), p. 228. While I disagree with von Hallberg's criteria for poetry, his book is far the best account yet written of the post-World War II poetry scene in America. Also, its readings of a number of poets—especially Robert Lowell and Edward Dorn—are impressive and important. Differences of criteria aside, its only notable deficiency is its failure to observe the development of L=A=N=G=U=A=G=E Writing through the seventies and eighties. See also Robert Pinsky's *Situation of Poetry* (Princeton, N.J., 1976). The best discussions to date of L=A=N=G=U=A=G=E Writing are Marjorie Perloff, *The Dance of the Intellect: Studies in the Poetry of the Pound Tradition* (Cambridge, 1985), chap. 10, and Lee Bartlett, "What Is Language Poetry?" *Critical Inquiry* 12 (Summer 1986): 741–52.

4. In a letter to me Ron Silliman suggested that this work be designated *Language* (rather than L=A=N=G=U=A=G=E) Writing because the latter term is associated with a specific journal (which only began relatively late in the day, so far as this movement was concerned), and because the name calls attention to institutional rather than stylistic matters. Though the first point is important and persuasive, I disagree with the second, in this sense: I think the institutional character of this movement should be emphasized. One of the most salient characteristics of the movement has been its determination to disseminate itself outside the traditional institutional structures (that is, outside the New York publishing centers, on one hand, and the academic network on the other). L=A=N=G=U=A=G=E Writing developed its own infrastructure, in reading centers and publishing ventures which are variously located, but whose two chief points of reference are New York and San Francisco. These social and institutional networks were painstakingly constructed between approximately 1970 and the present.

are almost *all* situated—economically and institutionally—outside the academy, their counterparts—critics and poets alike—occupy important scholastic positions. The difference between pre- and post-1973 American poetry lies in the extremity of the ideological gap which separates the traditionalists from the innovators in the post-1973 period. As will be very clear from the discussion below, L=A=N=G=U=A=G=E writers typically foreground their oppositional politics in ways that the New American Poets did not. The latter were more socially disaffected than politically opposed.

The two divergent lines in American poetry since 1973 are usefully contrasted in terms of the shape of Ashbery's career and their relation to it. Throughout the seventies and even into the eighties, the single most influential figure in American poetry has been Ashbery. But there are certainly two Ashberys to choose from. For L=A=N=G=U=A=G=E writers, all of his work should be read out of—by means of—the experimental projects developed from *The Tennis Court Oath* (1962) to *Three Poems* (1972). Not that he has ceased to write important work since, but in those early years his innovative stylistic repertoire had been fully deployed. Indeed, Ashbery's style—established in the sixties—has come to seem an early exponent of a postmodern sensibility. As such, it was (properly) taken as a swerve away from the poetries of the fifties and sixties—a presage of things to come.

The problem, however, is precisely the political significance of Ashbery's "postmodern" stance. The heated controversy which has developed around the idea of the postmodern—is it or is it not a reactionary social phenomenon?—throws the problem of Ashbery's work into sharp relief.[5] His unmistakable style has been read as the poetic equivalent of a deconstructive mode; and yet deconstruction in America, though seen in many traditional quarters as a socially subversive movement, has been centered in the Yale School, which has never made any efforts to develop or practice an oppositional politics.[6] So far as Ashbery is concerned, a similar type of "nonpolitics" is discernible throughout his career—even as his work has been used by many younger writers whose oppositional politics are clear. But Ashbery himself has not exploited or even fore-

5. The literature on the question of postmodernism is now quite large. The best account of the debate—an essay at once descriptively acute and critically significant—is Andreas Huyssen's "Mapping the Postmodern," *New German Critique* 33 (Fall 1984): 5–52. The argument is sometimes made that postmodernism, though outwardly accommodational, mounts an *implicitly* critical comment upon contemporary society. But no one who has taken part in this debate—not even Peter Bürger, Jean-François Lyotard, or Fredric Jameson—has discussed the postmodernism of the L=A=N=G=U=A=G=E writers, who are aggressively and openly oppositional in their political stance. See the discussion which follows.

6. The best (critical) account of the Yale school is in *The Yale Critics: Deconstruction in America*, ed. Jonathan Arac, Wlad Godzich, and Wallace Martin (Minneapolis, 1983).

grounded his own work's "oppositional" features and potentialities; and in the period from 1973 to the present his work (for example, in *Vermont Notebook* [1975], *Houseboat Days* [1977], or *As We Know* [1979]) has moved instead along lines that parallel the suburban and personal interests of poets like Pinsky, James McMichael, and Turner Cassity.

Ashbery's avoidance of a conscious political position defines the style of his postmodern address. Not without reason has his work been canonized in academic discourse about contemporary poetry. As earlier Lowell became the exegetical focus of high/late New Critical discourse, Ashbery has become the contemporary touchstone for deconstructive analysis. What we confront here, however, is not so much an issue of poetic style or poetic quality as it is a problem in ideology—the kinds of cultural ideas that are to be propagated through that crucial ideological apparatus, the academy. In postmodern work we become aware of the many crises of stability and centeredness which an imperial culture like our own—attempting to hold control over so many, and so widely dispersed, human materials—inevitably has to deal with. The response to such a situation may be either a contestatory or an accommodational one—it may move to oppose and change such circumstances, or it may take them as given, and reflect (reflect upon) their operations.

"The test of a 'politics of poetry,'" Barrett Watten has observed, "is in the entry of poetry into the world in a political way."[7] Watten has been a prominent L=A=N=G=U=A=G=E writer for some time, so that for him "politics" means "opposition" rather than "accommodation." What we must recognize is that both types of writing, whether contestatory or accommodating, are political in character, and represent a certain type of political stance toward life in imperialist America. Furthermore, from the vantage of a writer like Watten, the poetries of accommodation of the seventies represent a retreat from the critical responsibilities of art, and perhaps even an active celebration—properly hedged or refined—of immediate social and political circumstances.

One cannot write about these matters neutrally. Neutrality here will in fact be a choice of the position of accommodation. And while I find much to admire in that kind of poetry, I think that far the most important work is now being done elsewhere in American writing. Nor does its importance lie solely in its oppositional politics. The most innovative work stylistically is now to be traced in the journals, chapbooks, pamphlets, and—increasingly—the books of various poets associated with L=A=N=G=U=A=G=E Writing. The eventuality is hardly a surprising one; for this work has been actively forging, over the past ten or fifteen years, writing procedures which seek after a *comprehensive* account of the American experience during that period.

7. Barrett Watten, "Method and Surrealism: The Politics of Poetry," *L=A=N=G=U=A=G=E* 4, ed. Bruce Andrews and Charles Bernstein (Open Letter, Fifth Series, no. 1), p. 129.

Of course, much of this work is weak, some of it is trivial, and a great deal has only a formal or aesthetic significance—despite its political urgencies. My interest here, however, is not in such matters. Rather, what I want to indicate is the kind of intervention L=A=N=G=U=A=G=E work typically seeks to make—*how* it tries to enter the world in a political way, and what it means to carry out through that entrance.

In the eyes of eternity—if eternity is interested in art—Wordsworth and Blake will each find their appropriate place, and later ages will find in each those various resources appropriate to a later moment. But between 1789 and 1815 the work of Wordsworth and Blake entered the world very differently, and their art stood for two correspondingly different "politics of poetry." Each is part of the same cultural structure, but each imagined that culture—its past, present, and future alike—in radically different ways. When they produced their work they were carrying out a struggle of the imagination, ultimately a social and political struggle. Just so is all writing engaged in immediate disputes that have broad and long social implications—in contests of the present for the resources of the past and the possibilities of the future. As such, we too have choices to make. Histories of our moment are currently being written by various poets, and within those histories alternative histories of poetry are being carried out. Because I believe the history that is L=A=N=G=U=A=G=E Writing is extremely important, I want to indicate here, in a brief and polemical way, the context and import of its antithetical venture.

I shall begin this inquiry at a tangent, by looking at a passage from a recent essay by Richard Rorty. The essay has nothing as such to do with contemporary American poetry.

> There are two principal ways in which reflective human beings try, by placing their lives in a larger context, to give sense to those lives. The first is by telling the story of their contribution to a community. This community may be the actual historical one in which they live, or another actual one, distant in time or place, or a quite imaginary one. . . . The second way is to describe themselves as standing in immediate relation to a nonhuman reality. This relation is immediate in the sense that it does not derive from a relation between such a reality and their tribe, or their nation, or their imagined band of comrades. I shall say that stories of the former kind exemplify the desire for solidarity, and that stories of the latter kind exemplify the desire for objectivity.[8]

8. Richard Rorty, "Solidarity or Objectivity?" *Post-Analytic Philosophy,* ed. John Rajchman and Cornel West (New York, 1985), p. 3.

Rorty, as we know, is committed to "stories" of what he calls "solidarity"—"pragmatistic" stories of the here and now. Or we should rather say that he *reads* all the stories that interest him out of the framework of his "cultural peers," the group he also calls "postmodern bourgeois intellectuals." This is the locus of his allegiances and conscious "solidarity." Though I shall later have some comments on Rorty's ideas about postmodernity, I must first call attention to the privilege Rorty gives to narrative itself. Rorty assumes—the passage is, in this respect, typical of all his work—that "human being" is fundamentally a social rather than a rational function. He goes on to say that we "give sense to" our human being in only two communicative forms. This thought is striking enough, but even more so is the idea that both of these forms are narrative ones.

As Michel de Certeau and others have pointed out, narrative is a form of continuity; as such, its deployment in discourse is a way of legitimating established forms of social order, as well as the very idea of such established forms.[9] Within discourse structures, critical alternatives to the orders of narrativity characteristically emerge from various types of non- and antinarrative. Such forms have grown especially prominent in the discourses of postmodernism. As we shall see more particularly in a moment, however, while non- and antinarratives both move counter to regularized, normative, and "accommodating" orders, they exemplify distinct forms of discourse. Antinarrative is problematic, ironical, and fundamentally a satiric discursive procedure. It *engages* a dialectic, and its critical function is completed in a structure of antithesis, which may include the double irony of a self-antithesis. Nonnarratives, on the other hand, do not issue calls for change and alterity; they embody in themselves some form of cultural difference. To adapt (and secularize) the terminology of Blake, nonnarrative is the "contrary" (rather than the "negation") of narrativity. Its antithesis to narrative is but one dimension of a more comprehensively imagined program based in the codes of an alternative set of solidarities. Byron's *Don Juan* is one type of antinarrative and Blake's *Milton* is another type. *The Marriage of Heaven and Hell,* on the other hand, is decidedly nonnarrative.

The special relevance of nonnarrative and antinarrative lies within the horizon of postmodernism, when such forms (and their correspondent terminologies) began to be elaborated. Nevertheless, because nonnarrative

9. See Michel de Certeau, "La Fiction de l'histoire," *L'écriture de l'histoire* (Paris, 1975), pp. 312–58 and "History: Science and Fiction," *Heterologies: Discourse on the Other,* trans. Brian Massumi (Minneapolis, 1986), pp. 199–221. Robert Scholes has a good discussion of the ways "post-modernist anti-narratives" move antithetically against the continuities of narrativity, in "Language, Narrative, and Anti-Narrative," *Critical Inquiry* 7 (Autumn 1980): 211; see also Nelson Goodman's essay "Twisted Tales; or, Story, Study, and Symphony" in the same issue (pp. 103–20). Some of the more general forms of non- and antinarrative are also treated in my own earlier essay "Some Forms of Critical Discourse," *Critical Inquiry* 11 (March 1985), pp. 399–417.

and antinarrative were not contemporary inventions, their presence in certain previous literary works can help to define their special currencies. Consider antinarratives, for example, whose structures depend upon, reflect, and thereby maintain the forms of narrative continuity which they bring under critical examination. The digressive structure of *Don Juan,* for example, is intimately connected to the fate of that poem's narrative—which is, fundamentally, the recollective narrative of Byron's own life told via several displaced and putatively fictive narratives involving the poem's hero Don Juan. Similarly, Blake's *Milton* is a critical examination of English history between approximately 1640 and 1810. That history is presented as a system which replicates itself in its various subsystems (for example, the events of Milton's life, the events of Blake's). Furthermore, these histories are placed within the context of the more comprehensive narrative of human history as set forth in the redemptive mythos of Jewish-Christian polemics. The critique of history in *Milton* appears as a secret narrative moving antithetically to the known and apparent narrative: Blake represents this structure as a pair of cogged wheels, with the destructive wheel (of nature) turning in one direction, and the redemptive wheel (of art)—attached to it—turning in the other.[10] That image itself suggests the intimacy of the relation between narrative and antinarrative.

Nonnarrative is different—for example, Blake's *Marriage of Heaven and Hell.* Among all of Blake's works it most closely resembles the *Songs of Innocence and of Experience* both in its ideas and its form. Both works explore the significance of what Blake calls "contraries." Furthermore, both are collections of diverse materials—anthologized structures where the relations between the parts are not determined by narrativities. This odd character of the *Marriage* in particular is underscored in several ways. The work opens with an "Argument," which ought—by poetic convention—to be a brief summary of the work to follow. But the "Argument" is a small narrativized unit whose relation to the rest of the *Marriage* can only be arranged by the reader's ingenuity in drawing different kinds of verbal and tropaic analogies of the "Argument" (and parts of the "Argument") with other parts and pieces of the work. The *Marriage* contains as well a number of other brief narrativized units, but all are self-contained; their interrelations, once again, have to be consciously constructed because the work provides no narrativized structure, either express or implied, within which they find their coherence.

This fact about the internal form of the work is emphasized by the heterogeneity of the particular writing-units. Some are narrativized, one is a collection of proverbs, and four others are expository presentations of different kinds of ideas. Furthermore, the subject matter taken up in

10. The image appears in both *Milton* and *Jerusalem;* see, e.g., *Milton,* pl. 27, ll. 9–10.

these different textual units is equally heteronomous. The "Argument" (pl. 2) is a spare allegorical narrative based in the biblical mythos; the "Song of Liberty" (pls. 25–27), also narrativized, is a polyglot piece whose primary location is in contemporary history; and the other narrative units (for example, pls. 12–13, 15, and the two narratives embedded in pls. 17–23) are equally diverse with respect to type and subject matter. The differentiating inertia of the *Marriage* operates as well within the specific textual units. Plates 12–13, for example, narrate a personal anecdote, but the location of the event—in some kind of spiritual hyperspace—forces a reorientation of certain fundamental categories of thought (spatial, temporal, social).

Finally, one must observe the variable order of the text as a whole.[11] Most copies of the *Marriage* are arranged in the sequence plates 1–27, but copies E and G deploy perfectly acceptable alternative orders, and copy G was in fact foliated by Blake himself. The shifting plates are 4, 14, and 15, which are so moved that two other orderings are created for the work. One should note here that a similar indeterminacy of textual relations is found throughout Blake's work: no copy of the *Songs* has an order which corresponds to that of any other copy, and variations are the rule in almost all of his engraved works. There is no question that these variances in sequencing are deliberate, and there is every reason to think that he was encouraged to this kind of textual experimentation by recent biblical and classical scholarship.

Whatever the order of this wild diversity of material, then, it is clearly not a narratological one. Indeed, narrativity is short-circuited from the moment that the reading process is spatialized as a field of illuminated printing. It is not simply that the "text" is illustrated or illuminated; rather, the verbal discourse evolves *as a set of images, decorations, and pictures.* To say that one "reads" Blake's works is to invoke a metaphor, as we do when we speak of "reading" a painting. Of course, if Blake's work is delivered over to us simply in typographical forms we are likely to end up as nonmetaphoric "readers" of the "texts." This commonly happens when Blake is "taught," but it is a type of misreading—an abstracted form—which has nothing to recommend it as an imaginative activity. In short, Blake ought to be "read" in facsimile.

What, then, *is* the order which pervades a work like the *Marriage*? Blake called it the order of Imagination—the order generated through the faculty or process which discovers previously unapprehended relations of things. And in fact one of the most striking aspects of the *Marriage* is that it encourages the reader to draw all kinds of unusual substantive and grammatological materials into relationships which convention normally keeps separate. Antinarrative calls those conventions into question

11. For information on the different copies of *The Marriage of Heaven and Hell,* see *William Blake's Writings,* ed. G. E. Bentley, Jr., 2 vols. (Oxford, 1978), 1:692–95.

and develops the premonitory conditions for imaginative activity. Indeed, antinarrative frequently generates imaginative localities and incommensurate particulars which escape the imperialism of narrativity. But nonnarrative alone will establish, among the kingdoms and principalities of narrative, the proper world of what Blake called Imagination.

Once again we must ask, however, what is the order of that world? An answer may be glimpsed if we reflect for a moment on one of the most striking variations in the plate sequencing. Plate 15 (the Printing House in Hell episode) comes last in copy E of the *Marriage,* immediately after the "Song of Liberty," which is the work's traditional conclusion. This dramatic placement clearly calls attention not merely to the work's own productive processes, but to the satanic view of what all knowledge—imaginative or otherwise—must be: mediated language forms generated through specific social—specific material and institutional—processes. In all copies of the *Marriage* the subject of Blake's own productive processes is prominently and recurrently treated. This subject calls attention to the inherently material and social character of imaginative work. Placing plate 15 at the end is one way of giving such ideas paramount and conclusive importance.

A poem like the *Marriage,* then, urges us to see that the order of nonnarrative is the order of production (as opposed to the orders of reflection and reproduction). This order foregrounds itself in the *Marriage* through the pervasive thematic of the printing and engraving processes: the meaning of the *Marriage* is its means and modes of production. It is as one might say "a poem about poetry," but not about the "idea" of poetry. The *Marriage* is praxis-oriented, and thus it is "about" poetry only in the sense that poetry is understood as a set of socially engaged material practices.[12] In the *Marriage* poetry "practices itself," poetry is carried out; and this work of poetry as a productive social practice is self-consciously brought before the attention of the "reader." This sort of thing happens in Blake's work all the time—for example, in *Jerusalem,* part of whose wit involves the understanding that Albion's "emanation" is in literal truth the work Blake produces and calls *Jerusalem.*

This example of Blake is a useful point of departure for considering a large and important body of contemporary writing where antinarrative and nonnarrative figure prominently. Blake is useful not merely because his example is familiar, but perhaps even more because his is a problematic case. In the *Marriage* a redemptive myth is essayed which is based in forms of creation rather than forms of atonement. Within the general

12. I use the word "praxis" here because its Marxian meanings are peculiarly apposite to Blake's work. Nowadays the term is applied fairly loosely—or perhaps metaphorically—to a wide variety of poems. In Blake's case, however, the material and institutional dimensions of the work are made an integral *thematic* part of the poems. Thus the production process, in a specifically Marxian sense, is a constant subject of Blake's work.

framework of Judeo-Christian culture, a production-based redemptive order is unusual—and extremely difficult to maintain. Blake's work is most emphatically carried out within a Judeo-Christian culture, and although the work moves at a strange diagonal to that culture, it never wholly escapes its gravitational field. Atonement, rather than creation, is a form of thought—a mode of action—which recurs throughout the work, most prominently, I suppose, in *Milton* and *Jerusalem*. To the extent that Blake is interested in creation rather than redemption, he is hostile to the theory of atonement. In the end Blake arrived at a compromise: he rejected the traditional theory of atonement, but he embraced a heterodox theory which held, essentially, that a general redemptive scheme would emerge through the practice of continuous self-atonement.

Insofar as works like the *Songs* and *Marriage* are nonnarratives which do not involve themselves in forms of atonement, they resemble various kinds of post-structural discourse, and in particular the work now commonly known as L=A=N=G=U=A=G=E Writing. Since antinarrative and nonnarrative forms abound in this work, it exemplifies a significant strand of postmodernist writing. But unlike certain other forms of postmodernism—and prototypically the academic postmodernism associated with the Yale School, on the one hand, and with Richard Rorty on the other—L=A=N=G=U=A=G=E Writing typically deploys a consciously antithetical political content. It always situates itself, therefore, to the left of Rorty's "postmodern bourgeois intellectuals."

Though an extraordinarily diverse group, all L=A=N=G=U=A=G=E writers are involved with writing projects which fracture the surface regularities of the written text, and which interrupt conventional reading processes. Thus, Richard Foreman writes a theoretical essay carrying the imperative title "Trying To Be Centered . . . on the Circumference."[13] If the Word of God issues from that famous circle whose center is everywhere and whose circumference is nowhere, these new words come from a circle of human writers whose circumference is everywhere and whose center is nowhere. Abigail Child declares, in an aphoristic manifesto, that the poetic object is to set "UNITS OF UNMEANINGNESS INCORPORATED ANEW // VS. A COMMUNITY OF SLOGANEERS" (p. 94). The sense is that poetry and writing generally have been colonized by imperial forces, and that the power of this monopoly has to be broken. The object of writing must be to set language free, to return it from the domains of the abstract

13. See Richard Foreman, "Trying To Be Centered . . . on the Circumference," in *The L=A=N=G=U=A=G=E Book*, ed. Bruce Andrews and Charles Bernstein (Carbondale, Ill., 1984), pp. 50–51. This important book is a generous selection of pieces reprinted from vols. 1–3 of the journal *L=A=N=G=U=A=G=E*. All further references to this work will be included in the text.

and the conventional (the communities of SLOGANEERS, whose name today is Legion) to a world of human beings and human uses.

The program of these writers, consequently, has a strong—usually, an explicit—social and political orientation. I want to leave that aside for the moment, however, in order to concentrate on its more local and even technical aspects: for example, on Tina Darragh's forms of "procedural writing" which she adapts from the work of Francis Ponge. Darragh produces arrangements of textual forms—they are literally unreadable, as is much other L=A=N=G=U=A=G=E Poetry—by selecting, via an orderly but arbitrary plan, sequences of verbal materials that appear on a single page of a dictionary. The point of this kind of operation becomes very clear if we read a few of Bernadette Mayer's practical writing injunctions as set forth in her mini-manual "Experiments":

> Systematically derange the language, for example, write a work consisting only of prepositional phrases, or, add a gerundive to every line of an already existing piece of prose or poetry, etc.
>
> Get a group of words (make a list or select at random); then form these words (only) into a piece of writing—whatever the words allow. Let them demand their own form, and/or: Use certain words in a set way, like, the same word in every line, or in a certain place in every paragraph, etc. Design words.
>
> Write what cannot be written, for example, compose an index. (Read an index as a poem).
>
> Attempt writing in a state of mind that seems least congenial.
>
> Consider word & letter as forms—the concretistic distortion of a text, for example, too many o's or a multiplicity of thin letters (lllftiii, etc.)
>
> Attempt to eliminate all connotation from a piece of writing & vice versa. [Pp. 80, 81, 82]

The final injunction in Mayer's list of writing experiments is appropriately, summarily, placed: "Work your ass off to change the language & dont ever get famous" (p. 83). The message is clear: the celebrated writing of her time appears in digestible and accepted forms; indeed, at this time (at any time, one wonders?) fame, conventionality, and the regularities of narrativized discourse are functionally related to everything that must be judged unpoetical, inhuman, a failure—even, perhaps, a betrayal. To revive poetry, "to change the language," means that one must try to "Write what cannot be written," to produce what cannot be "read" (an "index," a "multiplicity of thin letters")—in short, to "derange the language" from its current (truly "deranged") conventionalities.

Mayer's "Experiments" speak very clearly about a number of the most important characteristics of L=A=N=G=U=A=G=E Writing. In the first place, writing is conceived as something that must be done rather than as something that is to be interpreted. The vantage is Horatian rather than Plotinian. The "meanings" sought after in this work are neither ideas which lie behind (prior to) the texts nor residues left over from their operations. Meaning occurs as part of the process of writing—indeed, it *is* the writing. Thus Charles Bernstein will say of such poetry that it "emphasizes its medium as being constructed . . . designed, manipulated, picked, programmed, organized" (p. 39):

> Whatever gets written gets written in a particular shape, uses a particular vocabulary & syntax, & a variety of chosen techniques. . . . Sometimes this process takes place intuitively or unconsciously. . . . Sometimes it is a very conscious process. . . . In either case, various formal decisions are made & these decisions shape the work. [P. 43]

This kind of statement—it appears repeatedly in the manifestos of L=A=N=G=U=A=G=E Writing—argues that discourse, including poetic discourse, is not meaning-referential but meaning-constitutive. Writing is an event, a praxis, and in our day one of its principal operations involves the dismantling of the ideology, reified in so much that passes for "writing" (the SLOGANEERS), that language—which in this context means producing and reproducing texts—is an object, an icon. "The signs of language . . . are not . . . mere structures," Bernstein says; "they do not sit, deanimated, as symbols in a code, dummies for things of nature they refer to" (p. 41). We are to think of poetry as "making a path" rather than "designing a garden" (p. 39). "Texts are themselves signi*fieds,* not mere signifiers. TEXT: it requires no hermeneusis for it is itself one—of itself" (p. 34).

A second crucial feature of the L=A=N=G=U=A=G=E approach to poetry and writing centers in its preoccupation with nonsense, unmeaning, and fragmentation. As writers they practice language experiments which generate and promote such conditions. As readers their approach is archaeological. Their reviews and critical comments on poetry display little concern with "interpretation," that positive obsession of academic discourse. Rather, they elucidate as it were the behavior, the manners, the way of life that various kinds of writings perform and live. When Alan Davies and Nicholas Piombino see poetry as a locus of "indeterminate intervals," they develop a method for encountering and illuminating texts which they call "Field Reading."[14] One recalls Darragh's work with "pro-

14. See Alan Davies and Nick Piombino, "The Indeterminate Interval: From History to Blur," *L=A=N=G=U=A=G=E* 4, pp. 31–39.

cedural writing" whereby the page of a dictionary is suddenly exposed as a field of strange and unrecognized deposits—odd bits and pieces scattered across a surface whose depths and layers and correspondences escape the notice of the dictionary's ordinary users.

This archaeology of knowledge represents a deliberate intervention in and through the processes of writing. Field reading and procedural writing are stochastic immediate events that intervene with writing deposits, equally stochastic, which are already situated. What is crucial to the immediate acts of intervention, however, is that they are conscious of their own relative status. These writers deploy an archaeology which does not stand in an objective and superior relation to the fields they are exploring. There is a "transmutative effect" (p. 49) between writings and readings, feedback loops that persist and expand their operations as the random and the deliberate intersect in the dynamic field of language use:

> There's a place that you're going from and a place that you're going to; to get to that place, that tracking, is as worthwhile as the endpoint of going, because while you're going there you find other things and those things are related to the final place; that helps to define what it is when you get there. New combinations and connections are experienced. In finding your locus you redefine it again each time, systematically finding new coordinates.[15]

This passage reminds us that, in the view of L=A=N=G=U=A=G=E Writing, the time is always the present. Nevertheless, past and future are permanent concerns of these writers, whose work would be travestied if it were represented as the imperialism of the here and now, or the immediate self. The textual activism that is promoted in L=A=N=G=U=A=G=E Writing places the writer inside the writing process. The writer manipulates and deploys his or her texts, but in so doing the writer is also, necessarily, made subject to their inertia as well. "Texts read the reader," Bruce Andrews observes (p. 36), which means, in this program, that they read the writer as well. The activist writer/reader, by operating on and in texts, is forced to undergo and deal with the limits and the significance of that activism. As a consequence, "meaning" emerges not as an appropriation or institution of truth but as "the enabled incapacity to impose a usage" (p. 35). The program is precisely conceived to reveal the power of writing and the production of meaning as human, social, and limited in exact and articulable ways. Indeed, it is designed to demonstrate and *practice* such a conception.

Thus we can see the general context—political and stylistic alike—within which the antinarrative and nonnarrative procedures of

15. Ibid., p. 37.

L=A=N=G=U=A=G=E Writing are deployed. Narrativity is an especially problematic feature of discourse, to these writers, because its structures lay down "stories" which serve to limit and order the field of experience, in particular the field of social and historical experience. Narrativity is, in this view, an inherently conservative feature of discourse, and hence it is undermined at every point. Bernstein's poems, for example, typically begin with an attack upon conventional "beginnings." In traditional texts, the "beginning" signals the text's sense of itself as a "unitary document" within which "continuity is possible."[16] Because the fundamental codes of the reading procedure are established at every beginning, Bernstein's poems typically start by throwing up barriers and creating problems. His initiating codes are always antithetical, as we see at the outset of one of his most astonishing poems, "For Love Has Such a Spirit That if It Is Portrayed It Dies":

> Mass of van contemplation to intercede crush of
> plaster. Lots of loom: "smoke out", merely
> complicated by the first time something and don't.
> Long last, occurrence of bell, altitude, attitude of.
> The first, at this moment, aimless, *aims.* To the
> point of inordinate asphalt—lecture, entail.
> These hoops regard me suspiciously.[17]

From this apparently scattered set of texts one scarcely knows how to proceed. We are at the outset of a "poem"—this much we know, from having decoded other attendant bibliographical conventions—and hence we assume that "continuity is possible." Bernstein counts on that assumption and then attacks it. To "go on" with this text in itself means that the reader has assented to the justice—the poetic justice—of Bernstein's initial move. And if we *do* in fact go on with his text, we will discover that relationships and forms of order can only be had if they are actively made by the reader. We will also discover that such relationships and forms of order are multiple, and that they will shift from reader to reader and from reading to reading. Continuities do not lie in wait for us, and the idea that we should expect continuities is specifically rejected.

This is the antinarrative mode of L=A=N=G=U=A=G=E Writing, and it is Bernstein's most typical form of stylistic address. The nonnarrative mode is perhaps best displayed in the elaborate forms of serialized writing produced by Ron Silliman. This is how *Tjanting* begins:

> Not this.
> What then?

16. Edward Said, *Beginnings: Intention and Method* (New York, 1975), pp. 58, 48.

17. Bernstein, "For Love Has Such a Spirit That if It Is Portrayed It Dies," *Controlling Interests* (New York, 1980), p. 48.

> I started over & over. Not this.
> Last week I wrote "the muscles in my palm so sore from halving the rump roast I cld barely grip the pen." What then? This morning my lip is blisterd.
> Of about to within which. Again & again I began. The gray light of day fills the yellow room in a way wch is somber. Not this. Hot grease had spilld on the stove top.
> Nor that either. Last week I wrote "the muscle at thumb's root so taut from carving that beef I thought it wld cramp." Not so. What then? Wld I begin? This morning my lip is tender, disfigurd. I sat in an old chair out behind the anise. I cld have gone about this some other way.[18]

In an important essay on Silliman's work, "Narrating Narration," Bernstein points out that Silliman's nonnarratives consciously work against "the deep slumber of chronology, causality, and false unity (totalization)."[19] He elaborates this idea in a general comment which might well serve as the basis for a particular exegesis of the passage I just quoted:

> Detail is cast upon detail, minute particular upon minute particular, adding up to an impossibility of commensurable narrative. With every new sentence a new embarkation: not only is the angle changed, and it's become a close-up, but the subject is switched. Yet maybe the sound's the same, carries it through. Or like an interlocking chain: A has a relation to B and B to C, but A and C have nothing in common (*series not essence*). ["NN," p. 93]

Silliman's text commits itself to the "Not this," to a productivity that starts over and over again. But while the work is clearly a processive text, its movement is not governed by a narrativized totality. At the same time, if the work is oriented toward "the future," toward "what comes next," it firmly grounds itself in both the present and the past: what it denominates, in its first two sentences, as the "this" and the "then." The chief effect is a brilliant sense of immediacy which is not, however, fixed or formalized. The text is restless in its presentness, restless in a presentness which at all points vibrates with its relations to the past and its commitments to the future.

In fact, Silliman's energized present-ation will gradually show that the past and the future are themselves open to many possibilities. "I cld have gone about this some other way," he writes, and in that very statement we observe a change of direction.

18. Silliman, *Tjanting* (Berkeley, Calif., 1981), p. 11; all further references to this work, abbreviated *T*, will be included in the text.

19. Bernstein, "Narrating Narration: The Shapes of Ron Silliman's Work," *The Difficulties*, Ron Silliman Issue 2, no. 2 (1985): 93; all further references to this work, abbreviated "NN," will be included in the text.

In a work like *Tjanting* language is carrying out—dramatizing—certain fundamental realities of social space and social relations. Silliman's text is a vast trope of the human world. Events in the past continually impinge upon the present and possibilities beyond the present: words and phrases recur in slightly altered forms and circumstances, as do syntactical forms, images, and sound patterns. As a consequence, we confront time, or the sequence of eventualities, in a highly pressurized state. The shifting forms of the repetitions open the textual field to greater possibilities. They also locate startling interventions in the text's immediate moments:

> The yellow room has a sober hue. Each sentence accounts for its place. Not this. [*T*, p. 11]

But perhaps most remarkable of all is the translation of the past—that is to say, earlier textualizations—out of this generational process. So, while "earlier" textual forms appear in various "later" transforms, a reciprocal transformative process operates backward, as it were, changing the "earlier" texts within their memorial "later" constitutions. Thus in the next paragraph of *Tjanting,* when we come upon the statement "Each sentence accounts for all the rest" (*T*, p. 12), the "rhyme" of the sentences forces a new perspective on the earlier form "Each sentence accounts for its place." Minimally we observe that the particular "places" of "each sentence" are functionally integrated with "all the rest." Out of the play of language emerges an idea of history as profoundly dialectical—as dialectical as Silliman's textual presentation. The "past" is no more fixed than the present or the future. All time is open to transformation.

Silliman's poem, in its largest sense, aims to represent through textual enactment a redemption of the *localities* of human history. Marxist in his orientation, Silliman's politicized writing has passed through the filtering critique of the Frankfurt school, and especially through the work of Walter Benjamin. His Marxism is "Western" in the concrete sense that it is carried out within the arena of advanced capitalism and American political imperialism. As a writer his struggle against these exploitive social formations appears as a critique of the modes of language which produce and reproduce the "reality" of a capitalist world and history.

Silliman is especially interested, then, in that paradigmatic bourgeois form of writing, the novel, along with those correspondent breezes "referentiality" and "narrative." Silliman does not attack "reference" in language—all language is social—but that deformed and repressive form of reference called referentiality wherein language is alienated from its use-functions:

> What happens when a language moves toward and passes into a capitalist stage of development is an anaesthetic transformation of

> the perceived tangibility of the word, with corresponding increases in its descriptive and narrative capacities, preconditions for the invention of "realism," the optical illusion of reality in capitalist thought. These developments are tied directly to the nature of reference in language, which under capitalism is transformed (deformed) into referentiality.[20] [P. 125]

Silliman calls poetry "the *philosophy of practice in language*" (p. 131) because its procedures are performative, "gestural," and nonnarrative. Poetics is, therefore, the critical instance through which narrativized forms are to be understood. In every novel is concealed its true poetic, screaming to get out:

> Repression does not, fortunately, abolish the existence of the repressed element which continues as a contradiction, often invisible, in the social fact. As such, it continues to wage the class struggle of consciousness. [P. 126]

But the novel, dominated as it is by referentiality and narrativity, is always moving within the medium of its own self-occlusion. The function of poetry is to provide an example of language in conscious pursuit of complete self-transparency. At this particular juncture of late capitalism, poetry represents the "social function of the language arts" as a liberating rather than a repressive structure: "to carry the class struggle *for* consciousness to the level *of* consciousness" (p. 131).

Because "*all meaning is a construct*" (p. 168), however, this self-transparency of the word is not an Idea or a priori form which the poem tries to accommodate. Self-transparency, like social justice, is a practical matter—a form of accomplishment rather than a form of truth. It has to be carried out. In Silliman's writing, this "constructed" procedure appears most frequently in his resort to various artificial numbering systems to order his work. Two procedural rules govern the form of *Ketjak,* for example. First, the work moves by a series of paragraphs in which each successive paragraph has twice the number of sentences as the previous one. Second, each new paragraph must contain, somewhere, all the words used in the preceding paragraph. The method is designed to generate a network of accumulating and interconnecting details. New material is continually being generated, but always within the context of the body of materials which has already been developed.

Of *Ketjak* Bernstein has acutely noted that "the narrative rules are not taken to be of intrinsic interest" ("NN," p. 94). Indeed, these are not "narrative rules" at all, but generative ones. Furthermore, they do not

20. Silliman's two important essays, "Disappearance of the Word, Appearance of the World" and "If By 'Writing' We Mean Literature," from which these prose quotations are taken, can be found in *The L=A=N=G=U=A=G=E Book,* pp. 121–32 and 167–69.

occupy the reader's attention as such, they provide the framework within which acts of attention are carried out. Therefore Bernstein observes, in a brilliant turn of critical wit, that "Definition is a posteriori" in Silliman's work, "arising from a poetic practice in which the reader is acknowledged as present and counting" ("NN," p. 95). What "counts" are the multiple perspectives processed through the text along with the reader who takes part in that processing. This is why Bernstein says that a Silliman poem is "not reductive to a single world viewed" but is "participatory, multiple" ("NN," p. 95).

Yet in *Tjanting,* written four years after *Ketjak,* Silliman deployed a numerically based rule for generating his materials which clearly held something more than a procedural interest for him. The work, he has said, grew out of a problem he had been pondering "for at least five years: what would class struggle look like, viewed as a form. Would such a form be usable in writing?"[21] The answer was that it would look like the Fibonacci number series—that is to say, the series in which each term is the sum of the preceding two.

> What initially attracted me to the series were three things: (1) it is the mathematical sequence most often found in nature, (2) each succeeding term is larger, and (3) the quantitative difference between terms is immediately perceptible, even when the quantities are of syllables or paragraphs.[22]

Such a sequence came to embody for Silliman an *objectively based* dialectical process:

> The most important aspect of the Fibonacci series turned out not to be those gorgeous internal relationships, but the fact that it begins with two ones. That not only permitted the parallel articulation of two sequences of paragraphs, but also determined that their development would be uneven, punning back to the general theory of class struggle.[23]

But what must be noted is that *Tjanting* does not tell the/a "story" of "class struggle." It does not reflect the operation of "the general theory of class struggle" in a projected "fiction" (first-person or otherwise). Rather *Tjanting* is a localized instance of class struggle itself: not merely Silliman's

21. "Interview [with Ron Silliman]," *The Difficulties,* p. 35.

22. Ibid. Silliman's interest in the Fibonacci numbers may well have been generated through his reading of Olson's "The Praises," or—alternatively—through a reading of the book which was the chief source for Olson's poem: Matila Ghyka's *The Geometry of Art and Life* (New York, 1946). See von Hallberg, *Charles Olson: The Scholar's Art* (Cambridge, Mass., 1978), pp. 24–27 and nn.

23. "Interview," p. 36.

personal act of struggle, but his deployment of an artistic occasion within which such struggle may take place. In the end, as Bernstein observed, it is the reader in the poem who "counts."

As with other L=A=N=G=U=A=G=E writers, Silliman's work engages adversely with all that means to appear authoritative, fixed, and determined. These antithetical projects function within the world of language because language is taken as the representative social form per se—the social form through which society sees and presents itself to itself. Thus, the "languages" within which these writers live and move and have their being are quite specifically the "languages" of the cold war West after the debacles of the Korean and the Vietnam Wars. This is important to realize for it helps to explain the extremity of their work. In them poetry appears at a crisis of its traditional modes of expression. So false and self-conflicted seem the ordinary public forms of discourse—in the media, the policy organs of government, and the academic clerisy—that the artistic representation of such discourse must either be subjected to their one-dimensionality or it must activate a critical engagement.

That L=A=N=G=U=A=G=E writers have chosen the alternative is clear not only from their poetic practice, but from their theoretical and exegetical work as well. Though they discuss and comment upon each other's work quite frequently, this mode of their discourse almost never takes the form of "interpretation." Interpretive remarks are of course embedded throughout such commentary, but these are invariably subordinated to various types of pragmatic and performative modes of discussion. As often as not the "commentary" will take the form of another poem or poetical excursus; or of an explanation of how some particular text "works" (rather than what it "means"); or, as we have already noticed in the work of Darragh and Mayer, of a set of directions and procedures, a mini-course in how-to-write.

The special character of Silliman's nonnarrative texts is nicely dramatized if we set a work like *Tjanting* beside an academic text like John Hollander's *Reflections on Espionage* (1976).[24] This may seem an odd comparison, but it is in fact quite apposite. In the first place, both poems are fully conscious of their placement within the sociohistorical field of cold war America. Correlatively, both imagine and reflect upon the function of poetry within such social circumstances. Finally, both resort—in an extraordinarily odd conjunction of purposes—to the Fibonacci number

24. See John Hollander, *Reflections on Espionage: The Question of "Cupcake"* (New York, 1976); all further references to this work, abbreviated *R*, will be included in the text. The poem first appeared—in a shorter version—in *Poetry* 125 (Nov. 1974), where it took up the entire issue.

sequence as an important procedural device within which their poems' meanings are carried out.

Reflections on Espionage is a narrativized text made up of a series of code messages sent by the spy Cupcake to various other persons in his espionage network. The poem tells the story of Cupcake's increasing psychic disaffection—partly concealed even from himself—with his work as a spy. Eventually Cupcake comes under the surveillance of his own organization's internal security apparatus, and at the end—his reliability as a spy hopelessly compromised—the organization calls for his "termination."

The story involves, of course, an elaborately executed allegory in which "spying" is equated with "being a poet," and vice versa. The text is full of coded references to American poets and writers, mostly Hollander's contemporaries. Its distant progenitor—Robert Browning's "How It Strikes a Contemporary"—underscores, by contrast, the special character of *Reflections,* for Hollander's story—like his hero—is dominated by nostalgia and a pervasive sense of ineffectuality. The poem's world is graphed along an axis of "them" and "us" which reflects both the political situation of the cold war, and the typical antagonisms and divisions between "schools" or groups of poets. All this would merely be amusing were it not that Hollander's hero continually reflects upon the social function of poetry; and from these reflections he draws the most mordant and disheartening conclusions. In fact, *Reflections* argues—or rather demonstrates—that poetry under the social circumstances "reflected" in this poem has, like spying under the same circumstances, only an alienating effect. This poetry of "reflection" preserves, and ultimately reifies, the world-as-alienation, and it does so by failing to imagine that poetry might struggle with, rather than merely reflect (upon), its world.

Cupcake's meditations on his work as spy/poet lead him to a sharp sense of his own isolation. In his loneliness he calls into question the whole enterprise to which he has given himself:

What kind of work is this
For which if we were to touch in the darkness
It would be without feeling the other there?
It might help to know if Steampump's dying
Was part of the work or not. I shall not be
Told, I know.

[*R*, pp. 3–4]

Cupcake's question is rhetorical and will not—cannot, in his imagination of the world—be answered. This social alienation mirrors a correspondent crisis of the personality:

Names like ours leave no traces in
Nature. Yet what of the names they encode, names

> One's face comes in time to rhyme with, John or James?
> The secret coded poem of one's whole life rhymes
> Entirely with that face, a maddening
> Canzona, every line of which sings in the
> Breaths we take and give, ending with the same sound.
> As with the life, so ridiculously, with
> The work. But, after all, which of them is the
> Enciphered version of the other one, and
> Are we, after all, even supposed to know?
>
> [*R*, p. 28]

In the end Hollander's "master spy" will watch the system he has served send out a broadcast order for his execution. His final coded transmission is a frightening poem constructed partly on the use of the Fibonacci number series. Its principal message, secreted away in the poem's initial and terminal syllables, is revealed by using the Fibonacci number sequence as an index to those syllables. It is a plea for death, and it is answered in the poem's final line—a series of *X*s which, decoded, translate: TERMINATE CUPCAKE.

Silliman's imagination, as we have seen, found in the Fibonacci numbers an image of class struggle and social dialectics. The numbers confirm his search for signs and modes of social dynamism. But when Cupcake uses the Fibonacci series in his final transmission, he interprets his own usage in these terrible terms:

> and I have sat watching
> Key numbers in their serial dance growing
> Further apart, outdistancing their touching,
> Outstretched arms.
>
> [*R*, p. 71]

Hollander's alter-ego "editor" of Cupcake's story supplies a gloss to Cupcake's final transmission. The exegesis remarks on the desperation of the passage but can only replicate the master spy's own sense of helplessness:

> This disturbing and disturbed transmission seems to be a kind of cry for help. But to whom?
>
> [*R*, p. 75]

The interpretation here is congruent with the poem's self-conception. Hollander characterizes cold war America and its poetry as a world of desperate (rather than rich) ambiguities. It is a poetic world whose own highest value—close interpersonal relations—is contradicted by the social structures and practices it takes for granted. To Hollander, the march of the Fibonacci numbers is the apocalypse of such a world, the prophecy of its desperation and its even more fragmented future.

Hollander's poem imagines what it knows (or thinks it knows) about poetry and society alike. Such an imagination, however, can mount no effective resistance against its own terrible revelations: vacancy in luxurious words, dismemberment in the way we live now. It is all mirror and meditation, a story and a set of reflections on the story. In this respect the contrast with writers like Bernstein and Silliman is striking and unmistakable. In them antinarrative and nonnarrative continually work against and move beyond the enchantments of what has been given and what is taken to be "real." They are the true inheritors of Blake's early attempts to dismantle those prisons of imaginary beauties: social and personal life in its cruel apparitions, and art as what reflects upon such things. Hollander's poem is a work of decadence in that it refuses to press the charges called for by its own investigation. Pleading "no contest," it is properly found guilty. *Reflections on Espionage* is not, however, a trivial poem. Its analogues are, for example, Edward Fitzgerald's *Rubáiyát* and Dante Gabriel Rossetti's *House of Life,* and all those works which deliver us over to luxurious and unlivable things. The highest form of such poetry is reached in the work of artists like Baudelaire, the mayor of the City of Pain over whose gates is written the legend "Anywhere Out of the World."

Poetry can and does offer alternatives to such desperate forms of idealism, however. I do not have in mind work which celebrates or reflects the "solidarity" of "postmodern bourgeois intellectuals," though we certainly have a great deal of that today. Charles Bernstein's "For Love Has Such a Spirit . . ." is too long to quote in full, or even at length, but it certainly represents such an alternative: a Shelleyan performance, not unlike *Epipsychidion* or the great "Life of Life" lyric, in which love burns through all the vests which seem to hide it from us.

> For love I would—deft equator.
> Nonchalant attribution of all the, & filled with
> such, meddles with & steals my constancy, sharpening
> desire for that, in passing, there, be favorite
> in ordinary, but no sooner thought than gone. My
> heart seems wax, that like tapers burns at light.[25]

This is a "deconstructive" poetry, fully postmodern in its style, but in its nervous erosions it moves the "Spirit" of a love that, settled in what is "ordinary" and given, will not settle for anything.

Silliman's nonnarratives are also exemplary alternatives, and a number of other significant writers might be named: Alan Davies, Lyn Hejinian, Susan Howe. They are all distinctive and distinguished writers. In each of them, however, writing is used to contest and disrupt those forms of order which are always replicated in the "realism" deployed through

25. Bernstein, "For Love Has Such a Spirit . . . ," pp. 48–49.

narrativities. These disruptions take antinarrative as well as nonnarrative form. In the latter, however, the critique of fixed orders ("reality") is carried out simultaneously with the deployment of new orders and "realities":

> The mind evolves a blueprint out of what is already there, doesn't recognize where to go next, then explores and enumerates the possibilities. . . . The odd connection permits a reexperience of what was originally recorded but not really experienced. The mind (language) reshuffles its fragments in order to attain the original hierarchy; reassembling it permits reprocessing from the new perspective.[26]

This might have been a specific commentary on Silliman's *Tjanting,* for the process sketched here is precisely what we discover in Silliman's poem. But Davies and Piombino are making a general statement about L=A=N=G=U=A=G=E Writing. It is well put. And though it does not talk directly of a "politics of poetry," the politics of such writing—the theory and the practice of it alike—are plain for anyone to see.

26. Davies and Piombino, "The Indeterminate Interval," p. 39.

Political Poetry and the Example of Ernesto Cardenal

Reginald Gibbons

Perhaps the subject of political poetry is so inextricable from specific poems and poets at particular historical moments that one can discuss only examples. Ernesto Cardenal is an interesting one, not least because the cause for which he long spoke, the release of the Nicaraguan peasantry from the oppressive burdens of economic exploitation and arbitrary rule by force, was victorious; the Sandinista victory gave him an opportunity, or an obligation, to become a poet of praise and victory after he had been a poet of compassion and wrath:

> De pronto suena en la noche una sirena
> de alarma, larga, larga,
> el aullido lugúbre de la sirena
> de incendio o de la ambulancia blanca de la muerte,
> como el grito de la cegua en la noche,
> que se acerca y se acerca sobre las calles
> y las casas y sube, sube, y baja
> y crece, crece, baja y se aleja
> creciendo y bajando. No es incendio ni muerte:
> Es Somoza que pasa.[1]

This essay has benefited greatly from the comments and conversation of Robert von Hallberg and Terrence Des Pres.

1. Ernesto Cardenal, *Poesía de uso (Antología 1949–1978)* (Buenos Aires, 1979), p. 59; all further references to this volume will be included in the text.

Suddenly in the night there's a siren
of alarm, long, long
the gloomy howling of the siren
of a fire engine or the white ambulance of death,
like the cry of a mourner in the night,
that comes nearer and nearer over the streets
and houses and rises, rises, and falls
and grows louder, louder, falls and goes away
rising and falling. It's neither fire nor death:
It's Somoza going by.

In Latin America Cardenal is generally regarded as an enduring poet. He brought a recognizably Latin American material into his poetry, and he introduced to Spanish-language poetry in general such poetic techniques as textual collage, free verse lines shaped in Poundian fashion, and, especially, a diction that is concrete and detailed, textured with proper names and the names of things in preference to the accepted poetic language, which was more abstract, general, and vaguely symbolic. But what is notable in Spanish-language poetry is not only Cardenal's "craft," in the sense given this word by Seamus Heaney to mean manipulation of poetic resources; there is also this poet's "technique," which in Heaney's sense means a "definition of his stance toward life."[2] Cardenal's characteristic poetic stance has been admired because he addresses the political and social pressures that shape—and often distort, damage, or destroy—life and feeling. This is apparent even in the earliest poems Cardenal has chosen to preserve. "Raleigh," for example, is a dramatic meditation from 1949[3] in which the treasure-hunting explorer marvels at the expanse and wealth of the American continents and out of sheer pleasure recounts some of the triumphs and hardships of his travels. Although his alertness and wonder make him sympathetic, this Raleigh's vision of the New World as a limitless source of wealth is forerunner to the economic exploitation of the land and people.

2. Seamus Heaney, *Preoccupations: Selected Prose 1969–1978* (New York, 1980), p. 47.
3. The date is from Joaquín Martín Sosa, "Breve guía (para uso) de lectores," preface to *Poesía de uso*, p. 9.

Reginald Gibbons is the editor of *TriQuarterly* magazine and teaches at Northwestern University. His most recent books are his third volume of poems, *Saints*, one of the winning books in the National Poetry Series (1986), and two edited collections of essays—*The Writer in Our World* (1986) and, with Gerald Graff, *Criticism in the University* (1985). He is at work on a critical study of modern and contemporary poetry, as well as new poems and fiction.

One might ask, What are the political and social circumstances which, rather than distorting and damaging life and feeling, nurture and preserve them? Perhaps one might answer that, paradoxically, destructive conditions of life have many times proven insufficiently powerful to prevent the creation of poetry. And some poetry has even arisen in reaction to the destructive: such conditions produce resistance, which, if it cannot heal the spirit, can lend it strength. One might answer further that it is not Cardenal's or any artist's responsibility to establish what circumstance will form a fruitful matrix for art, but only to work as honestly and as hard as political, social, and artistic circumstances will permit.

Poetry, perhaps of all arts, is least demanding of physical materials: mere scraps of paper and a pencil, or nothing at all but a good memory, may suffice for its creation. Its medium is the currency of our thinking and feeling, language; and its creation is individual, solitary, and takes place in response to, or despite, every known social and political situation. States may seek to suppress it by making publication difficult or impossible and by attacking its creators, the poets. But no state has found a way to expedite the writing of great poetry or to improve the quality of poetry generally.

However, one sees Cardenal seeking at times, especially in his most recent works, to praise conditions and possibilities which he regards as favorable to life and to art, and which he locates in the promises and principles, if not always the achievements, of the Sandinista government. Most such poems are less convincing than those which speak not for any form of social organization but for other persons in their suffering or happiness, or which represent a critical intelligence and speak against the destructive.

Indeed, in Cardenal's work as a whole there are two recurring contradictions which are never resolved convincingly, as far as I can tell. The first is between on the one hand poetic experiment and on the other hand a desire to write as accessibly as possible; that is, a contradiction between the poet answering his own expressive needs or the political needs of the audience (as he conceives them). The second is between on the one hand poems of anger and hope which speak *against* (against injustice, suffering, materialism, oppression both historical and contemporary, and so on) and which enjoy the advantages of a stance of independence, critical thinking, and resistance, and on the other hand poems which speak *for* (for compassion, for justice, for delight, and—or but?—for revolution, then for the Sandinista victory) and which may adopt a voice of consensus or even obligatory ideals. Both of these patterns of contradiction are also congruent with the modern dilemma of the artist-intellectual: "the unresolved conflict at the heart of the Romantic-democratic concept of art" is a "dual commitment both to 'high' literature (as the expression of transcendent personal genius) and to a literature that represents 'the people' at large," in the succinct wording of Sacvan Bercovitch, writing of the classic (North) American writers.[4]

A common though blandly favorable reaction to Cardenal's poetry outside Latin America goes like this: "His poems deserve attention both for the ideas expressed (whether one agrees with them or not) and for their intrinsic poetic merit."[5] We are often so asked to divide poetry into two constituent parts, its technical virtues and its expression of belief, and to suspend or qualify our judgment of the latter. But is the division desirable, necessary, useful, or reliable as a representation of how we read, experience, and evaluate poems? How do the two elements function? What part of poetic *meaning* is constituted by belief? How is that meaning created and conveyed, how far is it subject to evaluation apart from the poem, and how generally may the poem be evaluated if it expresses belief?

These questions go beyond the broad notion of the inherently "subversive" nature of art, as in Marcuse's formulations. All art may indeed stand in a subversive or at least critical relationship to established institutions, to ideology, to "common sense," conventional wisdom, and habits of feeling. (I will return to this idea below, in discussing the rhetoric of poetry.) But that antagonistic relationship is flexible enough to permit artworks to decorate corporate buildings or to please tyrants. Equally problematic is the intention of authors whose essentially subversive works (such as surrealist poems) prove too difficult to be understood by those whom they would either attack or liberate. And when art, including poetry, professes belief or takes a perceptibly political stance toward life or allies itself explicitly with certain historical figures, movements, or causes, there can also be surprising contradictions. If Pound and Cardenal are, for instance, completely opposed politically, they nonetheless share not only a poetic technique but also the (related?) assumptions that the structure of society and of institutions, if changed, could improve the spiritual and material conditions of man, and that poetry may participate in the attempt to change what exists. How may the devices and powers of narrowly read literary works so participate? One answer derives from Kenneth Burke: literature may function as a kind of "symbolic action" which confronts that which cannot be effectively confronted by "real"

4. Sacvan Bercovitch, "The Problem of Ideology in [North] American Literary History," *Critical Inquiry* 12 (Summer 1986): 650. In proposing that answers lie in the posing of the questions, the solution in the very problem of ideology, or rather in "problematizing" aspects of literary study which were previously neglected, like ideology, Bercovitch happens to participate in the ascendant literary-critical ideology of our time.

5. Robert Pring-Mill, introduction to Cardenal, *Apocalypse and Other Poems*, ed. Pring-Mill and Donald D. Walsh, trans. Thomas Merton et al. (New York, 1977), p. ix.

action, either categorically (such as death) or effectively (such as a war). (Symbolic action joins in spirit other forms of action that confront mutable realities such as the social and political organization of the human community.) This symbolic action has the power to satisfy our impulse to act, to *move* (as in political "movements"), our desire to be moved (as in "[e]motion"), and our need for solace and joy, which we seek even in "emblems of adversity." By no means does this amount to a mere "acting out," which would be a kind of blindness to reality; it is instead a clearer seeing of the world, an elucidation of reality by artistic means.

An example is the poem quoted at the head of this essay. This early work of Cardenal's uses the devices of poetry, including the enacted rhythms of perception, the chimes of similar sounding phonemes (especially assonance on the vowels *e-a* and *a-a*), and the dramatic possibilities of syntax to create first a perceptible sense-impression and then to reveal the source and thus the meaning of that sense-impression. Especially significant is the assonance on *e-a,* which links the words *suena* ("it sounds"), *sirena* (the siren), *cegua* (the "mourner"—a deliciously complicated word, of which more in a moment), *acerca* ("it comes near"), *calle* ("street"), and *aleja* ("it goes away").

Cegua is a Central American regionalism, a word indigenous to the world Cardenal is describing. It derives from the Aztec *cihautl,* "woman," and means a woman weeping, or even a hired mourner; but it's also a kind of apparition, a village bogey with the body of a woman and the head of a horse, which screams in the night and is popularly believed to be a ghost.[6] The *cegua*'s presence in folklore is pre-Columbian, so with this word Cardenal establishes the cry in the night as an ancient protest, heard by the humblest persons (to whose imagination and lives the *cegua* mostly speaks). The *e-a* assonance *is* the *cegua;* the assonantal words enact its approach and withdrawal through the streets. Cardenal plays on contradiction at the end of the poem, when he writes that the sound is not in fact that of a fire truck or an ambulance rushing to some emergency with which a mourner might be associated. The siren comes from Somoza's convoy of police, yet the ghost-soul in torment cries out at the passing of the tyrant, as if at fire and death. The tyrant is not the fact of fire and death but the ever-present threat. The *cegua* is not only his announcement of his passing but also the curse laid on him by the common people through the image of this supernatural mourner.

The terrible sound moves, as Somoza does, and the unmoving listener who hears it escapes simply because Somoza goes by without stopping. Is the deftness of the manipulation of expectation and surprise simply an ornament to the poetic contention that Somoza is an active, destructive force, against whom the passive citizen can do nothing except bear bitter

6. On the authority of Francisco J. Santamaría, *Diccionario general de americanismos* (México, D.F., 1942), vol. 1, and other sources.

witness? Or is this oscillation between opposites or containment of them something essential to the poem, and even to poetry generally?

The poem is "political" in that by means of its allusion and devices it attacks the dictator of Nicaragua. In terms proposed by Thomas McGrath, this would appear to be more of a "tactical" revolutionary poem, aimed at local and specific circumstances, than a "strategic" poem, whose effect is to "expand" the consciousness of the reader:

> One [. . .] kind of poetry [. . .] might be called tactical, about some immediate thing: a strike, let's say; some immediate event. The poet should give it as much clarity and strength as he can give it without falling into political slogans, clichés, and so on. I also thought we needed another kind of poetry that is *not* keyed necessarily to immediate events, a poetry in which the writer trusts himself enough to write about whatever comes along, with the assumption that what he is doing will be, in the long run, useful, consciousness raising or enriching. A strategic poetry, let's say. There have been a lot of tactical poems directed to particular things, and those poems now are good in a certain sort of way, but the events they were about *have moved out from under them.* Somebody asked Engels, "What happened to all the revolutionary poetry of 1848?" He replied: "It died with the political prejudices of the time." That is bound to be the fate of a lot of tactical poetry. [. . .] On the other hand, we take a poem like Neruda's *Canto General,* a marvelous big poem, but it's not there to help in some immediate kind of situation; it's a *strategic* poem. But anyone who reads it will have his consciousness expanded by the reading of it. . . . The ideal thing of course is to bring the tactical and the strategic together so that they would appear in this massive poem of pure lucidity, full of flying tigers and dedicated to the removal of man-eating spinning wheels from the heads of our native capitalists—absolute lucidity and purest, most marvelous bullshit. That's the poem I would like to have, because there's a place where those two are the same. That's in the archetypal heavens of course.[7]

The value of Cardenal's best work, even when it is most specific to Nicaraguan life, is that it is—in McGrath's terms—strategic as well. For does one have to know who Somoza is for the poem to make sense? Doesn't an inference of his nature suffice? One cannot substitute the name of a humane benefactor—Mother Teresa, Hippocrates—without introducing an absurd contradiction into the poem; but it *is* possible to substitute the name of any historical or literary figure identified with state terror, or any political figure identified by some audience, somewhere,

7. Thomas McGrath, "The Frontiers of Language," reprinted in *North Dakota Quarterly* 50 (Fall 1982): 28–29.

as tyrannical and violent, without changing the poem's meaning, only its focus.

Nonetheless, the poem's strongest gesture is in its naming of Somoza, and if a substitution of names reveals a deeper value, still the act of naming—ancient and consecrated to poetry—is crucial. Here the naming is not, as in some poems, a blessing, but a curse. And the poem is political not only in delivering the curse that is Somoza's name but also in its demonstration, within the terms of the descriptive diction, of a political relationship between the one who listens passively, powerless and vulnerable, and the one who raises sounds of fright and threats of harm. Both Somoza and the listener are "political" agents in their participation in Nicaraguan society. But the powerless agent—namer, witness, and giver of detail—has only the language and his poem, which by virtue of its artistic effectiveness is emotionally empowering, with which to "act" (symbolically), while the agent of power acts but has no voice of his own (in the poem), only the accompanying mournful cry of the *cegua,* which is at once the sound of his own destructiveness and the wail of those whom he harms. In life, Somoza's voice rules persons; in poems, Cardenal's can hope to rule only time (as poets have always hoped their poems would outlive themselves and their subjects).

When, with his fellow poet José Coronel Urtecho, Cardenal formulated his new poetics, which was intended in part to make a kind of political comment aesthetically possible in poetry, he gave it the name *exteriorismo* and offered a rationale for density of detail, use of documents, and free form. Aesthetically, "exteriorism" was influenced not only by Pound's introduction of materials formerly foreign to poetry but also by his advice to the Imagists to avoid subjectivity in their work and to prefer a precise description of the thing outside the self. One of several explanations:

> *Exteriorismo* is a poetry created with images of the exterior world, the world we see and sense, and that is, in general, the specific world of poetry. *Exteriorismo* is objective poetry: narrative and anecdote, made with elements of real life and with concrete things, with proper names and precise details and exact data, statistics, facts, and quotations. . . . In contrast, interiorist poetry is a subjectivist poetry made only with abstract or symbolic words: rose, skin, ash, lips, absence, bitterness, dream, touch, foam, desire, shade, time, blood, stone, tears, night.[8]

But beyond this aesthetic influence and preference, exteriorism seems also shaped by unmistakable political considerations. In the context of long-suppressed civil liberties and gross economic exploitation of the

8. Quoted by Mark Zimmerman in "Ernesto Cardenal after the Revolution," introduction to Cardenal, *Flights of Victory,* ed. and trans. Zimmerman (Maryknoll, N.Y., 1985), p. x.

peasantry, exteriorism looks like an attempt to find a poetic principle that would disallow the kind of language that was characteristic of, or acquiescent to, political and commercial powers. The acquiescence of poetic interiority and ethereality to arbitrary state power or capitalist exploitation would be forestalled if a poem contained the true names of things and the textures of perceived reality. No one who is unfamiliar with the clichés of bad poetry in Spanish can appreciate how bitter is the gesture of Cardenal's list of despised "subjectivist" words.

While it is unfair to expect manifestos to be reasonable, there are two objections to this one. First, if subjectivist words are indeed a poetic liability (as, in our poetry, the repetitive later work of W. S. Merwin seems to demonstrate with a similarly reduced symbolic vocabulary), it was nonetheless with such a brief poetic word list that Paul Celan created powerful—but not at all "exteriorist"—responses to the historical reality of the German concentration camps and the murder of so many Jews. A prescription for poetic diction cannot guarantee the truth of poetry, even if the example of Cardenal shows how one poet freed himself from an oppressive poetic context with just such a prescription (which excluded a few things and, more important, included many things). Second, as Czeslaw Milosz has written, "Not every poet who speaks of real things necessarily gives them the tangibility indispensable to their existence in a work of art. He may as well make them unreal."[9] I take him to mean that the mere naming of things is insufficient to suggest their reality to the reader, and such a failing has little to recommend it over its opposite poetic failing, mystification. But however valid these two objections may be generally, Cardenal's exteriorist poetics nonetheless empowered him to write a kind of poetry, and a poetry of distinct successes, not seen before in Spanish. The exuberance and plenitude of descriptive detail even in the early "Raleigh," and the American materials and occasions of this and other poems, attest to this. If these same two objections have more weight against Cardenal's later poems, that is another issue in a poetic career inextricably rooted in his changing political circumstances in Nicaragua, to which I will return.

The influence of both the ventriloquistic and autobiographical passages in Pound's *Cantos* is also apparent in Cardenal's early "La vuelta a América" or "León," although Pound's poems are denser and more far-ranging in their allusions. The irony of Cardenal's use of Pound's poetics—the leftist poet profiting from the reactionary's poetic achievements and discoveries—shows that those devices have no inherent relation to any particular political position but in larger terms simply accommodate the presence of political and historical materials in poetry. McGrath has warned against unthinkingly equating traditional poetic forms with reactionary political belief and has pointed out that "most of the inventors [of free verse]

9. Czeslaw Milosz, *The Witness of Poetry* (Cambridge, Mass., 1983), p. 71.

were political reactionaries, even Fascists. Why should they smash up the traditional forms?" (Indeed—why should they? The topic is complex. The communist Hugh MacDiarmid, for example, used both traditional forms and meter, and free verse.) McGrath suggests unexceptionably that free verse "has often been used to bring new materials, attitudes and feelings into poetry. In this century, it always flourishes when poets interest themselves in social-political matters, when they take sides, even tentatively or unknowingly, in the class struggle."[10] McGrath doesn't specify on what side, and one thinks not only of Pound but also of Williams Carlos Williams, Allen Ginsberg, Aimé Césaire, and others in this context.

In keeping with this more general connection between free verse and political *materials,* and even before his political position is as clear as it will later be, Cardenal employs poetic detail in his early work simply to suggest the complex and unhappy effect of the first Europeans on the native cultures of America. His judgment of them as individuals is not at all sweeping; in "Los filibusteros" ("The Freebooters") he writes:

> Hubo rufianes, ladrones, jugadores, pistoleros.
> También hubo honrados y caballeros y valientes.
> [P. 27]

> There were rogues, thieves, gamblers, gunmen.
> There were also decent men, gentlemen, and brave men.

So these early poems are "political" in the sense of being concerned generally with a moral judgment of social and political relations and therefore with the historical record of conquest and governance in America. For, as Kenneth Burke puts it in an early essay, "The Nature of Art Under Capitalism," both "pure" art and "propaganda" arise partly out of the relationship between "work-patterns and ethical patterns."[11] That is, all poetic response is in some way tied to the ways in which the people around the poet live, work, and die. But, despite our being able to invoke Burke's symbolic action and McGrath's terms "tactical" and "strategic," the artistic accomplishment of a poem may well seem insufficient to a poet whose daily life brings him the sight of peasants debilitated, impoverished, and even murdered by their own government. Some poets and readers will always feel that in terms of its concrete effect on life, the poem is arguably of less value than bread would be, even though

10. McGrath, "Notes, Personal and Theoretical on 'Free' and 'Traditional' Form," *Poetry East* 20/21 (1986): 18, 20.

11. Kenneth Burke, *The Philosophy of Literary Form: Studies in Symbolic Action,* 3d ed. (Berkeley and Los Angeles, 1973), p. 314.

Milosz says that the experience of Poland shows that when bread is scarce, poetry becomes most valuable. Cardenal's exteriorism, as a linguistic gesture, seems to be an attempt to bring the power of naming—as when he cursed Somoza in the poem quoted above—to bear on everything that could be named in the life around him, and his poetic faith in the power of naming is striking, one might even say touching, in the face of hopelessness. But exteriorism was an artistic solution to an artistic problem, not a political solution to anything.

After the successful revolution, Cardenal can be seen to move from the anecdotal and narrative textures of some of the exteriorist poems, juxtaposed against each other and against other kinds of quotation and poetic material, toward something simpler with, if anything, a renewed presence of names and naming, but more like homily that includes exemplary incidents or facts. The short postrevolutionary poems, while they sometimes have a lyric intensity missing from Cardenal's exteriorist poems, can also seem pieces of a larger work that he has not accomplished, perhaps hasn't wanted to accomplish. He prefers the tactical to the strategic *after* the revolution, one might say. Under the surface of many of the later poems is a felt, implicit obligation to make use of poetry as an inspiriting, uplifting kind of exhortation and for praise of revolutionary accomplishment.

Cardenal's case is less unusual in Latin American terms than in North American ones. The Latin American tradition of education and art differs from our own, first in grouping the artist with the relatively small caste of intellectuals, and second in expecting the intellectual (and artist) to be sensible of a social obligation to the rest of society. Latin American intellectuals and artists tend to be more involved in political activity than their North American counterparts: when governments are sufficiently acceptable to them, writers have often served them, and when governments are unacceptable to persons with humane values, writers have tended to oppose them not only with words but also with acts. When Cardenal writes in a spirit of solidarity with the revolutionaries against Somoza or the impoverished peasants or later the Sandinista government, he is keeping faith with the intellectuals' social responsibility as he has inherited it. Is he likely to be charged with breaking faith with a responsibility more familiar and more highly touted among North American writers—to independence from all constraints, from all responsibilities but those felt as personal? He might answer that the responsibilities he feels are indeed, to him, the stuff of conscience. Is the objection then to conscience itself, when conscience brings not only consciousness of "wrong," but also responsibilities of "right"? After all, in his major early work, *Hora 0* (1960), we see, as the poem itself says of Sandino, "poeta convertido en soldado por necesidad (a poet converted by necessity into a soldier)"

(p. 77). In the social context in which Cardenal has lived and written, preserving a strictly "personal" independence might be regarded not as a responsibility but as an intellectually irresponsible withdrawal from social and political life.

Cardenal's position as the first minister of culture of Nicaragua, dating from his appointment by the Sandinista government in 1979, is a circumstance that one cannot help pondering when reading his most recent work. After all, his poems closely identify him with the contemporary history of Nicaragua. The trajectory of his work moves from outrage and lament over suffering and injustice to a sense of triumph and an active encouragement of those who rebelled against Somoza, overthrew him and his army, and took control of the nation's government. With these views many North American literary intellectuals have no complaints. Ernesto Cardenal has done the right thing, has been politically correct—this is the viewpoint of the North American left (and, of course, of others whose stand is political because it arises out of moral repugnance at the inhumane dictatorship which the Sandinistas overthrew).

It is far more common in Latin America than in North America for a writer to join a political party or cause; this is the accepted, indeed expected, course of political conscience. If a party wins power, it may be just as common for those who have joined or supported it to find themselves in the position of having to choose to work for the new government or to be considered an enemy for having declined to serve. I do not know either the nature of the Sandinista government's invitation to Cardenal or his feelings about accepting it. But if his present position is no surprise, it is probably a reflection not only of conviction but also of political necessity. For this reason I am not sure Cardenal can be considered an architect of the political regime which eventually was established, insofar as it is not ideal. The practical necessities and compromises of political power will crush the scrupulosity of intellectual and artistic inquiry and experiment, even where these have had the apparent advantage in their formation of a consciousness of social responsibility. And even if ministers of culture had much power, the historical record shows few such officials who could bring their artistic scruples to the exercise of their personal power. But we so seldom see a serious artist in a position of state power that we may forget the inevitable conflicts of conscience that must face any intellectual whose public being is not outside power and devoted to critique but subservient to a power group and at least partly conscripted for the presentation and protection of that power.

Speaking in Chicago in 1985, Cardenal ridiculed as a perversion of the humanistic tradition the bizarre appendix on "Literary Resources" in the contra pamphlet circulated by the CIA. His justifiable scorn for this absurd little essay and its author follows from the assumption that poetry by definition can have no hand in violence against the innocent or in violation of humane ideals such as the sanctity of life or the desirability of education or medical care. Yet because of Cardenal's own conversion from poet to soldier—and understandably—there come moments even in his poems when some of these values are abandoned. If a revolution is to win a military victory it must usually succeed in killing and capturing a sufficient number of the ruling forces. Revolutionaries weigh the violence they must commit against the violence suffered by those on whose behalf they fight. Others weigh the justice of that cause. Poets may side with revolutionaries, or against them, or neither; but their weighing of the same moral dilemma remains a "symbolic" act, in that poems, even when they move readers, do not carry arms. If it is true, as has been said, that Che Guevara carried poems of Pablo Neruda in his pack, it is also uncertain whether poems are sought in such circumstances because they encourage, or console.

It is no surprise when a great and political poem like Neruda's "Alturas de Macchu Picchu" prizes life over death, but a political (and especially a revolutionary) poem must also begin to say *whose* life. When Pound bitterly laments in poems the waste of life in World War I, the "enemy" is not Germany—no more than it is England—but a deadly failure that the political leadership of both nations share. In Cardenal's earlier work the lives of the powerless, the vulnerable, and the persecuted are movingly memorialized; perhaps, in such fierce work, it is impossible not to prize their lives above the lives of their tormentors or oppressors. In his postrevolutionary work the compassion narrows further. If it was true that there were no "innocent" victims on the side of Somoza, and that one cannot invite the murderous oppressor into one's own house, there is nonetheless something disappointing in the poet who makes such frequent reference to a Christian commune based on love, but who, in "Preguntas frente al lago" ("Questions Beside the Lake"), sounds not wise but strained when he writes that "God is something that is in everyone, / in you, in me, everywhere."[12] The exteriorist poetic cannot justify or redeem some of Cardenal's later poems, nor convince the reader to admire them solely for their value as sentiment or statement.

Another recent poem recounts the young Sandino's fury at seeing a trainload of American soldiers come to occupy Nicaragua for the benefit of American investment:

> y el chavalo se puso furioso
>   y dijo que deseaba colgarlos a todos de los palos.
> Lo interesante de este cuento es que este chavalo
>   después pudo realizar lo que deseaba.[13]

> and the boy became enraged
>   and said he wanted to hang them all from the trees.

12. Cardenal, *Flights of Victory,* p. 92.
13. Ibid., p. 96.

The interesting thing about this story is that this boy
later was able to do what he wanted.

Again, one doesn't by any means expect to see a forgiving hand offered to the contras and ex-Somocistas who are still committing crimes of violence; one wonders only if the prophet of democratic, humane ideals can sustain his vision when he must speak for a regime—any regime—rather than against one. The lives of "men and women who find themselves in history's path" tend to be so much expendable currency to those who rule, and even to those who would rule. Cardenal's deep—and convincing—allegiance was to those who *are* ruled. In his much earlier poem "Apocalipsis" ("Apocalypse," published 1973) he rewrites the Revelation of Saint John and includes these lines:

y el ángel me dijo: esas cabezas que le ves a la Bestia son dictadores
y sus cuernos son líderes revolucionarios que aún no son dictadores
pero lo serán después
y lucharán contra el Cordero

[P. 114]

and the angel said to me: those heads you see on the Beast are dictators
and its horns are revolutionary leaders who are not yet dictators
but will be afterward
and will fight against the Lamb

This frightening prophecy only confirms, to my mind, the humane sensibility and values in Cardenal's work. It does not alter my own understanding that the revolution against Somoza for which he hoped and which he supported did indeed rescue many people from violent or impoverished death, and has led to a life at least marginally better—especially regarding education and medical care—for many, perhaps most of the citizens of Nicaragua. But these early lines seem dangerously ironic in the present political context.

Cardenal's comments in Chicago sought to establish an intimate, essential link between poetry and the Sandinista revolution. Yet the U.S.-sponsored counterrevolution of the contras against the Sandinista government, which has put the former revolutionaries in the position of defending an established order, had inevitably driven him to a position we often call in English "artistic compromise." Now, in Spanish the word "compromised" does not have a pejorative connotation but means the same as the French *engagé*—committed to a belief and to a participation in the possibilities for action that follow from that belief. *Comprometido* connotes not "I will yield my interests and in part accept yours" or "I have cheapened my character" but "I am committed to what I have promised, in solidarity with you." Does this merely rationalize, or does it justify, not only Cardenal's lament for the deaths and deprivations suffered under Somoza but also his desire to find glory as much as tragic loss in revolutionary death?

Among poems that present us with the issue of the "political," then, there are those which express identifiable party, ideological, or historical positions (the tactical poetry of a revolutionary). There are others that happen rather to represent human life in such a way that inevitably some of the social and political contexts of feeling and action are depicted, pondered, or enacted by the poet (the strategic poetry of a socially conscious writer). There may also be implied politics in a poem caught willy-nilly in a powerful sociopolitical context. Even the poem intended to be "pure" (a species deriving from Mallarmé and Valéry, and one whose value was much debated in Spain in the first half of this century) may come to seem political or reveal its political meaning (and its strategic value) in the context of repressive state power. The state, in permitting, perhaps undermines some art and, in attacking, foregrounds in art the humane values it would destroy (as with Mandelstam or Lorca). Less apparently political art may be attacked as forcefully as overtly oppositional works because its expressive power can be just as memorable, and because it too threatens to bear witness far into the future against the state.[14]

I think what distinguishes the strategic sort of poetry is that it *resists* ideology in favor of an insistence on the intrinsic value of life and the political value of life lived freely. Such poetry often shows an encompassing compassion. These very values can of course be claimed by an ideology—and as Burke notes, "the ideal act of propaganda consists in imaginatively identifying your cause with values that are unquestioned."[15] But the political practice of ideology will inevitably belie the rhetoric. (For example, Cardenal has said that there is no poetry of the contras, nor could there be; but even if there were, it would be bound up with the likes of Ronald Reagan's absurd claim of virtue for the contras when he calls them "freedom fighters" while at the same time condemning black revolutionaries who have far greater cause to rebel against the South African government.) The values that can truly claim the widest adherence,

14. "Purity" is a much larger topic than can be addressed here. Some might argue that all "pure" poetry, or poetry intended to be "pure," masks implicitly conservative politics, but I find that attitude simplistic. However, it is of course true that even poetry long judged to be nonpolitical, like Emily Dickinson's, conceals social and political content, whether of the sort hidden in "I like to see it lap the miles" representing the intrusion of industry and mechanization into a pastoral landscape, or that hidden in "Because I could not stop for death" representing crises of domestic, male/female politics. Yet another topic related to political poetry, but one that must be postponed to another, lesser occasion, would be poems of deliberate collusion with state power.

15. Burke, *The Philosophy of Literary Form*, p. 87 n.

and which repressive states will strive actively to eradicate, or with bureaucratic structures will wear down, or with the manipulation of language and image will subvert and discredit, are those which in essence make a plea for peace, freedom from danger, mutual respect and compassion between persons, and an orderly social organization that forbids arbitrary power and fosters justice. Thus artistic works expressive of these values must unavoidably offer witness to the relationship between individual and state; to memory, as against forgetting (the cardinal point of Milosz's conception of poetry); and, quite simply, to life as against death.

I believe there is an identifiable rhetoric of poetry—a poetics, general across several historical periods, languages, and cultures (at least in the West), which is subtly and complexly entangled with these values. It is a rhetoric of observable techniques common to many poets—perhaps all of which belong to a general intention to write in such a way as simply to please the memory that recalls the poem. Perhaps the pleasure to memory of the wrought thing, the poem, partly accounts for the admiration and preservation even of poetry whose ostensible subject is pitiable or unpleasant. This does not mean subject is secondary or irrelevant; on the contrary, this shows that the poet's manipulation of poetic devices and resources (Heaney's "craft") tends to please the senses and to evoke one's admiration for the poet's gift, while the poet's "stance toward life" (Heaney's "technique") gratifies the spirit and emphasizes one's overcoming, with the poet, the distances between men. Thus Heaney says one can find poets of wobbly craft who nonetheless have a strong technique, like Patrick Kavanagh, but the most common failing is the poet of some craft who is lacking a technique, a stance toward life. Technique implicates the poet's materials, subjects, and occasions: Homer's craft becomes a source of pleasure and the vehicle of ancient lore, while Homer's technique makes one reread the poems to feel again our astonishment at them.

Obviously, poems of the sort that present what Terrence Des Pres calls "the *concrete* relations of men and women who find themselves in history's path" tend no less than any others to utilize this rhetoric, and we often call these poems "political" only in the most general sense of the word.[16] But to see this is nonetheless to catch a glimpse of the politics indeed inherent in all use of language. In English, the poetic rhetoric seems generally to privilege acute discriminations and vividness of detail, memorable freshness of diction, and strength of syntax. No better description of it exists than Coleridge's in chapter 14 of his *Biographia Literaria,* which implies the power of poetry to contravene the *habits* of perception, feeling, and thought and thus to confront us with a more profound sort of truth than we are used to, as well as giving us pleasure in the art. This quality of newness ("defamiliarizing," in the critical vo-

16. Terrence Des Pres, "Poetry and Politics," *TriQuarterly* 65 (Winter 1986): 17–18.

cabulary) is what William Carlos Williams meant when he wrote in "Asphodel, That Greeny Flower":

> My heart rouses
> thinking to bring you news
> of something
> that concerns you
> and concerns many men. Look at
> what passes for the new.
> You will not find it there but in
> despised poems.
> It is difficult
> to get the news from poems
> yet men die miserably every day
> for lack
> of what is found there.[17]

The values inherent in such a poetic rhetoric would inevitably contend on some level with all bureaucratic and state powers. Is it for this reason that tyrants prefer music to poetry for their aesthetic pleasure? Music draws one, sometimes dizzily, into the self, as one responds to what Suzanne Langer called music's formal "morphology of feeling"; but poetry is unavoidably an utterance that presumes a connection between the one who writes and the one who, when reading, experiences not only a kind of dynamics of feeling but also the recognition of the referents outside the poem and of the concrete being of others. Totalizing powers, such as those of governments and bureaucracies, must be blind to the feelings and suffering of others in order to function; they fail to respond to individuals except as antagonists whom they would distract, coopt, suppress, or destroy. The rhetoric of poetry, in this context, is inherently critical; and its essence is a kind of quicksilver gleaming that cannot be eradicated.

Perhaps the poetic rhetoric I have described is natural to all literary works of enduring value; it collects, constellates, presents, transforms, and otherwise alters the names and descriptions of things, acts, and mental states in such a way as to produce in us a responsiveness to the descriptive detail and to the minutest functions and powers of language. To take an outwardly unlikely example, even such a programmatically generalized work as Samuel Johnson's *Rasselas*—where in chapter 10 Imlac offers a famous definition of a poetic rhetoric quite opposite to the one I have just sketched—presents us nonetheless with a literary text to which we respond as to none other: we apprehend not only the descriptive specificities of the text and the unique substance and embodiment

17. William Carlos Williams, *Pictures from Breughel and Other Poems* (New York, 1962), pp. 161–62.

of Johnson's thinking but also the admired and inimitable rhythms and textures of Johnson's sentences. Thus the poetic rhetoric of details and oppositions, in congruence with the moral values with which I have associated it, suggests that the nature of literary works is to resist tendencies in the reader to totalize, summarize, paraphrase, or abstract, just as the nature of those values is to stand against the effort of states and bureaucracies to oppress individual citizens, to generalize and quantify them, and thus to convert them from unique individuals to manipulable groups. Poetry's nature is to prize its own contravention of the political or social norm, even in a period when the poet considers himself an exponent of the norm, for the great poem defies above all the mediocrity of the other poems that form its literary context.

Even though individual poetic temperament may often be more important than any other factor in the poet's craft, some interesting generalities about individuality itself can be seen. In much eastern European poetry, the idea of privacy seems a defiance of state powers of surveillance, an insistence that individual powerlessness imposed by the state will not succeed in eradicating identity. The laconicism and antitraditionalism of such poetry are a kind of refusal of any tone of voice that might be interpreted as august, formal, "stately." What is wanted by the poet is the right to a thoroughly private life. This value, expressed in a poem, is political. In poetry written under parliamentary governments the idea of individuality seems often to be a defiance of market manipulation and an insistence on the irreducible identity constituted by genuine feelings. Yet what this poet wants is the ability to speak *for* others (beyond those found in the publishing "marketplace" as the relatively few buyers and readers of books of poems), to associate with others on terms of feeling rather than on grounds of economic or other statistical status (what the staffs of American commercial magazines call "the demographics"). The categorizing of the individual by either state power or advertising analysts is no more accurate, and no less false, than a précis of a novel or a paraphrase of a poem, for these always fall into more general categories of types. (My having to summarize in this discussion some of Cardenal's works and certain positions, opinions, and attitudes in those works is unfortunately also false, although imposed necessarily by the limited space of an essay.) To pursue this parallel: in some sense, paraphrase and literary taxonomy are census—and we might recall that after a census, the ancients felt a need to bathe, to cleanse themselves in order to restore their identities.

Now, compared to English, the Spanish language has less of the sort of concrete texture that I have been saying was a defining aspect of poetic rhetoric; by this I mean simply that Spanish has a smaller number of words for the naming of things, and that these tend to fall into less various levels of diction. Is it merely a coincidence that when less precision is wanted in English, diction can become latinate and periphrastic, as in bureaucratic prose that aims at an authoritative and procedural, even ceremonial tone? Borges thought English a superior medium for poetry to Spanish, for reasons related to the poetic rhetoric I have characterized above. In formulating "exteriorism," Cardenal was reacting artistically against an apparently narrow tonal range in Spanish, *so that* poetry could speak against social and political circumstances which the old poetic diction had been inadequate either to resist or criticize. In order to attack more forcefully the "subjectivity" of accepted poetic diction, he exaggerated it somewhat; in truth it can indeed be physically evocative in Antonio Machado, even if etherealized in Juan Ramón Jiménez. But Cardenal found his preferred poetic models in Pound and other North American poets. I think the artistic defense of this poetic posture is that, in requiring poetry to refer to the tangible and historical world in a literal as well as a symbolic way, it draws attention to the *occasions* of poems as well as their *subjects;* Cardenal requires that there be an apprehensible occasion outside the poet, not solely an interior "poetic" subject like love or longing or death. Bad poems, in this view, are simply too vague and misty, and ask of the reader a familiar rather than a fresh response of feeling and thought. This would imply that poems bearing traces of ideology (of any sort) would also tend to echo propagandistic points of view (wrong not because they are already established but because they falsify with slogans and simplifications). The rhetoric of politics may prize either action or passivity, depending on the nature of the structure of government, and in either case a familiarity of statement, a mere reference; the rhetoric of poetry prizes the vital re-experiencing of feelings and thoughts, and vision—in both senses, and vividly. The rhetoric of politics prizes persuasion; that of poetry prizes perception (the sight of what is visible) and insight (the understanding of what is hidden). Of course this does not rule out political content in poems, but it does discount those poems bearing a heavy load of the ideological.

How one means to use the word "ideology" is crucial. The conflict is very wide—between the rhetoric of poetry and, on the other side, the highly developed modern rhetoric and media of persuasion, cultural and political amnesia, and the falsification of information by those who control its preservation and dissemination. Before the successful revolution of the Sandinistas against Somoza in 1979, Cardenal frequently used the word "propaganda" in the customary pejorative sense to mean precisely the language of state power and advertisements, as for instance in his first psalm:

> Bienaventurado el hombre que no sigue las consignas del Partido
> ni asiste a sus mítines
> ni se sienta en la mesa con los gangsters

ni con los Generales en el Consejo de Guerra
Bienaventurado el hombre que no espía a su hermano
ni delata a su compañero de colegio
Bienaventurado el hombre que no lee los anuncios comerciales
ni escucha sus radios
ni cree en sus slogans

Será como un árbol plantado junto a una fuente

[P. 161]

Blessed is the man who does not follow the orders of the Party
nor attend its meetings
nor sit at the table with gangsters
nor with Generals in councils of war
Blessed is the man who does not spy on his brother
nor inform on his school-mate
Blessed is the man who does not read advertisements
nor listen to their radios
nor believe in their slogans

He will be like a tree planted beside a fountain

Paradoxically, this moral high ground remains to some extent a luxury of the powerless, who in challenging ruling powers exercise a critical function that is more congruent with the rhetoric of poetry, with the artist's "criticism" of life itself. A successful revolution brings with it meetings and slogans, although these are certainly the most innocent of the sins denounced in this first psalm. As I have already noted, Cardenal's poetry falls perhaps unsurprisingly into two groups; there is a troubling difference between poems condemning injustice, mostly written before Somoza's fall, and poems praising the new political and social order, written afterward. Take Yeats as a counterexample: one can go so far as to ignore the contours of his (reactionary) politics and note simply that as an individual who actively sought to intervene in the political history of his nation, he remained relatively powerless because he was in the opposition. Therefore his two critical functions, as poet and as opposition political figure, were in a crucial way not at odds with each other, and he did not experience the torsions of the poetic impulse felt by Cardenal, who went from being a hunted conspirator against the Somoza regime to being the minister of culture of Nicaragua.

Earlier, I suggested a congruence between art's critical nature and a "speaking against." Harold Rosenberg's analysis of the relationship between the artist's engagement with politics and the use by political power of artistic method led him to hold that the artist is the most valuable critic of propaganda, for "as an expert in the fabrication of appearances and realities, he has the training needed to penetrate the fabrications of politics." Some of Cardenal's prerevolutionary poetry, aimed against the manipulation of politics and political information by Somoza, demonstrates this critical impulse. Such artistic expertise is needed, according to Rosenberg, because

> politicians have become fiction makers, competitors and collaborators of fiction writers. One recalls, for instance, that mystery-story writers were invited to participate in think tanks on national military strategy [just as, I would add, more recently some science fiction writers have had a hand in advocating the so-called Star Wars Strategic Defense Initiative, in opposition to the expertise of some genuine scientists]. . . . A former assistant secretary of state declared on a radio program in which I participated that propaganda can no longer be successfully carried on by waiting for events to happen, and then interpreting them to support one's policies. It is necessary, said he, to create the events that verify the soundness of the policies one advocates.

Rosenberg held in the same essay that art could have almost no impact on politics, but that "the impulse to intervene in political life hovers like a ghost over the art of our century, perhaps because of the crisscrossing of fact and illusion which art and politics share."[18]

But as one can infer from Milosz's *The Witness of Poetry,* the impulse to bear witness *is* a kind of indirect intervention—a small act, at the very least, in the larger discourse of which politics forms a sometimes dominant part. It is in the realm of politics, too, that the only decisive answer to this indirect intervention may be given, either as persecution or state approval, neither of which should be wanted. The task of criticism, then, in addition to pondering artistic intervention in political life, should be to weigh political intervention in imaginative life, to which political poetry is in part a response. With regard to poems, criticism should consider not only expressed belief or conviction or political position but also the expressive significance of the poem's formal qualities *and* the formal value, in the overall structure of the poem, of the expressed belief or conviction.

And no one should suppose that an opposition between poetry and a state that uses literary devices to manipulate information and opinion leaves poetry altogether unharmed. The "competition" of opinions and of versions of information, like that of products, extends—as a circumstance of commercial life and also as an ideology dear to the industrialized, parliamentary states—into the very production and distribution of books of poems. The effect of this incursion is destructive because in the frenzies and failures of publicity it promotes not a genuine sorting out of artistic value but a race between public images and literary fashions. Inevitably,

18. Harold Rosenberg, "Art and Political Consciousness," *Art and Other Serious Matters* (Chicago, 1985), pp. 293, 281, 282, 284.

competition in this sense affects in a dubious manner the dissemination of artistic works in society, by whatever means (including all the phenomena related to the writing and reading of poetry: readings, workshops, writers' conferences, and so forth).

Therefore, even if poetry can usefully preserve humane values which stand against the inhumane, which show men and women suffering in the path of history, this political engagement of the art is not free from a reverse damage which the marketplace and the pervasive manipulated language of politics work on all language. The fundamental contradiction of poetry's engagement with politics is that if, especially when it's "political," poetry tries to intervene in history, then in all its forms poetry is subject to the intervention of politics and economic relations—both in terms of language and in terms of the very conditions of life (and sometimes death) of the poet. So in some sense writers generally work *against* "history"; for if, as Des Pres writes, "history has often shown us the long-term victory of truth,"[19] we might also concur with him in noting, less cheerfully, that history (that is, the surviving record) has also—and often—concealed the long-term victories of falsehood.

The critic is not immune to this sometimes unwitting falsification. It is the victor and his beneficiaries, however removed, who enforce the context of historical interpretation, which includes even poetry. Many examples testify to the susceptibility of evaluation and canon formation to political distortion. The phrase "evaluation of political poetry" can only suggest the phrase "political evaluation of poetry." We can play a game with adjectives revealing how difficult it is to untie the knots already tightly pulled at the heart of the evaluation of poetry. If one can speak of the "evaluation of a political poem," one might also substitute for "political" such words as "historical," "psychological," "philosophical," or "religious" without suggesting anything out of the ordinary in the history of literary criticism. But if one takes the altered phrase, "the political evaluation of poetry," and makes the same substitutions for "political," a whole range of different *sorts* of criticism presents itself, not many of them practiced with distinction. To place any adjective in front of "evaluation" is to play the victor, to abdicate a larger and more significant responsibility in favor of a smaller and less significant one (albeit more immediately *useful* to the concerns of various intellectual fields of inquiry), and to enforce an unresponsive, partial context of evaluation on the work evaluated. Our task should be, instead, to read the poetry for the sake of investigating every aspect of its participation in the life of the people in whose society it was created (even if that is our own); then to ask what it brings to those (even ourselves, in our most conscious moments) not overly distanced from that society and that poem by history or by greater or smaller cultural heritage, or by our individual formation as

19. Des Pres, "Equipment for Living," *TriQuarterly* 65 (Winter 1986): 91.

readers; then to ask what it brings to those who are indeed at such a distance. In such contexts of expectation, what was once tactical may turn strategic—the poem written in response to a given historical and political circumstance may finally reveal its resonance to wider human situations and command our admiration, evoke our pleasure, and compel us to preserve it.

Cardenal has written political poetry of both a general and a partisan kind, and some of the poems (mostly, but not entirely, written before the revolution) are enduring work, while others seem flawed by simplification and service to a political position enforcing idealization. (This is a practical judgment, an evaluation—the result of my reading his work through—which I must assert for lack of sufficient space to demonstrate.) Is it possible to go further and to open a generally valid theoretical avenue to the problem of evaluation of "political poetry"? I do not believe so.

The individual reader's judgment and evaluation are much shaped by experience and temperament. This acknowledgment may come less readily from critics, who tend to prefer theoretical consistency, than from writers, who are often and unavoidably engaged in informal evaluation and make little pretense to being "objective" about it. Their own artistic needs compel them to evaluate the work of others so as to determine whether and how to make use of it. Cardenal did this with the works of Pound and other English-language poets and took from them what he needed—but not Pound's politics, or his entire aesthetic, and certainly not his technique (his stance toward life).

Barbara Herrnstein Smith has noted how thoroughly the question of evaluation has been neglected by academic criticism for decades, and she has expounded an impressive theoretical examination of evaluation.[20] Her essay leads me to two points. First, neglect of evaluation is itself an ideological and evaluative act which, in removing the question of evaluation from ostensible concerns while continuing unavoidably to participate in a myriad of implicitly evaluative acts, is partly responsible not for "the decline of the humanities" but for the general decline of *regard* for the humanities (even among some engaged in humanistic study). When literary criticism shows no overt concern for the evaluation of individual works but only for abstract goals like "critical thinking" or "humanities," it contributes to the opinion held all too widely that there is little *value* in the humanities, only a teachable method. Thus the scientistic longings of criticism, when they do achieve some result, end merely in a self-destructive explosion.

20. See Barbara Herrnstein Smith, "Contingencies of Value," in *Canons,* ed. Robert von Hallberg (Chicago, 1984), pp. 5–40.

Second, it is not possible to construct any theoretical model of evaluation because the terms "theoretical" and "evaluation" are at odds. Can there be a "theoretical," that is, often "hypothetical," evaluation, except as a kind of mental role playing? Evaluation is an act of mind that may issue in conviction as well as proceed from it—a specific act of a specific individual, who if he or she evaluates a literary work solely in terms of a theoretical position may violate his or her own identity as a person, for we pursue evaluation—as Smith notes—with a larger portion of our being than that which contemplates theoretical possibilities, and rightly so. In Christopher Lasch's terms, we might say that we cannot evaluate solely as voices of reason, but do so also as voices of conscience and imagination.[21] To do otherwise is to narrow the critical act of evaluation to a partial act of analysis, as I attempted to demonstrate with my lists of adjectives for the phrase "the ______ evaluation of poetry."

Thus evaluation is always, in larger terms, the incorporation into criticism of the assessment and judgment of beliefs. But whereas a technical analysis or theoretical disquisition requires, for interest's sake, almost no prior or anticipated consensus except around the notion that criticism should be interesting to read, evaluation and judgment do require prior or anticipated consensus on the standards or values by which poetry, or any human endeavor, is to be judged as good, fruitful, acceptable, mediocre, bad, destructive, or whatever.

To substantiate a claim with regard to value, one can argue from verities perceived as eternal, as from religion, or from those perceived to survive over time, as from tradition, or from those perceived to lie in scientifically validated evidence, as from the natural world. The first method tends to seek its justification in the divine, the second in the people, the third in principles deduced to be inherent in the human creature because inherent in the physical universe. There is no great clarity here because from any one of these one can also argue to another—if there are apparently universal principles governing the nature of life on this planet, I can infer a divine order. If there is, as in Kenneth Burke's view, a "constellation" of human values such as courage, love, freedom, which are demonstrably present in cultures widely separated in time and space, I can infer from this tradition some universal and eternal aspects of human nature. And so on.

Sociological and Marxist thinking have insisted on the "socially constructed" nature of every value. Although based on the incontrovertible evidence that most human experience and all values held in common by human beings are affected by historical circumstance, finally this seems

21. See Christopher Lasch, "A Typology of Intellectuals: I. The Feminist Subject," *Salmagundi* 70/71 (Spring/Summer 1986): 27–32. My reading of this issue, titled "Intellectuals," was a rich occasion for my thinking about political poetry and Cardenal, and I am indebted to the contributors and to the editor of the magazine, Robert Boyers.

to lie just beyond the point of truth. (It would be hard to prove that the experiences of the rush of adrenaline when one is in danger, of the wearying heaviness of grief, of the ecstasy of orgasm, are socially constructed in any appreciable way.) Essentialist and politically reactionary thinking has insisted on the firm, inalterable, and flawed core of human nature, and, although based on incontrovertible evidence that across huge barriers of history, culture, and race, certain central human experiences find their unmistakable echoes in others, this too of course lies beyond the point of truth. (It would be hard to prove that the particular choices of one's active response to physical aggression, one's outward behavior at the death of one's child, or one's notions of romantic love, are not socially constructed almost in their entirety.)

So if a poem is called "political" and presents itself to our eyes as a tangle of poetic craft (which we judge by one conventional set of standards) and poetic technique, or "stance toward life," or "belief" (which we judge by another, subtly related set of standards), our response is diagnostic not only of the nature of the poem but also of the nature of our assumptions about art and politics. Most valuable among these, perhaps, is the assumption that works of art and human actions may be—should be—judged against one another, some to be preferred and some abhorred. Because evaluation is the act of an individual mind at a given moment, to evaluate Cardenal's political poetry is to evaluate individual poems against other individual poems, and to do so in the realm of both conviction and pleasure, both solace and connoisseurship, as well as that of literary history. Persons will disagree on the priority assigned to human values and will disagree on poems: I believe that some of Cardenal's poems are enduring works, and perhaps more important than that, I see his poetry as a sphere in which we are called as individuals to react not only to a poet's perceptions but also to feeling, conviction, and belief as they may be related to us in our own lives. Work like Cardenal's forces us to make ourselves as conscious as we can of the implicit assumptions affecting our evaluative decisions. Poetry, with its peculiar rhetoric, calls us thus to respond to an intense and vivid presentation of the human condition, and Cardenal's poetry is a particularly compelling instance of this. When criticism denies or ignores this call, it turns against its own subject.

Without Consequences Is No Politics: A Response to Jerome McGann

Charles Altieri

As someone who thinks he is committed to experimental poetry yet has a great deal of trouble considering L=A=N=G=U=A=G=E Writing worth the labors it demands, I looked forward to Jerome McGann's essay, "Contemporary Poetry, Alternate Routes." Looking back on it I find myself in a very different frame of mind. McGann not only failed to convince me of the value of the poetry, but made me wonder about my own commitments. With such defenders, experimental poetry needs no enemies: indeed, McGann's blend of political naïveté and latent aestheticism risks confirming those suspicions that keep most intellectuals from reading any poetry at all. It therefore becomes crucial that one try to specify where McGann has gone wrong, if only to restore attention to essays—like the one he mentions by Marjorie Perloff—which challenge the political claims while offering concrete elaborations of the specific writerly intensities and reflexive qualities that can justify some of the difficulties in the poetry.

Let me be as concrete and brief as possible. We ought notice first that there are good reasons to think that McGann's version of literary history is accurate neither to the actual contours of contemporary writing nor to the politics which the authors project. McGann posits two homologous distinctions—between personal poetry and L=A=N=G=U=A=G=E Writing, and between poetry that ultimately accommodates the political order and writing that makes possible an "oppositional politics" capable of assuming the "critical responsibilities of art" in order to produce "a *comprehensive* account of the American experience" over the past ten or fifteen years (p. 257). The facts, however, are not so tidy: L=A=N=G=U=A=G=E writers like Lyn Hejinian or Rae Armantrout or Douglas Messerli are far more personal than very traditional "impersonal" poets like John Hollander or assertively political ones like Ed Dorn, and poets like Robert Hass, Gary Snyder, and Adrienne Rich are at least as oppositional in their politics as Ron Silliman or Charles Bernstein. There are differences in their understanding of the relationship between the personal and the political, but these should not be reduced to such gross categories as accommodation and opposition without substantial arguments on just what makes poetry effectively political.

McGann's version of the necessary arguments concentrates on spelling out the possible political significance of adapting an adamantly nonnarrative poetry. Nonnarrative is not merely another self-reflexive idea about poetry. Rather it offers a concrete "productive social practice . . . self-consciously brought before the attention of the 'reader'" (p. 262) as a formal alternative to the way in which the "continuity" of narrative legitimates "established forms of social order, as well as the very idea of such established forms" (p. 259). Adapting this practice makes it possible for writing to assume the critical responsibilities of art and through that to pursue the following values: (1) making literal the energies of Blake's "order of Imagination" so that the dominance of a limiting rationality gives way to an "order generated through the faculty or process which discovers previously unapprehended relations of things" (p. 261); (2) using such processes to have works "embody in themselves some form of cultural difference" (p. 259)—this is accomplished by presenting a number of brief narrative units, all "self-contained," whose interrelations have to be "consciously constructed" because the work provides "no narrativized structure, either express or implied, within which they find their coherence" (p. 260); (3) making the embodiment a vehicle for changing the audience's attitude toward language by " 'deranging the language' from its current (truly 'deranged') conventionalities" (p. 264). McGann envisions these specific values all combining ultimately to make possible contemporary versions of Blake's ability to project an alternative to traditional theories of atonement by embracing "a heterodox theory which held, essentially, that a general redemptive scheme would emerge through the practice of continuous self-atonement" (p. 263). Keeping readers attuned to the constant productivity of language will then provide the terms for performing this self-atonement by refusing sense and the narcissistic ego any secure resting place within the established political and epistemological modes of understanding.

The appeal of such abstractions is obvious. Unfortunately, the problems that accompany them are equally obvious, so obvious in fact that

---

Charles Altieri is professor of English and comparative literature at the University of Washington. He is the author of *Act and Quality: A Theory of Literary Meaning and Humanistic Understanding* (1981) and *Self and Sensibility in Contemporary American Poetry* (1984).

they provide a superb context for spelling out some of the fundamental confusions and blocks that underlie most of contemporary criticism's efforts to develop a sophisticated model for the political work that the experimental arts can accomplish. On the most general level, McGann's own professional affiliations with Victorian values, evident in his claims about the critical responsibility of the arts and the necessity that they offer comprehensive accounts of their culture, makes visible a crucial seam in postmodern political visions. For if L=A=N=G=U=A=G=E Writing, or any other stance based on modernist experimental principles, is to satify those demands, it must do so largely on the basis of whatever powers its formal principles can make available. The culture's most grandiose claims about art must be realized within its most skeptical and minimalist sense of the resources available for that task. The task may not be impossible, but the direct assertion of political ends makes it extremely difficult to show how forms of meaning not devoted to representing social conditions can carry such broad implications. But McGann, shored up by his opening truisms about the global political order, disdains modernist discipline for Victorian generalizations attributing political content to those formal principles. In the process he reduces the best in L=A=N=G=U=A=G=E Writing to its most pious analogies claiming to link art as a mode of production and the psychic economies governing basic forms of social life.

That reductiveness is clear in the problematic models of meaning that McGann must invoke for his task. Traditional art locates its social and political force in the capacity of the medium to give distinctive force to certain implications of what the work represents, so that art grapples with the same concerns and codes adapted in other social practices. Like much of modernist art, McGann's L=A=N=G=U=A=G=E Writing finds those practices so contaminated that it must base most of its energies on deranging the language from its conventionalities. But much of that art can also go on to reject the claims of the political which are normally carried in such language, putting in its place a range of individualist and spiritual states whose difference from the practical order warrants these experiments in deranging and reconstructing sense. But McGann's L=A=N=G=U=A=G=E Writing must claim direct political significance for its ways of rejecting the prevailing political theater.

McGann proposes two basic strategies for that task. First of all he calls attention to the concrete energies mobilized for a reader by those material properties that L=A=N=G=U=A=G=E Writing can free from the idealizing habits of traditional art. Here, rather than projecting interpretations of the world, the work literally enacts certain relational principles within that world which make us aware of certain powers we have within it. Thus Silliman's *Tjanting* is not a fiction about class struggle but a "localized instance of class struggle itself" (p. 271). In the same vein McGann can claim that "Silliman's imagination . . . found in the Fibonacci numbers an image of class struggle and social dialectics. The numbers confirm his search for signs and modes of social dynamism" (p. 274). For not only do they engage us directly in self-reflexive signifying practices; they also rely on the fact that "language is . . . the representative social form per se—the social form through which society sees and presents itself to itself" (p. 272). On this basis McGann can proceed to the more particular claims he derives from these writers' second strategy of replacing narrative structures with the modes of relationship articulated within nonnarrative. There false continuities give way to a constant process of construction in which language pursues "complete self-transparency"; readers must take responsibility for the meanings produced; and writing assumes a complex temporality combining an intense immediacy, unframed by the exigencies of story, with a constant sense of the reader's responsibility to connect that present to a past and a future (see pp. 268–70).

Each strategy, however, seems to me both trapped by its modernist heritage and conceptually overextended as it tries to free itself of that heritage. Consider first McGann's claims about language. Modernist arts had stressed a variety of powers made available by concentrating on the medium rather than the message. But the medium was rarely so rarefied, so confined to the properties of the physical. Even in painting, the paradigmatic example of what Harold Osborne calls modernism's shift from semantic to syntactic principles of organization, we find the cubists less concerned with the properties of the medium per se than with the modes of compositional intelligence and the affective complexes that they could mobilize by treating the physical as components fitted to carry the play of mind. Similarly, while Mondrian stresses the "dynamic balances" which artworks literally embody once the painter frees the elements to define their own relational structures, his aim is not to free the audience but to bind it more intensely and abstractly to certain dominant forces. Finally poets like William Carlos Williams, Guillaume Apollinaire, Gertrude Stein, and Wallace Stevens all adapted those principles to two fundamental pursuits—freeing composition so that the mind could explore new principles of relationship, and treating those relationships less as comments about the world than as literal testimony through which the experience of the work became substantial evidence for the claims the work asserted. When Stevens speaks of "this endlessly elaborating poem" displaying "the theory of poetry / As the life of poetry," and Williams of poetry at once freeing and dynamizing the word, they imagine the presentational level of the poem not simply as pointing to language but as showing how language can give substance to intentional states that define new modes of understanding the powers of human agency. McGann's L=A=N=G=U=A=G=E Writing, on the other hand, is so suspicious of continuities and intentions that it puts all the burden of meaning on the reader. Thus it has as its only metaphoric ground the analogies McGann can draw with the forms of relationship that the syntactic and connotational features of the linguistic structures suggest. What had been the means for presenting testimonial acts becomes only a weak stimulus for audience associations.

That focus on language per se has two seriously limiting effects. First, it reifies language by treating it as "the representative social form" itself, which these poets try to make as "transparent" as possible (pp. 272, 270). Language is obviously the basis for social interactions, but it is not in itself anything except a set of abstract relations within which certain meanings become possible. In all probability there is no one social form—that hypothesis is pure Platonism, not Marxist materialism. The most one can say about the relation of language to social structures is that it comes to articulate a range of practices that we must master in order to move fluidly through the social order. But that is a question of content, not of form, and the range of practices will not stand still for any one ethical metaphor. Language does not have ethical content; only its speakers do, and then only when we can attribute intentions enabling us to characterize and to assess actions. This then sets off as the second limitation of McGann's claims about language his tendency to make language itself replace all other metaphors. McGann narrows the field in this way because his writers so distrust all the interpretive contents one might impose on or locate within any given linguistic practice that they must turn for their political metaphors primarily to analogies drawn from specific syntactic effects. But in fact grammar contains as many instances of dominant logical hierarchies as it does figures for an open and communal temporality, and it offers as many models of constant tension among subjects because of its play of differences as it does instances of integrating particulars with a collective order.

Even more important, whenever such abstract analogies are required to make one's political point, one has stripped one's claims of all effective social content. Notice in this regard that many of McGann's images of class struggle and projections of audience freedom and responsibility can easily be recast to support or reflect basic capitalist practices. Why is the process of audience freedom not best understood along the lines of neoconservative economics: is not such freedom to recast inherited materials a perfect exemplar of the right to treat language as a commodity to be manipulated in whatever ways I can get away with? That too is a social relation all too much in keeping with an order in which there is no responsibility to the continuities imposed by received disciplines or respect for the intentions of others. And shouldn't I be able to make what profit I can from this field of economic possibilities, on the assumption that if each of us bends the law to our own interest the dynamic competition will prove in society's best interests? Finally, is not the irreducibly social coding of language precisely what every advertising genius must learn to control for his or her own purposes?

It is important to realize that these openings to conservative retranslation are not mere impositions on L=A=N=G=U=A=G=E Writing but are deeply woven into the modernist logic that McGann tries to make serve Marxist roles. This is clear when we shift to the problems in his claims about the assertive force made possible by cultivating nonnarrative modes. For he must then be able to say how these structures will have semantic force through their evading or overthrowing the standard practices of intentional communication. McGann finds no trouble locating that force in the activity of "self-containment," of embodying in the work itself its productive capacity to define a difference from the commodified ways of the social order. But how then attribute to value that productive difference? If, as McGann usually puts it, the force of the difference lies in the reader's sense of his or her interpretive freedom to produce meanings rather than be bound to a commodified language, he comes dangerously close to relying on the idea of the free, pleasure-seeking consumer that L=A=N=G=U=A=G=E Writing's doctrines so pompously revile. After all, the basic dodge of capitalist advertising consists in promising an undefined freedom that depends on a person's thinking that he or she is the only one on the block to compose a certain order or possess a certain way of arranging his or her world. But if McGann were to stress instead the power of the object to compose its own order in resistance to the contaminating force of social narratives, he would come dangerously close to the very conservative models of modernist autonomy and self-containment proposed by Clement Greenberg and Michael Fried.

By contrast with McGann's, those conservative positions begin to look reasonable, if not desirable. At least they show how particular works can dramatize concretely certain exemplary powers. And while their model insists that these powers are primarily individual and not social—matters of grace that are dimensions of our struggles with ourselves rather than with others—the specific readings it encourages can suggest ways of treating those powers as worth trying to make available for the polity. But the actual arguments, the relation between what art discloses and politics can be made to pursue, will depend first on a responsible criticism, then on a willingness to submit its descriptions to the analytic and narrative modes of discursive judgment required for serious political thought. If, on the other hand, one refuses that mediating role for art and, with McGann, seeks more direct political authority, it is likely that one will end up with little more than a very thin formalism desperately proclaiming in theory the significance it cannot locate in the specific works. Brecht loses to Lukács.

Look once more at McGann's triumphant claim that "Silliman's imagination . . . found in the Fibonacci numbers an image of class struggle and social dialectics" (p. 274). What kind of an "image" is this and what possible force can it have? At best it is a picture of an idea or an analogy to another abstraction which has only a minuscule claim on either feelings or intellect. Does the ability to manipulate these sequences, or even to make formal literary analogies for them, demonstrate anything at all about actual class struggle or intensify the reader's hopes and commitments in that practical sphere? Yet McGann presumes to disparage the political force of the narratives that Marx and his followers used to elaborate that image and work out some of its possible consequences. Perhaps McGann would have advised Marx to take the more revolutionary route of encouraging readers to produce their own meanings rather than work analytically through the contradictions of the existing social structure.

Clearly poetry will not do Marx's work. But poetry did to a considerable extent shape the values at stake in Marx's work, primarily because it did not become so ambitious as to pursue the self-canceling project of making empty rhetorical claims that deprive it of the powers it can muster. McGann's essay, by contrast, shows one of our keenest critics now taking a route all too traveled which makes the grandeur of the critic's claims and affiliations a substitute for careful poetic and conceptual analysis. McGann's emphasis on a semantics preoccupied with "nonsense, unmeaning, and fragmentation" (p. 265) allows him to learn very little from actual poems. Indeed despite his generalizations about the social order, his actual accounts of production and his interpretations focus almost exclusively on metaliterary abstractions about the nature of meaning, on the force of formal analogies like the Fibonacci series, or on assertions that "relationships and forms of order can only be had if they are actively made by the reader . . . and that they will shift from reader to reader and from reading to reading" (p. 267). Just as McGann treats language as an entity distinct from the many language practices which constitute social life, he abstracts poetry from its capacities to enter and use the range of attitudes and beliefs implicated in those social practices. He thereby denies the best L=A=N=G=U=A=G=E poetry its considerable force as exploration of new imaginative investments not bound to the narcissistic ego-formations that govern contemporary life. Such reductive accounts are hardly the stuff on which to dream of carrying " 'the class struggle *for* consciousness to the level *of* consciousness' " (p. 270). In fact consciousness is reduced essentially to metapoetic discourses having very little to do with any real world, individual or political (even when a poem like Bernstein's "For Love Has Such a Spirit That if It Is Portrayed It Dies" makes clear personal and philosophical demands on the reader). McGann's version of a new ideal of meaning emerging "not as an appropriation or institution of truth but as 'the enabled incapacity to impose a usage' " (p. 266) proves all too easy, and all too incapacitating. And his ideals of readerly freedom do little more than curry favor with an audience already committed to the radical gestures of an avant-garde. Such ideals actually prevent poetry from challenging that audience or forcing McGann to confront the individualism inherent in his Blakean vision of self-atonement. This claim to an oppositional politics actually resists those accommodations to a collective that are the precondition of effective social action.

Response to Charles Altieri

Jerome J. McGann

Though Charles Altieri faults my essay on a number of particular points, I don't see, in most cases, that I need to add anything to what I have already written. Readers can judge for themselves whether my representations or his criticisms seem more persuasive.

In two instances, however, I feel that my essay did not make itself clear enough. That failure of clarity seems to have led Altieri into a pair of (related) misjudgments. These misjudgments are important not so much because they are directed at what I have written, but—more crucially—because they may lead to confusions about what is involved in the project known as L=A=N=G=U=A=G=E Writing.

It is probably my fault that Altieri can say, as a critique of my discussion of L=A=N=G=U=A=G=E Poetry, that "language does not have ethical content; only its speakers do, and then only when we can attribute intentions enabling us to characterize and to assess actions" ("Without Consequences Is No Politics," p. 305). I take it that Altieri here uses the word "language" in a general way, and not with a specific reference to L=A=N=G=U=A=G=E Writing. And I take it that his remarks seem to him a critique of my paper (and perhaps even—I cannot tell—a critique of L=A=N=G=U=A=G=E Writing) because he thinks I use the word "language" in the phrase "L=A=N=G=U=A=G=E Poetry" in the same sense that he uses it in the sentence I have quoted.

Let me only say that the term "language," in the phrase "L=A=N=G=U=A=G=E Writing/Poetry," would be tautological if it meant what Altieri takes it to mean—or if he takes that meaning as my understanding of the word, or indeed as the understanding of any of the writers associated with such work.

L=A=N=G=U=A=G=E Poetry has as much "ethical content" as any other kind of poetry. It has no special privilege to freedom from ideology, any more than Romantic poetry does, or modern poetry. The phrase "L=A=N=G=U=A=G=E Poetry," as I understand it, gestures toward the effort on the part of certain writers precisely to highlight, to foreground, "to language" the ethical/ideological dimensions of their own work. L=A=N=G=U=A=G=E Writing tries to short-circuit the distinction between "content" and "form," to show that the material and institutional structures of transmission are indices—or as Olson once said, "extensions"—of content. This effort often appears in their (theoretical) work as an attack on the speaking subject in the poem, or as an attack on "the referent." The critical moves against the speaking subject and the referent, however, are part of the effort to draw both into the framework of the total poetical action. These moves are made in order to withdraw from the reader all ethical or ideological resorts.

Reading this kind of work the reader is meant to feel that, when one is engaged in communicative action, the act of communicating is itself heavily invested in ethics and ideology. This is (as it were) "the moral" of the story of L=A=N=G=U=A=G=E Writing. "Language does not have ethical content," Altieri says, and if one means by "language" the abstract system of communication, of course the statement is true. But if one means by "language" "communicative action," or "language" as it is actually and actively engaged, then obviously it does have ethical content and is invested in ideology.

My interest in L=A=N=G=U=A=G=E Writing lies precisely in this fact: that such work demonstrates how every particle of the language we use—lexemes, phonemes, letters, separate marks of punctuation, spacings, paper, format, institutions and media of communication, and so forth—all are "always already" involved in a structure pointed toward communicative action. None of these things ever have a purely formal existence. In everyday life people often "use" their languages, or think of their languages, as if they were neutrally instrumental—means that forward certain ends (getting things done, coming to understandings). And in fact this is one framework within which communicative action can take place. L=A=N=G=U=A=G=E Writing is critical of that instrumental and pragmatistic/use conception of language, and its critique ultimately rests in the argument (and belief) that the instrument and the action, the medium and the message, are totally interinvolved.

L=A=N=G=U=A=G=E Poetry is important, I think, because it does not allow a reader to deploy it in those instrumental ways that were

---

Jerome J. McGann is Commonwealth Professor of English, University of Virginia. His most recent critical work is *Buildings of Loss: The Knowledge of Imaginative Texts.*

taught to us through the Kantian and Arnoldian traditions. The L=A=N=G=U=A=G=E Poetry that matters to me does not yield to (or issue in) either the imagination of disinterested formalities or the imperatives of significant meanings. It does not operate under those ancient forms of completion, Truth and Beauty. Rather, it moves through an endless field of various truths and different beauties (these always including many erroneous and unbeautiful reciprocals). In this process it involves the reader in a correspondent set of activities. To read the poetry is to "communicate with" it, to participate in an action which is an engagement of the conflicts of authority, intention, and interest that are set in motion through the communicative interchange.

The second point I want to address is Altieri's critique of the position of the reader in L=A=N=G=U=A=G=E Writing. "Why is the process of audience freedom not best understood along the lines of neoconservative economics: is not such freedom to recast inherited materials a perfect exemplar of the right to treat language as a commodity to be manipulated in whatever ways I can get away with? . . . Finally, is not the irreducibly social coding of language precisely what every advertising genius must learn to control for his or her own purposes?" (p. 305).

Altieri can ask these questions, I think, because of the ineffective way in which I represented the theoretical work of the writers I was discussing. I believe now that my discussion of "audience freedom" was too abstractly presented—so abstractly, in fact, that it licensed Altieri to his equation of the reader of L=A=N=G=U=A=G=E Writing with the writer of advertising copy, and ultimately to his equation of the reader with the Late Capitalist consumer.

In a sense, of course, all texts are subject to the crass manipulations which Altieri calls attention to. Indeed, much literary criticism is plainly a consumer activity, and much of it is (equally plainly) a (self-)advertising discourse. He who is without sin here may cast the first stone. The question is: does L=A=N=G=U=A=G=E Writing *in fact* promote that kind of activity? (And the further questions—which I shall not address here—might also be raised: does Altieri himself think that it does, or does he only think that I have represented it so? And if he only thinks the latter, then what is *his* view on the issue, and why does he never give his view?)

It is difficult to imagine a style of work less like advertising copy than L=A=N=G=U=A=G=E Writing. Perhaps Altieri is led to this imagination by the appearance of the page in many L=A=N=G=U=A=G=E texts. The whole field of the page is held open for poetic disposal; indeed, the page itself is not taken as a given, but may be conceived anew at any point, or deconstructed altogether. In advertising copy, however, the communicative action is directed to a single goal; success is measured by the degree to which that goal has been secured; and the audience is imagined as uniform (just as the text is designed to promote further the uniformity of the audience).

The "audience freedom" which is the object of L=A=N=G=U=A=G=E Writing has nothing to do with the stimulation/satisfaction dynamic which is the foundation of advertising texts. On the contrary, what one first recognizes about so many L=A=N=G=U=A=G=E texts is that their surfaces, their appearances, are disaffected (in both senses), and that the reading experience moves through complex and ramifying networks of difficulty. They hold out nothing but problems. Milan Kundera once said that the point of poetry is not to give answers but to ask questions. In L=A=N=G=U=A=G=E Writing those questions become the field within which the reader will move freely—if the reader is to move at all.

The relation of this style of work to politics should be very clear, though Altieri seems not able to see it. "Audience freedom" in these texts is to be experienced as one experiences "political freedom" in any communicative or agenting framework. In this case one has to be very particular, has to see (or judge) what the political situation is in the United States, and what is the place of communication in that situation today.

To reckon freedom along a pleasure thermometer, as Altieri seems to do, is to misunderstand what freedom is—at least in the United States and the West generally. In such contexts freedom has little as such to do with pleasure. Freedom may be imagined as pleasure when one is living in circumstances where pleasure is removed or curtailed or forbidden. In societies (like our own), however, where pleasure (and happiness) are generally constructed not as deprivations but as illusions, poetry will not survive as A-Thing-Of-Beauty; and the politics of poetry will lie in its ability to expose those illusions, to open areas in which one may gain a certain freedom from their power.

The strength of L=A=N=G=U=A=G=E Writing, I think, arises from its involvement of the audience in the deconstructive maneuvers of the texts. It does not propose for its immediate object pleasure, as Coleridge once said all poetry does. Its immediate objects are the illusions of pleasure. Furthermore, the freedom it offers requires initially that readers experience an evacuation and failure of their customary reading privileges. Freedom in L=A=N=G=U=A=G=E Writing begins when those privileges are laid open to critique; and the critique is founded at the level of "language," that is, at the level of the forms of communicative action in which everyone is enmeshed. Readers in L=A=N=G=U=A=G=E texts operate most freely—and of course such a text can be any text, a poem by Donne as much as a poem by Bob Grenier—when their responses to the texts are finally seen, by the readers themselves, as equally involved in the problematics of the discourse as the initiating text itself.

Freedom would be achieved when the reading/writing subject stood transparent to those forms of communication, and vice versa. That condition of transparency is an unachievable ideal, of course, like complete self-consciousness. But insofar as it is achievable, it is a social and a political condition, not merely a personal one. Even Socrates, our byword for a person who set a supreme value upon self-knowledge, saw the political and social dimensions of that knowledge. His life, and his death, are an enduring testimony to the necessary relation—for good as well as for ill—that always operates between the personal and the political. L=A=N=G=U=A=G=E Writing has simply thrown that relation to the foreground of our attention once again.

The Politics of, the Politics in

Jed Rasula

> A writer will find that the more precisely, conscientiously, appropriately he expresses himself, the more obscure the literary result is thought, whereas a loose and irresponsible formulation is at once rewarded with certain understanding.
>
> —THEODOR ADORNO, *Minima Moralia*

The vexing issue of politics *in* and the politics *of* contemporary American poetry is perennially aggravated by the ambiguity of domestic political discourse in the first place, and by the constantly shifting planes of attention which various literary strategies forward, obscuring the view of their ideological parameters. The nature of American politics precludes poetry as a significant social discourse, and the choice of poetry as a medium instantly sidelines the poet as a voice of any political consequence.[1] As George Oppen remarked, reflecting on his decision to abandon poetry during the Depression, a poem is simply not a politically efficacious form: "If you decide to do something politically, you do something that has political efficacy. And if you decide to write poetry, then you write poetry, not something that you hope, or deceive yourself into believing, can save people who are suffering."[2]

Possibly the most consequential—because the most visible and unmistakable—political act relating to poetry in the United States in recent decades was Robert Bly's use of the 1968 National Book Awards ceremony

1. We lack, for instance, a tradition of political song, which in Latin American countries provides the material base for a genuinely political poetry followed by a mass audience.

2. George Oppen, interview, in *The Contemporary Writer: Interviews with Sixteen Novelists and Poets*, ed. L. S. Dembo and Cyrena N. Pondrom (Milwaukee, 1972), p. 187.

to denounce his publisher's tacit support of the war in Vietnam and hand over his prize money (for *The Light around the Body*) to the draft resisters' league. But this was a rare forum, the fortuitous coupling of public occasion and the will to assert political values. Other readily acknowledged political functions for American poets would include the public-personality activism of Allen Ginsberg, Adrienne Rich, and Amiri Baraka, and the region-specific ecological positions of Gary Snyder, Wendell Berry, and Michael McClure. Another politically consequential practice has evolved which is not dependent on fame or public persona; this is the issue-oriented, socially expository poetry of women, gays, ethnic minorities, and other groups bonded by debates outside aesthetics. Ron Silliman has speculated that the yearly total of reported rapes in the United States exceeds the total number of volumes of poetry sold.[3] An appalling statistic, it nonetheless suggests one reason for the preponderance of topical, personal-experience women's poetry; whether it conveys experiences of rape or simply delineates feelings of vulnerability, such work clearly leads to solidarity, dialogue, and political conviction.

The phrasing of the topic as "Politics and Poetic Value" adds an intriguing but different emphasis to the issue. Politics depicted in or by means of poems may reflect poetic value; but then, poetic value (as in William Blake or Ezra Pound) is likely to generate its own matrix of political reference. And poetic value is a kind of capital invested in the genre itself, genre as institution. "Genres are essentially literary *institutions,* or social contracts between a writer and a specific public, whose function is to specify the proper use of a particular cultural artifact."[4] While Fredric Jameson has done much to illuminate the "political unconscious" of the novel, it would be expedient to consider the lingering contractual arrangements between readers and writers of lyric poetry—particularly in light of the ways in which the poem (as Jameson says of narrative in the novel) is an "ideologeme whose outer form, secreted like a shell or exoskeleton, continues to emit its ideological message long after the extinction of its host."[5] We have grown accustomed to hearing repeated declarations of the "continuity" of a tradition. Such claims may be recognized as precisely the sort of ideological emission Jameson means,

3. See Ron Silliman, "The Political Economy of Poetry," *L=A=N=G=U=A=G=E* 4 (Winter 1982): 59.

4. Fredric Jameson, *The Political Unconscious: Narrative as a Socially Symbolic Act* (Ithaca, N.Y., 1981), p. 106.

5. Ibid., p. 151.

Jed Rasula is a Ph.D. candidate in the History of Consciousness program at the University of California, Santa Cruz. He is the author of *Tabula Rasula: being a book of audible visual matters* and an associate editor of *Sulfur*. He is completing a book on postwar American poetic practice, *Composting Poetry*.

particularly in this century of the permanent avant-garde and the revoking of genre as social contract.

Charles Altieri appears to believe in the social contract that stipulates for poetry a role in public life commensurate with its concessions to public discourse. He insists that poetry is devoid of political consequence unless it submits itself to "those accommodations to a collective that are the precondition of effective social action" ("Without Consequences Is No Politics," p. 307). But as Altieri must realize, politics in the United States has itself made continual "accommodations" to the ascendant public discourse of self-promotion and advertisement. If we look for accommodations of this order in contemporary poetry, a caterwauling legion of candidates presses forward, including the Care Bears soft touch of Hugh Prather, the carnival geek antics of Charles Bukowski, and the Age of Aquarius spell-casting of Bly, among others.

The distinction Jerome McGann draws from Robert von Hallberg between a poetry of accommodation and a poetry of opposition ("Contemporary Poetry, Alternate Routes," p. 255) is highly misleading as a political measure. As Altieri readily sees, formally conservative poets can be just as oppositional in their politics as any Language Writer.[6] The problem with this distinction is that it posits politics as a realm separate from poetry, which poetry can only report on or represent, by means of "analogies drawn from specific syntactic effects" (Altieri, p. 305). In this scenario, poetry is invariably secondary, diminished, and stripped of whatever political issues might be found intrinsic to its own arena of action. But there is, in fact, a politics *of* poetry, and this is what Language Writers have largely chosen to address from the outset.

Language Writers have been investigating the politics *of* poetry for over fifteen years now, abiding by Charles Bernstein's dictum: "All writing is a demonstration of method; it can assume a method or investigate it."[7] The language of description and representation is by no means eschewed, but in Language Writing the conventional work of exposition is conducted through a text that at the same time examines its own materiality. This self-exposition is recovered as an event charged with partisanship *beyond* the neutrality which any (re-)presentational transparency would suggest. These principles have been adhered to with admirable diligence, but

6. I am here emphatically deleting the equal signs from the spelling of "Language" in order to register my disagreement with McGann on this point. He says "I think the institutional character of this movement should be emphasized" (p. 255 n. 4), graphically marking his choice by retaining the spelling spawned by the magazine *L=A=N=G=U=A=G=E*. By iterating institution, McGann contaminates his reading of Language Writing by alleging an ideological consistency antithetical to what even he refers to as a "loose collective enterprise."

7. Charles Bernstein, "Writing and Method," in *In the American Tree*, ed. Ron Silliman (Orono, Me., 1986), p. 590.

they are not new. This century's project in American poetics has been a continual reexamination of assumptions and testing of methods, from Pound, William Carlos Williams, Wallace Stevens, e. e. cummings, and Gertrude Stein through Louis Zukofsky, Charles Olson, Robert Duncan, Robert Creeley, to such immediate progenitors of Language Writing as Jack Spicer, Jackson Mac Low, and Jerome Rothenberg.

Given the tradition of a radical, investigative poetics the most confounding thing is the continuing prevalence of formally conservative (not necessarily "accommodational"), self-expressive, family-snapshot verse. This tendency is surely indebted to the proliferation of workshops, at both professional and recreational levels, in which poetry acquires the accessory functionalism of arts and crafts. A Marxist analysis might recognize in this a good example of the continued existence of an obsolete mode of production. The work of Amy Clampitt or Alfred Corn, then, would prove more interesting in comparison with a bestselling fiction author like John D. McDonald than with the poetry of John Ashbery or Lyn Hejinian. Considering such work from the point of view of dialectical materialism, it is what Raymond Williams calls "writing of a residual kind," adding that "most writing, in any period, including our own, is a form of contribution to the effective dominant culture."[8] Jonathan Raban has characterized such poetry as "low, mimetic realism," stating that it "deliberately compromises itself by submitting to the only common, available language that we have . . . [that of] the submerged and mortgaged middle class, that is promoted by property developers, television advertisements, feature-writers for popular newspapers, and politicians with the common touch."[9] Such writing has as its main purpose the maintenance of recreational literacy: Auden's passion for crossword puzzles is symptomatic. It appeals at its highest level (James Merrill, Robert Lowell) to a certain nostalgia for the civilizing pleasures of style, taste, and sensibility; and at its lowest (Bukowski, James Dickey) to a faith in literary realism masquerading as a viable way of life.

The greatest liability of the mode of low mimetic realism is its unexamined urge to find the emotional center of its issues. But as Brian Fawcett noted in *L=A=N=G=U=A=G=E*, "the emotional is the least reliable source of information we now have, because it's the most thoroughly manipulated."[10] Poetry that is readily acknowledged as "political," such as that by Carolyn Forché or Rich, is primarily tied to mood and is formally cautious in direct proportion to the anticipated size of the audience. Such work awkwardly attempts to be politically responsible while at the same time struggling to sustain a swollen poetic intensity.

8. Raymond Williams, *Problems in Materialism and Culture* (London, 1980), p. 45.

9. Jonathan Raban, *The Society of the Poem* (London, 1971), pp. 137, 72.

10. Brian Fawcett, "Agent of Language," *The L=A=N=G=U=A=G=E Book,* ed. Bruce Andrews and Charles Bernstein (Carbondale, Ill., 1984), p. 154.

What does it mean that we so easily succumb to politics in poetry if it's grounded in methods of emotional manipulation? The ultimate "accommodational" argument would be that this is consistent with the dominant culture of movies, records, and television; as such, it has its proper historical role to play as an unwitting chronicle of its time.

The resentment within some poetry circles that Language Writing has caused in recent years is a sign of rudimentary alarm at the specter of a group, particularly one so efficiently organized. It's a singular phenomenon that poets should come together as active *readers* and conceptually adroit *critics* of one another's work rather than, as is the custom, mutual celebrants of poetry as initiatory cult. The term "Language Writing" should be taken strictly as a historical marker for the willingness of a few dozen American poets to go public, in the 1970s, in a mutually supportive way. But there was no manifesto of party doctrine in the manner of Surrealism. If anything, the heterogeneity of the group was its most significant bonding agent. Debates within the group have periodically resulted in withering assessments of a kind rarely associated with supposed "members" of a doctrinal league. Yet now, with articles by such scholar-critics as Lee Bartlett and McGann, "Language Writing" is given a portable new facade, this time reconstituted from the outside. Language Writing is made to speak in a unified or typical voice, in which the internal disputes and diversity are erased.

Reading through the mass of theoretical statements and position papers in *The L=A=N=G=U=A=G=E Book, In the American Tree,* and the booklength issue of *L=A=N=G=U=A=G=E* (volume 4), it's evident that the only issues about which a consensus was reached among Language Writers were the restoration of the reader as coproducer of the text and an emphasis on the materiality of the signifier. Yet even these have proven subject to reconsideration. Recently, Steve McCaffery has indicated that "in the light of the Baudrillardian 'proof' that use value is but a concealed species of exchange value, I would say now that the gestural 'offer' to a reader of an invitation to 'semantically produce' hints at an ideological contamination."[11] This same contamination, I would suggest, is what Altieri notices when he contends that "many of McGann's images of class struggle and projections of audience freedom and responsibility can easily be recast to support or reflect basic capitalist practices" (Altieri, p. 305). These practices value "freedom" only insofar as (in Altieri's words) there is an assumed "right to treat language as a commodity to be manipulated." *L=A=N=G=U=A=G=E* magazine can be regarded as a concerted communal effort to explore a literary "bill of rights" that would *not* consent to such a "right."

11. Steve McCaffery, *North of Intention: Critical Writings 1973–1976* (New York, 1986), p. 124.

If one concedes a right to manipulate language, a concession has already been made to the manipulation of human beings. And it is here that the fulcrum of the reader/writer alliance central to Language Writing comes to bear. Bernstein writes: "The question is always: what is the meaning of this language practice; what values does it propagate; to what degree does it encourage an understanding, a visibility, of its own values or to what degree does it repress that awareness? To what degree is it in dialogue with the reader and to what degree does it command or hypnotize the reader?"[12] On the one hand Bernstein is cautioning against the hypnotic lure of language-as-commodity (a cereal called Kix, a car called Cougar), but he is also addressing a venerated principle germane to the poetic tradition of the high sublime: the hypnotic reverie, the stupefied assent of the reader drugged with bewitching words. As Brecht would remind us, a self-critical method of delivery need not entail a less impassioned spectacle; it simply serves as a way of maintaining a functional perspective that visibly operates alongside the passion it conveys. The point is to resist the demagoguery that saturates an emotive deluge of first person (singular *and* plural) fixations. The reliance on means of distancing that splinter the textual surface has the beneficial effect of destabilizing the central authoritarianism of the writer.

A textually fractured surface, however, does not always clearly exhibit its theoretical superstructure. The robust critical and conceptual energies of Language Writers have been applied, by and large, outside the context of the poetry itself.[13] Given the rigor of the theoretical work and its relevance as direct stimulus to the poetry, this is an awkward lacuna. Ironically, this shortcoming fills Altieri's prescription for political responsibility. He suggests that "the actual arguments, the relation between what art discloses and politics can be made to pursue, will depend first on a responsible criticism, then on a willingness to submit its descriptions to the analytic and narrative modes of discursive judgment required for serious political thought" (Altieri, p. 306). Altieri, remember, is reproaching Language Writing not directly but as accounted for by McGann. McGann indicates repeatedly that Language Writing is non- or antinarrative and that it is antagonistic to description and representation. He frequently speaks of "oppositional politics" in Language Writing, but what he does

12. Bernstein, "Writing and Method," p. 589.

13. This separation of poetry from theory was maintained throughout the tenure of *L=A=N=G=U=A=G=E,* which functioned as a theory depository while *Hills, Roof,* and *This* published the poetry. It persists in the essay collections *Content's Dream* by Bernstein, *Total Syntax* by Barrett Watten, *North of Intention* by McCaffery, and the straightforward, conventionally marked poetry collections by the same authors. And despite Silliman's recursive and self-examining procedures in his prose-poems *Ketjak* and *Tjanting,* he perpetuates the theory/praxis schism in his anthology *In the American Tree* by relegating the theoretical pieces (otherwise brilliantly chosen) to the back of the collection under the unflattering heading "Second Front."

not make clear is that this political assertiveness is largely carried out through what Altieri calls "responsible criticism" in which analytic and narrative modes are indeed applied in the service of "discursive judgment."

McGann, misled perhaps by the separation of theory and praxis among Language Writers themselves, makes the mistake of reading the theoretical pronouncements as a supplementary aid to reading the "real" work. It is apparent from the existing body of Language Writing that poetic praxis and theoretical exactitude have rarely been so intimately bound together in American poetry. And here, in the structural integrity of this symbiosis, is the specific political dynamic of Language Writing. The writers themselves, by adhering to a clean separation of theory and practice, have regrettably followed a long tradition in which "poetry" retains a kind of mystical primacy. In the process, they have unwittingly filled Altieri's requirements for a politically responsible criticism, but at the cost of having the poetry isolated with its fractured "surface regularities . . . which interrupt conventional reading processes" (McGann, p. 263). And as Altieri is quick to point out, such work is particularly exposed to the charge that it treats language as a manipulable commodity. Short of the embedding of the *poiēsis* in the praxis (as in Silliman's work) there is no certain way to counter the accusation.

Because of the prodigious critical writing undertaken by most of the Language Writers, the above charges are less damaging than would be the case with many other poets who shroud their work in decontextualized, atmospheric silence. This critical activity has often been directed at the clouds of mystification endemic to much contemporary verse practice. And in this it participates in a long and conscientious critique sustained by Pound, Williams, and others up to the present. The continuity of this critique is what constitutes the politics *of* poetry, and it is best exemplified in the social history of American poetry publishing.

In 1934 Williams could find no publisher willing to bring out his *Collected Poems* in the United States until a group of younger admirers—including Charles Reznikoff, Oppen, and Zukofsky—consented to produce it themselves. This private initiative was followed up a few years later when James Laughlin founded New Directions to bring Williams, Pound, and others into print. These are the roots of an alternative publishing tradition that has quite literally been the lifeblood of American poetry for half a century. This deliberate practice of forming a network outside the mainstream is what McGann misleadingly implies has been "painstakingly constructed" within the past fifteen years in Language Writing circles. While credit is obviously due the admirable thoroughness of the Language Writing publishing and distribution network, the full extent of an alternative or oppositional publishing tradition in American poetry is obscured by McGann's partial perspective. This is regrettable because the politics *of* poetry has been waged as a social struggle of this tradition. The scale may be small, relative to other cultural activities, but it's no mean thing to sustain an alternative system of production and distribution within a capitalist society. This has been managed with considerable difficulty, but the unique result has been a more authentic community-audience than is customarily generated by the atomistic marketing practices prevalent in the general economy.

A politics in and a politics of American poetry can never arrive at a full collaboration between writer and reader without the deliberate location and cultivation of an audience. The poetry printed by mainstream publishers (New York trade houses and university presses) is, in practice, abandoned to the marketplace like a note in a bottle. Any functional correlation between poet and potential reader is randomized (and becomes a different sort of alienation effect in the reification of commodity relations) by the marginal status poetry has in that publishing world.[14] For fifty years now, the most vital American poetry has operated *on* those margins that it has consciously allied itself with, rather than haphazardly submitted itself to. Considering the suffocating monotones that official (or statistically dominant) cultural media have spawned in our time, it's a good thing—and a politically expedient strategy—that some members of the culture have *elected* to inhabit the margins and learned to cultivate modes of production and communication at the edge. If we can dispense with the oppressively institutional urge to speak of "Language Writing," we may be able to recognize the salutary gestures of a number of new citizens of this strategically declassed American zone which, after all, is Whitman's "liquid rims and wet sands," where "the spirit that trails in the lines underfoot" is endlessly rocking.

14. For a sociopolitical account of these parallel publishing practices—mainstream and alternative or "small" press—see my essay "The Role of Critics and the Emperor's New Clothes in American Poetry," *Sulfur* 9 (1984): 149–67.

Comment: Without Admonition

David Bromwich

We can make everything end in politics if we choose. Poetry is as likely a candidate for this sort of translation as medicine or epistemology. "Value" remains another matter. Could we still mean *poetic* value, once we saw it end in politics? The foregoing essays suggest that credible terms do not exist for reckoning what is gained or lost in the translation. But even before starting on the subject, critics ought to distinguish among several paths of inquiry, any one of which may go by the name of "politics and poetic value": (1) the interest poems have in politics; (2) the politics an individual reader may find in poems; (3) the good of politics in intensifying a poet's motive for writing; (4) the manifest political uses of poems, regardless of what the poet may have aimed for; (5) the imperative, always shared by a few, and sometimes by many readers, to defend or attack poetry in general on political grounds. Commonly, I think, (1) and (2) are collapsed together and the critic is thereby enabled to slide from (3) to (5). Any interpretation that follows will be a trivial instance of (4), buoyed up by a comfortable moralism. Poets and critics are, however, nearly enough allied for judgments like this to carry some conviction. Both poets and critics are citizens. The trouble is that an analysis governed by some such analogy between the mental work of poets and critics is apt to underdetermine the general character of the object it means to study. Often, to judge by the conclusions alone, a given poem might just as plausibly have been a documentary film.

Empson seems to me the only modern critic who wrote about politics without implying special or parochial demands. It would take a lot of quotation to show how he did it; and there is no occasion here for that. The place to look is his writing on seventeenth- and eighteenth-century authors: *Milton's God,* and the essays on *Religio Laici, The Beggar's Opera,* and *Tom Jones.* In all of these he avoided a tendency that has been prominent in criticism of the last several years: the habit, namely, of looking on politics now as an inclusive circumstance of life, now as an urgent commitment of the moment; of discovering evidence of the former in a poet's career (it is bound to turn up anywhere); and then testing the poems for their service to the latter, from the perspective of the present. Anachronism, of course, is a necessity of historical thought, but it is apt to take its full swing here. The result may be a tone of confident dismissal that has not been earned by the critic. And indeed, how could it be? A feeling for politics as a vocation has always been as rare in critics as it is in poets. What is strangest in today's climate of political criticism is that a poet like Wordsworth, who really did have a political vocation, should be judged by the canons of a severe republicanism that no one would think of invoking against psychiatrists, policemen, or thinkers-at-liberty in institutes for advanced study.

Poetry, as many of the contributors here agree, is risky work because its relation to politics is equivocal. Whatever a poem says may be read as political-*and-yet.* In the short view, this does not matter: a poet's works are still less answerable than those of, say, a speech writer or a composer of popular songs. In the long view, if, that is, one believes that poetry tells something significant about the way life is going in a culture, then its testimony counts like nothing else that is said or done. (To be accurate, we need to include as poetry all written works of imagination—a broad definition that Shelley encourages in his *Defence.*) And yet the long view ought to induce a more than parochial receptiveness to the possible sympathies of a time different from our own. What happens on the contrary, in a good deal of the work I have seen, is that an up-to-date bigotry is employed in the prosecution of a timeless "answerability."

The sentence by Auden that Robert von Hallberg quotes in his introduction may seem to license researches of just this pattern. "A society," Auden observed, "which was really like a good poem, embodying the aesthetic virtues of beauty, order, economy and subordination of detail to the whole," would actually be a modern fascist police state. This looks like a paradox and is therefore liable to abuse: take it one way and it will lead to a programmatic distrust of all poetry in all circumstances. But Auden's aim probably was to disenchant critics, then in the thrall of Yeats, Pound, and other high modernists, by reminding them that every thing is what it is and not another thing. The extension (he was telling them) of symbolist and modernist aesthetics into politics ought to have been suspect from the first, since it proceeded from a confusion of discrete

---

David Bromwich is Mellon Professor of English at Princeton University. He is the author of *Hazlitt: The Mind of a Critic* and editor of *Romantic Critical Essays.*

tasks (with their discrete virtues). The deduction von Hallberg makes, "that a poet could not be a responsible critic of liberal democratic society" ("Introduction," p. 1), does not necessarily follow. Rather, the poet has no special exemption as a poet. He or she may be a responsible critic merely as a citizen, even if certain acts of citizenship are only imaginable in poetry. At this point, it is true, the boundary that conventionally separates poetry from eloquence would seem to have vanished. Where and how that occurs is a matter of wide interest. It belongs I think at the focus of current debates about poetry and politics, and we would find it there if the terms of the discussion were derived less than they now are from Marxist theory, and more from the republican and democratic language we share in our daily lives.

Eloquence differs from propaganda (the eloquence, I mean, of Edmund Burke or Abraham Lincoln or Martin Luther King, as against the propaganda of Pablo Neruda or William Safire). It binds together the members of a community who may have felt no connection with each other until they saw their common response to an utterance. Propaganda is a cheer (a war whoop, usually) destined to be taken up by a community that is already defined from within. Indeed, for a work of propaganda, the differences between author and audience are wholly accidental. Where poetry and eloquence most converge, and where both exclude propaganda, is in their supposition of an audience whose exact character cannot be anticipated, an audience that has not only to be touched, but moved. Milton's sonnets are a good field of exercise for a critic who wants to explore such matters, and Janel Mueller's essay shows how fresh some of the results can be. She allows no strong distinction between Milton's reading of the ancient rhetoricians and his interest in finding a stance both true and credible for the various occasions of his poetry. She may trust too much to another kind of distinction when she remarks, of the sonnet beginning "Captain or Colonel, or Knight in Arms," that as an inscription it belonged safely to a genre whose "funerary and memorial associations tended to make it apolitical." Poets have seldom believed that the decorum of a poem would keep its politics genre-specific, as MacDiarmid reminds us in his reply to Housman's epitaph on an army of mercenaries. Nor will the political sincerity of a poem assure its aesthetic rightness three centuries later. These goods simply need not harmonize. But it does seem possible now and then to free oneself from modern pedagogic criteria for judging the aptness of an utterance. The paw/maw rhyme which Mueller regrets at the end of "Cromwell, our cheif of men" taps a genuine vein of pulpit eloquence that was audible well into the nineteenth century, as Wordsworth surely knew in spite of his depreciatory comment. You can hear it still going in the speeches George Eliot wrote for Mr. Lyon, the dissenting minister in *Felix Holt.* But there probably are readers even now who will appreciate this without instruction and without turning Milton into a "character" like Mr. Lyon.

Only if one neglects the relation between eloquence and poetry and if, in turn, one assumes that poets as a rule cherish high-modernist ambitions with respect to politics, can one adopt George Steiner's view that in the nature of their work they are bound to be reactionary. Von Hallberg summarizes a recent article in which Steiner seems to say this. But he has been saying it all his life. And his worries are evidently the product of a convulsive shock, from the revelation that deep culture and responsible citizenship do not reliably inhabit the same person. Following the same line of argument, inquisitors of poetry are fond of citing the case of the SS officer who returns from work at the gas chambers to read and admire Goethe. As it happens, there is a live instance of it now in Klaus Barbie, who, when he asked to be excused from appearing at his own trial, let be known through his lawyer (a cultivated left-wing anti-Semite) that his time would be better spent in his prison cell, reading Homer. I agree that it is a good thing in cases like this not to weigh culture in the balance with crime. But the reaction of convulsive shock at the very existence of such persons—the reaction that says: because culture cannot save us, its heroes must be secretly bent on our ruin—misrepresents not only the reality of things but also our feelings about the reality. We are surprised by the SS man who reads Goethe, because we continue to think him an exception, and not because he overturns all our previous assumptions. We feel, in short, that culture tends to discourage this kind of subhuman behavior—if only because it is a mode of knowledge and knowledge tends to reduce prejudice, just as ignorance tends to increase it. This Enlightenment belief I freely confess my own. Unless one holds some version of it, I cannot see the logic by which one consents to work as an educator.

That the shocking example proves nothing seems to be borne out if we look into more familiar cases. A writer like Pound, who clamored for the slaughter of Jews and whom no amount of culture could civilize, again appears as the exception compared with T. S. Eliot, whose virulent prejudices were mitigated by a belief in the final worth of a plurality of cultures. For thinkers like these a generation ago, discussions of culture sometimes took on a political complexion because they were *not* an academic affair. By contrast, academic critics now are able to talk of a political "intervention" by professors in the "production and reception" of literature, implying that this would be a pleasant development if it could really be achieved. I am not sure. Given the number of poets who are themselves academics, it is odd to think of any further widening of the academy as an intervention. A PTA might as well intervene in the protocols of visiting day (they will be welcomed if they try). When the terms of the proposal are framed more stringently, they do not appear such as to foster unexpected work in either poetry or criticism. Anne McClintock, near the end of her article on black South African poets, speaks of "forcing poetry and criticism to step outside the magic circle of immanent value, into history and politics where criteria of judgment remain perpetually to be resolved" ("'Azikwelwa' [We Will Not Ride]," p. 225). But *pace* Terry Eagleton, Barbara Herrnstein Smith, and the others who are cited in support of the usefulness of such a step, poetry may be judged irrespective of "immanent value" without the criteria of judgment being "perpetually to be resolved." As Hume pointed out in his essay "Of the Standard of Taste," the criteria can be resolved for a long time, provided one looks for them to be formed by judges who know something about poetry. It is not clear from McClintock's argument whether, in discussing work by writers who testify directly to an experience of oppression, she thinks that people who know something about poetry are in fact to be trusted; or, if not, whether their judgments are to be suspended in these circumstances, or in lots of similar circumstances. "Perpetually" sounds like a long time. To make a defense of these poets, I do not think she needed in any case to allude to poetic value generally.

Jerome McGann's subject comes closer to home for an American. There is a problem, perhaps a minor one, about "the L=A=N=G=U=A=G=E poets," the heroes he selects to represent poetic radicalism today. They do not appear, as yet, to write good poems. McGann allows as much space, however, to their manifestos as he does to their poems: understandably, for, in a movement of this kind, there is apt to be a high proportion of manifestos to poems. In dealing with any "school" whose aims and theories have been well publicized, a sympathetic critic stands in peril of taking the wish for the deed. This tendency is always part charity and part convenience. Many of the L=A=N=G=U=A=G=E poets are politically radical. They also say that they are poetically radical. Their poetry, McGann explains, makes a "conscious attempt . . . to marry the work of the fifties' New American Poetry with the post-structural work of the late sixties and seventies" ("Contemporary Poetry, Alternate Routes," p. 255). Plainly, this is a marriage of convenience. Must the critic therefore be charitable? The twenties were full of poets who set out to "marry the intense individualism of the Romantics with the almost impersonal grandeur of the Machine." Their intentions have had a fair trial, and their poems have not worn well. In poetry as in politics, the consciousness of an attempt cannot finally be credited, any more than the unconsciousness of an attempt can be blamed. McGann seems mostly occupied with what the L=A=N=G=U=A=G=E poets want to do, their commitment to "procedures which seek after a *comprehensive* account of American experience during that period" (p. 257). And yet, it is hard to know what a comprehensive account of experience would be like, in poetry or in any other branch of writing or knowledge.

By "procedures," however, what appears to be meant is techniques. Here one cannot help noticing the rather narrow textual or technological grounds on which alone McGann is prepared to assign radical interest to a work of literature. His leading earlier example comes from Blake's

Marriage of Heaven and Hell. What particularly recommends that work, to this way of thinking, is the nicely varied disposition of certain plates in different copies that Blake printed; these, it is argued, call "attention to the inherently material and social character of imaginative work" (p. 262); though to extract such a meaning requires close scrutiny of the plate containing, for example, the Printing House in Hell, which in just one copy ("copy E") is placed at the end of the poem. Presumably, in this analysis of Blake, the ideal reader he looked for was someone of Alexandrian capability and resources like McGann, someone who could leaf from copy to copy and check for the plates in some copies that raised the "material and social character" of his work to the foreground. This conclusion is so implausible as to mark a challenge to the whole enterprise of political interpretation as McGann conceives of it.

As to the sheer possibility of our ever encountering a "nonnarrative"—McGann's word for the aspect of radical postmodern writing that produces its radical postmodern character—various opinions may be held by tactical admirers of a new avant-garde. Nontactically, they are likely to assent to Marx, Freud, MacIntyre, Rorty, and others who have argued that narrative affords a way of understanding which we cannot escape, though we can alter its conventions (for example, by seeing a tragedy as a farce). To go outside narrative altogether, outside a story-connected motive for thinking, except at the bidding of another story that has yet to emerge, is insanity or just mindlessness but anyway the end of argument, and not the beginning of a new kind of argument. What we can choose for ourselves are the narratives which seem to us either *more* or *less* worth talking about. This holds as true in making a story about the relation of texts in a sequence as it does in forming the list of texts we want that story to cover. Bad, already existing, stories are a waste of time even for polemical purposes. I am not familiar with the critics who classified Wilfred Owen as a "masculine" poet, as Susan Schweik tells us some of them did, but they were obviously poor readers and poor observers of character. A better-informed cliché about Owen used to say that of all the World War I poets, he was possessed of the most "feminine" sensibility: this gave a depth to his sympathies, though it had earlier been a vice to be reformed. Neither of these judgments comes close to a truth about his poetry, and Schweik, in expounding "In Distrust of Merits," is right to dispose quickly of a similar pair of counters.

Randall Jarrell was a fine appreciator of Marianne Moore's poetry. But as a reviewer of "In Distrust of Merits," he appears to have suffered a rare lapse into commonplace, and he invoked versions of both war-poet clichés: male-particular-actual suffering versus female-general-abstract sympathy. These pairs, which can be altered at pleasure depending on the culprit, have never helped anyone to read a poem. Occasionally a poem itself will help us to see past them; Schweik brings this out forcibly in her interpretation of Jarrell's "Eighth Air Force." Even so, to alter the sense of a narrative, as Jarrell did there by adapting Moore's poem, or as Schweik has done by interpreting it, points no moral concerning the probable uses of a given narrative (hierarchical, antihierarchical, or whatever). To take the most striking available instance, the argument Schweik uses to restore appreciation to Moore's great poem would be adaptable in some respects to a defense of bad antiwar poetry, such as sections 4 and 5 of "Hugh Selwyn Mauberley." Equally, if we move from a concern with public and hortatory language to a concern with allegorical meditation, it would be adaptable to a defense of a great martial ode like Collins's "How Sleep the Brave."

In a celebrated phrase, Auden said that poetry was "a way of happening; a mouth." When he wrote those words, he was, for reasons all his own, ready to acquit poetry entirely of the charge that it sometimes made things happen other than itself. But there is still wisdom in his injunction, and in the sense it carries that poetry, so far as it persists in any social function at all, is neither didactic nor impartial but exemplary. At times, to be a way of happening may seem not to be enough, as if to do so were to sympathize with the processes of social decay; and at such times, poets who work without a self-conscious politics will seem to be giving in to a temptation that ought to have been resisted. It is possible that we are now living in or getting near to such a time. In what seems to me an accurate summary of the tenor of a recent didacticism in critical theory, von Hallberg writes of the demand that poets "refuse to collaborate with their readers in the establishment of values." This has a stirring sound. But do poets, or, for that matter, any of us have this choice to make? Trotsky observed in his debate with Malraux: "You may not be interested in dialectics, but dialectics is interested in you." Let poets and critics, then, refuse to collaborate in the establishment of values; all the while, the establishment of values will be collaborating with them. If one accepts this as a general truth about poetry, the only political failure that ever matters in a poem is a failure of observation.

There is a mean way and a generous way of drawing attention to such a failure. Donald Davie exemplifies the generous way when he compares the politic decency of *The Deserted Village* with the precise realizations of *The Traveller*. For him, a comparative judgment of the two poems is a matter of listening closely: the accusation that *points,* in Goldsmith's earlier attempt ("useful sons exchang'd for useless ore"), is displaced in the later by a generalized atmosphere of nostalgic eulogy ("a bold peasantry, their country's pride"). We have been taught to think of the less sharp, less intimately satirical language of *The Deserted Village* as somehow more poetic and more resonant with eighteenth-century moral aspiration. Davie invites us to reconsider, and once again the problem has to do with a relation between eloquence and poetry. His verdict, for the works in question, is that where the motive for eloquence was deeper, the observation of poetry was truer.

It is useless to ask whether Goldsmith hoped for a more immediate effect, thought himself more productively "meddling in politics," in *The Traveller* or *The Deserted Village*. The latter has certainly eclipsed its predecessor in anthologies of the last two hundred years. It has also been serviceable, any time in that interval, for a brief and telling citation in works of social history. But a recovery like Davie's has the character of an acknowledgment, for it brings to light a political design which, we feel, was never altogether hidden from readers, and which may once have been known with an assurance too implicit for commentary. A rule without exceptions in criticism, but specially pertinent to writing on politics and poetry, is that the effort of acknowledgment outlasts the effort of admonition. I have in mind the kind of work that Shelley spoke of, work that has its end in a future that cannot be known.

Of all the poets treated in this volume, Pindar is doubtless the least politically assimilable to readers today. And yet Anne Burnett is able to close her impressive survey of "poetic scrutiny" in his odes by recalling that "in every generation since his own, certain men have been moved afresh by Pindar's vision of government by men who were both strong and fine" ("The Scrutiny of Song," p. 36). How is that possible? Pindar instructed the favorable aspect of his hero: "Now BE what you have learned yourself to be." Men read the words and found a vision—through restraint, and action—of what it would be to justify the praise in such a command. Political transitions just as strange have followed from great writing, where no god was addressed and none was expected to intervene; where all that seemed in agitation was only the frolic of wits,

> In evening dress on rafts upon the main,
> Not therefore uneventful or soon drowned.

Gandhi tells us that the reading of Thoreau made him think for the first time of "Civil Resistance" as a principle of action. Thoreau, a white man, idealizer of nature and apologist for the very individualism Gandhi would reject: but who will say what collaborations took place on that occasion? Professional critics may contribute a little, perhaps, to narrow the margins of thought in which similar meetings of smaller consequence have occurred in the past. They can do it by inculcating a generation of university-trained readers with the precept that words alone are never certain good. If success in this venture could ever be complete, we would not have Thoreaus as writers, and we would not have Gandhis as readers.

Index